The University of Iowa
in the Twentieth Century

The University of

Iowa

in the Twentieth Century

An Institutional History

BY STOW PERSONS

University of Iowa Press Iowa City

University of Iowa Press, Iowa City 52242

Copyright © 1990 by the University of Iowa

All rights reserved

Printed in the United States of America

First edition, 1990

Design by Richard Hendel

Printed on acid-free paper

Library of Congress Cataloging-in-Publication Data

Persons, Stow, 1913–

The University of Iowa in the twentieth century: an institutional
history/by Stow Persons.—1st ed.

   p. cm.

Includes bibliographical references.

ISBN 0-87745-282-2 (alk. paper)

1. University of Iowa—History.   I. Title.

LD2568.P47   1990   90-10771

378.777'655—dc20   CIP

TO THE MEMORY OF

MAY BRODBECK

1917 – 1983

CONTENTS

PREFACE

Although I am not an alumnus of the University of Iowa I taught history at the university for thirty-one years and came to have a feeling of close identification with it. Following retirement in 1981 it seemed appropriate that I should put my sense of attachment into the form of a history, since no work of this kind had yet appeared. The book concentrates on the period when the university established its place among the major American universities. It was a substantial achievement, and I hope that my account conveys a proper feeling of appreciation for the dedication of those who brought it about. This was also the period in which the university assumed its own distinctive profile. Several scholars and administrators placed the stamp of their unique personalities on the institution, and I have attempted to indicate their accomplishments and to establish for them the place in the history of the university that they deserve.

In ultimate terms, a university is a company of scholars and their students. The history of a university should ideally be an account of what was taught and what was learned. Goethe might have written such a history at the end of the eighteenth century, but I doubt that even that formidable polymath could have mastered the modern university in all of its specialized complexity. In any event, it has been impossible for me to write such a history. This book is primarily an institutional history. Because no such history of the University of Iowa has yet been written, I like to think that the present work may serve as a starting point from which someone may eventually produce a more comprehensive account of the university as a learning experience.

During the 1930s and 1940s the late Professor Harrison J. Thornton supervised a number of doctoral dissertations and master's theses on aspects of the history of the university which I have used with profit. In 1976–77 James Beilman interviewed some thirty-five senior and emeritus faculty members and administrators whose recollections provide an invaluable record for the immediately preceding decades. But the major source of information is of course the university archive, a rich and extensive collection of manuscript and printed material, including records of the governing boards, presidential papers, faculty papers, collegiate files, student publications, newspaper clippings, and much miscellaneous material. In finding my way through this vast storehouse I have had the invaluable assistance of the university archivist, Earl Rogers, whose intimate acquaintance with the material and generous response to my innumerable demands greatly lightened my task. Robert McCown, Barbara Siebenschuh, Judith Macy, Vevalee Voots, and Susan Hansen of the Special Collections Department were all exceedingly helpful. Many friends and colleagues have provided valuable information and helpful suggestions: Robert L. Alexander, Myrtle K. Aydelotte, William O. Aydelotte, the late William B. Bean, Arthur Benton, Richard Bovbjerg, the late Howard R. Bowen, Willard L. Boyd, Michael Brody, Joan Cantor, Carl Cone, Hamilton Cravens, Ralph Ellsworth, Paul Engle, Samuel Fahr, G. Edgar Folk, the late Robert Hardin, R. Palmer Howard, Sydney James, George Kalnitsky, Jerry Kolross, the late Baldwin Maxwell, Julia Mears, Hunter Rawlings III, the late Leland Sage, Gordon Searle, and Lyle Shannon.

A Provincial University

The practice of establishing state universities at federal expense was well established by the time Iowa became a state of the union in 1846. The federal land grant of 1840 setting aside two townships for the support of a university when Iowa Territory should achieve statehood was the twelfth such grant.[1] The founding of institutions of higher learning was a universal impulse of mid-nineteenth-century America. Few citizens, however, thought of public higher education as an ongoing burden to be borne by the taxpayers. In view of the prevailing hostility of rural communities to professional and learned elites it may seem surprising that Iowa should have seized the federal offer of aid with such alacrity. One has to assume that few of the pioneers had a clear idea of what a university was or what it would cost. In any event, the First General Assembly of the legislature, on February 25, 1847, established a state university and located it in Iowa City. With the wisdom of hindsight we must regard it as a blithely premature and ill-considered act, the consequence of which was a prolonged and frustrating struggle extending over many decades to bring a true university into being.

Since the first prerequisite for the survival of an educational institution was a student body, it was an awkward fact that the state in 1847 was preparing virtually no students for college. Of the estimated population of about 100,000, some 20,000 were of school age. In the absence of a state-mandated public school system, which did not come into being until 1858, a few local academies were providing elementary education on an individual tuition basis.[2] Although the population of the state grew rapidly, doubling or tripling in each decade as the frontier of settlement pushed westward, it was a growth almost wholly rural, in which the interests and outlook of freehold farmers struggling to establish themselves in a new country prevailed. The creation of a public school system to serve the needs of a population thinly distributed over thirty-five million acres of farm land was indeed a formidable challenge to be met initially only in the most rudimentary terms.

At about the same time, within each of the ninety-nine counties a comparable struggle for survival and growth among fledgling communities ensued. Railroad connections were crucial, as was the location of state and county facilities. To become the seat of the state university or a branch of it was a prize which might well mean the difference between survival and demise. Intense community competition focused on the legislature, influencing educational decisions of far-reaching consequence. Mount Pleasant, Fairfield, and Yellow Springs as well as Iowa City all contended vigorously for the university. When the decision to locate at Iowa City was made, Dubuque and Fairfield were consoled with "branches," while Andrew, Oskaloosa, and Mount Pleasant were awarded normal schools.[3] Fortunately, these plums failed to ripen, saving the state from the dissipation of its meager educational resources.

The choice of Iowa City, the territorial capital, as the location of the university proved in some respects to be an unfortunate one. Ideally, the university should have been located near the geographical and future center of population where it would be able to develop as an educational institution unencumbered by extraneous problems which would work to its disadvantage and slow its growth. The State Agricultural College at Ames near Des Moines was more fortunate in this respect. Johnson County, of which Iowa City was the county seat, came to possess large German and Irish populations and became the focus of a deep underlying ethnic conflict with the Anglo-American element in other parts of the state. Expressing itself first in local politics as Democratic and Copperhead opposition to the majority Republican party's management of the Civil War, the ethnic tension was perpetuated by the struggle over prohibition, which persisted through the later decades of the nineteenth century and gained for the people of Johnson County the unenviable reputation of being saloon keepers and scofflaws. Faculty members themselves became embroiled in these controversies, to the undoubted detriment of the university.

Of even more momentous consequence than the matter of location was the struggle between proponents of agricultural and liberal education. The struggle focused at first on the question of whether there should be a professorship of agriculture at the university or a separate college of agriculture. Vocal spokesmen for the agricultural interest stressed a class conflict between farmers and professionals, contending that students educated at a university would not deign to dirty their hands at honest manual labor.[4] Prevailing in the legislature, they secured in 1858 the establishment of a separate agricultural college, including the provision that each student should engage in manual labor not less than two hours daily in winter or three in summer. Ten thousand dollars was provided for the purchase of a farm for experimental and pedagogical purposes. The struggle was renewed in 1862, following passage of the Morrill Act providing federal land grants for the support of colleges of agriculture and the mechanic arts. Again the agricultural interests prevailed over those who would assign all or a portion of the income from the grant to the university. Iowa joined Michigan, Indiana, and Kansas as states maintaining separate colleges of agriculture and the mechanic arts.

If Iowa was not always first in agriculture as measured by output it was first in the proportion of its population and resources devoted to agriculture. It was not surprising that in such a state the agricultural college should enjoy a favored position. It could always count upon a strong rural representation both in the legislature and in the press. A succession of able leaders promoted its rapid development. In no other state where the state university and the agricultural college were separately organized did the latter achieve the equality of status, both locally and nationally, that was enjoyed by the Iowa State College. Once established, the college at Ames moved steadily away from the narrow conception of agricultural education that the legislature had originally prescribed. In the 1870s the college was awarding master's degrees in literature, philosophy, and social science. Finally, in 1884, the legislature revoked the act of 1858 mandating the narrow practical curriculum and prescribed "a broad, liberal and practical course of study" in the arts and sciences.[5] Thus at the beginning of its history the state provided itself with two institutions of higher education when it lacked the resources to support one adequately; simultaneously it witnessed within these institutions the curricular convergence that would pose the problem of duplication of programs and facilities and poison the educational atmosphere for a century to come.

The recruitment of students in the early years would have been difficult enough had the university been the only institution of higher learning in the state. Apart from the agricultural college, however, there quickly sprang up a host of denominational colleges—twenty-two of them by 1870—all engaged in the scramble for students. Of necessity they all organized preparatory departments, and most of them admitted women students. Each of them regarded a particular denominational group as its special clientele, and each cultivated a distinctive moral and social atmosphere to distinguish itself from the others and from the public university. Throughout the latter half of the century the denominational colleges kept a wary eye on the "godless" institution in Iowa City. In the face of such competition the university was able to grow only very slowly.

The university was also obliged to open a preparatory department which for some years enrolled a substantial portion of the student body. Women were admitted from the beginning, and there were no racial or ethnic barriers, although very few minority students enrolled. Because of the need for schoolteachers the normal department was for some years the university's most flourishing branch.[6] The shortage of lawyers and doctors was also recognized, and one of the first acts of the university trustees was to designate the College of Physicians and Surgeons of the Upper Mississippi as the medical department of the university. A proprietary institution, that college shortly moved from Davenport to Keokuk, where it flourished during the Civil War. Its connection with the university was merely nominal. After the war the trustees under the leadership of John P. Irish became persuaded that if the needs of the university were to prevail in the face of a hostile or indifferent public it must have a loyal and influential body of supporters who could be counted upon to support its claims in the press and legislature. Doctors and lawyers who were alumni were the most obvious source for such support. Chancellor William G. Hammond, proprietor of a law school in Des Moines, was persuaded in 1868 to relocate the school in Iowa City as the law department of the university. In the following year, and over the strenuous opposition of Keokuk, a medical department under the vigorous leadership of Dr. Washington F. Peck was organized in Iowa City, and the Keokuk school was left to wither on the vine. Technically speaking the Iowa City institution was now a university, although the status of its liberal arts program remained highly uncertain.[7]

Iowa's neighbors faced comparable problems in the development of their systems of public higher education, and a study of their experience might have helped in confronting the difficulties that Iowa was to face, although the day of the professional educational consultant was still far in the future. Wisconsin, Minnesota, and Iowa were all carved out of Michigan Territory, and it was only appropriate that University of Iowa president George MacLean should hail the University of Michigan as "the mother of us all." Many of the precedents as well as the problems of public higher education in the upper Midwest were revealed in the early experience of the University of Michigan. The demographic blend of Yankee settlers and educated French priests in Detroit produced the strong educational impulse that expressed itself in a drive to create a university while Michigan was still in the territorial stage of institutional development. The Yankee element with its strong educational tradition was also evident in the university movements in Wisconsin and Minnesota. In Iowa, on the other hand, a large population movement from Missouri, Kentucky, and Virginia pushed northwestward up the tributaries of the Mississippi to confine Yankee settlers to the northern counties.

Michigan was the first state to conceive of its university as the capstone of the public educational system. As an expression of the democratic ideal of an educated citizenry the concept of a unified series of grades from primary to the highest university levels may have commanded widespread allegiance in principle, but its practical implementation required a bureaucratic authority that most states hesitated to invoke. The forces of local autonomy rejected Prussian educational centralization and compelled the public universities to devise means of "articulating" their standards with those of the lower schools from which they drew their students. In a sense, they were to remain captives of the public schools so far as their admissions standards were concerned. But at the outset, where the newly established universities antedated public secondary school systems, it was necessary to create preparatory departments for collegiate-level work.

Considerable freedom was left to the states for the management of the federal educational land grants. The efficiency with which the lands were converted into cash furnished revealing insight into the determination and skill of state officials in obtaining a maximum yield for their respective university establishments. Michigan, Wisconsin, and Minnesota managed their land sales so as to realize significant funds for the support of higher education, whereas Illinois and Iowa yielded to pressure from land-hungry settlers and largely squandered their grants.

In the early years of development, before the institutions had achieved stability, the accidents of leadership had much to do with the relative degrees of success in surmounting the many obstacles confronting the fledgling universities. Henry Philip Tappan at Michigan, John Bascom at Wisconsin, and John M. Gregory at Illinois provided their universities with the aggressive leadership necessary to achieve rapid development. At Minnesota leadership was assumed by a public-spirited political leader, John S. Pillsbury, who established himself as the benevolent patron and protector of the state university. In Iowa, on the other hand, the only leader who might have played a comparable role, James Grimes, was diverted by other pressing problems, and the infant state university was left to languish.

In a predominantly agricultural region it was inevitable that each state should feel the competing pressures of vocational—that is, agricultural and other occupational—and liberal-professional education. Each state university organized programs in arts and sciences, law, and medicine; and

each faced the question whether agricultural, engineering, and other occupational subjects should be provided by the university or by separate institutions. Wisconsin, Minnesota, and Illinois combined all programs in
their state universities. Michigan organized the first state college of agriculture, and Iowa followed closely upon its heels.

THE LIBERAL ARTS

Tom Paine had innocently declared that the American republic had
been blessed with the unique opportunity to begin the world anew
and avoid the mistakes of all previous regimes. It might similarly be said
that the newly settled western states were privileged to offer their citizens
a higher education appropriate to their needs unencumbered by the weight
of outmoded traditions. On the Iowa prairies there was no entrenched
classical tradition to be sloughed off. There were no elite patrons to be
placated. Governor Grimes sensed the possibilities when he declared that
it would be a mistake to create a "literary institution" to compete with the
private colleges of the state which were entirely capable of preparing students for training in the professions. What was needed was a practical scientific or polytechnical school to educate farmers, mechanics, engineers,
chemists, architects, metallurgists, and geologists. But in the absence of a
local leadership capable of implementing Grimes's vision it proved impossible to prevent the eastern clerical and educational interests from controlling the university curriculum and transplanting in the new soil the elements of the older liberal arts curriculum.

When the university opened its doors in 1855 it offered, at least on
paper, a comprehensive program drawn up by its president—or chancellor, as he was designated—Amos Dean. Instruction was to be offered in
nine departments: ancient languages; modern languages; mathematics; intellectual philosophy; moral philosophy, including international law and
politics; history; natural history; natural philosophy; and chemistry. A
two-year program emphasizing scientific subjects would lead to the B.S.
degree; four years of classical subjects, the B.A.; and six years of work in all
nine departments, the Ph.D. Both sexes were to be admitted: girls at fourteen and boys at fifteen. In fact, however, a faculty of four professors
offered courses in ancient and modern languages, mathematics, and natural philosophy, with assurances that additional work would be offered "as
fast as the people of Iowa will furnish students to be instructed." The catalog for 1856–57 listed 83 gentlemen and 41 ladies for a total student en-

rollment of 124. Chancellor Dean, who was also professor of history, had condescended to visit the campus but then returned to his home in Albany, New York, where he continued to reside. Since the state proved slow to furnish students the university was closed between 1858 and 1860, except for the normal department.

It reopened in 1860, with hardly more promising prospects. The historian of the early years, Vernon Carstensen, has aptly observed that "with a faculty consisting of four professors and the President, the Trustees proposed to open a University which had more offices than officers, more departments than professors, and almost more courses than qualified students."[8] The new president was the Reverend Silas Totten, formerly president of Trinity College in Hartford, Connecticut. Totten organized a somewhat more modest program with six departments: intellectual and moral philosophy and rhetoric; history, political science, constitutional and international law; mathematics and astronomy; ancient and modern languages; natural philosophy and chemistry; and natural history (geology, mineralogy, botany, agricultural chemistry, and zoology). Each department determined its own courses and requirements for admission. The student was free to elect courses, subject to departmental approval. This so-called departmental plan of instruction was in effect an elective system, anticipating by ten years Eliot's advocacy of a more modest version of the plan at Harvard. Alternatively, however, the student was given the option of choosing a "class" plan of study, a fixed curriculum with little choice: mathematics and ancient languages in the freshman year; more of the same, together with science, rhetoric, and logic in the sophomore year; history and philosophy for juniors; with literature, economics, and political science as well as more science and mathematics for seniors.[9]

In view of Totten's announced preference for the departmental plan it seems likely that the traditional class pattern was forced on him by a conservative faculty. The principal justification of the class plan, in the president's opinion, was that it allowed for the arrangement of the entire course of study "so as to cultivate all the faculties of the mind in due proportion." Nor would students be permitted to avoid subjects in which they might be weak. The idea that the mind consisted of faculties to be developed through exercise had long been used to justify a fixed curriculum. It was a functional idea in which mental discipline was strongly emphasized. It should be distinguished from the twentieth-century theory of general education conceived as acquiring the essence of a culture. Totten's principal objection to the class plan was that because students were unequal in preparation and ability the professor must pitch instruction to the average, neglecting both the best and worst. It pained the president to think that some students might fall by the wayside, for he "would no more turn a youth out of College for poverty of intellect than for poverty of purse." All deserved the opportunity to make the most of what they had. Given the crucial need for students at that moment Totten's generous allowance for human frailty had its practical side.[10]

The departmental plan as Totten conceived it afforded several practical advantages. A struggling young institution need offer only as many fields of study as its resources permitted. Students could progress at their own pace, choosing such courses as their interests and aptitudes indicated. The specialized skills so much in demand could be acquired with maximum speed and efficiency. Students who lacked adequate preparation in certain fields need not be held back as would doubtless be the case under the class plan.[11] Totten's conception of the university as a place to foster advanced learning in specialized fields placed him in the mainstream of university development. But in the absence of a faculty committed to research the departmental plan merely introduced competition for students resulting in jealous backbiting and faculty turmoil.

In the absence of a general consensus of what a university should be it was inevitable that the model of the traditional liberal arts college should have great influence in the early years. Presidents Oliver Spencer and James Black taught the course in moral philosophy which had become almost obligatory in eastern colleges.[12] At the same time, the university was obliged to stand in a parental relationship to its students who, although officially classified as ladies and gentlemen, were in fact treated as children. The early catalogs assured the community that wholesome moral influences would prevail on campus. Attendance at daily chapel and at the Sunday church service of the student's choice were required. Study hours were to be observed with strict decorum. There would be no drinking, card playing, gambling, profanity, entering a saloon, or attending the theater. Rooming houses in the town were to be subject to inspection and certification as to safety and suitability.[13] Nevertheless, the philosopher-psychologist George T. W. Patrick, who graduated in 1878, later recalled that if any of his classmates either smoked or drank he knew nothing of it. His account of the simple student life of those days does not suggest a repressive atmosphere. Most students had grown up in religious homes with a firm moral code, and the disciplined pattern of university life seemed natural to them.[14] As late as 1888 a committee of the legislature observed that the citizens expected professors to be "relatively at least perfect models after whom their children can be safely trusted to pattern."[15] It seemed only appropriate that a clergyman should preside over such an institution, and the four presidents who followed Totten were all clergymen.

As conservative and clerical influences gained the upper hand during the 1860s and 1870s the curriculum of the academic department was shifted away from the freedom of the departmental plan toward the prescribed pattern of the class plan. Choice of two programs was offered, classical or scientific, the former consisting for the most part of prescribed courses, the latter completely so. In 1873 a philosophic program was added, substituting modern for ancient languages and adding some work in philosophy, psychology, and science. The Reverend George Thacher, who became president in 1871, epitomized the conservative impulse. A Congregationalist clergyman and graduate of the Yale Divinity School, Thacher brought to Iowa Yale president Noah Porter's conception of higher education as mental discipline. Echoing Porter, he declared that students most needed what they were least inclined to study and that the faculty should be firm in indicating what those studies should be. An important consequence of the curricular changes was the restriction of the development of the science program and the beginning of a decade of increasingly bitter controversy, culminating in the explosion of 1887.[16]

One of the first Iowa faculty members to enjoy more than a merely local reputation was Gustavus D. Hinrichs, professor of natural philosophy and chemistry. German born and educated, Hinrichs joined the Iowa faculty in 1863. A strong and vivid personality, he was a highly successful teacher who introduced laboratory methods of instruction and infected students with his zeal for investigation. His scientific reputation rested largely upon an early compilation of the periodic table of chemical elements. His textbooks were widely used, and he maintained extensive contacts in the scientific community. Blunt and irascible, he engaged vigorously in the controversies over the curriculum; as the president and classical members of the faculty gained the upper hand he became increasingly vituperative. To make matters worse, he was a freethinker who did not hesitate to ridicule the "Sunday School boys" on the faculty whom he identified with low academic standards and moral censoriousness.[17] He was also an ardent opponent of the prohibition movement in Iowa, an explosive issue that cut across many concerns and touched both public and private morality.

A state prohibition law passed in 1855 had provided for county referenda, exempting those counties that chose to continue the sale of alcoholic beverages. Johnson County, with its large Irish and German element, voted against prohibition, thus in the eyes of many setting itself apart from the decent and law-abiding regions. These circumstances undoubtedly worked to the disadvantage of the university. As late as 1888 Governor William Larrabee informed the legislature that the university enrollment was not larger because students avoided an institution in a community where the liquor law was not more "rigorously enforced," apparently forgetting that the law itself provided for the exemption.[18]

Turmoil within the faculty reached the point where in 1885 the regents removed Hinrichs from the collegiate faculty and reassigned him to the medical faculty and in the following year dismissed him from the university. He thereupon opened a slashing press and pamphlet war against "the university of darkest America," denouncing it as "rotten to the core!"[19] The taste of Hinrichs's blood seemed to whet the appetite for more. Following a regents committee report critical of the quality of instruction in elocution and Greek, professors Leonard F. Parker, Nathan R. Leonard, and Stephen N. Fellows were summarily dismissed in 1887. Although President Josiah Pickard as well as alumni and students testified to the competence of the professors, certain regents confided that "new blood" was needed to reinvigorate the faculty. The *Vidette Reporter*, the campus newspaper, noted that the hapless professors were temperance men and suggested that they had been fired to placate the antiprohibition party.[20] These events received national publicity unquestionably damaging to the reputation of the university. Widespread criticism of the regents led to the creation of a legislative investigating committee which held public hearings in May 1888, heard 200 witnesses, and took 2,500 pages of testimony. After the washing of much dirty linen the committee concluded that while the specific charges lacked substance there was much to indicate that the Board of Regents was both inefficient and incompetent. It recommended that the large board of part-time nonsalaried members be replaced by a small five-member, full-time, salaried board with governing powers over all three state institutions of higher learning.[21] The proposal was too drastic to be immediately acceptable, but a seed was planted which would eventually blossom twenty years later.

THE SEEDS OF GROWTH

Many years were to pass before the citizens of Iowa were prepared to accept the fact that the maintenance of a state university involved a significant outlay of public funds. Owing to a combination of mismanagement and public demand for cheap farm land the initial federal land grant yielded an annual income of less than $12,000 to support the university. It was nevertheless expected to be sufficient. The faculty complained in 1855 of the public misconception that the university was wealthy. Although it proved to be impossible to implement the ideal of a tuition-free university, student fees in the early decades were nominal. The collegiate department fee of $5.00 per term in 1865 had risen to only $8.33 in 1880, and to $25.00 a year in 1890. No student, however, was to be denied a college education on account of poverty, provision being made for remission of fees for those demonstrating inability to pay. Law department tuition during the nineteenth century remained at $20.00 per term, while medical department tuition increased from $55.00 for the full two-year course to $65.00 per year. With an enrollment of only 887 students in 1890 it is clear that student fees contributed relatively little to university operations.

Although requests of the legislature for operating funds were made from the beginning, the legislature considered its obligation to be limited to providing buildings. It was not until 1878 that a modest appropriation of $20,000 was made for operating expenses. Thenceforward there ensued an annual or biennial struggle to increase the appropriation. Frequent comparisons with the support afforded universities in surrounding states showed how far the University of Iowa was lagging behind. President Josiah Pickard, who succeeded Thacher in 1878, urged the legislature to emulate Wisconsin and Minnesota by imposing a small university tax which would bring increasing revenue as the state grew in wealth and population, but without success.[22] The State College and the Normal School each had its own Board of Trustees, and in the absence of a single administrative agency it proved impossible for the legislature to determine a comprehensive policy for public higher education.

Following two earlier reorganizations the Board of Regents, which was created in 1870, continued to govern the university until 1909, when it was replaced by the State Board of Education. The regents consisted of the governor, superintendent of public instruction, and university president serving ex officio, together with one member from each congressional district chosen by the legislature. The number of such regents increased from six to eleven as the state increased in population. A secretary and a treasurer appointed by the board and resident in Iowa City provided liaison between the board and daily operations at the university. For thirty-eight years until retirement in 1903 the secretary was "Major" William J. Haddock, a testy character who came to have a strong possessive feeling for the institution. He also served as business manager. In 1886, doubtless as a result of the turmoil within the university, the legislature removed the president from membership on the board. Thereafter he attended board meetings only by invitation.[23] Although some questioned the wisdom of it at the time, the removal of the president probably contributed to the gradual development of the necessary distinction between board as policy maker and president as administrator, although the distinction would become clear only after long and painful turmoil. As previously noted, the board took quite literally its authority to hire and fire the faculty, fix salaries and tuition, and manage financial operations in minute detail. As the university grew the board subdivided itself into as many as sixteen standing committees each charged with supervision of a specified area of the university program.[24] Growing dissatisfaction with the board, as well as with the management of the State College and the Normal School, led to the creation in 1904 of a joint legislative committee to study the three institutions and make recommendations for the improvement of their management. It was the recommendation of this committee that resulted in the establishment in 1909 of a single board for the government of all three institutions.[25]

The slow but steady growth of the university during the later decades of the nineteenth century seemed to assure its survival even though the enrollments were hardly great enough to sustain significant expansion of the educational program. From an initial enrollment of 89 students in 1860, all of them in the normal department, the growth by decades saw 523 students in 1871, 560 in 1881, 887 in 1890, and 1,542 in 1900. The combined enrollments in law and medicine generally accounted for about half of the totals. There was a corresponding growth in the size of the faculty. From 7 in 1860, the number of faculty members increased to 30 in 1871, 42 in 1880, 73 in 1890, and 102 in 1900, exclusive of teaching assistants.

In the absence of systematic searches for academically qualified candidates, the recruitment of a scholarly faculty remained for many years a hit-or-miss affair, in which the gradual formation of a nucleus of scholars has to be seen as a series of happy accidents. The process began in 1873 with the appointment of Samuel Calvin as acting professor of natural science. Born in Scotland, Calvin spent his boyhood in Buchanan County, where he taught school briefly before attending the Lenox Collegiate Institute at Hopkinton. Essentially self-taught in science, he developed a distinguished career as geologist and paleontologist, making important contributions to Pleistocene paleontology and receiving national recognition in election to the presidency of the Geological Society of America.[26] Calvin remembered a bright pupil named Thomas Huston Macbride and brought him to the university in 1878 as assistant professor of natural science and botany, although Macbride's training had been in mathematics and languages. Six years later the chair of natural science was divided, Calvin becoming professor of geology and zoology and Macbride, professor of botany. Calvin's good judgment was confirmed as Macbride went on to do widely recognized work on slime molds, inaugurating investigations continued by his successors into the twentieth century. Calvin also secured appointments for his students Gilbert L. Houser in geology and C. C. Nutting in zoology.[27] Bohumil Shimek, who graduated from the university in 1883 with a degree in civil engineering, turned to the study of geology and botany, joining the faculty in 1890 as professor of botany. A native of Shueyville, near Iowa City, Shimek specialized in prairie ecology. His paper on the "Theory of the Loess" (1896) displaced the prevailing theory of the aqueous origin of loess deposits with the theory of aeolian (wind) origin. His botanical work was also recognized internationally.[28]

Personal association similarly accounted for the early appointments in psychology, inaugurating a distinguished Iowa tradition in that field which lasted for nearly a century. George T. W. Patrick, who had grown up on an Iowa farm and graduated from the academical department in 1878, went on for graduate work in philosophy at Yale and in psychology at Johns Hopkins under G. Stanley Hall, one of the American pioneers in experimental psychology. Patrick had told Dean Amos Currier that after graduate work he would be ready for a faculty appointment, and Currier obligingly arranged for his appointment as professor of philosophy and psychology in 1887, succeeding Stephen N. Fellows, who had just been dismissed by the regents. Then known as mental science, psychology had traditionally been an integral part of academic philosophy. Fellows had taught both mental science and "Moral Science and Evidences of Christianity," as well as the history of philosophy. Patrick immediately introduced a course in experimental psychology and a seminar in 1888, probably the first seminar at the university. He opened a psychological laboratory in 1894 and three years later launched the *University of Iowa Studies in Psychology*, in which the research would be published. Although he continued to teach both philosophy and psychology his publications were primarily in the former subject. It was Patrick who in 1897 recommended the appointment of Carl Seashore.[29]

These pioneers of academic scholarship at the university understandably felt the need both for mutual support and for a local forum in which their work could be brought to the attention of the university community. In 1885 they organized the Baconian Club, at the weekly public meetings of which the members read papers on their research. In addition to Calvin, Macbride, Nutting, Houser, and Patrick, the membership during the early years included Laenas G. Weld in mathematics; Andrew A. Veblen, physics; E. W. Rockwood, chemistry; and J. G. Gilchrist, homeopathic medicine. Calvin read over fifty papers in this forum, and Patrick also contributed a number on psychological topics.[30] The importance of "The Baconian" as evidence of the emergence of a scholarly community at the university cannot be overestimated. Papers read to the club served to disseminate ideas locally, but in order to reach a wider audience publication in print was necessary. Beginning with the *Natural History Bulletin* of 1888, a series of periodical publications was established which by the end of the century included the *Transit*, the *Law Bulletin*, the *Bulletin of the Homeopathic Medical Department*, the *University of Iowa Studies in Psychology*, and the *State University of Iowa Studies in Sociology, Economics, Politics, and History*.

THE EMERGING UNIVERSITY

The appointment of Charles Ashmead Schaeffer as president of the university in 1887 marked an important turning point in the history of the institution. A chemist trained at the University of Pennsylvania and Harvard as well as at the Sorbonne and Göttingen, Schaeffer came to Iowa from Cornell University where he had been vice-president and dean. He was well received by all factions of a faculty weary of infighting. When he declared that "the faculty is the one necessary part of a university" he sounded a new note in administrative-faculty relationships. "The college professor of today," he said, "must be a specialist; he must first have obtained a broad, general education, and then, while not neglecting to keep himself abreast of the general progress of the world in the arts and sciences, in literature and philosophy, he must concentrate his higher powers and expend his best efforts on some single line of study."[31] The full implications of academic specialization were not to be realized for some years to come, but the path was now charted toward a professionalized faculty. It was not surprising that the new president found that teaching loads at Iowa were too heavy and too diversified. Many subjects in the humanities and social sciences were being neglected or treated inadequately. Schaeffer recognized the promising beginnings already made in the sciences and was determined to achieve similar results in the other fields.

Charles Bundy Wilson, a specialist in German literature whom Schaeffer had known at Cornell, was brought in to develop the program in modern languages. Isaac A. Loos and Benjamin F. Shambaugh joined the faculty in political science, William R. Perkins in history, and George Cram Cook in

English literature. Loos in particular played a prominent role in the development of the social sciences at the university. A former student of William Graham Sumner's at Yale, he had ambitious designs for courses in economics, sociology, and anthropology, as well as political science. Schaeffer wished to form a School of History and Political Science, whereas Loos preferred to orient political science toward the other social sciences. He prevailed with the regents and was made director of a School of Political and Social Science, but without administrative control of the other social science chairs. It was left to Shambaugh to develop the association of history and political science, achieved in part through the State Historical Society of Iowa, which was brought into close association with the university. In 1890–91 Loos offered a course in Socialism; the title was changed in the following year to the less sensitive Recent Economic History and Theory. But he continued to discuss such currently controversial topics as bi-metalism, railroad regulation, and the single tax.[32]

The struggle for more adequate financial support continued through the later decades of the nineteenth century. During the first forty-eight years of its existence the university had received only $248,000 for buildings. Schaeffer proposed an ambitious program including a liberal arts building, library, museum, hospital, and gymnasium. The legislature responded in 1890 with an appropriation of $125,000, the largest up to that time. It also provided funds for the liberal arts building which was to bear Schaeffer's name. In 1896 a one-tenth mill tax to be assessed for five years was to provide a university building fund. In his report to the board for 1887–89 the president pointed out that from the beginning the state had spent just under fourteen million dollars on its public institutions: forty-one percent of this for its three mental hospitals; thirty-four percent for charitable institutions; fourteen percent for its two penitentiaries; and nine percent for its three educational institutions, of which four and one-half percent had been devoted to the university. Critics nevertheless complained that it cost the public more to maintain a student at the university than to support a boy at the reform school. Schaeffer observed that it would be more appropriate to compare the university's costs with those of comparable institutions. Among seven such universities Harvard ranked at the top with an annual cost per student of $445. Iowa ranked at the bottom with $126 per student.[33]

The status of the president as chief executive officer of the university continued to be highly uncertain. In 1896 the regents ruled that faculty appointments were to be made by the board upon recommendation of the dean "in connection with" the chairman of the relevant regents' departmental committee and the executive committee of the board. This action appeared to circumvent the president and was so understood both by Schaeffer and by Henry Sabin, the state superintendent of public instruction and ex officio board member. The president could hardly have been reassured by regent A. W. Swalm, who informed him that his exclusion from the appointment process was not intended; it was assumed that the president was an "advising" member of all committees.[34]

President Schaeffer died in 1898, his life cut short at the relatively early age of fifty-five. He had come to the university at a time of crisis when the faculty ranks were decimated and its public repute was at its lowest ebb. He had nevertheless succeeded in restoring morale and in enunciating principles which would lead to a university in fact as well as in name.

Since the university was a public institution standing at the head of the state's educational system, its relationship to the public secondary schools had always posed difficult problems of "articulation." There was always agreement in principle that students should be able to advance by regular steps from the elementary schools to the highest university level. The state superintendent of public instruction was appropriately an ex officio member of the university governing board. But in the beginning, if the standards of admission to the university were to approximate those of the more securely established institutions, few if any Iowa students would be adequately prepared. In order to meet this problem the legislature in 1855 authorized the university to open a preparatory department. For over twenty years a two- or three-year program in mathematics, science, and classical languages prepared students for college-level work. In 1878, when the legislature deemed the high schools to be sufficiently competent to the task, the preparatory department was abolished.[35] It quickly became apparent, however, that many students were not adequately prepared, obliging the university to evade the legislative intent by instituting a subfreshman year. Relations with the schools would be greatly improved if the university could assure itself that high school graduates were indeed prepared, obviating the necessity for entrance examinations. A high school inspector was appointed whose duty it was to inspect and certify those schools where adequate preparatory work was offered. But in the absence of a common governing board and administration the difficulty of articulating school and college programs remained a source of friction between the public schools and the university. In the long run the university had little choice but to adapt itself to what the schools were able to accomplish in the way of preparation for college.

At a distance of more than a century it is difficult to determine with assurance what kind of academic standards prevailed in the early years. Critics of the university, many of whom were biased on other grounds, did not hesitate to ridicule it as the "Iowa City High School." The idea of a university as a company of scholars may have begun to permeate the consciousness of the midwestern academic community, but little was done at Iowa before the 1890s to bring such a company into being. No evidence survives of deliberate and systematic searches for faculty appointees of scholarly achievement or promise. Indeed, the few true scholars who stand out by virtue of their very isolation—Hinrichs, Calvin, Macbride, Patrick—must be regarded as happy accidents of a casual and unfocused process of recruitment. Nevertheless, when we inspect the collegiate curriculum, especially for the underclass years, it is hard to withhold a grudging admiration for an institution that required its students to confront such solid subjects as Greek, Latin, mathematics, and science undiluted by the froth that decorates the modern course of study. The early faculty members may not have been great scholars, but there is evidence that many of them were dedicated and capable teachers who earned the respect and affection of their students.

THREE STAGES OF DEVELOPMENT

The modern university as an institution is a complex pattern of behavior dominated by an animating idea. It incorporates people and structures, money and skills. It exhibits hierarchical authority balanced by extraordinary autonomy in its functioning parts. It processes a product—students—while simultaneously championing timeless ideals. It fosters a continuing tension between the divergent demands it makes on its faculty for "teaching, research, and service." It is singularly dependent on the outside world for its very existence, yet it is a haven for scholars who pursue their arcane mysteries in cloistered seclusion. The formation of such a complex institution was obviously not the work of a day. In Iowa it was the outcome of a process of slow growth, a process which was in fact coterminous with the history of the state itself.

Three stages of development may be readily discerned. The earliest, beginning with the founding of the university, was characterized by arbitrary and often capricious management by those in positions of power who may have had no well-considered or coherent idea of the purposes or possi-

bilities of the institution. Because they were laymen—regents or legislators—who divided their time among a wide range of activities their
interventions were sporadic, and sometimes motivated by considerations
having little to do with the purposes of the university. In the early stage
there was little understanding of the importance of what might be called
the integrity of the institution as a functioning entity. Conflicts within the
university were often open and bitter, provoking intervention from outside. The distinction between policy making and administration was not
understood. Even more important, no one at first grasped the significance
of the principle of delegation of authority, the principle which made possible the preservation of formal power in the hands of the governing body
while delegating its practical exercise to subordinate levels of management. Delegation indeed presupposed the presence of such levels, which
did not exist in the early years. The duties and authority of the university
president remained uncertain until well into the twentieth century, while
the president in the early years had no colleges, schools, and departments
to which responsibilities could in turn be delegated. In the absence of
delegation the exercise of power often assumed an arbitrary form that
amazes the modern student of university practices. Eventually, after more
than a century of development, the practice of delegation would be
so firmly established that certain Engineering College faculty members
would claim to possess governmental powers, and it would be necessary
for a latter-day president to remind them that they possessed only such
authority as the regents had directly or indirectly delegated to them.[36]

The successive boards of trustees and regents had been charged by law
with the responsibility of governing the university. Initially they did so directly, adopting and changing curricula and hiring and firing professors. It
became accepted practice for faculty members to go directly to board
members with their needs and complaints.[37] The minutes of board meetings show with minute detail how the board supervised operations, approving the purchase of chalk, or denying the librarian's request for a
bookcase. Until 1886 the president was an ex officio member of the board,
thus in a practical way blending their respective functions and rendering it
difficult to determine in retrospect what the president's powers and duties
actually were. Although professors expected to teach as long as their services were deemed satisfactory there was nothing to prevent the board
from terminating them at its pleasure. The legislative investigating committee of 1888 chided the board for the summary manner in which it dismissed professors, but it did not question the board's authority to do so;
nor did it stipulate that dismissals be justified by appropriate causes.

The second stage of institutional development, the era of creative anarchy, began at least symbolically in 1908 with the appointment of Carl Seashore as dean of the Graduate College. By that time the university had achieved sufficient size and stability to support its own internal life relatively free from arbitrary interventions. The principal institutional forms of colleges, schools, and departments based on the precedents of the older institutions to the east were now in place. Within these forms was room for local variations. The situation was now ripe for exploitation by a generation of aggressive, creative individuals who would seize the opportunity to pursue their own purposes within the institution, initiating new programs and leaving a long-lasting stamp on the overall profile of the university. More than a half-century later the activities of Seashore, Loos, Fitzgerald, Steindler, Alcock, Foerster, Mabie, and Clapp would still be readily discernible, if only in the continuing efforts to undo some of the bonds they had so securely tied. They may appropriately be called anarchists because unlike Eliot at Harvard or Harper at Chicago, men with dominating conceptions of what a university should be, each of them single-mindedly pursued his own interests and in doing so imparted to the university a distinctive character.[38]

The third stage, which stretched through the middle of the twentieth century to the present, is the age of institutional inertia. The organization has now become thoroughly stabilized. The governing board, which since 1909 has been charged with the management of three universities as well as schools for the blind and deaf, can no longer oversee the details of operation as in earlier times. Externally, the relations among the legislature, regents, and university president have become regularized. Internally, a settled pattern of colleges, schools, and departments has become fixed. Faculty duties and expectations are clarified in the triune formula of teaching, research, and service. Terms of faculty appointment are specified, with security assured by the principle of "indefinite tenure." The type figure of the period was President Virgil M. Hancher, who considered among his principal achievements during a presidency of twenty-four years the adoption of a funded faculty retirement system and a plan for medical faculty compensation. During the period of inertia the institution tended to run on its own momentum. Appropriations, though always inadequate, were relatively dependable and were used chiefly to meet fixed commitments. Administration, now for the most part in the hands of lawyer-presidents, was judged by standards of efficiency rather than academic leadership. The faculty became professionalized, which was doubtless the reason why the university came to look much like every other university.

CHAPTER ONE

George MacLean and
the New University

On September 29, 1899, George Edwin MacLean was formally installed as the eighth president of the State University of Iowa. The inaugural exercises were held out of doors, before the east front of the Old Capitol building which the state had bequeathed to the university when the seat of government had been removed to Des Moines. It was a chilly fall day, and a sharp wind characteristically swept around the corners of the building in its exposed location on the bluff above the meandering Iowa River. It was a raw wind that blew MacLean no good, for the exercises were protracted—the chief feature was an address by the new president in which he set forth his ambitious plans to elevate the institution to equal rank with its peers in the region. A chill settled upon the audience, an event which proved to be of both practical and symbolic significance. Practically, it fixed the president's resolve to build a suitable auditorium, an objective which was to become a source of bitter controversy. Symbolically, the chill alienated a portion of the faculty who resented or feared his proposed innovations.[1]

Upon the sudden death of President Schaeffer in 1898 the regents had designated Amos Currier, professor of Latin and dean of the collegiate faculty, as acting president pending the choice of a successor. Schaeffer had been a popular president who had secured modest increases in appropriations and salaries without burdening his faculty with new programs. There was strong faculty sentiment in favor of a president chosen from their own ranks. The botanist Thomas Huston Macbride and an ambitious young political scientist, Benjamin F. Shambaugh, were reported to be the faculty candidates. The regents, possibly fearing factional repercussions, thought it best to pass over the local candidates and bring in an outsider.[2]

A search committee consisting of Governor L. M. Shaw, State Superintendent of Public Instruction R. C. Barrett, Acting President Currier, and five regents conducted a broad and careful search. Advice was sought from eminent educators. Candidates were interviewed both by the committee and by the entire board. A favored prospect was Dean Harry B. Hutchins of the University of Michigan Law School, who visited the campus and conferred with the committee but then withdrew his candidacy.[3] The search was concluded with the choice of Chancellor George E. MacLean of the University of Nebraska, who was characterized by the board as "in the prime of life, a refined, cultivated, Christian gentleman; a pleasing and effective public speaker; a thoroughly educated and enthusiastic scholar; an administrator of proven ability; and a man who will be a positive moral force in the university." He was to be paid a salary of $6,000 annually. Although this was less than the amount paid to the presidents of the state universities in neighboring states the board felt defensive about paying such a substantial sum. The full board accepted the recommendation of the search committee by a vote of nine to four, with three members of the search committee voting against the recommendation.[4] The new president thus began his administration with something less than the solid confidence of regents and faculty.

Whatever the reservations may have been, the critics could hardly have faulted MacLean's formal credentials. A Connecticut native and graduate of Williams College in 1871, he had taken theological training at Yale and had held brief pastorates in New York state. He had then abandoned the ministry and had gone to Europe for graduate study, receiving a Ph.D. in philology at the University of Leipzig in 1883. For twelve years he had been professor of English and chairman of the department at the University of Minnesota. In 1895 he had gone to the University of Nebraska as chancellor and had had a vigorous and successful administration before coming to Iowa at the age of forty-nine.[5]

Apart from what they may have learned of MacLean's tenure at Nebraska the regents also had available for inspection a newly published little volume entitled *A Decade of Development in American State Universities*,[6] in which MacLean set forth certain basic educational principles which might be expected to characterize his administration. He noted that the new university that was emerging in the more progressive American states was an educational institution for serious-minded adults and would no longer stand *in loco parentis* for juveniles. Its structure consisted of departments, schools, and colleges. It was rapidly raising the standards of professional education to full graduate status. Its faculties were scholars as well as teachers who acknowledged the obligation to disseminate the results of their investigations through publication. The leader of such an institution was a new type of scholar-administrator who knew how to serve both the scholarly community and the world of public affairs.[7] Each of these prin-

George MacLean. Courtesy of the University of Iowa Archives.

ciples if applied to the University of Iowa would result in significant innovations. It is reasonable to assume, therefore, that in their discussions with the candidate the regents understood and approved at least in general terms the kind of university MacLean would wish to develop for the state of Iowa.

THE UNIVERSITY IN 1899

The Iowa City of the turn of the century was a placid and somewhat isolated community where life moved easily through its appointed rounds. Delight Ansley, who was born in 1906, later likened life there to "a sedate game of croquet just before the eruption of a volcano."[8] Her father had come to the university in 1900 as professor of English at a salary of $2,000. They lived in a comfortable ten-room house on a large lot with a barn. There were no live-in servants; "hired girls" came in to help with the cleaning and laundry. Junior faculty members on less munificent salaries found that living expenses were correspondingly modest. Stephen Bush, who joined the faculty in 1901 as instructor in modern languages at a salary of $800, obtained board and room for $34 a month.[9] Although business and professional people were beginning to drive automobiles university people did not own them and were accustomed to walk to their destinations. Ansley was certainly mistaken in thinking that almost everyone in town was connected with the university. There was in fact a fairly rigid separation of town and gown; her own life was lived wholly within the circle of university families. Both faculty and students, who were almost all native Iowans, shared a conviction as to the superiority of Iowans and the Iowa way of life, balanced by a somewhat morbid sensitivity to the presumed condescension of easterners.[10]

The university in 1899 was a modest institution consisting of six departments: collegiate, legal, medical, homeopathic medical, dental, and pharmacy. The collegiate department was the largest, enrolling 615 undergraduates and 83 graduate students. As the capstone of the state's educational system the collegiate department sought to articulate itself as widely as possible with the high schools, publishing in the catalog a list of 120 accredited and 66 approved high schools whose graduates would be admitted without examination. Six courses of study were offered by the department, each consisting of a combination of required work and electives. All required military drill for male students. The classical course emphasized ancient and modern languages, science, history, and some mathematics.

The philosophical A course was similar, except that Greek was not required. The philosophical B course substituted modern for classical languages. The courses in general science, civil engineering, and electrical engineering emphasized those subjects. The department also offered graduate work in various subjects leading to master's and doctoral degrees.[11]

The professional departments at that time were not yet graduate programs. Admission requirements of the two medical departments were rather less rigorous than those for admission to the collegiate department. High school graduates, provided that they had had a year of Latin, were admitted without examination. Each department offered a four-year course for the M.D. degree. Each also offered jointly with the collegiate department a combined six-year course leading to B.S. and M.D. degrees.[12]

The law department, while affirming legal practice to be a learned profession and recommending prior collegiate study, nevertheless admitted students with a high school education "or its equivalent." The two-year course of study leading to the L.B. degree coincided with the legal requirement for admission to the state bar, and the bar examination set by the state Supreme Court's bar examiners also served as the final examination for the degree. Although collegiate study was encouraged, no combined collegiate and legal course was available since the bar requirements mandated a full schedule of legal study during the two years of the course.[13]

The dental department offered a three-year course leading to the D.D.S. degree. A high school diploma was required for admission. A refresher course for practitioners and a dental assistant's course were also offered. The pharmacy course of two years was not of collegiate grade. Admission was gained by examination in English, penmanship, geography, and arithmetic or by submission of evidence of having studied such subjects in grammar school. Graduates received the degree of Ph.G. (Graduate in Pharmacy), and were duly registered as pharmacists by the State Board of Pharmacy.[14]

The administrative structure of the university was lean, not to say gaunt. President Schaeffer had followed tradition by continuing to teach, although he found it increasingly burdensome to carry on all of his functions without secretarial assistance. He enlisted the aid of his family, teaching his son the most efficient way to lick stamps and seal envelopes.[15] A student recalled that when he enrolled as a freshman in 1895 Professor Patrick had registered him by writing his choice of courses on a card and tossing it into a shoe box.[16] While the president served as chairman of the executive committee of the collegiate department and was closely involved in the affairs of that department, the professional departments were oriented toward their respective professions and were only marginally involved in the institutional life of the university.

The new president commenced his inaugural address with a rather florid celebration of the history of the state and the virtues of its stable, homogeneous, and democratic citizens. He emphasized the great wealth of Iowa: first in agriculture and seventeenth in manufacturing. Among the north-central states only Ohio and Illinois were richer. There was a purpose in his recitation of material blessings, for the newcomer intended to prod the state into more generous support of its university.

The principal burden of the address, however, was to set forth the chief characteristics of the new university MacLean proposed to develop in Iowa City. As part of the public school system it would be truly a people's university, coeducational, nonsectarian, and free. At the same time it would serve the private academies and church-related colleges with its professional and graduate schools. The most important and distinguishing feature of the new university would be its separate graduate department, which would displace the collegiate department as the central focus of university activity. The undergraduate programs would now gain coherence and purpose as they oriented the students toward graduate and professional work. Eventually the high schools would do collegiate-level work while the graduate school would absorb the upperclass undergraduate work. It seems unlikely that an American educator at that time could have arrived at such a vision without a German university experience.

MacLean's vision extended beyond the campus to the state and national context of higher education. Articulation of high school and college had already been achieved largely through the agency of the State Teachers Association. MacLean was hopeful that the college section of that organization would achieve the same result in articulating the state's colleges with the university's graduate and professional programs. Other public institutions should also be coordinated with university programs. Museums, public libraries, learned societies, and philanthropic and penological institutions should all be brought into a federated relationship with the university for scientific and educational purposes. At the national level, all of the state universities and A & M colleges in effect constituted a national university which should be recognized as such and coordinated by the federal government.[17]

There were elements both of style and substance in the address that were disturbing to many of the faculty who gathered on the lawn before the Old Capitol. The speaker's orotund manner of delivery reminded them unhappily of the succession of clergyman-presidents under whom the university had for so long languished. More ominously, the projected absorption of the collegiate department by the high schools on the one hand and the graduate program on the other, however fanciful it might be, suggested a boldness, not to say rashness, that disturbed those who were comfortable with the present arrangements. Although there was nothing new in the assertion that a university was a company of scholars there was some uneasiness lest the new president apply the principle literally in such practical matters as salary determination and promotion policy.

The faculty's reservations about MacLean would soon come to the surface, but in the meanwhile the president moved vigorously to implement his program. The six existing departments were designated colleges, while graduate study was separated from the former collegiate department, now liberal arts, and assigned to a college of its own under a newly designated graduate dean, the mathematician Laenas Weld. Within the colleges subject-matter departments were created, and in certain instances groups of departments with related interests were designated schools.[18]

The process of elevating the professional colleges to the status of graduate programs was also inaugurated. MacLean echoed Charles William Eliot's warning that liberal education was not safe in a country in which the vast majority of professionals were not liberally educated. The law course was extended from two to three years, while the academic year in medicine and pharmacy was extended from seven to nine months. As an inducement to future students in law and dentistry to undertake liberal arts study before enrolling in the professional colleges the principle of the combined course in liberal arts and medicine was extended to those subjects. By taking five hours in law, together with five hours in history, economics, political science, or philosophy, liberal arts seniors would be able to complete requirements for both degrees in six or six and one-half years. Lengthening the law program beyond the minimum set by the bar requirements introduced the distinction between legal study as a professional and as an academic pursuit. A comparable combination was made available to predental students.[19]

Twelve new departments and thirty-three new faculty positions were created. The new departments in liberal arts were economics and statistics, Scandinavian languages, physical education, speech, and Greek art and archaeology. In medicine, lectureships were added in pediatrics, sur-

gery, and electro-therapy; in homeopathic medicine, lectureships in pe-
dology and the diseases of women; in dentistry, professorships in dental
anatomy and orthodontia.

The administrative structure was greatly enlarged with the addition of
new specialized offices. Following the appointment of the Graduate College dean new deanships were established for the summer session, for men,
and for women. New offices of registrar, examiner (admissions), university
editor, university publisher, superintendent of grounds and buildings, and
high school inspector were established. Some of these functions had previously been performed by the on-campus secretary of the Board of Regents, William J. Haddock, who had held the office for thirty-eight years.
In divesting Haddock of his various duties the president created one of his
bitterest critics.[20]

A University Senate originally consisting of all members of the faculty
had been in existence since 1887, but it had met only infrequently to discuss matters of little consequence. MacLean proposed to reinvigorate it,
both as a forum for consideration of general university matters and as a
means of building faculty morale through involvement with issues of common concern. Senate boards on general university needs, auditing, athletics, library, and publications were created. He found, however, that the
faculty members did not welcome what they presumably perceived as a potentially intrusive agency.[21] Each academic unit preferred to go its own
way with a minimum of interference. The rivalries and personal jealousies
rife within the faculty were effective barriers to the development of a sense
of collegial identity.[22] Over the years the two issues that received the lion's
share of Senate attention were athletics and student intoxication. The organization of a Student Council encountered comparable apathy in the
student body. The president reported, no doubt with a mixture of disap-
pointment and relief, that students were concerned primarily with their
personal affairs and took little interest in student government. In the absence of dormitories or commons for dining, fraternities and sororities
provided many practical and social necessities.

To accomplish all of this in a single biennium and in the face of faculty
and student hostility or indifference was a striking testimonial to Mac-
Lean's energy and effectiveness. It was unquestionably the most important
biennium in the university's entire history. Whatever reservations about
him the regents may have had at the outset were now put to rest, and until
it was dissolved in 1909 the board firmly supported him in his forthcoming
struggles with faculty and alumni groups. Financing the innovations required a strenuous campaign to persuade the legislature to provide addi-

tional funding. MacLean took charge of the lobbying, and for the remainder of his tenure regularly occupied a Des Moines hotel room during the days when the university appropriation was under consideration, buttonholing legislators and directing the efforts of regents and influential alumni.[23] At the top of the president's list of needed physical facilities stood a library, museum, gymnasium-armory, and assembly hall. He reminded the legislators that while students in the professional colleges might properly be expected to pay their way, exclusive of buildings and equipment, the Liberal Arts College should not be thus financed. As the capstone of the state's educational system, and in order to serve rich and poor alike, it should be as nearly tuition-free as possible. It should not be necessary for young people to leave the state in order to receive a liberal education.[24]

In comparison with neighboring states Iowa ranked at the bottom in financial support of its university. For the academic year 1897–98 Michigan supported its university most generously, providing an income from all sources nearly four times greater than that of the University of Iowa. Wisconsin and Illinois were next in rank, followed closely by Minnesota. Even Nebraska and Missouri outranked Iowa.[25] Comparisons such as these were regularly made over the years by successive presidents and regents when justifying requests for increased appropriations. Their effectiveness depended upon the sensitivity of legislators and the public to Iowa's standing in the competitive educational struggle. Relative standing meant little to those with only modest expectations. MacLean identified four explanations for the state's meager support of its university, probably in reverse order of importance. First, the state's constitution prohibited public indebtedness, which prevented it from borrowing for educational purposes as was done in many states. Second, the decision had been made to give priority to penal and charitable institutions. As MacLean put it, the state had chosen to favor "reformative" over "formative" institutions. Third, the large number of denominational colleges in relation to the population blinded Iowans to the need for a university. The public had come to think of the university as simply one among many, instead of being higher than the others. Fourth and most important was the state's determination to maintain separate agricultural and teachers' colleges. If the three state institutions were combined, Iowa's higher educational statistics would compare favorably with those of surrounding states; separately, the appropriations were usually inadequate for each of them. In spite of the handicaps MacLean was determined to push vigorously for more generous public support.[26]

PRESIDENT AND BOARD

MacLean's achievements were the more remarkable when the ill-defined nature of regental management of the university is considered. The board consisted of the governor and superintendent of public instruction, ex officio, and one member from each congressional district. The latter were unsalaried citizens usually deeply immersed in their respective occupations. According to a gentleman's agreement the political balance among the members would shift as it shifted in the legislature. Although formally elected by the legislature board members were in fact designated by district caucuses at the state conventions of each party. Under these circumstances educational considerations were likely to be irrelevant in the selection of board members.[27] Nor was the board effectively organized to perform its functions. It had no full-time salaried staff except for the secretary and treasurer, who were located in Iowa City, where they performed regular administrative functions. Nevertheless, the board persisted in its traditional practice of involving itself in the daily routine of administrative decision making. It organized itself in twelve standing committees, each of which actively engaged in the management of one of the colleges or some other aspect of university operations. The deans reported directly to these committees, which in turn forwarded recommendations on salary and other budget items to the finance committee. No distinctions appear to have been made between important and trivial matters. MacLean might protest an attempt by the Law College committee to make a faculty appointment which in the opinion of law chancellor Emlin McClain would have jeopardized the college's commitment to the case method of instruction. At the same time the board would be busily approving the purchase of old gold decorative bunting and issuing a key to the liberal arts hall to Professor William C. Wilcox, head of the history department.[28]

Under these circumstances the situation was ripe for a strong president to seize the initiative and attempt to establish an efficient allocation of functions between president and board. MacLean drew upon the analogy of corporate management. The board should determine policy and exercise a general oversight of university operations. The president should be the chief executive officer in all educational and business matters. But the corporate analogy hardly sufficed to define the delicate position of the president between his two constituencies. He was admittedly the servant of the board and should always be prepared to modify his position to suit its wishes "except in matters of principle."[29] At the same time he was the leader of the faculty and its representative in dealings with the board. He insisted that faculty members bring their business to him and not go directly to the board as had been their custom. This became a major faculty grievance against him, although it undoubtedly strengthened his position as a mediator positioned to play faculty and board off against each other.[30] In his pivotal position MacLean was able to establish strong leadership. After surviving a faculty challenge in 1904, thanks to the board's support, he consolidated his position, and by 1909 when the board was abolished he was in firm control.

THE NEW LIBERAL ARTS PROGRAM

Perhaps the most controversial of MacLean's proposed reforms was the prospective minimizing of the role of the collegiate department in the university structure. From the beginning this department had been the largest and most important unit of the university. It had absorbed the early preparatory and teacher-training programs and had fostered the beginnings of graduate study within its own departments. But the new president now anticipated the time when the high schools would provide the general education of the underclass college years while the graduate and professional schools would offer the specialized work of the upperclass years. It was little wonder that the collegiate faculty should have received the newcomer with less than complete enthusiasm.

If MacLean anticipated the disappearance of the Liberal Arts College as an organized entity he was, of course, quite mistaken. That college would continue to be the foundation stone of the university and as the principal magnet in the ongoing struggle for student enrollments its importance could not be denied. But with the rapid growth of graduate and professional programs the undergraduate college was forced to yield an increasing share of budget and administrative attention. Some elements of the new relationships were well established before MacLean's arrival. The detailed specification of admissions requirements laid the foundations for a conceivable extension of high school programs into the underclass college years.[31] At the senior level the combined course in liberal arts and medicine, already noted, paved the way for similar combinations with other professional subjects. Combined undergraduate and graduate courses were also offered in the various subject-matter fields of the liberal arts. The cumulative effect of these developments might conceivably lead to the result MacLean envisioned.

A change of fundamental importance in liberal arts occurred in the academic year 1905–1906 with the introduction of a required departmental "major" in the upperclass years, a pattern which has survived for nearly a century. With the passage of the years undergraduates and faculty alike have come to take the major concentration for granted, little realizing that, in the minds of those who introduced it, it had been intended to serve as an introduction to graduate work. Under the previous plan of study in which the student chose one of four "courses," or fields, the mandatory work had been concentrated in the underclass years, while elective freedom was granted to juniors and seniors. The catalog for 1898–99 had noted that the student was free to concentrate the electives in a single field, thus constituting a voluntary major, although it is not known how many students availed themselves of this opportunity. In the following year the science faculty specifically discouraged the practice.[32] The new plan of study required English in the freshman and sophomore years together with an ancient or modern foreign language in the absence of previously earned credits. Freshmen were also required to take a course in history or in economics and government; a course in animal biology, botany, chemistry, or zoology; and a course in mathematics if later work in physics, chemistry, or commerce was contemplated. The surviving records are singularly barren of evidence of faculty discussion of the change, which, however, was clearly in the wind. The engineering departments and the School of Political and Social Science had already introduced major concentrations, as had the philosophical B course prior to its abandonment in 1900–1901. The old nineteenth-century curriculum quietly expired, and the classical languages were the principal casualties.

The new plan of underclass distribution and upperclass concentration had both practical and theoretical implications. Whatever the educational rationale of the old plan it had had the practical effect of assuring a fairly even distribution of students among the various subject fields. Under the new plan, in order to offset potential enrollment imbalances consequent upon the free choice of major field, it was stipulated that the student must take twenty-four hours of work in areas remote from the major subject. Theoretically, the major concentration served to orient the student toward advanced study, thus furthering MacLean's objective of merging the upperclass years with graduate work. The offering of courses open to both undergraduates and graduate students also pointed to the same end. This practice also antedated MacLean's administration. It was always clouded with a certain ambiguity: was it intended to introduce advanced undergraduates to graduate-level work or was it to provide unprepared graduate students with the preliminary work necessary for graduate study? The question could presumably be answered only by examining the preparation of each graduate student as well as the content of each course. Nevertheless, the introduction of the upperclass major as the focal point of the liberal arts curriculum cemented a new and intimate relationship between undergraduate teaching and research. Professors who offered the specialized courses to major students in their departments were likely to be research scholars whose academic standing among their peers was a source of pride to the university and an attraction to ambitious students.

While the Liberal Arts College was thus assuming its modern form under his administration MacLean continued to stress its transitional character. As chairman of the Committee of Standards of the National Association of State Universities he drafted the 1908 report defining the characteristics of the standard American university.[33] In the ideal pattern the standard college consisted of two years in which high school work was completed and two more in which specialized work pointed toward graduate study. The combined courses with the professional fields established a similar relationship with the professional colleges. Nothing was said to indicate a distinctive role for the Liberal Arts College as such. MacLean acknowledged that his conception of the undergraduate program would leave the independent liberal arts colleges in an awkward position, but he professed to believe that they could find suitable affiliations with the "greater university," whether public or denominational, which he envisioned.[34]

Nevertheless, however uncertain in MacLean's mind the institutional status of the Liberal Arts College may have been, he remained a firm believer in liberal education as that term was understood at the turn of the century. It rested upon the heritage of classical, Christian, and Renaissance traditions. Its aim was to liberalize, to bring one's capacities to full fruition, to emancipate from provincialism, to understand and react effectively to the general culture, and to orient the student "to nature and to God." He condemned both the mercenary view of education as having cash value and the specialist's impatience with general education. In his talks to students MacLean constantly emphasized character formation as the great aim and end of liberal education. Moreover, he faced if he did not solve the problem inherent in the situation in which the same individuals functioned simultaneously as the liberal arts and the graduate faculties. The Stanford president, David Starr Jordan, had expressed the view that the kind of teaching required by the theory of liberal education could not be combined with the scholarly commitment to the strict disciplinary research required by membership in the graduate and professional faculties. The Harvard philosopher Josiah Royce had taken the opposite side, insisting that a close association of the two was essential. MacLean leaned to the latter view. He believed that the state universities had demonstrated conclusively that liberal education and specialized graduate and professional training could successfully be combined in a single faculty.[35]

Amos Currier retired as liberal arts dean in 1907, and MacLean offered the position to the graduate dean, Laenas Weld. The memorandum that Weld submitted in response set forth his recommendations for what he considered to be the completion of the college organization. He noted that at that time there was but one school, Political and Social Science, which he believed to exercise undue influence in collegiate matters. He proposed to create five additional schools: Education and Philosophy, Language and Literature, Fine Arts, Physical Science, and Biological Science. The directors of these schools together with the liberal arts and graduate deans and the chairman of the Committee on Admissions would constitute a collegiate executive committee. Weld doubtless knew that MacLean regarded such schools as germs from which colleges would grow. Nevertheless, little came of Weld's proposal. Education was shortly to be set apart in a college of its own. An affiliated School of Music and a School of Fine Arts were organized. Save for the College of Education, however, these visions of schools and colleges came to nothing, as liberal arts continued to grow as a single administrative unit under its dean.

Weld also believed that there must be a more distinct identity for the Graduate College. Graduate study had emerged within the liberal arts departments and was fostered or neglected according to the whims of each department. The Graduate College, he insisted, should have the authority to impose scholarly research standards in all departments. At the moment, research was being vigorously promoted in psychology, but not in physics or chemistry. It was appropriate that Weld should recommend as his successor for the graduate deanship the energetic young psychologist Carl Seashore.[36]

The Graduate College from the beginning occupied an anomalous position among the seven colleges of the university. The graduate faculty as originally constituted consisted of those offering graduate courses, namely, liberal arts and preclinical medical faculty members. Weld noted that in establishing a college without a faculty exclusively its own the university was acting out of practical necessity; he seemed to imply that eventually a separate graduate faculty would come into being, thus neatly solving the problem of teaching versus research. Seashore, on the other hand, was to make a virtue out of necessity. He celebrated the relationship of the

Graduate College with the Liberal Arts College as a "unique partnership" based not upon separate faculties or formal allocations of functions and responsibilities but upon a feeling shared by the deans of both colleges of mutual obligation to build up the arts and sciences. The liberal arts dean had the salary budget and the formal authority to make faculty appointments, but at least during Seashore's tenure no major recommendations on appointments, programs, or policies were formulated without consultation with and concurrence of the graduate dean. As the colleges of Education, Engineering, and Commerce developed graduate programs similar relationships with them were established. It is apparent that in the absence of formal authority much depended upon the personal influence of the graduate dean with both the collegiate deans and the president. Seashore, who was not a man to minimize his sense of his own importance, attributed his influence to his scholarly prominence. MacLean's strong commitment to research undoubtedly strengthened the graduate dean's position.[37] In later times, however, when the administrative offices were occupied by men of lesser stature the weakness of the graduate dean's position became only too apparent.[38]

PRESIDENT VERSUS FACULTY

In spite of his abilities and the record of his accomplishments on behalf of the university MacLean always remained unpopular with a substantial majority of his faculty. The trivial nature of many of their complaints put the faculty in a most unfavorable light. They complained of the president's flamboyant personal style, which they found offensive or ridiculous. Charges of deviousness and dishonesty rested upon the casual manner in which he was said to make oral promises that were not recorded and were subsequently forgotten.[39] A list of MacLean's offenses compiled by secretary Haddock following his resignation in 1902 reflected the petty nature of much of the faculty criticism. The president had converted departments into colleges, allegedly an illegal act. In the absence of a suitable auditorium he had introduced the practice of holding commencements under a tent, with pomp and ritual all too reminiscent of a circus. He had greatly increased the size of the university catalog, a needless expense. By strengthening degree requirements he had caused a decline in student enrollments. He had introduced a weekly student assembly with overtones both of a prayer meeting and a pep rally. While he no longer taught a class in his academic specialty, he had nevertheless provided himself with the luxury of two secretaries.[40] In order to recover enrollments lost elsewhere he had affiliated with the university a proprietary music school, which Haddock regarded as a frivolous activity. Finally, the director of physical culture and athletics had become involved in a domestic scandal, and it was alleged that MacLean had protected the offender rather than firing him promptly as he should have done, although the president had in fact managed the matter with the full knowledge and approval of the regents.[41]

A more significant cause of dissatisfaction was the determination of building priority. With the exception of the Old Capitol the university had always been inadequately housed in cheap and flimsy buildings. The first substantially constructed fireproof building had been authorized during the Schaeffer administration to house the liberal arts program and was subsequently named for Schaeffer. The science faculty expected that a matching building on what was later to be known as the Pentacrest campus would be provided for them. MacLean, however, had his own priority list. Recalling the inaugural chill, he proposed to build first a combined assembly hall, armory, and gymnasium. Thanks to the one-tenth mill building tax he had persuaded the legislature to provide, he would be able to proceed with a law building, a fireproof museum, and a library.[42] In March 1901 a fire in the medical building west of the new liberal arts building spread to the adjacent engineering building and destroyed both structures, a loss MacLean privately considered to be a blessing in disguise.[43] Temporary sheds were provided for medicine and engineering, while a new medical building became the first in a medical campus located on the north side of Iowa Avenue. When in 1903 the regents affirmed MacLean's priority list, proposing to build first a combined assembly hall, armory, and gymnasium, followed by a library and museum, there was a vigorous faculty protest resulting in a revision of the plan. Thanks to a doubling of the millage tax it would be possible to begin two buildings simultaneously: an armory-gymnasium and a science building containing an assembly hall and quarters for the library. As soon as permanent buildings for the latter functions were provided the entire building would be turned over to the science departments. The science faculty was not pleased with this solution, although it was hardly anticipated that the library would remain in the science building for half a century, while the assembly hall (Macbride) would survive to the present day.[44]

Beyond the general unhappiness left by the building controversy there were individual grievances resulting from MacLean's handling of certain appointments. The search for a law dean following the resignation of chancellor Emlin McClain in 1901 resulted in the alienation of attorney general Milton Remley, who had apparently aspired to the position. After Charles Noble Gregory was appointed to succeed McClain the president assured Remley that his name had never been under consideration, when in fact it had been discussed with at least one of the regents.[45] Whatever the facts may have been, Remley, who was publisher of the *Iowa City Citizen*, became a bitter critic of the president and may well have been one of the sources of the flow of hostile press reports that emanated from Iowa City. Arthur V. Sims, head of the department of engineering, was another enemy. Following the fire of 1901 Sims had angered MacLean by lobbying vigorously for a new science-engineering building. Two years later, when the engineering department was reorganized as the School of Applied Science Sims was passed over as director, the appointment going to the mathematician Laenas Weld.[46] MacLean also incurred the enmity of the professor of chemistry, Launcelot W. Andrews. Prior to 1901, when Wilbur J. Teeters joined the pharmacy faculty, there had been no specialist in pharmacy except the dean, Emil Boerner; the others, including Andrews, were drawn from liberal arts and medicine. When the pharmacy department was elevated to collegiate status and Boerner retired, Andrews aspired to the deanship but was passed over for Teeters. These estranged faculty members took the lead in organizing a movement to oust MacLean.[47]

The president's troubles were compounded by the coarse and venal character of the Iowa press of that era. It was an age of highly personal journalism in which small-town editors did not hesitate to allow their personal grievances to color their coverage of the news. MacLean had early alienated the press by declining to place advertisements on the ground that he had no funds for that purpose when in fact he did have a small budget which was used to place ads through an agency in a few strategically located papers. On other occasions he carelessly said that it was not the policy of the university to advertise. Indignant editors refused to print university news items which they chose to regard as attempts to secure unpaid advertising. They heaped abuse on the president in exaggerated accounts of his troubles that President Bradley of Grinnell characterized as "wolfish" and "brutal." Rumors of conflicts with the regents and impending resignation were widely circulated.[48]

Matters came to a head after several local alumni groups, urged on by Sims and Andrews, passed resolutions criticizing MacLean's administration and demanding an investigation by the regents. Finding that they could not ignore the matter the regents announced a hearing for June 14, 1904, to investigate criticisms of the university administration by the press and alumni groups and invited critics to appear and air their complaints.[49] At the closed hearing held in the Old Capitol Milton Remley repeated the criticisms of MacLean's personality and policies that have already been indicated. He alleged that the president had made slanderous charges against professors Macbride, Shambaugh, Andrews, and Sims, but declined to reveal the sources of the information.[50] F. W. Beckman of Des Moines then made the mistake of mentioning the names of faculty members who were said to be critical of MacLean. It was a list of some fifteen senior professors, all but the medical dean James R. Guthrie members of the liberal arts faculty. There is no way of knowing how many of them would have appeared voluntarily, for the regents under the leadership of Parker Holbrook immediately shifted the focus of investigation from press and alumni complaints to faculty grievances and summoned the named faculty members to testify, much to the discomfort of several of them. Out of testimony often extracted reluctantly came the mixture of personal dislikes and policy disagreements that reflected rather more unfavorably on the faculty than on the president.

Dean Currier provided a relatively balanced and dispassionate assessment of the situation. He acknowledged that while there was considerable unrest and dissatisfaction in the liberal arts faculty the press reports were inflated and wholly unreliable. In addition to the matter of building priority he noted that the hostility of science and engineering faculty members was explained in part by MacLean's determination to balance the strong science departments with comparable appointments in the humanities, which one might have expected the scientists to have welcomed.[51] Dean Weld uncovered another source of dissatisfaction when he revealed that in an early faculty meeting the president had indicated that he wished to be mediator between faculty and board and that he expected faculty members to bring their business to him rather than to the board directly.[52] Law dean Gregory believed that MacLean's determination to strengthen the graduate and professional programs alienated the liberal arts faculty.[53] Finally, Carl Seashore testified that MacLean had always dealt candidly with the faculty; that the majority always prevailed in faculty meetings; and that the discontent could be traced to a small number of disgruntled faculty members. The names of Andrews and Sims regularly recurred in these enumerations.[54]

After two days of hearings the regents unanimously adopted a resolution declaring that they found no cause for making a change in the presidency of the university. They condemned improper and unwarranted criticism of the administration by faculty members. Complaints should be directed to the board and not made on the streets. The resignations of professors Andrews and Sims were requested and accepted. Governor Cummins, who had attended part of the hearings, brought the good news to MacLean, who thereupon submitted his own resignation, which the regents rejected.[55] The outcome of the hearings was greatly to strengthen the position of the president as the principal administrative officer. Faculty opinion and grievances must now be voiced through established channels of communication over which the administration could, if it chose, exercise a good deal of influence. So long as the university continued under its own governing board MacLean remained in firm control. After 1909, when the new board decided to dispense with his services, faculty restiveness was not among the specified causes of dissatisfaction with him.

SCHOOL SPIRIT

The cultivation in the student body of university spirit and pride in the institution was a matter about which MacLean felt strongly. He was not content to allow institutional patriotism to grow naturally as the university became a stronger and more visible institution. School spirit should vigorously be promoted by substituting a variety of sponsored activities for the informal diversions by which students had traditionally amused themselves. There should be convocations addressed by noted scholars and public figures, intramural and intercollegiate forensics, and athletic contests. Shortly after taking office MacLean formed a Board of Delegates consisting of a student representative of each class in each of the seven colleges, together with one from each literary society, fraternity, and club. He proposed to consult the group on matters of student interest. There proved to be little business of concern to students, however, and the board became a semiannual social gathering. Had the board been offered something more than consultation the response might have been more enthusiastic. MacLean believed that government should be in the hands of regents and faculty, with open channels of communication to the students.[56]

A more ambitious attempt to promote university spirit was the Greater University movement. County Clubs of students and alumni had been formed in 1904, and three years later, at the suggestion of alumnus Herbert M. Harwood, MacLean appointed a Greater University Committee of students and faculty members to coordinate the activities of the County

Clubs and support university projects. During 1908 over fifty meetings were held in various counties. One of the projects promoted by the movement was to obtain funds for a women's building; another was a clubhouse for men, a project that would eventually become the Student Union.[57]

Conceiving of the university as an institution for adults, MacLean was particularly displeased with manifestations of boyish behavior. He was less offended by what might be considered the adult offenses of entering saloons or drunkenness than by the traditional adolescent practice of hazing. For some years the sophomores had abducted members of the freshman class on the eve of the annual freshman banquet. They were ordered to desist from the practice, and when, in 1901, they abducted the president of the class and held him captive for two days ten offenders including the son of Chancellor McClain were suspended for the remainder of the year. In order to curb behavior of this kind MacLean encouraged organized contests and sports as a substitute.

Athletics assumed its modern form in university life, both at Iowa and elsewhere, during MacLean's administration. The president and many faculty members displayed the ambivalence toward intercollegiate athletics that has been characteristic of thoughtful educators ever since. Isaac A. Loos, professor of political science and an enthusiastic supporter of athletic competition, found organized sports altogether preferable to hazing and "other crude exhibitions of animal spirits." He did not claim that former hazers now personally found an outlet for aggressive impulses in active participation in sports, but at least it seemed persuasive to assume that such impulses found vicarious gratification in the activities of the teams. Without making explicit reference to the playing fields of Eton Professor Loos correlated the sturdy Anglo-Saxon devotion to outdoor sports with the "dominance of the English race in winning the world to a higher civilization."[58] For his part, MacLean believed that athletics made a salutary contribution to the development of school spirit. He never knew of a player to be "degraded" by football; on the contrary, the athlete was often elevated morally and intellectually by participation. The preaching of "muscular Christianity" had often resulted in athletes joining the YMCA. "The support of football and athletics," he told an inquirer, "is a significant straw as to which way the wind blows in a university in all the lines of its activities."[59] In short, as football goes, so goes the higher learning.

In the intervals between such bursts of exuberance MacLean acknowledged that there were difficulties having to do almost entirely with football. There was no doubt that playing football interfered with studies and that minimum scholastic standards were necessary. He believed that the athletic program should be under the supervision of a director with academic credentials and that in Dr. Alden A. Knipe he had such a person. Nevertheless, the recruitment of students with athletic ability was not always easy to reconcile with the ostensible purpose of the university. An official who refereed a football game with Grinnell in 1905 complained to MacLean that Iowa players abused and threatened him for enforcing the rules. The Iowa team, he reported, had an evil reputation. In the previous year one of the players had informed the president that he had been paid only half the amount promised him to enroll and play for Iowa.[60] However preferable it may have been to other "crude exhibitions of animal spirits," football clearly presented the university with problems of control that would continue to vex it long after MacLean's time.

Not only was it necessary for the university to take control of athletics from the students, but it was also apparent that the formation of athletic conferences was necessary to assure uniform conditions of competition.[61] In 1899 the universities of Iowa and Indiana joined the universities of Chicago, Illinois, Michigan, Minnesota, Northwestern, Purdue, and Wisconsin in the Western Athletic Conference. MacLean boasted that it maintained the highest academic standards of any conference. Membership in the Missouri Valley Conference presented problems of a different order. President A. Ross Hill of the University of Missouri informed MacLean in 1910 that his team would not play an opponent whose team included a "nigger." Iowa had recently played Washington University in St. Louis, where Iowa's black player had been banned from the game and had been unable to sleep with the team. Although MacLean had no sympathy with those who would exclude blacks, he readily acquiesced in the practice when playing in communities where exclusion was the custom. He proposed to "meet Missouri half-way" by using black players when playing in Iowa but excluding them when in Missouri.[62] This compromise was unacceptable to President Hill, and football games with Missouri were broken off. It was problems of this sort that prompted the new Board of Education president James H. Trewin to say publicly that athletics gave the university a bad name.[63] Perhaps the best that could be said for intercollegiate athletics was that it helped to orient the university toward institutions whose standards and achievements it needed to emulate. The University of Michigan had little to gain academically from association with its fellow members in the Western Athletic Conference; but at the bottom of the heap the University of Iowa had everything to gain.

EDUCATION AND RELIGION

The celebrated nineteenth-century controversies over science and religion precipitated by evolutionary theories were hardly echoed on the Iowa campus, where the local conflicts involved less exalted matters. Although the strength of the faculty following the dismissal of Hinrichs continued to reside in the scientists, they were not men with a theoretical or philosophic orientation, but rather represented the last generation of field naturalists engaged in exploration and classification. They were also men of exemplary religious orthodoxy whose impulse was to minimize rather than maximize the impact of science on religion. As recently as 1909, doubtless because it was the fiftieth anniversary year of the publication of *The Origin of Species*, Samuel Calvin addressed a small audience at the university's Lakeside Laboratory on the subject of geology and revelation. He said nothing that geologists had not been saying for at least two generations. His purpose was to insist that science and theology were not in conflict as long as each confined itself to the search for truth in its own proper sphere. Only with respect to the material facts of nature could science insist that its findings take precedence over the account of origins found in Genesis. On the other hand, science could not touch the great spiritual truths of the Bible. Calvin remained secure in the conviction that "when the fullness of time was come, God sent forth His Son." This was his only reference to distinctively Christian teaching, and he left it to his auditors to wonder how the science of biology would deal with the miracles of virgin birth or resurrection.[64]

Although in most respects a modern academic man, MacLean also retained certain traditional attitudes that gave his administration a somewhat archaic flavor. The most striking of these was his steadfast belief in the religious dimension of the higher learning. Education to him was essentially a religious experience since it was concerned with the development of the spiritual nature; in fact, the distinction between spiritual and secular was held to be purely nominal. He believed that the Founding Fathers had incorporated this conviction in the organic law of the nation when they declared in the Northwest Ordinance of 1787 that "religion, morality, and knowledge, being necessary to good government and the happiness of mankind, schools and the means of education shall forever be encouraged." The American people had taken this mandate to their hearts, with the result that their public school systems had experienced a "silent conquest" by religion. The fusion of education and religion, MacLean as-

serted, had been accomplished without impairment of liberty of conscience or of the freedom of the individual, since religious values were inherent in the content of the curriculum itself and were to be clearly
distinguished from exclusive sectarianisms. He found it significant that the
modern state universities had taken over virtually intact the curricula of
the older liberal arts colleges with their deep religious roots.[65]

But MacLean was not content to let the traditional curriculum bear the
full burden of the religious spirit of the university. He was prepared to take
positive action. At Nebraska he had fired Professor Harry K. Wolfe for
"proclaimed agnosticism." Wolfe, one of the pioneers of experimental
psychology in America, might have survived as a closet agnostic, but to
make anti-Christian remarks in his classroom was incompatible with the
"university spirit," and he had to go.[66]

The president did his best to refute the oft-repeated charge that the
university fostered infidelity. He assured an inquiring parent that such
charges were wholly unfounded. Although perfect freedom prevailed in
religious matters, he pointed out that a large proportion of the faculty
members were active in church and YMCA work. The professors of Greek,
sociology, and philosophy were graduates of the Yale Divinity School. The
professor of public speaking was an ordained Congregational minister.
The professor of history was a trustee of the Congregational church. The
noted scientists Calvin, Macbride, and Nutting were staunch Presbyterians. Seashore was a Lutheran, and the venerable Currier a Baptist. The
botanist Bohumel Shimek, whom some enemies of the university alleged
to be an infidel, publicly denied the slander. The president himself of
course was an ordained clergyman.[67]

These somewhat defensive protestations of orthodoxy did not shield the
university from pious critics in the evangelical denominations. For them it
was not enough to insist that learning was instinct with religious values.
MacLean distinguished between the fundamental religious beliefs that all
shared and the specific formulations of the sects, which had no place in a
public university. But to conservative spokesmen religion as conviction or
feeling apart from doctrinal or creedal affirmation was suspect—it smacked
of Unitarianism. In their minds religious liberalism all too readily accommodated itself to the secular outlook that was becoming increasingly apparent on the campuses of public universities.

Suspicions such as these came to the surface in April 1908, when the Des
Moines papers reported the remarks of E. C. Mercer, an itinerant YMCA
evangelist, who said that it was easier to carry on his work in Ames than in
Iowa City. He found Ames to be "closer to the soil," a place where an agri-

cultural rather than a philosophic mode of thinking prevailed. In Iowa City irreligion and consequently immorality reigned. The work of Professor Edwin D. Starbuck was singled out as "unconsciously dangerous to faith."[68] Starbuck, professor of philosophy and former student of William James and G. Stanley Hall, was a pioneer in the study of the psychology of religion. A religious man himself, Starbuck's purpose was not to explain away religion, but to gain a better understanding of it in modern terms by applying to its study the techniques of a scientific discipline. But he was said to have remarked that Iowa students lived double lives, accepting traditional religious teachings as well as the truths of science without being able to reconcile them. To the evangelicals this was dangerous doctrine.[69]

MacLean was furious to see his carefully cultivated image of the university as a center of religious values shattered by the evangelicals. It was little consolation to him to be told that the university had been caught up in the ongoing battle between religious conservatives and liberals. He assured the clergy of Des Moines that the philosophy department of the university exerted "positive, constructive religious influences."[70] It did not apparently occur to him to tell the ministers that the teaching of philosophy had no necessary connection with religious convictions. Nor did it occur to him that the generalized religion presumably fostered by the university underlay anything more than Christianity in its various forms. Provincial Americans in those days rarely encountered non-Christians. When asked in 1908 whether it would be useful for a rabbi to visit Jewish students MacLean responded that there were not enough Jewish students to justify such a visit. As an afterthought he added that there was perhaps one Jewish instructor in the faculty.[71]

In spite of the hostility of the conservatives MacLean continued to promote his conception of a spiritually rooted public university. He insisted that he was "not afraid that religion and morality in the schools will trench upon liberty of conscience and degenerate into sectarianism."[72] The university continued to sponsor a monthly Sunday vesper service, while the weekly University Assembly opened with brief religious exercises. In the academic year 1908–1909 the Iowa Plan for Religious Education was inaugurated. Under the supervision of a University Committee on Religious Education of which Macbride was chairman, pastors of Iowa City parishes were invited to offer two-hour credit courses on religious topics, with examinations to be set by the committee. Students were allowed a total of eight credit hours for such courses. The pastor of the First Presbyterian Church offered a course on Christian Ethics. Literature of the Bible was offered by a Methodist clergyman. A university professor offered Modern

Interpretations of Religion. Present-Day Religious Problems was offered by the pastor of the Christian church; Historical Development of Religion by the Episcopal rector. The Catholic bishop of Davenport agreed to designate a priest to offer a course acceptable to Catholics, but apparently the course did not materialize. Macbride was disappointed in the small enrollments, and the clergymen complained of the burden added to their regular pastoral duties. They received no compensation for their services. It was clearly not a permanent solution to the religious education problem, although MacLean continued to anticipate strictly denominational courses offered in a "scientific and thorough manner." [73] It was one thing to maintain that the spirit of instruction in the university was inherently religious, but quite another to introduce explicit instruction in religious topics. By MacLean's time the general tone of instruction was thoroughly secular. To introduce courses in religion was not necessarily to influence the life or atmosphere of the university beyond the confines of those courses. Religious courses or, later, a School of Religion, simply assured a place for religious studies alongside the various secular disciplines. The overall or pervasive spirit of the institution was no longer religious. The formula later adopted to justify religious courses in a public university—studying *about* religion—tacitly acknowledged the not so subtle distinction between religion as lived and religion as perceived, a mere cultural phenomenon.

THE FACULTY

MacLean knew that in the final analysis the reputation of the university was determined by the quality of its faculty and that if he were to succeed in elevating the institution to a position of parity with the leading universities of the region he would have to make strong faculty appointments. He took this responsibility seriously, involving himself personally in the search for deans and full professors. His criteria were unexceptionable, if somewhat unrealistic. Possession of the doctorate and a record of significant scholarly publication were indispensable qualifications for a senior appointment. The professor should be the best authority in the world on a particular subject, with a commanding personality, broad culture, and a sterling character. [74] The regents also interested themselves in faculty appointments, working through their relevant committees with the president, deans, and department heads. They were particularly active in law and medical appointments. There is no evidence, however, that members of the faculty were involved in these searches. Among MacLean's first important appointments were deans for the colleges of Law, Medicine, and Engineering. Law dean Charles Noble Gregory was appointed in 1901, without faculty consultation, and regent C. E. Pickett advised MacLean to proceed with the choice of a medical dean also without consulting the faculty. He believed that to involve the faculty "might tend to subsequent embarrassment." For their part, members of the medical faculty seemed to be less concerned with the quality of faculty appointments than with the consequences of the introduction of new practitioners into the competitive local market.[75] The exclusion of the faculty from the recruitment process no doubt reflected the assumption on MacLean's part, probably well taken, that the faculty as then constituted would not seek out the active scholars he was determined to recruit. At the same time it is not surprising that faculty morale should have been low, nor that an atmosphere of apathy in institutional matters should have prevailed when members of the faculty were not involved in decisions central to their functions.

Looking back in later years MacLean expressed satisfaction with the faculty appointments he had made. In addition to Gregory and medical dean Guthrie, William G. Raymond was appointed dean of the newly created College of Applied Science, as engineering was called. Clarke Fisher Ansley was brought from Nebraska to build up the English department. Arthur Fairbanks and his successor Charles H. Weller were strong appointments in Greek and classical archaeology. Stephen H. Bush in Romance languages began a tenure of nearly half a century. In medicine, in addition to internist Campbell P. Howard, the anatomist Henry J. Prentiss and the surgeon William Jepson were strong appointments. Undoubtedly MacLean's most important accomplishment was to support and promote the young psychologist Carl Seashore. When the University of Illinois attempted to lure him away MacLean reacted vigorously, assuring the regents of Seashore's worth and securing the support necessary to retain him. Had Seashore departed, the subsequent course of the university's development would have been markedly different.

The terms of faculty appointment were beginning to assume their modern form during MacLean's administration, although nothing was codified. In the eyes of the governing board the faculty consisted of the professors only; assistant professors, instructors, and other assistants had no faculty status.[76] "In theory," according to the president, a professor's tenure was permanent, as distinct from that of lower ranks where annual appointments were made. A more accurate adjective than "permanent" would have been "indefinite," the term which later became official with the Board of Education. MacLean felt constrained to add that the power of dismissal always rested with the governing board, a power which the board had not hesitated to exercise on various occasions. He admitted that in fact the professor had only the same security as that of people in business whose employment was assured so long as their performance was satisfactory and there was need for their services. The board itself, in 1911, assured security of tenure to the faculty and assistant professors with good behavior and satisfactory performance.[77] The American Association of University Professors was founded in 1915 and addressed itself at once to the codification of tenure rights, which were perceived to be a basic ingredient of academic freedom. But many years were to pass before its formulations would obtain general acceptance by educational governing bodies.

The university had no formal salary scale, and when in 1899 certain faculty members proposed one the regents expressed their displeasure by freezing all salaries for the coming year. MacLean reported that in 1902 the nominal full-time professorial salary was $2,000, although the extremes ranged from $1,600 to $2,400. Assistant professors received $1,200, and instructors, $600 to $1,000.[78] When Edwin D. Starbuck was asked in 1906 to head the philosophy department his request for an increase in his $1,800 salary was refused by the regents, despite his burden of a family of eight children. MacLean was able to arrange an appointment for Starbuck's wife, an organist, in the affiliated School of Music.

The idea of formal retirement with appropriate compensation was only beginning to appear in educational circles at the turn of the century. In the absence of such a provision the university often faced the unhappy task of providing for elderly faculty members who had become incapacitated by reason of age or infirmity. Were he able to do so MacLean would retire all professors at seventy, assigning to them some slight duties as teachers or researchers for which they would receive appropriate compensation. Ideally, they should be retired outright on pensions at half pay, although he was certain that Iowa taxpayers were not ready for any such arrangement, and he did not press for it. Samuel Calvin continued to teach until his death in 1911 at the age of seventy-one. When Amos Currier retired in 1907 at the age of seventy-three after forty years of service he was designated professor emeritus without stipend. MacLean was able to secure a pension for him from the Carnegie Foundation. The same was done for the philosopher Patrick, who had suffered a nervous breakdown. But these were exceptional events, there being no evidence that other faculty members were similarly assisted.[79]

The Carnegie Foundation recognized the problem as national in scope, and in 1905 it established a pension fund for teachers in private institutions. Working through the American Association of State Universities of which he was serving a term as president MacLean mounted a vigorous campaign to persuade the foundation to include the faculties of public institutions. As spokesmen for the private schools Charles William Eliot and Woodrow Wilson strenuously resisted the proposal, arguing that state institutions were a public responsibility. MacLean replied that in the Midwest, except for Northwestern and the University of Chicago, the leading universities were all public institutions and that by excluding them the foundation would be guilty of a regional bias. Whether or not it was sensitive to such a charge the foundation agreed in 1908 to include any public university faculty provided that the governor and legislature of that state would agree to take over the burden of pensions after a period of ten or fifteen years. The Iowa legislature consented to this proviso, and in 1909 the university faculty became eligible for Carnegie pensions.[80]

Teaching loads in MacLean's time were heavy by the standards of a later day. The average assignment was thirteen class hours per week. Full professors taught between eight and twenty hours, while assistant professors and instructors taught from fifteen to twenty hours. (The rank of associate professor had not yet been introduced.) No provision was made for sabbatical leaves of absence, although under exceptional circumstances such a leave was occasionally granted with half pay to a full professor.[81]

The scholarly strength of the faculty continued to be concentrated in the sciences. Macbride, Shimek, Nutting, and Wickham continued to lend distinction to the departments of botany and zoology. George W. Stewart joined the physics department in 1909, inaugurating important work in acoustics. Carl Seashore, who was appointed dean of the Graduate College in 1908, was already well launched on the career of research in the psychology of music which was to have such important consequences for the future development of the university.

Although not a scholar, Ansley inspired a group of disciples whose popularity in the classroom drew the increasing number of students who found in English and American literature an attractive alternative to the stricter discipline of the sciences. The popularity of literary studies among both undergraduates and graduate students was to become a distinctive feature of the twentieth-century university. Among Ansley's pupils was John G. Bowman, who was to succeed MacLean as president. Another popular teacher of English was Sam Sloan, who had also come from

Nebraska and who for many years taught large and enthusiastic classes. Percival Hunt, Ellen Geyer, and Walter Meyers would eventually follow Bowman to the University of Pittsburgh. John T. Frederick and Edwin Ford Piper inaugurated the long and fruitful tradition of creative work in poetry and prose for which the university was to become notable.[82] In philosophy Edwin D. Starbuck joined Patrick to launch a scholarly tradition that would endure for nearly a century.

These promising beginnings in the humanities were hardly duplicated in the social sciences and history. The misnamed department of political science under the headship of Isaac A. Loos was in fact a department of economics and sociology. The name was subsequently changed to political economy and sociology, which more nearly reflected its real function. The department of government and administration under Benjamin Shambaugh offered the work in political science. The head of the history department, William C. Wilcox, who was appointed dean of liberal arts in 1909, had done nothing to enlarge the faculty or to expand the curriculum in that small department. All of these programs were drawn together in the School of Political and Social Science, one of the several schools which emerged from time to time in response to some vaguely felt need for interdepartmental collaboration. The constituent departments of these schools insisted upon retaining control of their own budgets and upon having direct access to the dean, which left to the directors of the schools little more than moral suasion.

Two of the schools which did emerge into collegiate status were the schools of Engineering and Education. Engineering had been introduced as early as 1857, with a course in civil engineering offered in the mathematics curriculum. Other branches were added in later years under various administrative auspices. A School of Applied Science was organized in 1903, in the Liberal Arts College. In the following year an investigating committee of the legislature, determined to eliminate duplicating programs, recommended that all work in engineering be concentrated at the State College. Believing strongly that as a professional discipline engineering belonged in the university along with the other professional fields MacLean responded to this threat by strengthening the university's hold upon the subject. The School of Applied Science was elevated to collegiate status with eight departments and four new faculty appointments.[83]

The School of Education was organized in 1907. The first director, Frederick E. Bolton, boasted that Iowa was the first university in the country to have established instruction in pedagogy on an equal footing with the academic subjects in the collegiate department (1862). More significant than the equality implied by separate status was the fact that from the early years onward education was an integral part of the undergraduate and graduate curricula, first in the collegiate department and later in the Liberal Arts College and Graduate College. The object of the school, which functioned as a liberal arts department, was to bring together all of the subject-matter programs that contributed to the preparation of teachers and administrators for high schools, normal schools, urban superintendencies, and colleges. Its students majored in the subject-matter departments. The curriculum was based on the assumption that high school teachers should have a broad liberal education and mastery of the particular subject they were teaching, as well as the necessary pedagogical training. The superiority of this plan to that of the conventional teachers' college was manifest.[84]

THE BOARD OF EDUCATION

The momentous decision of 1857 to establish a separate College of Agriculture initiated an ongoing rivalry with the state university that lasted for a full century. Over the years, as the two institutions grew and initiated new programs, the biennial requests for legislative support became the focal points for intense competition. Students, alumni, and friends of each institution formed themselves into solid blocs of patriotic supporters who fought vigorously for the legislative dollar. Since each institution had its own governing board there was no way for the state to arrive at a common policy for higher education. MacLean recognized the danger in the situation, and his first act upon accepting the presidency was to visit President Beardshear at the State College and pledge cooperation, especially when presenting askings of the legislature.[85] There is no evidence, however, that his good intentions bore fruit.

In addition to the competition for financial support there was the vexing problem of duplication of programs and facilities. No doubt it seemed feasible in the beginning to maintain separate institutions for teacher training and for agriculture and the mechanic arts without overlapping university programs. Over the years, however, duplicating programs grew up in engineering and in liberal arts, giving rise to complaints of needless expenditures for staff and facilities.

Supported by what it considered to be a mandate of the Morrill Act, the State College claimed to be the proper place for the study of engineering. As we have seen, the university had also initiated courses in engineering at an early date. It maintained that as a professional subject engineering properly belonged at the university in the company of the other professional subjects. Its supporters claimed that the "mechanic arts" referred to in the Morrill Act designated such practical skills as surveying, road building, bricklaying, metalwork, and carpentry. There would be no duplication if the State College were to accept this modest definition of its role. Needless to say, that college had no intention of restricting its program to humble crafts.[86]

The State College and the Normal School had both developed liberal arts programs that duplicated what the university felt to be its proper responsibility. At the State College programs in general science and in home economics seemed to require a broad range of supporting subjects of the kind found in a liberal arts curriculum. At the Normal School, where the original purpose had been to train teachers for the common schools, new programs at the collegiate level were transforming the school into a teachers' college.[87] President Van Hise of the University of Wisconsin remarked that a College of Education without a Liberal Arts College was unthinkable; but to develop such a program at Cedar Falls entailed a major expense.

Impatient with the institutional rivalry and legislative lobbying, members of the legislature proposed to get control of the problem of duplication by abolishing the three separate boards and replacing them with a common governing body. A bill to this effect was introduced in the General Assembly in 1902. All three of the presidents testified against it. In his testimony MacLean took the position that the proper question to be addressed was not the matter of single or separate boards, but rather the differing functions of the three institutions and the proper allocation of responsibilities among them. He may well have foreseen the possibility that a single board might not necessarily be able to solve the problem of duplication. He reaffirmed the principle enunciated in his inaugural address that there should be one state university, the center for advanced study and research, drawing its students from the colleges, public and private. Michigan and Kansas together with Iowa maintained A & M colleges and normal schools separate from their universities. Michigan was the best of these and provided the model to emulate. Wisconsin, Illinois, Minnesota, and Nebraska all incorporated the A & M college with the university, with obvious economies of operation. The experience to be avoided, in MacLean's judgment, was provided by Ohio and Indiana, states which dissipated their resources among two or more public universities. He warned that the establishment of a professional grade engineering school at the State College would precipitate the inevitable transformation of the college into a university, with the consequence that neither institution would receive adequate support.[88]

Bills providing for a single governing board were introduced in four successive legislative sessions. The Senate generally favored the proposal, while the House, in which partisans of the institutions were heavily represented, blocked passage of the first three bills. Each group feared that the other might dominate a common board. MacLean actively opposed the plan in 1902 and 1904, but thereafter adopted a noncommittal position.[89] A joint legislative committee in 1906, under the chairmanship of Senator W. P. Whipple, reported the results of a detailed study of the operations of the three institutions. In addition to visiting the three campuses the committee visited or received information from a number of state universities of the region. It found considerable duplication of work between the university and the State College, some of it necessary but much of it unnecessary. Moreover, "a spirit of rivalry is engendered that is, in many respects, detrimental to the educational interests of the state." It also found that the State Normal School had become a "miniature university," where much of the program duplicated that of the Iowa City institution. In order to control the duplication and restrict competition the committee recommended that the three governing bodies be replaced by a single board of fifteen unsalaried members to be appointed by the governor for six-year terms. For its assistance the board should be empowered to appoint a three-member executive committee of full-time salaried employees who, however, would not have independent authority. If the board were to meet only four times annually, as the committee proposed, it could hardly expect to exercise the close supervision of operations that was characteristic of the existing boards. Senator Whipple was reported to favor appointment of a single chancellor for all three institutions, but he withheld what he knew would be an additional rallying point for the opposition.[90]

A bill incorporating the Whipple Committee proposals was passed by the Senate in 1906, but was defeated in the House. MacLean continued to insist that the problem was not the existence of separate boards but the duplication of programs. As a substitute for the Whipple bill he proposed the creation of a Board of Visitors with specific powers to inspect the institutions, review accounts, approve building plans, concur in the creation of new departments and chairs, and review appropriations requested by the three governing boards. Such a board, he believed, would be able to contain the proliferation of duplicating programs.[91] At that point, without obtaining approval by the legislature, the regents unwisely authorized the construction of a home for the president on the bluff at the head of Church Street. Proponents of a single board seized upon this relatively minor matter and made much of it as an indication that the separate boards were out of control. In the 33rd General Assembly they gained control of the House and in 1909 replaced the three boards with a single Board of Education.[92]

The law establishing the new board substantially incorporated the recommendations of the Whipple Committee. The nine unsalaried members, not more than five of whom were to belong to the same political party, were to be appointed by the governor for staggered six-year terms and approved by two-thirds vote of the Senate. The membership at any time should include no more than one alumnus of each institution. The board was empowered to elect a president from among its membership, as well as a president and treasurer for each institution, together with other officers, professors, and employees. It would make necessary rules and regulations, manage property, determine salaries, and direct the expenditure of appropriations. The board was also authorized to appoint a Finance Committee consisting of three full-time employees who would visit each institution monthly and maintain a close supervision of financial operations.[93]

In providing for a close balance of political party affiliation among board members it was the intent of the legislature to assure a nonpartisan approach to the management of public higher education. In this it was gratifyingly successful, at least in the earlier years, to the occasional annoyance of political leaders who would have liked to bend the board to their legislative programs. Observers testified that one could never tell the party affiliation of members from their work on the board.[94] At the same time, the stipulation that the board should contain not more than one alumnus of each institution indicated a firm intention to break with the previous pattern in which the institutional boards had been dominated by their respective alumni. This provision also implied that there would be little if any continuity between the old boards and the new. Judge W. I. Babb, a former university regent, urged Governor Beryl F. Carroll to provide for minimal continuity by appointing one member from each of the old boards. The governor adopted this suggestion, appointing from the Board of Regents Parker K. Holbrook, an Onawa banker who had served on the board for fourteen years. From the State College Board of Trustees he appointed the Dallas Center banker Charles H. Brenton, and from the Normal School board the Cedar Falls banker Roger Leavitt. The board itself elected as its president James H. Trewin, a Cedar Rapids lawyer and former state senator. The Finance Committee chosen by the board was headed by William R. Boyd.[95]

As it went about its work, beginning July 1, 1909, the new board quickly indicated its faithfulness to the legislative intent by adopting a detached and at times critical stance toward the institutions under its control. It seemed to be determined not to become the partisan promoter of educational programs after the manner of the old boards. Although it was required to meet only four times annually, with other sessions as called by its president, the heads of the three institutions were not at first invited to sit with the board but were summoned individually as needed. No lobbying by institutional representatives was to be permitted, the board reserving to itself the formulation of needs to be presented to the governor and legislature.[96]

Although the law prescribed the functions of the Finance Committee, that body quickly came to exercise a much broader range of powers than had been contemplated. As full-time officials the committee members were available for duties that would have been impossible for board members. Moreover, the president of the committee, William R. Boyd, proved to be an unusually able and determined man whose dedication to public higher education won the full confidence of the board and earned him an ascendancy over its operations that endured for many years. A Cedar Rapids journalist and banker, Boyd was an alumnus of the university who was to become one of its strongest and most influential supporters. It was his friendship with Abraham Flexner and Henry S. Pritchett which cemented the close association between the university and the Carnegie Foundation and Rockefeller Foundation, resulting in the financial support crucial to the development of the modern Medical College. Nevertheless, as the wide range of educational functions assumed by the Finance Committee began to unfold, MacLean became increasingly critical of what he felt to be encroachments upon his authority. The board delegated to the committee the task of formulating a plan for interinstitutional coordination of programs, by far the most important piece of business before it.

If the board was fortunate in its choice of Boyd it was unfortunate in electing Trewin as its first president. A dominating personality and a self-made man who had worked his way up from plowboy to leadership at the bar, he had little feeling for or sympathy with academic life. Although he was reputed to be a partisan of the State College he was equally contemptuous of presidents Storms and MacLean and was determined to get rid of both of them.[97]

Early in its regime the board, no doubt acting on the suggestion of Boyd, invited Henry S. Pritchett of the Carnegie Foundation to advise it on its proper course with respect to its educational and administrative responsibilities. Pritchett spent two and a half days with the board in March 1910, discussing a wide range of issues. He urged the board to conceive of itself as a governing but not as an administrative body. It should determine policies after consultation with the executive officers of the three institutions. Administration should be left to the executives so long as they were judged to be competent. The board should, of course, act independently and resist politicization. Its most important immediate task would be to allocate programs among its institutions in order to minimize duplications. In its *First Biennial Report* the board formally endorsed these recommendations as its own policy.[98]

It quickly became apparent, however, that the board was either incapable of or unwilling to distinguish between policy making and administration, especially in matters of faculty personnel and curriculum. During the first three years of its management it was constantly intervening in routine institutional operations, presumably in the interests of economy. As chairman of the board's Faculty Committee President Trewin was the moving spirit in what often seemed to approach an inquisition. Reports were demanded on the liberal arts summer session, on the combined programs of liberal arts and the professional colleges, on the organization of an employment placement office for graduates, and on plans to provide for the welfare of students.[99] The board wanted to know how many hours were spent by faculty members in their various academic activities and the average daily attendance in each class. It wanted to know the cost of proposed course changes and insisted that promotional material be eliminated from the catalog. Great interest was shown in formulating a "plan" for student activities. Each dean was asked to describe the student organizations in his college.[100]

On the resignation of Laenas Weld as liberal arts dean, in 1909, Trewin informed MacLean that the board would designate a successor from among four nominees to be selected by MacLean. The importance of personal contacts with students was stressed, and from among MacLean's candidates the historian William C. Wilcox was appointed. MacLean was authorized to make such junior nonfaculty appointments as instructors and assistants, but the board reserved faculty appointments to itself.[101] Further erosion of the president's authority came from the Finance Committee, which involved itself directly in departmental affairs. MacLean found it necessary to insist that business to be brought to that committee be transmitted "in regular order" through the deans and the president.[102] There can be little doubt that his resistance to encroachment upon his administrative authority contributed to the rapidly growing estrangement between president and board.

If the major issue confronting the board was the duplicating programs of the institutions under its charge it was diverted from confronting this matter at the outset both by its inability to determine its proper priorities and by extraneous events that could not be foreseen. The Flexner investigation of the university's medical program was underway when the board took office, and it was imperative that medical reforms receive the board's immediate attention. It wisely allowed itself to be guided by Boyd and MacLean, although it was subjected to a certain amount of pressure from dissenting medical faculty members to resist reforms.

When the legislature replaced the three governing bodies with a single board it was frequently rumored that the new board would replace the institutional presidents with its own men. The presidents were identified with the competitive tradition that the legislature was determined to end, and they had publicly opposed the creation of a common board. It was understandable that the new board should wish to replace officers who had established intimate working relationships with their respective regents or trustees with new men who would readily accommodate themselves to the more formal and impersonal relationships that would now prevail. Had the board candidly announced this to be its intention it would have gained much needed public respect as well as relieved the presidents of uncertainty and bitterness. It chose rather to express its mounting dissatisfaction with their services through Trewin's peremptory commands and acerbic comments. President A. B. Storms of Iowa State College submitted his forced resignation on February 20, 1910. He complained that he had been unable to meet with the board for discussion of policies; that faculty members had been hired and fired without consulting him; and that the Finance Committee had invited departments of the college to circumvent him. He could not remain in office and retain his self-respect.[103]

MacLean could make the same complaints, but he clung to his position for another year. Without consulting him the board, in August 1910, dismissed Charles R. Fischer, director of the School of Music. Fischer reported to MacLean that Trewin had referred to them both in insulting and contemptuous terms.[104] The signs clearly indicated that the board wished to be rid of him, but MacLean refused to take the hints. Rumors of his dismissal were reported in the press.[105] Finally, on January 24, 1911, Trewin summoned MacLean to his Cedar Rapids office and requested his resignation. Neither in private correspondence nor in public statement did MacLean acknowledge that the resignation had been forced, and consequently the board was not obliged to indicate the reasons for its action. Perhaps as a reward for going quietly the board obtained for him a pension from the Carnegie Foundation.[106]

The replacement of the university's own regents with a new board that "knew not Joseph" was the immediate occasion for MacLean's downfall. Beyond that, however, it is apparent that neither the board nor the public was ready for the "larger university" that he envisioned. In spite of the eloquence with which he expounded the idea of a scholarly institution composed of graduate and professional schools he proved unable to organize and hold the constituency that was vital to success. His conception of the place of the university as the capstone of the state's educational system was sufficiently far-reaching to bring him to the point of forcing the hand of a new board that had not yet established its proper role or formulated its own policies. It was a moment in the history of the state when the problem of the proper relationship of the three institutions of higher learning had come to a head, and MacLean's proposal for the solution of the problem was not the one chosen by the board.

CHAPTER TWO

The Reign of Walter Jessup

The brief and unhappy tenure of President John Gabbert Bowman (1911–1914) was significant for bringing to a head the
problem of the relationship between president and governing
board. An Iowa native and university alumnus (B.A. 1899,
M.A. 1904), Bowman had taught English briefly at the university before
going to Columbia for his Ph.D. For four years he had served as secretary
to the Carnegie Foundation, maintaining close contact with President
MacLean and strengthening the bonds between foundation and university.
He had facilitated MacLean's campaign to secure participation in the
foundation's pension plan and had advised him on how best to approach
Carnegie for support of a Library School at the university.[1] He was, according to his friend Stephen Bush, an exceedingly tough, ruthless individual, "a little Napoleon." Following MacLean's forced resignation on
January 24, 1911, it took the Board of Education only a month to offer the
position to Bowman. Clearly, no very extensive search had been deemed
necessary. President Pritchett's recommendation of Bowman had been
sufficient to secure the appointment.[2]

The new president was well aware of the nature of MacLean's problems
with the board. His acceptance of the appointment was accompanied by a
statement addressed to the board setting forth his understanding of the
proper relationship between board and president. It emphasized the distinction between board as policy maker and president as administrator.
The board should determine the character and relationships among the
institutions under its charge, while the president should implement its
policies. While the board should indicate the type of faculty and administrative appointees desired and fix salary scales, the president should initiate all staff nominations for board approval. The same procedure pertained to dismissals. The president should be the sole avenue of official
communication between the university staff and the board.[3] These stipulations presupposed a measure of delegation of authority which the board
and its predecessors had never previously conceded. Nevertheless, Trewin

John Bowman. Courtesy of the University of Iowa Archives.

declared himself to be in full agreement with them. A year later, when Raymond A. Pearson, who was considering the board's offer of the presidency of Iowa State College, raised similar questions about the president's relationship to the board, Trewin quoted Bowman's precise language in indicating the board's policy.[4]

The removal of presidents Storms and MacLean paved the way for the board to address itself to the problem of duplication, the principal issue which had led to its creation. Its initial plan, formulated during the first year of its tenure and announced in its *First Biennial Report*, September 1910, had been a modest and sensible one which in all likelihood could have been implemented without insuperable difficulty. Two problems were identified: engineering duplication between the university and the State College and duplication in pedagogy between the university and the Teachers' College. While in principle there needed to be but one Engineering College, two in fact existed; the board proposed to coordinate their offerings so as to reduce duplication to a minimum. This would be achieved by designating one a graduate college which would offer advanced work only. It did not indicate to which institution the graduate work would be assigned. The board recognized that some time would be necessary to accomplish the differentiation. Likewise, the duplication in pedagogical training would be eliminated in time by making the university School of Education a graduate college.[5]

Two years then passed without any attempt to implement the plan. The board excused itself with the plea that deliberation was necessary in carrying out so important a reallocation of functions. In fact, it was preoccupied with matters which it felt to be more pressing. When in 1912 it again took up the problem of duplication it amplified and substantially altered its earlier plan. The Finance Committee had been instructed to study the matter, and it had consulted a number of educational experts. The revised plan was apparently the work of William R. Boyd.[6]

The new plan dealt with the problem of engineering in a much more drastic fashion. Although instruction in engineering had been offered at both the university and the State College from an early date the program at Ames was much more extensively developed in terms of faculty, students, and facilities. At the university engineering had been accorded collegiate status only in 1905, and at the expense of other programs more deserving of support, in the board's judgment. The assertion that advanced engineering properly belonged at the university was now seen to lack merit: MIT, Rensselaer Polytechnic Institute, and other independent schools provided ample evidence that engineering could flourish outside the university setting. The board decided consequently to discontinue the College of Engineering at the university and to concentrate all engineering studies at the State College, where the terms of the Morrill Act seemed to mandate it in any event. The state would save a substantial sum in salaries and upkeep since no transfer of staff was contemplated.[7]

Duplications in liberal arts involved all three institutions. The board found that the Teachers' College had departed substantially from its original purpose of training teachers for the elementary schools and was offering a bachelor's degree program inferior in quality to that of the university. A School of Education at the collegiate level belonged at the university. All work in education and liberal arts beyond the sophomore level at the Teachers' College should be discontinued. In order to provide needed elementary and rural teachers the board recommended that additional normal schools be established. At the State College the bachelor's degree program in general science duplicated university programs and should be abandoned. Work in home economics at the State College should be transferred to the university, although no program in that field existed there. Home economics, in the board's judgment, properly belonged in the liberal arts setting where work in fine arts, education, and other related subjects would be available. The transfer would reduce the proportion of female students at the State College to one in ten, a ratio that seemed to the board not inappropriate for a college of agriculture and the mechanic arts. The board even went so far as to acknowledge that ideally all three institutions should be located in one place, although it recognized that this was now water over the dam.[8]

On October 8, 1912, the board announced its intention to carry out the proposed reorganization and was immediately greeted with a storm of protest. Faculty, students, and alumni of the three institutions mounted a vigorous campaign of opposition in the press and legislature. Both of the candidates for governor denounced the plan. In April of the following year the legislature by joint resolution requested that the board rescind its order, which was declared to be "unwise." The resolution specifically approved duplicating programs "to such extent as will advance the educational interests of the State." Although the resolution did not have the force of law the board realized that it had no choice but to yield, and on April 3, 1913, it rescinded its order.[9] Thus failed the first major attempt to control duplication by differentiating the functions of the three institutions. Duplicating programs now proliferated rapidly, and the board showed little inclination to attempt to control them. The university expanded its engineering program and established a home economics department, while the State College created new departments of journalism and structural design and recruited more women students.

In later years W. R. Boyd attributed the failure to the inability of the board to act promptly on what he considered to be the mandate of the 33rd General Assembly to eliminate duplication by placing the three institutions under a common board. He believed that had the board moved promptly its decisions would have been supported by a legislature that felt strongly about the need for reform. But after three years of delay the composition of the legislature, especially the House, contained many who had not been present earlier and who did not have the same sense of urgency in the matter.[10] The new members were more susceptible to pressure because less impressed with the importance of eliminating duplication. Boyd had apparently forgotten that the board's initial proposals would have been far less disruptive and might well have survived the changes in legislative personnel. In any event several factors accounted for the board's failure to take prompt action. Perhaps most important was its inability to define its policy-making role, thus allowing itself to become preoccupied with administrative details to the neglect of more important concerns. Its determination to dismiss Storms and MacLean obliged it to devote the time necessary to choose successors. The unexpected crisis in medical affairs occasioned by the Flexner investigation required immediate attention. Finally, because the board mistakenly assumed continued legislative support for reform it felt no urgent need to act promptly. MacLean's prediction that a common board might not necessarily be able to control duplication proved to be all too accurate.

President Bowman had originally supported the board's plan to consolidate engineering at the State College and to discontinue liberal arts work at the Teachers' College. He told MacLean that he saw much virtue in concentrating on the arts and sciences at the university. But following the board's announcement of its plan, in October 1912, he changed his mind. Stephen Bush reported that A. O. Finkbine, a prominent alumnus, persuaded Bowman to abandon the board's plan.[11] It is more likely that Bowman was impressed by President Pearson's opinion that if engineering study at the State College was to be of high quality, courses in general science must be continued there. In urging the board to reverse its decision Bowman noted that it had lost the confidence and good will of its three constituencies, and he urged it to address the problem in open consultation with the institutions and their alumni.[12] Under fire from all sides, board members felt that Bowman had betrayed them, and their trust and confidence in him were fatally impaired.

During 1913 the gulf between president and board steadily widened. The tension was certainly not alleviated by the attitude of the board toward the institutions under its control. Instead of making common cause with them on behalf of higher education the board seemed to regard them as fractious subjects to be governed and disciplined as might be necessary. The presidents met with the board only when invited to present matters pertinent to their respective institutions, and each received only such portions of minutes of board meetings as pertained to his own institution. Given these restrictions Bowman had little opportunity to develop the relationships of mutual understanding and trust that were essential. It was hardly surprising that he should have formed a low opinion of the board, confiding to Flexner that it preferred to do politically popular rather than educationally sound things.[13]

Conflict with the board over appointments in medicine led directly to Bowman's downfall. The board had difficulty in grasping the new conception of the Medical College as primarily a teaching and research institution. Board members had personal contacts with physicians in private practice who were concerned with problems arising from the care of private patients at the university hospital and who were interested in faculty appointments in that context. On occasion board members proposed appointments for their friends which Bowman was obliged to reject, saying that distinctions should now be made between practitioners and teachers of medicine and that only the latter were properly qualified for faculty appointments. While such proposals by board members may not have violated the understanding that recommendations for appointment were to be initiated by the president, his rejection of them certainly did not endear him to the board.[14]

Following the resignation of Dr. Jepson as head of surgery Bowman came directly into conflict with the board. J. H. Trewin, now chairman of the board's Faculty Committee, ordered the president to promote Dr. Howard L. Bye, a recently appointed instructor in surgery, to a full professorship. Bowman held that the promotion should await the appointment of a new head of the department, who should be free to assemble his own staff. Trewin pointedly reminded Bowman that only the board had the power of appointment and dismissal. A divided board accepted Bowman's recommendation that the promotion await the appointment of Dr. C. J. Rowan as head of surgery, but it was now clear that Bowman must go.[15]

Instead of dismissing him directly the board chose to force the president's resignation by deliberately violating its agreement with him. Without consulting him the board at its meeting on March 11, 1914, voted to make the affiliated School of Music an integral part of the university and to dismiss its head, Professor Gustav Schoettle, whom it declared to be incompetent. Publicly, it subsequently insisted that it had not intended to precipitate a conflict with Bowman and that its action had been taken in accordance with what it understood to be the president's wishes. Privately, however, board member Parker K. Holbrook, always a staunch friend of the university, told Bowman that if the latter were aware of the depth of the board's dissatisfaction with him he would resign forthwith. This Bowman did, on March 20, 1914, to take effect at the board's earliest convenience.[16]

MACBRIDE'S BRIEF TENURE

With the abrupt departure of President Bowman it became necessary for the board to make an interim appointment while searching for a successor. It had little hesitation in choosing the botanist Professor Thomas Huston Macbride, for at the same meeting on March 27, 1914, at which Bowman's resignation was accepted Macbride was designated acting president and asked to assume office five days later.[17] It was understood that he would serve until the board was ready to make a regular appointment. He had been a faculty candidate for the office in 1899, following the death of Schaeffer, and had been passed over again in 1911 in favor of the ill-fated Bowman. He was now sixty-six years old and in poor health. In the first five years of its existence the Board of Education had compiled a dismal record of incompetence and vindictive hostility toward its principal employees. It was well that it should now give itself breathing room in which to take stock of itself and give careful thought to the kind of person with whom a more effective working relationship could be developed.

In academic terms Macbride was perhaps the most distinguished of all Iowa presidents, and he was certainly the most literary. As a protégé of Samuel Calvin's at Lenox College in the 1870s he had learned his natural history at a time when its various specialized subdivisions were emerging, but when its devotees still shared a consciousness of engagement in a common enterprise. His scientific interests originally ranged from mathematics to historical geology, zoology, and botany. Calvin brought him to Iowa as his assistant, and eventually the older man specialized in geology, while

Thomas Macbride. Courtesy of the Iowa Lakeside Laboratory.

the younger concentrated on botany. His work on slime molds earned him an international reputation. He was largely responsible for the university's *Natural History Bulletin*, to which he was a frequent contributor.

As an undergraduate Macbride had concentrated on ancient and modern languages and had at his command a wealth of literary materials seldom found among scientists. He was one of the last of the nineteenth-century romantics, suffusing his feeling for nature with the warm sense of ultimate purpose which permitted him to view the universe as the creation of an all-seeing intelligence. Those who in his judgment mistakenly dismissed Darwinism as degrading and atheistic simply failed to appreciate the fact that Darwin had only revealed the divine method of ordering natural processes. Where others saw in natural selection the chaos of chance governing a universal struggle, Macbride saw inevitable progress along "the pathway of spiritual unfolding." [18] On a narrower scale, human history similarly revealed "the march of mind," or progress in some profound sense. Culminating moments of history came when some new aspect of truth was discovered, as, for instance, with the teachings of Christ, the work of the Italian Renaissance, and the publication of *The Origin of Species*. Our own time is distinguished by the rapid spread of the scientific method, which has changed our thinking from an anthropocentric point of view to the idea of universal growth. We now believe that although life will never reach perfection it will find ever fuller realization in an infinite future.[19] Dispensing such comforting sentiments in the rather florid rhetoric of which he was a master, Macbride was a welcome participant in the school and college ceremonial gatherings which played an important role in the institutional life of the times.

It was not to be expected that during the brief period of his presidency Macbride would undertake significant educational initiatives. The establishment of the School of Commerce, the separation of speech from the English department, and the abandonment of the abortive College of Fine Arts were events foreordained by developments prior to his administration. The most important event, the formal decision to sponsor the creation of a Child Welfare Research Station, was made with a singular lack of enthusiasm on Macbride's part. He considered it to be a project of "other people," namely, Cora B. Hillis and her friends, and he informed Senator Frederic Larrabee that if authorized and financed by the legislature the station would simply find shelter at the university. He did not consider it a matter of high priority.[20]

Macbride's views on the vexed question of duplication of programs among the three public institutions were notably balanced and free from partisanship. Interest in the subject was widespread, especially in states like Iowa where the land grant college was separate from the university. In 1914 the National Association of State Universities asked Macbride to address its annual meeting on the subject. He pointed out that in the early days extensive duplications existed because no one considered it a significant problem. It was only as colleges and universities became more specialized that duplication of programs emerged as a central issue. Ironically enough, it was only as the State College sharpened its identity as the college of agriculture and the mechanic arts that duplication of university programs became controversial. Similarly, the creation of a separate Normal School resulted in a legacy of duplication with the university where teacher training had always been offered. The subsequent transformation of the Normal School into a Teachers' College intensified the competition as more liberal arts work was inevitably introduced.

Macbride believed that, so long as the state was growing and enrollments were everywhere increasing, duplication of programs was not necessarily a bad thing. It was understandable that the university should be on the defensive since by definition its educational mission was comprehensive, while the more specialized public institutions fought to escape the restraints of their limited functions. It was difficult for some friends of the university to understand why an A & M college should not be content to remain an A & M college. Be that as it might, however, to Macbride the issue of duplication should be seen in the context of interinstitutional competition with all of its baneful consequences of alumni bitterness and legislative infighting.[21] The outside investigators who at the behest of the legislature studied the problem of duplication during the following year may well have taken their clue from Macbride's dispassionate assessment of the situation.

JESSUP'S PRINCIPLES

Although the administration of Walter Jessup (1916–1934) began in the shadow of World War I and ended in the depths of the Great Depression it was nevertheless marked by steady growth of the university. The new president possessed the qualities necessary to assure institutional stability and expansion. Macbride had accepted the presidency in 1914 with the understanding that his tenure would be of brief duration; when the board accepted his resignation, on August 9, 1916, it was prepared to announce simultaneously its choice of Jessup as his successor.[22]

Jessup had come to Iowa four years earlier as director of the School of Education. He was an Indiana native and graduate of Earlham College who had taken a Ph.D. in education at Teachers' College, Columbia University, in 1911, and had then served for a year as director of the School of Education at Indiana University before coming to Iowa in 1912. When he assumed the presidency at the age of thirty-nine he was already widely known in educational circles and was the campus choice to succeed Macbride. His presidency marked an important turning point in the history of the university. Thanks largely to his personal qualities the relationship between president and board was finally stabilized around the distinction between policy making and administration. A new board president, George T. Baker, a Davenport engineer, understood the collaborative nature of the relationship between the board and its educational officers and was an unfailing source of support. A warm friendship and mutual respect also sprang up between Jessup and W. R. Boyd.

The secret of Jessup's success lay in the fact that he was not a conventional academic type. It was a sad commentary on the public perception of the educator that those who knew Jessup reported that he looked and acted more like a businessman or a banker than the conventional professor or university president. His manner was brisk and incisive, conveying to observers the impression that he was in firm control. A keen political sense was perhaps his foremost quality. As the head of a public institution he understood the importance of cultivating effective relationships with the board, legislature, and citizens of the state, and he devoted much time to visiting with legislators and public figures.[23] Faculty members were encouraged to follow his example and accept every opportunity to speak to school assemblies, service clubs, civic groups, and alumni gatherings. He had a conventional mind, and there was nothing in his speeches to challenge or disturb the complacence of his auditors.

Iowa presidents generally, and especially the presidents during the early decades of this century, carried an enormous workload. Apart from the heavy flow of daily correspondence requiring their attention, the ongoing business with the board, and their frequent absences from the campus, they involved themselves directly in the daily management of the university. The deans reported directly to them, and faculty and students expected to have ready access to them. It was not until 1945 that President Virgil Hancher added to his staff a general administrative officer, called administrative dean, and even then the new appointee, Allin Dakin, was an old friend with whom the president could talk freely, as he put it, rather than someone in a line position who could relieve him of specified duties.

Walter Jessup. Courtesy of the University of Iowa Archives.

The first such officer, the executive dean for teaching and research (later called provost), was not appointed until 1948. Thus it was hardly surprising that given his heavy workload Walter Jessup had little time to think about—or at least to discuss—matters of general university policy. Nor is there any evidence that he wanted such an opportunity or regretted his immersion in the daily routine.

The Board of Deans in its regular meetings discussed administrative matters exclusively. No records survive to indicate what went on in the "Kitchen Cabinet," the small group of congenial associates with whom Jessup relaxed and played golf. It included Fred Higbee, professor of engineering and alumni secretary; William H. Cobb, university auditor; Paul Packer, dean of education; and Fred Pownall, university editor. In view of the miscellaneous character of this group it is highly unlikely that it was of direct assistance in the formulation of policy. The University Senate, which had originally been created as an advisory body to the president and had been revitalized by MacLean, was found by Jessup to be of little use and was allowed to wither. The fact was that Jessup took little interest in the issues of higher education. He was essentially a builder who concerned himself primarily with the problems of growth. He believed that a university sensitive to and responsive to the public should offer the range of instruction the public found desirable and useful, and he was determined to secure the strongest faculty that the budget would support.

As an educational leader and spokesman Jessup's principal preoccupations were with growth and change. His responses were conventional. He dismissed the traditional educational elitism as outmoded. The university must be sensitive to public needs, providing the programs and services to meet those needs. Extension programs, educational radio, correspondence courses, and other off-campus activities should bring the resources of the university to the home communities of the state. Other services included the hospitals and clinics, the Child Welfare Research Station, the psychological clinic, and the counseling services of the College of Education. The psychology of individual differences had a significant impact on educators in making them more keenly aware of the unique qualities and needs of each student. Jessup frequently emphasized the importance of recognizing and serving the varied needs of students. While he did not question the traditional standard curriculum prescribed for all students, the implication of the emphasis on individual uniqueness clearly pointed toward the rapid elaboration of programs which occurred during his administration.[24] He was content to say that in the midst of rapid and bewildering change educational leaders should display the combination of conservatism, adaptability, and idealism necessary to adapt traditional values to new circumstances. In his zeal to emphasize the responsiveness of the university to local needs Jessup expressed strong disapproval of federal intervention in educational matters. He vigorously opposed the creation of a federal department of education.[25]

The second stage of the university's institutional development emerged during Jessup's administration. Indeed, it was his principal accomplishment to stabilize the relationship between the president as administrative head of the university and the board as the governing and policy-making body. The proper nature of this relationship had been defined by presidents Bowman and Pearson, but it remained for a man with Jessup's personal qualities to command the confidence necessary to establish the principles in practice. In this he was ably assisted by an intelligent and public-spirited board led by President Baker. Within a stable institutional framework it became possible to develop the distinctive academic programs for which the Jessup years were to be notable.

A firm institutional structure made possible the practice of the delegation of authority. While authority legally resided with the board, it delegated to the president the authority to act in its name on a wide range of routine administrative matters. Delegation always remained a matter of practice rather than of principle. It took the form of holding the president responsible for the recommendations which he brought to the board. Initially delegation defined the relationship between board and president; in Jessup's time it functioned much less clearly in the relationships of president and deans and of deans and faculty. Jessup and his immediate successors were reluctant to delegate to their subordinates authority comparable to that which the board had granted to them, and the board showed no disposition to extend the practice to the lower levels of the administrative structure. Eventually, however, delegation became an important working practice throughout the university.

One of Jessup's top priorities was the building up of a high-quality faculty. He followed MacLean's practice of involving himself directly in faculty recruitment, especially in the liberal arts. The rapid growth of colleges and universities in the early decades of the century was a national phenomenon, and the competition for outstanding scholars was intense. To enter the competition required financial resources necessary to pay competitive salaries, and it introduced a measure of faculty mobility as institutions bid for the services of highly visible scholars. Jessup regarded the securing of a faculty equal to the expectations of the university as the greatest problem in higher education.[26] His instinctive response was to accept the competitive challenge, paying whatever was necessary to keep the outstanding people while hoping that those who fell by the wayside would be good enough to find employment somewhere else.[27] At the same time, however, he was reluctant to face the full consequences of unrestricted competition. He recognized and regretted the destabilizing effect of competition upon the teaching program and the students, going so far as to assure the National Association of State Universities that he would consider leaving open a last-minute faculty vacancy rather than cause a ripple-effect of vacancies by raiding another institution. He believed that in the long run the discrepancies among the salary scales of various institutions would even out, thus relieving the competitive pressure. The higher salaries being paid in medicine and law could be tolerated so long as universities with professional schools dealt with the situation in a similar manner. In the meanwhile competition for faculty members should force institutions to formulate and implement more precise standards of promotion. All too often advancement in rank and salary came in response to competitive offers. It seemed foolish and shortsighted to Jessup that administrators should allow competitive bidding to establish the standing of individuals on their own campuses, tempting the faculty members to attach greater importance to their standing elsewhere than at home. Each institution should establish an adequate system of advancement based upon the judgment of peers and designed to identify and reward faculty members and thus assure their loyalty.[28] In practice, however, the formation of nationally organized bodies of scholars and local reliance upon the advice of experts in matters of appointment made it virtually impossible for the university to isolate itself from competitive pressures. The abler the appointee, the more likely was the prospect of losing him. Friends of the university could console themselves with the reflection that it was better to appoint a good scholar who was subsequently lost than to appoint a mediocrity who remained forever.[29]

THE CAPEN COMMISSIONS

Chastened by the legislative rejection of its plan to control duplication of programs the board appealed to the Federal Bureau of Education for assistance. Without reopening the controversial issues of combining engineering or concentrating liberal arts it wanted advice on ways to reduce or control interinstitutional duplications. The bureau named a commission of seven distinguished educational administrators under the chairmanship of Samuel P. Capen. After a thorough inquiry the commission presented its report to the board in February 1916. The portions of the report dealing specifically with the university became in effect an agenda for the Jessup administration.[30]

The commission took up a number of specific topics on which the board sought advice, but it found that beneath all of the instances of duplicating programs lay a single organic defect which must be addressed if the various forms of competition were to be dealt with successfully. This defect was the failure of the board to define clearly a distinctive mission for each of the institutions under its control. In the beginning the state had created a single university, but successive legislative acts had gradually transformed the agricultural college into a formidable competitor. This was not unique to Iowa, but was a common development wherever the agricultural college was separate from the state university. The rise of the land grant colleges with their tendency to emulate the universities posed the major problem in American higher educational administration. The commission believed that to have two or more state institutions with comparable academic standards was not necessarily disadvantageous provided that academic functions were effectively allocated among them. It proposed the principle of "major and service lines" as a formula for allocating programs to each institution. A major line should be assigned exclusively to one institution, whereas service lines would be determined by the needs of the major lines. It proposed that the major lines assigned to the State College be agriculture, veterinary medicine, home economics, and, preferably, engineering. All other subjects were to be classed as service subjects not to be developed beyond the needs of the major lines. Work in the humanities, social sciences, and certain of the natural sciences should not be developed at Ames beyond the introductory collegiate level. At the university the major lines would include the liberal arts and professional fields together with certain engineering subjects. The commission acknowledged that there were certain "problem" fields, such as chemistry, physics, zoology, bacteriology, and botany which were needed at both institutions. Here it recommended that conferences among board and staff members negotiate mutually satisfactory allocations.

Although the board had indicated that it had no stomach for reopening the vexed question of engineering, the commission boldly attacked that sensitive subject. It believed that work in advanced and professional fields should be concentrated on one campus. Just as it would be absurd to have two law or medical schools, so was it indefensible to maintain two engineering schools. Of the three possible solutions the commission favored concentration at the State College, which would eliminate friction, competition, and wasteful duplication. Failing this, the best alternative was to locate the undergraduate program on one campus and advanced work on the other, although for some unindicated reason it considered this not feasible in Iowa. The third alternative was to make a topical division of engineering fields between the two schools, with the advice of outside experts. It saw no need in Iowa to develop certain fields at all, especially marine engineering. Ironically enough, hydraulic engineering was to become the outstanding engineering field at the university.

In view of the board's prior decision not to disturb engineering, perhaps the most drastic of the commission's recommendations referred to the Teachers' College at Cedar Falls. It regarded the transformation of the old Normal School into a collegiate institution as a major mistake. The liberal arts work being offered there, while of inferior quality, clearly overlapped work at the university, and should be discontinued. The final two years of work leading to the bachelor's degree should be abandoned. The institution should reestablish its original character as a Normal School preparing teachers for rural and graded schools, not for high schools. It should abandon college preparatory work and devote three years to teacher training. The need for grade school teachers was in fact so great that the commission recommended additional normal schools in the western part of the state.[31]

These recommendations closely paralleled the ill-fated proposals of 1912, and the board quickly let it be known that it had no intention of reopening old wounds. Given its uncertainty as to its role it was unlikely that the board would be able to implement any of the commission's more comprehensive recommendations except for the distinction between major and service lines. For more than half a century this principle was to remain the official formula by which fields of study were to be allocated among the institutions.[32]

The commission was also concerned about the increasingly important role played by the board's Finance Committee. The law required the committee to visit each campus monthly to act on all transactions involving public funds. The board's attitude of suspicion toward the institutions under its charge as reflected in the decision not to admit the presidents to its meetings created a gulf which the Finance Committee could bridge. Under the able and aggressive leadership of W. R. Boyd the committee appeared to be in the process of taking over many of the functions normally exercised by the presidents. The high regard in which Boyd was generally held merely accentuated the trend. Educational and fiscal decisions often could not be separated, and the commission feared that the presidents were threatened with loss of educational control. It recommended that the presidents be made ex officio board members without vote and entitled to attend all board meetings.[33] The latter recommendation was subsequently adopted, while the continuing importance of the Finance Committee was largely a reflection of the forcefulness of its chairman.

The commission was far-sighted enough to see that the State College would inevitably achieve university status. A Graduate Division had been created at Ames two years earlier, and the college was already offering master's degrees in eighteen subjects and doctorates in nine. The principle of allocating major and service lines applied most obviously to graduate work, where duplication of programs would be unjustifiably expensive. The commission suggested that a standing committee with representatives of the board and the two institutions should review and approve proposed graduate programs in order to forestall duplication. It condemned in unmeasured terms the rivalry between the university and the State College, which it declared to be a "devastating blight fastened upon the whole educational system of the State." It suggested a temporary suspension of football and possibly baseball games between the two institutions as a means of dampening one of the more juvenile expressions of the rivalry. But there was nothing the commission could do about the organized alumni pressure, the newspaper partisanship, and the often bitter legislative infighting over institutional priorities.[34]

A formal organization for graduate work at the university had been in existence for only fifteen years when the commission visited the campus. Advanced study was being carried on in twenty-five departments. Work of good quality was being done in education, psychology, philosophy, history, and political science. In other fields the venture into graduate study was judged to be premature. This was a surprising conclusion in view of the traditional strength of the university in the sciences. The commission found that too much latitude had been given department heads to determine whether or not their departments should embark upon doctoral programs. It also recommended that a representative body, whether the graduate faculty (full professors engaged in graduate teaching) or the University Senate, be empowered to designate those departments qualified to offer strong graduate programs.[35]

The university chose to ignore certain of the commission's recommendations. The organization of a school or college of commerce was under discussion, and the commission sought to discourage such a development, finding no need for specialists in business in an agricultural state. It believed that departments of economics, accounting, and commerce should be sufficient. Disregarding this advice, the university established the College of Commerce in 1921. Similar advice not to establish a school of journalism was ignored. Following the board's original proposal to transfer home economics to the university a department in that subject had been organized in 1913. The commission considered this redundant and recommended that home economics be a service department, with no professional courses and no degree programs.[36] Again, this advice was ignored.

Even if the commission's recommendations had been adopted in full, constant surveillance would have been required to make certain that the restraints imposed by the board were observed. It remained to be seen whether it had the will and capacity to sustain such a function. It was, after all, a policy-making rather than a regulatory agency. Eight months after the board had received the commission's report W. R. Boyd informed it that Jessup was depressed and discouraged by the "unkind, unprofessional, almost dastardly things being done at Ames," where they were seeking to enter the university's field at almost every point. He urged the board to enforce the commission's formula concerning major and service lines.[37] Seven years later nothing had been done to curb the rivalry, and in a confidential memorandum Boyd rebuked the board for its failure to differentiate the functions of the three institutions. He reminded the board that it had been created to assure that the institutions should become less rather than more alike. To be sure, the legislature was largely at fault in that it was encouraging the rivals to pursue their ambitions "almost ruthlessly." Nevertheless, the board should steadfastly curb the trend toward the development of three universities. The Iowa City institution had relatively clean hands, if only because it was content to pursue its mission. The State College, on the other hand, had instituted programs in forestry, journalism, and architecture contrary to the wishes of the board and was offering graduate work in mathematics in competition with the university. At the State Teachers' College the duplications were particularly blatant. It was offering what was essentially a liberal arts rather than a teacher training program. As Boyd complained in despair to a board member, "they all want to be universities!" In view of the board's inability to control the situation he recommended that it appoint a chancellor with authority over all of the institutions.[38] There is no evidence that the board gave this serious consideration.

The legislature itself finally intervened and in 1925 asked the board to report on measures taken to curb the duplication of programs. The board again sought assistance from Samuel Capen, now chancellor of the University of Buffalo. Jessup and Boyd must have been surprised to learn from the visitors that remarkable progress had been made during the decade since Capen's previous visit. No other state could now boast of two public institutions of superior size or quality. Combined enrollments were four times what they had been ten years earlier, and the increased size tended to minimize the cost of operating separate institutions. Whatever they might be called, the state was in fact maintaining two universities, equal in standards, equipment, personnel, and advanced work. It was true that certain duplicating programs existed, but the visitors believed that the importance of the issue was overemphasized. They reaffirmed the principle of designating major and service lines as the best means of controlling duplication. The problem in engineering was not as serious as it had been earlier in view of the fact that both schools were filled to capacity. Instead of consolidation on one campus the visitors would encourage differentiation of engineering fields as an ongoing policy. Teacher training at the elementary level should be concentrated at the Teachers' College, and at the high school level at the university. Liberal arts work at the Teachers' College should be prohibited.

On the other hand, some duplication in graduate work was probably inevitable. Certain fields, such as chemistry and physics, needed at both the university and the State College, might perhaps be subdivided, while others, such as English, should be restricted to a service line at the latter institution. The visitors found that the earlier recommendation to create a standing committee to prevent duplications had not proved successful, and they urged that another effort be made.[39]

Under the leadership of President Baker the board chose to adopt the positive attitude of the Capen Commission, reporting to the legislature that the problem of duplication could be controlled by the allocation of major and service lines. A standing committee on the correlation of programs would examine new course proposals and report apparent duplications to the board. Such a committee was established in December 1926, consisting of one member from each institution with the board president himself as chairman. The university and State College were informed that each would be permitted to offer graduate work only in its major lines.[40] When State College spokesmen complained that the institution was being discriminated against the board issued comparative data showing that far from being put at a disadvantage it had regularly enjoyed larger appropriations (exclusive of building funds) in spite of its smaller enrollments. A comparison of course offerings in the liberal arts showed the curricula of the two institutions to be substantially alike. In short, the board found no evidence that its policies restricted the proper development of the State College.[41]

Thanks to the firm leadership of the board under President Baker the competition between the institutions was effectively curbed. The joint committee on graduate work was induced to make some fine discriminations, such as the distinction between pure and applied physics, in order to keep the peace. When the Brookings Institution surveyed the scene in 1933 it congratulated the board on its success in coordinating the functions of the three institutions. It had terminated graduate work in English at the State College; vocational training of teachers had been abolished at the university and the Teachers' College; elementary teacher training had been strengthened; and the joint committee on graduate work provided the machinery to control costly duplication of programs.[42] As the economic depression of the 1930s settled upon the state attention shifted from the irritations of institutional rivalry to the more somber issues of institutional survival.

THE PROBLEMS OF GROWTH

On assuming the presidency Jessup informed the board that he intended to make the university great in all of its departments, especially the Liberal Arts College, by bringing in the strongest possible faculty and by insisting upon high standards of scholarship and service. To achieve this laudable objective he would need an additional salary appropriation of $240,000 annually. The board acknowledged that the university had been less generously supported than the State College by some $360,000 annually and pledged itself to secure the necessary funds.[43] Thus began the frustrating and never-ending quest for money.

Throughout much of its history the university tied its appeal for financial support to the growth in numbers of its student body. Growth was the engine that powered the institution, and from MacLean's time onward university officials always kept an anxious eye on enrollment statistics. The high schools of the state were of course the principal source of students, and the Capen Commission commented favorably on a relationship between high schools and the university which was remarkably free of obstructions. About ninety percent of the university student body had been admitted without examination from accredited high schools. Iowa had achieved a well-coordinated system of public education which should go far toward maximizing the popularity and availability of higher education.

At the same time, however, the commission noted the absence of agreement on the standards of preparation for college work. It suggested three possible measures designed to strengthen academic standards: make the superintendent of public instruction a board member; extend the jurisdiction of the board to the public schools; and create an interinstitutional committee to evaluate high school programs. The first and third of these options had in fact already been tried, without notable success. The second was never seriously considered. The achievement of integrated academic standards was to remain an ongoing problem, and in their absence the university had little direct influence on the quality of high school programs.[44]

When Jessup became president in 1916 the university enrolled 3,523 students, 2,001 of them in the Liberal Arts College, 466 in the Graduate College, and the remainder distributed among the professional colleges.[45] Following a slight drop during the First World War, when the campus was largely given over to military programs, enrollments steadily increased year by year until the Great Depression of the 1930s brought a halt to the further growth of a student body of nearly 10,000. The annual increments may not seem large in terms of the university of the 1980s, but when it is realized that an institution which enrolled 3,300 students in 1917 had to meet the needs of more than twice that number in 1922 one can appreciate the problem of providing the necessary faculty and facilities. While the professional colleges remained relatively stable in size, the growth occurred chiefly in the Liberal Arts College and Graduate College. The greatest relative growth occurred in the latter, where the increase in the number of degrees granted during the 1920s was more than twice the increase in the number of bachelor's degrees. The same thing was happening in other state universities, and everywhere it was a tangible sign that work in the arts and sciences was achieving true university status. Jessup noted that the enrollment statistics correlated with the growth in research activities of the faculty and with the organization of research agencies and facilities, publication media, and library growth.[46]

The Capen Commission had noted that the prospect of steady growth necessitated corresponding increases in the state appropriation for higher education, which it rather blandly assumed would be readily forthcoming. State universities, it found,

> grow rich in material support with the growth in wealth or population, or both, of the states that maintain them. The appropriations for state higher education are everywhere greater every year. State legis-

lators as a rule are not only willing to pay larger amounts for higher education at each recurring session, but they do not hesitate to appropriate constantly larger percentages of the state's total funds. It is only necessary that the officers in charge of state institutions make a convincing showing that the money is needed and that it is being advantageously spent. As yet the probable limits of state generosity in this direction cannot be guessed. For all practical present purposes, therefore, state institutions have an unlimited source of support, even if the source does prove itself at times hard to tap. If this is true in general it is especially true of Iowa.[47]

The experience of the following fifteen years hardly confirmed the complacent expectations of the commission. Appropriations for operating expenses increased in rough proportion to the increase in enrollments. The commission had found, however, that the cost to the state per student in 1915 had been from $170 to $275 per year, which it considered to be too low, and this figure did not increase during the ensuing years.[48] With the inauguration of new academic programs and the intensifying competition for scholarly faculty members it was essential that increases in appropriations exceed by at least a modest amount the increases in enrollments.

Jessup was more successful in securing funds for new buildings than for educational purposes. His administration marked the first of the two major building periods in the university's history, the second coming half a century later during the Bowen and Boyd administrations. The man primarily responsible for determining the physical appearance of the university campus was the Des Moines architect W. T. Proudfoot, who served as supervising architect for some thirty years prior to his death in 1928. It was Proudfoot who fixed the gray stone neo-Renaissance style of the Pentacrest and surrounding east-side buildings to harmonize with the Old Capitol. He also determined the red brick with collegiate gothic trim which was to characterize the new west-side medical campus and dormitories, beginning in 1918 with the Quadrangle dormitory and the Children's Hospital, followed by the Westlawn nurses' dormitory, the Psychopathic Hospital, and the General Hospital with its dominating gothic tower. Jessup was able to relieve an acute shortage of classroom space for liberal arts by completing the "five-spot plan" (the Pentacrest) with the erection of University Hall (Jessup). He also secured funds for expansion along the North Capitol Street campus axis: the geology, chemistry-pharmacy-botany buildings, and the University Elementary School and High School. With the death of Proudfoot the university fell upon hard times, architecturally speaking. No one preserved the earlier conception of north-south and east-west axes, and a succession of nondescript buildings sprang up in available locations chosen with little apparent reference to an overall plan.

A major failure was Jessup's inability to secure funds for a library building. The central library collection in the well of the Hall of Natural Science (Macbride) had long outgrown the space provided, forcing the scattering of the collection among twenty-one departmental libraries, with loss of effective control. The Capen Commission had recommended that the building of an adequate library be given top priority.[49] Dean Seashore proposed that it be located in an extension of University Hall (Jessup) down the Jefferson Street hill to Madison Street, matching a similar extension of the physics building (MacLean) down Washington Street. These extensions, he believed, would provide a pleasing frame for the Old Capitol.[50] Nothing came of his proposals. By the time the last of the older buildings had been removed from the four-block square, in 1975, and the area actually became a pentacrest, the Old Capitol square had acquired a hallowed character forbidding additional construction and forcing campus sprawl as the institution expanded.

For many years the university enjoyed the dubious distinction of being the only major institution of higher learning without a library building. The board repeatedly included funds for a library in its requests for capital appropriations, but either the governor or the legislature refused to honor the requests.[51] Following the building of the Field House and Armory on the west side, the Old Armory and Men's Gymnasium at the foot of Washington Street was converted to library space for a Reserve Reading Room, serials, and government documents, to be known as the Library Annex. The librarian provided an eloquent description of working conditions in the annex.

During the summer months the unbearable heat in the main reading room . . . is unrelieved by a large number of noisy and gusty overhead and wall fans. Because the building is not equipped with screens, the months of September and October are chiefly noted for hordes of flies which keep the Librarians employed in such unprofessional tasks as arranging new sheets of fly-paper, spraying flit, etc. During the winter the building is inadequately ventilated, and it is always over- or under-heated. . . . At all times during the year the slightest shower of rain causes the roof to leak in a countless variety of places. . . . Early in January the melting snows entered the reading room via the walls and window sills. Many magazines out on shelves that lined the east wall of the room were badly damaged by water. . . .

[Three years later she renewed a plea for screens.] Due to the low location of the building and its closeness to the river, there is a real necessity for screens at the windows and doors. Without them the annoyance from bugs and insects (and on occasion bats) is very great, especially during the evening hours, when the electric lights are on. Although to help overcome this annoyance, patrons are sometimes supplied with fly swatters, the impossibility of carrying on serious study under such adverse conditions usually causes them to abandon their plans for working there.[52]

With the coming of the Depression of the 1930s capital appropriations for building were out of the question. It was possible, however, to secure funds from federal relief agencies such as the WPA for the construction of the theater and art building on the west bank of the river. The nuclei of what was to become the arts center, these buildings were erected prior to the construction of the Coralville flood control dam and were subject to occasional flooding of basements. Together with the Student Memorial Union on the east bank these were the first of the series of buildings in the floodplain which were to link the east and west campuses.

Initially the university had assumed no responsibility for the housing of students beyond inspection and certification of rooms in private homes. The limited capacity of a small community to provide for the growing number of students, however, eventually forced the university to provide dormitory facilities. Women students were the first to be accommodated, with the opening of Currier Hall in 1913. The Quadrangle dormitory for men was built with federal assistance during the First World War. These facilities housed some 600 students, while an additional 1,500 lived in fraternities, sororities, and private clubs. The board believed that the growth of the university was retarded by the lack of living accommodations, and in 1925 it persuaded the legislature to permit it to borrow money for dormitory construction.[53] Enlargement of the two residence halls enabled the university to accommodate over a thousand students by 1934, when the Depression brought a halt to further construction. While students of all races were accepted in its academic programs the university raised no objection when the residents of the Quadrangle adopted a constitution in 1919 limiting residence there to members who were white. Dean of students Robert E. Rienow explained that he did not wish to stir up dissension by imposing on the majority a policy of equal rights on behalf of a very small minority. The university preferred to assist minority students in finding housing in town.[54]

Prior to the First World War, the Iowa State College was the dominant institution as measured by every tangible index. In 1915 it enrolled 2,932 students as opposed to 2,690 at the university. It boasted a faculty of 302, 69 more than the university's. Its income from state appropriation was $1,055,840, as opposed to $767,200 for the university; and its total income of $1,365,481 exceeded that of the university by $412,366.[55] So long as university enrollments lagged behind, it remained very difficult to make the case for appropriations commensurate with the broader range of the university's educational responsibilities. Doubtless because of its strong condemnation of interinstitutional rivalry, the Capen Commission avoided emphasizing such comparisons; it was content to note that university salaries, especially in the liberal arts, were too low. Following the war, however, university enrollments regularly surpassed those of the State College, and it now became realistic to seek relatively larger appropriations.[56] Urged on by W. R. Boyd, who felt strongly that the university suffered unjust discrimination at the hands of the legislature, the board pressed for support commensurate with the university's responsibilities.

Jessup's determination to strengthen the faculty was premised on the assumption that the university would be able to offer attractive salaries in a highly competitive market. He reported in 1919 that Iowa salaries were somewhat lower than those at Illinois and Minnesota, about the same as those at Michigan and Wisconsin, and somewhat higher than those at Indiana, Ohio State, Missouri, Nebraska, and Kansas. Under these relatively favorable conditions it was possible to make several strong faculty appointments.[57] In the humanities and social sciences, Jessup could properly boast of the addition of Hardin Craig, John W. Ashton, and Norman Foerster in English; Arthur M. Schlesinger, Sr., in history; Philip Greeley Clapp in music; Edward C. Mabie and A. Craig Baird in speech; Frank H. Knight in economics; William F. Russell and Everet Lindquist in education; Edward Byron Reuter and Clyde Hart in sociology; Frank Luther Mott in journalism; Herbert Feigl in philosophy; Lee Travis and George D. Stoddard in psychology; and Amy Daniels, Beth Wellman, and Hornell Hart in child welfare. Strong appointments in the sciences included Wilbur Swingle and Emil Witschi in zoology; George W. Martin in botany; and Edward Bartow in chemistry. Professional college appointments included Edwin W. Patterson, Mason Ladd, and Paul Sayre in law; Samuel T. Orton and Henry A. Mattill in medicine; and Floyd Nagler in engineering. But as the

Iowa economy weakened in the agricultural depression of the later 1920s, the university lost its competitive position, and its salary scale sank to the bottom of the rankings. Several of these outstanding faculty members moved on to financially stronger institutions.

While Jessup wanted a strong faculty he wanted it to consist of scholar-teachers who would mind their own business and leave the management of the university to him. If he felt in need of advice he preferred to seek it privately from appropriate sources rather than from organized or representative faculty bodies. President MacLean had attempted to reinvigorate the University Senate, an advisory body consisting of deans, department heads, full professors, the librarian, registrar, and a representative of the board. But Jessup found the Senate of little use and summoned it for the last time on April 23, 1923, although certain of its standing committees continued to function. Similarly, the Board of Deans met thereafter at infrequent intervals. When the Capen Commission had visited the campus in 1915 it had reported that "the University presents rather strongly to the visitor the impression of a group of relatively autonomous departments and colleges, many of them going their own way, with little obvious regard to the interests of other departments and even less for the institution as a whole." [58] Jessup apparently found nothing undesirable in this situation and did nothing to encourage faculty involvement in the institutional life of the university. He noted a recent tendency in private universities for the faculty to take control of appointments, promotions, dismissals, and salaries, but he added with obvious satisfaction that no such trend was evident in public universities. In fact, he attributed the recently strengthened position of the president vis-à-vis the governing board to a faculty demand for an executive officer who viewed academic matters from a faculty point of view. There was, however, nothing in recent Iowa experience to sustain this interpretation of his own position. [59]

INTERNAL ORGANIZATION

As the university steadily grew in size and in the range and complexity of its operations it found itself somewhat cramped by its organization in departments and colleges. With the gradual clarification of the distinctions among undergraduate, graduate, and professional education it became increasingly apparent that the concentration of undergraduate work in the liberal arts departments made it difficult to address certain persistent educational needs. George MacLean had expected that the Liberal

Arts College would itself be fragmented into a number of more specialized organizations and that the formation of schools within the college would be steps in this process. Contrary to his expectation, however, the college proved itself to be a durable element in the university structure, spinning off certain specialized programs while at the same time nurturing others within its own administrative structure.

Three programs—engineering, education, and commerce—passed through the spin-off process. Some work in civil engineering had been offered in mathematics as early as 1857. It was organized in 1872–73 as an independent four-year "course" in the collegiate department, the first two years being identical with the scientific course. With the university reorganization under MacLean, engineering became briefly a School of Applied Science in the Liberal Arts College, and in the face of pressure to transfer the program to the State College it was hastily elevated to collegiate status, in 1905. A department of hydraulic engineering organized by Floyd Nagler in 1914 was to become recognized internationally and draw students from around the world.[60]

Education likewise had deep roots in the collegiate department. In the beginning the university had for all practical purposes been a teachers' college. Education became a department in the Liberal Arts College in the reorganization of 1901, a school in 1907, and was accorded collegiate status in 1913. At that point there was some sentiment in favor of separating teacher training from liberal arts in a college of its own with its own faculty, a pattern for which the Teachers' College of Columbia University furnished the model. Jessup, who was the newly appointed dean of education, believed strongly that prospective teachers should have a basic liberal arts education, and he insisted that they enroll in the Liberal Arts College for subject-matter training, taking only such pedagogical work in the College of Education as might be necessary for teacher certification. Only at the graduate level did the College of Education function independently.[61]

Another kind of controversy accompanied the emergence of what would eventually be called business administration. Isaac A. Loos, the professor of political economy (not to be confused with political science, which was Benjamin Shambaugh's field), had been instrumental in the organization in 1900 of the School of Political and Social Science. Loos envisioned a comprehensive interdisciplinary program in the social sciences, embracing history, political science, sociology, and economics. Among other options the school offered a four-year course in commerce, which was in effect a major in business administration. The title of the school was enlarged in 1907 to include the word "commerce." There was widespread opposition

in the liberal arts faculty to expansion of the social sciences, which as relative newcomers to academia lacked the prestige of the older established
subjects. Shambaugh capitalized successfully on this sentiment in his efforts to separate history and political science from the social science complex. The name of the school was changed in 1914 to the School of Commerce. Loos wished to retain the affiliation with liberal arts, believing that
only in the senior year should the student specialize in commercial subjects. He feared that full separation from the liberal arts would result in a
trade school mentality. Nevertheless, following the departure of Loos,
Jessup in 1921 approved the organization of the College of Commerce,
which offered courses in economics and sociology as well as the usual commercial subjects. It was rumored among the faculty that the decision had
been made in order to keep Chester Phillips, a specialist in money and
banking, who was made dean of the new college. If the rumor was true this
was not the only time when important institutional decisions turned upon
personnel considerations.[62] The creation of the new college may have succeeded in keeping Phillips, but it did not prevent the departure of the
economists Frank Knight and Henry Simon or the sociologist Ellsworth
Faris, all of whom moved to the University of Chicago.

Two "affiliated" programs which became schools in the Liberal Arts
College were music and religion. A small proprietary music school operated by Effie Mae Proffitt had become affiliated with the university in
1906. Faculty status was accorded to its staff members, who, however, received no university salaries. Students paid course fees to the school and
received university credit for their work. It had been President MacLean's
intention eventually to absorb the school into the university, which occurred in 1914, although not under the happiest of circumstances. As
noted previously, in that year the board chose to force the resignation of
President Bowman by dismissing the current head of the school, Gustav
Schoettle, and making the school an integral part of the university.[63] With
the coming of Philip Greeley Clapp in 1919 the School of Music was finally established on a firm footing.

The early history of the School of Religion illustrated some of the problems arising from the pattern of affiliation with organizations over which
the university exercised less than full control. The traditional nineteenth-
century union of religious piety with the higher learning gradually wore
thin as university scholars became increasingly preoccupied with their research. Public criticism of its "godless" character inevitably put the university on the defensive, although its critics would doubtless have been the
first to denounce it had it shown any sectarian tendencies. University

spokesmen like President MacLean made an implicit distinction between religion and sectarianism, hoping that the university might be perceived to be the friend of all faiths. In practice MacLean's program of affiliated courses in religion appeared to recognize several of the largest and most influential denominations whose clergymen provided the instruction. The program, as noted in the previous chapter, was handicapped by its reliance upon overburdened and unreimbursed local pastors and soon collapsed. Ironically enough, however, as the separation of church and public schools was becoming more clearly defined through a series of court decisions and legislative enactments in several states, the pressure to provide for religious instruction in public universities was steadily increasing.

Regardless of their secular character, public universities were not wholly without some forms of the study of religion. Thirty of the forty-two state universities in 1923 were offering courses in religion as part of their regular curricula. Most commonly offered were courses in the Bible as literature and in the history, philosophy, and psychology of religion. These courses were generally taught in the relevant academic departments by scholars whose specialties they represented.[64] But the detached and critical stance of a historian or philosopher dealing with religious topics was hardly calculated to satisfy the zeal of the religious community. What was needed was a firm base within the university to support courses in religion offered by faculty members with scholarly credentials who were also actively religious and acceptable to the churches.

The University of Iowa offered in the person of Professor Edwin D. Starbuck an excellent example of what the orthodox religionists hoped to circumvent. Descended from an old Nantucket Quaker family (Herman Melville immortalized the name by giving it to the first mate of the *Pequod*), Starbuck had joined the faculty in 1906 as professor of philosophy and psychology. Although he was a profoundly religious man, his faith was of a highly personal character, combining elements of Quakerism and romantic idealism. He believed that religious faith was indistinguishable from character and conduct; it was something that one lived rather than believed. He called his faith pantheism or panpsychism, the sense of an interfusing presence. At the same time he craved intellectual understanding; he wanted to make religion intelligible. To this end he sought to develop a science of religion by applying rigorous methods of scientific investigation to its central phenomena. His book *The Psychology of Religion*, a pioneer work in that field, applied empirical methods of investigation to the experience of conversion. His use of questionnaires elicited information which permitted him to reconstruct a careful analysis of conversion. Unfortunately for him, his method failed to satisfy the rigorous demands of the "brass-instrument" psychologists, among them his Iowa colleague Carl Seashore, who dismissed his work as unscientific.[65]

Undeterred by the disapproval of the experimentalists Starbuck pressed ahead with plans to develop a program for the scientific study of religion. He conceded that science could not deal directly with religion, only with ideas about religion. One's methods should be adapted to the nature of the material and would include historical, sociological, and psychological approaches. Orthodox religionists might not have objected strenuously to a strictly neutral study of religion, but as believers in divine transcendence they were offended by Starbuck's assertion that science itself supported a religion of immanence, a presumed cumulative revelation of divine purpose as life mounted from lower to higher forms. In 1913 he proposed the creation of a department of the science and practice of religion, only to be put off by President Bowman, who declared that the time was not ripe for it.[66]

Although he remained invincibly optimistic and never expressed discouragement Starbuck must have been distressed by his failure to find support where he might have expected to find it. His conflict with Seashore was an added source of dissatisfaction. He resigned in 1930 to accept appointment at the University of Southern California where he was assured of a more sympathetic environment for his work.

While Starbuck was waging a lonely one-man battle to introduce his brand of the study of religion into the curriculum the leaders of organized religion were bringing far more formidable forces to bear. In 1911 some nineteen Protestant denominations had organized a Council of Church Boards of Education which a year later formed a University Committee to explore ways in which religious education in the universities could be promoted.[67] These denominations, led by the Presbyterians, Methodists, Baptists, and Congregationalists, had reached a point in their institutional and theological development where they could agree on the value of a common effort to promote a basic or "least-common-denominator" Protestant Christianity in the expectation that students would discover or retain a religious commitment which would feed into the various denominations. The nonsectarian character of the movement would be greatly enhanced if Catholics and Jews could be persuaded to participate. The relatively small Jewish community of the Midwest, accustomed to living among Gentiles, was amenable to cooperation. For Catholics the decision was more difficult, but the bishop of the Davenport diocese agreed to participate on the apparent assumption that no compromise would be made with the church's faith and morals.

Tax-supported public universities which were of necessity secular in character offered a particular challenge. Professor Charles F. Kent of Yale and O. D. Foster of the Council of Church Boards of Education proposed to solve this problem by organizing privately financed schools of religion which would be affiliated with state universities, thus circumventing any restriction upon the use of public funds to pay professors of religion. Attention was focused initially on the state universities of Ohio, Michigan, Illinois, Texas, and Iowa. Foster in 1921 sounded out Jessup directly, but the chief contact was established through the secretary of the university's YMCA chapter, Rufus Fitzgerald.[68] An energetic promoter who enjoyed the confidence of Jessup, Fitzgerald rose rapidly through the administrative hierarchy. Instrumental in laying the foundations of the School of Religion, he then served successively as director of the Iowa Memorial Union and as director of the School of Fine Arts before following former President Bowman to the University of Pittsburgh, where he became provost.

Jessup's sympathetic response to the religious educators was consistent with his goal of serving the interests of Iowa citizens in every way possible. He declared that nothing was of greater concern to the university than providing "a wholesome religious and moral atmosphere which may influence the young men and women of Iowa." Although the university was a nonsectarian institution it aimed "to stimulate an intelligent and earnest consideration of the great religious principles." It encouraged the YMCA and YWCA, the Newman Club, and the Menorah Society. When completed, its Memorial Student Union would house campus religious organizations as well as other student activities with a serious purpose.[69]

A faculty Committee on Religious Education was appointed by Jessup in 1921. It recommended that the religious denominations be encouraged to establish affiliated courses or chairs of religion, and it sponsored two conferences to bring together religious leaders and university representatives. At these conferences a number of options were discussed, including pretheological courses offered in regular departments, religious courses of a broad character, and theological courses more narrowly defined. Among the organizational possibilities were affiliated denominational chairs or schools; an interdenominational school; or a nondenominational school on an independent foundation partly self-perpetuating and partly under denominational and university auspices. Degree-granting programs both liberal and professional were also considered.[70]

By 1923 the National Council of Schools of Religion was prepared to move more aggressively against the prevailing materialism of American higher education. Some ten independent schools of religion had by this time sprung up on state university campuses, and the council urged that they be incorporated within the universities and enjoy regular departmental status. It recommended a curriculum which would include Great Living Religions, Literature of the Bible, and Principles of Religion. Except for the first of these, the program had a strong Christian flavor, although there was no overt denominational emphasis. Graduate courses for the training of nonclerical religious leaders and teachers were also recommended.[71]

In the following year an enlarged faculty committee under the leadership of liberal arts dean Kay proposed the establishment of a School of Religion "just as soon as the religious organizations of the State have time to direct their energies into the joint enterprise," that is, to provide the money. The committee reported that "it is now generally recognized that religion has a vital relation to education in a democracy, and that every effort consistent with our principles and traditions as a democratic state should be made to develop and foster the religious growth of our future citizens. Religion is finding a place in every complete scheme of university education." The Board of Education promptly approved the plan, which provided for a school governed by trustees chosen by the churches and the university. Their principal function would be to raise the funds necessary to finance the school. The trustees would also employ a director and determine the policies of the school in cooperation with university officials. The school in turn would organize and staff a department of religion within the Liberal Arts College and Graduate College. The overall object of the program would be to provide a wholesome view of religion and create interest in religious activities; to serve the state by training religious leaders; to develop vocational expectations; to provide thoughtful insight into the nature and meaning of religion; and to provide graduate courses for the training of religious leaders.[72]

Sufficient funds were raised to appoint a faculty of four and to offer a number of courses in the year 1927–28. The director, Willard Lampe, had been the secretary for university work of the Presbyterian Board of Education. The other professors represented respectively Jews, Catholics, and Protestants. Courses were offered in Old Testament Religion, Judaism, Christian Apologetics, Christian Ethics, Comparative Religion, and Biblical Archaeology. Save for the course in comparative religion the courses were all Christian or Jewish, but were not narrowly sectarian. Thus the

Catholic representative, Fr. Henry G. Takkenberg, offered courses in Christian Apologetics and Christian Ethics. This was apparently going too far in the direction of ecumenism, and the Catholics withdrew from the school for a decade. When they returned in 1940 it was on their own terms: their representative, Fr. Donald Hayne, offered courses in Catholic Fundamentals and the Catholic Church.

Assurances had been offered from the outset that the school would be so organized as to eliminate the possibility of adverse criticism for using state funds or displaying sectarian bias. The financial problem was eased temporarily by receipt of a five-year grant of $35,000 from the Rockefeller Foundation for administrative expenses and the salary of the director.[73] The school was legally incorporated in 1927 with a governing board composed of denominational and university representatives. The object of the corporation was to maintain the school and to raise funds for its operation. As an independent legal entity its relationship with the university was an intimate but elusive one, to be manipulated by both religious and university interests as the occasion might suggest. The long-term objective of director Lampe was to transfer the costs of operations to the university budget, while university officials were content on occasion to evade responsibility by referring to the independence of the school.

President Eugene Gilmore, who succeeded Jessup in 1934, was an ardent advocate of religious education. He viewed with alarm the tendency of university students to fall prey to irreligion and cynicism. People without religion, he warned, were lacking in morale and were dangerous. "The revolt of youth against the established order has carried with it a revolt against religion." Science bore its share of responsibility for this situation, for although science might tell us much about life, it could not tell what life means; this was the function of a vital religion. The university, Gilmore declared, now recognized that religion was essential to a full and effective life, and he was prepared to promote it vigorously. Solomon's proverbial injunction to get wisdom and understanding, a fitting motto for any university, was altered by Gilmore to read: "With all thy getting, get religion!"[74]

Nevertheless, in spite of such somber bursts of piety Gilmore was a lawyer and a cautious man. He knew that complaints had been made to Governor Kraschel about the use of public funds to support the School of Religion, and he found it prudent to consult Professor Frank Horack, an expert on school law, as to whether tax funds could legally be used to support the school. Horack could find no law or court decision bearing directly on the matter, and he believed that a good argument in behalf of

Eugene Gilmore. Courtesy of the University of Iowa Archives.

such use could be made so long as the school did not teach a particular system of faith and worship.[75] Satisfied that the university was in the clear, Gilmore declared that if the school was indeed engaged in the teaching of sectarian religion it did so with funds other than those appropriated by the legislature. For its part the university recognized a responsibility for the religious and moral welfare of its students, providing a weekly vesper service and supporting a Campus Religious Activities Center.[76] The university in 1938 assumed the expense of the administration of the school, including the salary of the director.

Assured of Gilmore's support, Willard Lampe opened a vigorous attack on the secular university. In a university bulletin on the religious life of the university he quoted with approval the statement "Culture of intellect, without religion in the heart, is only civilized barbarism and disguised animalism." The American tradition of the separation of church and state was declared to be a blind alley. Lampe asserted that every teacher taught some kind of religion, however unenlightened; therefore it was essential that religion be taught properly. In other words, there was "true" religion and "false" religion, and the university should be on the side of truth. Religious instruction should be formally integrated with the university, which implied that it should be supported by appropriated funds. In the meanwhile he defended the organization of the school as an effective means of assuring the interests of both the university and the churches. To the objection that religion could not be taught objectively under the Iowa plan he pointed out that faculty appointments were made only on the recommendation of the dean of liberal arts and the president, which presumably assured the same standards of academic competence that applied to other faculty appointments.[77]

In fact, the status of faculty members in the School of Religion was subject to considerable confusion. They were identified in the university catalog as full professors, and their courses carried full credit. The director emphasized the joint participation of university and school trustees in their appointments. But unlike other professors, who enjoyed the security of appointment for indefinite terms—the so-called permanent tenure—professors in the School of Religion held one-year appointments without further security of tenure. Their appointments were not reported to the Board of Education, presumably because their salaries were not drawn from public funds.[78]

These circumstances came to light in 1939, when the Jewish patrons of the school terminated the appointment of the professor of Jewish studies, Moses Jung, who had served the school for ten years. The dismissal was not due to any deficiency of teaching or scholarship, but because Jung "was not qualified for all the responsibilities of a position which involves Judaism on the faculty of the School and among the Jews of the State." Jung appealed for assistance from the American Association of University Professors, which complained to Gilmore that Jung had been summarily dismissed without academic due process. Gilmore replied that the professor had not been appointed by the university and had received no money from it. In his opinion ample notice of dismissal had been given. There was nothing the association could do for Jung beyond asking some pointed questions: could the university justify the granting of faculty status and course credit for teachers whose appointments were less than official and whose tenure was subject to the wishes of those over whom the university exercised no control? Was it not engaging in a species of deception when it identified as faculty members teachers who were not subject to its regulations? Gilmore did not respond to these questions.[79]

If the School of Religion was at least in part a product of external pressure, so in another way was the short-lived College of Fine Arts, established in 1911. Mrs. Mark Ranney, the widow of a former lecturer in medicine, presented the university with a bequest in his memory which in the opinion of Clarke Ansley obligated the university to establish the new college. Ansley, who was appointed dean by President Bowman, drew up an ambitious plan for the Mark Ranney Memorial Institute, as the college was also called. It was to include the School of Music, a School of Design, including the graphic and plastic arts, a School of Architecture, and a School of Expression, embracing oratory and drama. Save for the School of Music none of these schools as yet existed. Central to Ansley's plan was the conception of literature as a fine art. The curricula which he drew up offered a number of four-year interdisciplinary programs leading to the B.A. degree: literature and architecture, literature and music, literature and painting, literature and aesthetics. It would also be possible to take a more conventional major in any of these subjects, based upon a broad humanistic foundation. Literature itself embraced all of the major languages then taught at the university, including English, German, French, Greek, and Latin. But the principal impetus came from the English department, which was to display an ongoing sense of the need to relate the study of literature to its social and historical context. The schools of design, architecture, and expression failed to materialize, probably because few students showed any interest in the programs offered by the new college, which quietly expired in 1915, leaving not a trace in the university catalog.[80]

Journalism was one of the bones of contention between the university and the State College. Both institutions sought to stake out claims to the field in the face of the widespread opinion that there was no need in Iowa for such programs. At the State College the emphasis was on agricultural journalism, while at the university courses were offered in the English department. Beginning with four courses in 1916–17, the offerings increased rapidly, including such technical subjects as editing, reporting, editorial writing, and circulation and advertising. The School of Journalism opened in 1926, with Charles H. Weller as its director. Weller was succeeded a year later by Frank Luther Mott, who added George Gallup to his staff.

Another attempt to integrate work in the fine arts resulted from the labors of that intrepid organizer Rufus Fitzgerald. A Student Union had existed as early as 1908, located successively in the former Unitarian Church and the St. James Hotel, both at the head of Iowa Avenue. The latter building burned in 1916. Fitzgerald, the director of the campus YMCA, persuaded Jessup to adopt an ambitious plan for a union conceived as a comprehensive fusion of the intellectual, cultural, and social aspects of campus life. Such a project seemed to be a suitable memorial to university students who had given their lives in the First World War. Fitzgerald was put in charge of fund raising, and the first unit of the Memorial Union, located on Madison Street at the foot of Jefferson Street, was opened in 1926. Fitzgerald, who had become director of student services the previous year, was made director of the union. He adopted Starbuck's proposal to associate the union with a program for character development. He also envisioned the union as a center for creative work in the arts, with studios for craft work and a theater. These projects were plagued by fund-raising difficulties and had to be drastically curtailed.[81]

What could not be achieved through the union might be accomplished by an integration of the regular academic departments in a School of Fine Arts, of which Fitzgerald was appropriately made director, in 1929. The new school embraced the dramatic art section of the speech department and the departments of graphic and plastic arts, music, and the history of art. The heads of these departments were to report to the director, who in turn reported to the dean of liberal arts. The purpose of the school, at first defined simply as coordination of programs and the prevention of duplication, was later amplified to include the affirmation that thorough training in one art should be accompanied by some work in the others. It was also the object of the school to create an indigenous American art using regional materials, an objective which reflected the presence in the faculty of Grant Wood. Scientific methods would be used to detect the presence of creative talent, techniques emanating from the laboratory of Dean Carl Seashore. And opportunities would be provided for performance, reflecting the influence of Mabie in theater and Clapp in music. It was rumored that one reason for creating the school was to impose a protective barrier of administration between liberal arts dean Kay and these abrasive personalities.

The idea of forming a number of schools within the Liberal Arts College persisted through the 1920s, but without George MacLean's assumption that they would supersede that college. When in 1930 the board authorized Jessup to organize the college in a number of schools it did so without announcing a rationale for a policy which may have reflected nothing more than a sense of the need to provide an intermediate layer of administration between the dean and the large number of departments under his jurisdiction.[82] Individuals within the university doubtless viewed the authorization in terms of their own interests. Seashore welcomed it as portending the breaking down of departmental barriers and opening opportunities for interdisciplinary cooperation. His vision, however, was not shared by those who were content with their roles within the existing structure and who felt threatened by proposed innovations, the consequences of which could not be foreseen.

These conflicting outlooks were brought to the surface in 1930 with the formation of the School of Letters, the first of the hypothetical new schools. It was to consist of the departments of English, Latin and Greek, German, and modern languages (French, Spanish, Italian). Jessup's vague statement of purpose referred to the "additional opportunity" to serve the needs of students that the school would afford.[83] No one seems to have considered the apprehensions of the small foreign language departments at the prospect of domination by the large English department. The director would presumably exercise the powers enjoyed by the director of the School of Fine Arts, denying department heads direct access to the dean. Each of the five individuals whose names were considered as candidates for the directorship were scholars in English literature, a fact which confirmed the dominant position of that department.

The fears of the foreign language executives were fully confirmed with the appointment of Norman Foerster, then professor of English at the University of North Carolina. Seashore, who had learned how to accomplish his purposes without occupying a position of strength in the administrative structure, sought to reassure the foreign language heads that they would not be deprived of any of their privileges and responsibilities, but that was certainly not Foerster's understanding of his authority. He complained bitterly that Bush in modern languages and Flickinger in classics took their business directly to Dean Kay and refused to collaborate in his comprehensive plan for language studies. In the English department, however, where his rank as full professor reinforced by his status as director of the school gave him great authority, he was able to make a number of innovations. The head of the department, Baldwin Maxwell, who disliked him cordially, acknowledged that Foerster was instrumental in securing the appointments of Austin Warren and René Wellek, and in introducing new courses in literary criticism. The new director was a firm supporter of Seashore's campaign to secure a place for creative work in the arts and humanities. He also organized an American civilization program which sought to integrate the methods of the humanities and social sciences using American materials.[84] Beyond the confines of the English department the School of Letters offered little more than catalog copy.

THE ATHLETIC SCANDAL

After a decade of generally successful administration the tide began to turn against Jessup. Although he was not personally involved in it the athletic scandal of 1929 cast a cloud over his presidency and strengthened the hand of those who demanded a legislative investigation of his administration. The Western Intercollegiate Athletic Conference—better known as the "Big Ten"—had pioneered in insisting upon faculty control of athletic programs. The University of Iowa had endorsed this principle even before joining the conference in 1899. In fact, however, "faculty control" simply demonstrated that university faculties acquiesced in practices of recruitment, certification, subsidization, and intensive training which set the athletes in the major sports apart from the student body and resulted in the elaboration of athletic programs grotesquely at odds with the ostensible purposes of the universities. A Carnegie Foundation survey of college athletics—an effort comparable in intent to Flexner's earlier survey of medical education—found the University of Iowa to be among some dozen institutions which had given the matter of control of athletics careful thought.[85] The Athletic Council, a standing board of the University Senate, was appointed by the president and given governing powers over the athletic program. Furthermore, it had seemed consistent with the principle of faculty control to incorporate athletics within the academic structure of the university, and to this end Jessup proposed in 1923 to create a Division of Physical Education which would include the departments of men's and women's physical education and the department of intercollegiate athletics. The coaches of major sports would hold faculty appointments. The successful football coach, Howard Jones, objected strenuously to these arrangements and resigned.[86]

The new director of physical education and athletics, Paul Belting, who had been a professor of physical education at the University of Illinois, was also appointed professor of physical education and chairman of the Athletic Council. He proceeded vigorously to develop the physical facilities for the athletic program. The remaining debt on the old stadium on the east bank of the river was paid off, a new field house at the head of Grand Avenue was built, the original Finkbine golf course was developed, and work on the new football stadium (Kinnick) was begun. Nevertheless, Belting's administration of the athletic program was bitterly criticized by the coaches and alumni boosters, who felt that he was not sufficiently supportive. The football coach, Burton Ingwerson, had not produced winning teams, but Belting and the Athletic Council continued to support him.

Early in 1929 several of the coaches threatened to resign if Belting were not dismissed. The Big Ten athletic commissioner, Major John L. Griffith, wrote to Belting that he had heard reports to the effect that certain Iowa alumni were attempting to gain control of the athletic program. He reminded Belting of the conference's commitment to faculty control and in effect offered the support of his office in resisting pressure from the boosters.[87] Nevertheless, in the face of threatened rebellion by the athletic staff, Jessup requested Belting's resignation as director, which was submitted on April 26, 1929. Belting declined to remain as professor of physical education and left town. E. H. Lauer was appointed to succeed him as director of the division, with George T. Bresnahan as assistant director for intercollegiate athletics. The suspension of the university from the Big Ten followed on May 28, 1929, to take effect at the beginning of January.[88]

By the standards of a later day the procedure of the conference in taking this drastic step was casual in the extreme. The university was given no opportunity to respond to charges; nor was the suspension accompanied by a statement of the university's offenses. When he left Iowa City Belting went immediately to the conference office and apparently gave Griffith and the athletic directors an account of the situation at the university that was favorable to himself and damaging to his enemies. Griffith informed Lauer informally that alumni interference was the crucial issue. He was reported to have characterized Lauer as a "stuffed shirt," and to have predicted that Bresnahan would run the athletic show for the "alumni gang." When queried about these allegations the conference committee of faculty representatives repudiated Griffith's comments as irrelevant and announced the reasons for the suspension. The major charge was their fear of the loss of faculty control. The dismissal of Belting was presumably the basis for this charge. There were also four "minor" charges: athletes had been given commissions for the sale of yearbooks; athletes were being subsidized from a slush fund; athletes had been permitted to draw on an illegal fund to make payments on tuition in arrears; and the registrar had failed to certify the eligibility of athletes as required by conference regulations.

The university immediately launched its own investigation, which was conducted by Fitzgerald at Jessup's request. The minor charges were found to be substantially correct. It was an open secret that alumni contributed to a "loan" fund administered by a local bank from which athletes could borrow small sums for incidental expenses. Jessup knew of this practice but took no steps to prevent it, thinking it sufficient to disavow any university involvement. But he did not know, until Fitzgerald discovered it, that Belting had transferred $1,703.50 of athletic department money to a trustee fund, also for the purpose of making loans to athletes. This was clearly a major offense, and the university sought to place the blame on Belting while exonerating the student-athletes who had unwittingly borrowed from the illegal fund.[89] When the university promised to clean house and sought reinstatement the conference rejected the petition and insisted that fourteen athletes who had borrowed from the fund be declared ineligible. Certain hotheaded alumni urged the university to renounce the conference and go its own way athletically, but good sense prevailed, and the university, on December 11, 1929, signified that it would take whatever punitive and remedial measures the conference might stipulate. The Athletic Council was replaced by a new Board in Control of Athletics whose chairman was to be a faculty member rather than the director of athletics. The position of assistant director was abolished, thus removing Bresnahan, who became the track coach.[90] The unlucky athletes were declared ineligible. The university was restored to good standing on Feburary 1, 1930, after one month of official suspension.

It was not an insignificant coincidence that the principle of faculty control which the conference declared to be its chief concern should at that moment have come under critical scrutiny by the Carnegie Foundation investigators. Faculty control was found to be rarely what it purported to be. Although the Big Ten proclaimed its devotion to the principle none of its member universities was among those cited by the report as having achieved effective faculty control. Ironically enough, the conference organization itself, which might have been expected to function in accordance with the principle, had surrendered to its athletic directors and coaches "nearly all official actions of the conference." The "minor" offenses for which Iowa was disciplined were rampant among the colleges and universities with highly developed athletic programs. A variety of methods of subsidizing athletes through scholarships, jobs, loans, and direct payments were found in 81 of the 112 institutions studied, several Big Ten universities among them. Northwestern in particular was cited for its direct subsidies to athletes. Faculty control simply put the stamp of legitimacy on these practices. In presenting the foundation's report to the public President Pritchett concluded that the current athletic situation was one of the consequences of superimposing graduate and professional schools on the traditional liberal arts colleges. The faculties were now oriented toward research and no longer concerned to provide undergraduates with a genuine intellectual experience. In an environment in which students and faculty were alike preoccupied with the preparation for and pursuit of careers "big-time" athletics with all of its abuses could flourish.[91]

THE GREAT DEPRESSION

The Great Depression which began for the country at large with the stock market crash of 1929 had begun for the agricultural region several years earlier. Overproduction stimulated by the First World War and the loss of export markets as European agriculture recovered by the mid-1920s combined to depress the prices of corn and wheat and bring on severe depression in the corn belt. The direct impact on the university was to make it increasingly difficult to obtain the funds necessary to sustain the growth of the institution. Indirectly, hard times brought out into the open much of the latent hostility to the university which had always been present and which could now take advantage of the widespread demand for economies in all of the state agencies.

The peak legislative appropriation came in 1925, when the university received $3,013,501. Thereafter there was a regular decline in the level of public support. By 1931–32 the university budget had been cut by eighteen percent, a per-student decrease of thirty-three percent, and in the face of the fact that graduate student enrollments, the most expensive type, had increased from 239 in 1918 to 3,083 in 1932. An increasing share of the cost of university operations was transferred to the students: in 1914–15 the state had contributed seventy-five cents to each dollar of university expenditures; by 1930–31 it contributed only fifty-seven cents. The library acquisitions budget, always a sensitive indicator of the university's economic health, was cut from $81,209 in 1924–25 to $47,136 in 1927–28, resulting in 10,000 fewer volumes added in the latter years.[92] One consequence was the steady drain of senior faculty members who moved on to more secure and better-paying positions elsewhere. The historian Arthur Schlesinger, Sr., left for Harvard; Berthold Ullman, head of Latin, moved to the University of Chicago; Dr. Frederick Falls, head of obstetrics and gynecology, to Illinois; Dr. Ruth Weller, head of nutrition, to Kansas. Others left for private practice or government service. The president reported in 1930 that thirty-six faculty members had recently received offers from other institutions.[93]

As the full grip of the Depression fastened upon the university after 1930 increasingly drastic measures became necessary. Faculty salaries were cut by five percent for 1932–33, and some 300 faculty positions were eliminated in the three public institutions. The board announced that in the 1933–34 budget salaries would again be reduced fifteen to thirty percent on a sliding scale and that dormitory rates would be reduced by twenty-five percent with restricted service.[94] In the national wave of bank failures in January 1932 all of the Iowa City banks closed their doors. The university account of some $112,000 in the First National Bank was fortunately covered by depository insurance, and no money was lost. University funds were transferred to the Iowa National Bank of Des Moines, and staff members continued to receive regular salary payments. At a time when many citizens had little or no income public employees, however reduced their salaries, were objects of envy and some resentment.

The prevailing public fear and unrest perhaps account for the attention given to the hysterical scandal-mongering journalism of Verne Marshall, editor of the *Cedar Rapids Gazette-Republican*, who in December 1930 launched a bitter attack on Jessup, his principal administrative officers, and the Board of Education. In a series of newspaper articles Marshall accused university officials of a number of offenses, some of them serious, others trivial. The major charge concerned the manner in which the Rockefeller grant for the construction of the medical buildings had been managed. The foundation had agreed to transfer the funds in advance of construction charges in order that the university might have the benefit of interest income for the support of medical research prior to receipt of construction charges. As of March 1929 the fund had earned $159,017.40.[95] The treasurer of the university, W. J. McChesney, who was also president of the First National Bank of Iowa City, had invested the grant in federal securities, keeping a small portion in the university's account at the bank with which to pay current charges. McChesney had served as university treasurer for many years without salary. By agreement with the board the bank paid no interest on the local Rockefeller account in recognition of the fact that McChesney received no commission for handling the grant.[96] It was these arrangements that Marshall found improper and possibly criminal. He also charged university officials with using university (i.e., public) property for private purposes. This allegation concerned small quantities of construction materials and apparently emanated from disgruntled local laborers. Other charges alleged the use of university employees on private projects and favoritism in the award of contracts. W. R. Boyd, a full-time employee of the board, was found to be holding another job, as president of a savings and loan association, simultaneously. Finally, Jessup was held to be responsible for the scandal which had recently rocked the athletic department and brought disgrace upon the university.[97]

Governor Dan Turner requested the legislature to appoint a joint investigating committee which met for six weeks in the spring of 1931, heard 75 witnesses, examined some 400 documents, and compiled a 6,000-page transcript of testimony. A majority of the committee was unfriendly to the university and would not have been unhappy to have found grounds for the condemnation of its officers. But it found no such grounds and had to content itself with complaints of lax administration. It recommended, appropriately enough, that the university treasurer be a full-time officer unconnected with any banking institution. It also found occasion to go beyond the investigation of charges to propose reforms that revealed something of its animus. It objected to legislative lobbying on behalf of public institutions. It complained of too much power exercised by the Finance Committee of the board. And it complained of the restraints upon its own investigative procedures, particularly the necessity of holding open hearings and admitting legal counsel. Had the committee been free to proceed in secret the university might well have been dealt with severely. One member of the majority, Senator H. B. Carroll, complained that the Board of Education was so loosely constituted that three individuals actually ran the university: its president, the president of the board, and the chairman of the Finance Committee. He proposed that the part-time unsalaried board be replaced by a small full-time salaried board of three or five members. What Carroll really objected to was not the inadequacy of the board, but its independence when its key positions were occupied by men of determination and ability, such as Jessup, Baker, and Boyd, who put the welfare of the educational institutions above political considerations.[98]

Behind the majority of the investigating committee stood Governor Turner, a Republican elected in 1930 who was struggling desperately to hold the office for his party in the face of the impending Democratic revolution born of the Depression. His principal objectives were to achieve economies in governmental operations and to reduce taxes. He resented the independence of the Board of Education, which he believed to be insensitive to the political necessities of the moment. In order to bring it under his control he broke with the well-established practice of reappointing board members whose terms had expired and replaced three long-time members with his own men.[99] One of the new members, Harry M. Neas, told Jessup candidly, "I want to do everything I can to help the governor." One way of helping was to consult the presidents of Iowa's private colleges about tuition, eliciting the not surprising response that university tuition was too low. Neas continued to be a thorn in Jessup's flesh, urging Iowa coal dealers who resented competitive bidding with Illinois dealers to bring their complaints to him. He opposed the practice of paying travel expenses of faculty members presenting papers at professional meetings and intervened in such routine matters as dormitory food service. When Jessup proposed to apply to the NIRA for funds with which to build the art museum and theater Neas attempted to persuade the board to transfer the fine arts and engineering programs to the State College.[100] Fortunately, a majority of the board was unmoved by these proposals.

In the midst of these difficulties the good name of the university was sullied by the misdeeds of its treasurer. W. J. McChesney had served the university for many years and had enjoyed the full confidence of the board.[101] Early in January 1932, prior to the failure of the First National Bank, the university auditor, W. H. Cobb, discovered discrepancies in McChesney's accounts, for which restitution was then made. Pleading illness, McChesney deputized Cobb to act as interim treasurer and left town. Subsequently it was discovered that the treasurer had embezzled funds from several accounts, and a warrant for his arrest was issued on March 31, 1932, by which time he had gone to Florida and taken his own life.[102]

These unhappy events added fuel to the fire of Turner's animosity toward the university, which, together with the board, he accused of incompetence, waste, and dishonesty. He had ordered an audit of university accounts by auditors of his own choosing, who made a hasty check and claimed to find numerous errors. None of these was confirmed by the board's independent auditors, save for the university's failure to collect payment on certain delinquent mortgages.[103] A legislative committee on the reduction of governmental expenditures also joined in the attack on the board, repeating the perennial charges that it had failed to control duplicating programs or the ambitions of the presidents. It had been uncooperative in the effort to reduce expenditures and continued to pay high faculty salaries. The committee's proposal to replace the board with a small full-time board was obviously intended to destroy its political independence.[104]

Beset by problems internal and external it was not surprising that Jessup should have welcomed the offer of the presidency of the Carnegie Foundation for the Advancement of Teaching. There he would be spared the abuse of politicians and editors and would enjoy the opportunity to dispense rather than to beg for money.

Seashore's University

When the Capen Commission visited the university in 1915 it noted the absence of any guiding policy for institutional development. This it attributed in part to the frequent changes in the presidency and in part to the lack of active faculty participation in the formulation and execution of institutional policy. The visitors found a university composed of relatively autonomous departments and colleges each going its own way with little regard for the others or for the institution as a whole. In the absence of strong and positive administrative leadership certain aggressive individuals had seized advantage of the situation to create privileged positions for their programs. The commission advised that there should be more faculty responsibility and less departmental autonomy.[1]

In some respects Jessup was able to provide the forceful leadership the situation required. He won the confidence of the board and legislature and during the immediate postwar years secured the support necessary to assure the growth of programs and facilities. But in a more fundamental educational sense he failed to meet the challenge posed by the commission. Although he was effective as an administrator he was not an educational thinker and therefore not a force in shaping institutional policy. His basic objective—to maximize growth by offering the range of programs demanded by the public—was in effect to surrender the shaping of the institution to those who knew what they wanted and were prepared to fight for it. Jessup reigned, but he did not rule. In the absence of intellectual leadership the university entered the second stage of its institutional development, the stage of creative anarchy whose seeds the Capen Commission had already detected. The institutional structure of colleges, schools, and departments was now sufficiently firm, and the practice of delegated authority so generally recognized and accepted, that it was possible for a new generation of able and aggressive faculty members working within its shelter to stake out claims to the exploitation of promising new subjects for teaching and research. The result of their activities was to give the university a distinctive academic profile. Previously the efforts of its leaders had been directed by the need to bring the university into conformity with the model established by the more prestigious institutions to the east. Now the new generation at Iowa was brash enough to strike out on its own and chart a path into unexplored territory.

Some years after he had left the university for Harvard Arthur Schlesinger, Sr., wrote to Walter Jessup that "never has it been more clearly demonstrated that the institution is the lengthened shadow of the man."[2] The man he had in mind was not the Iowa president, but the graduate dean, Carl Seashore. No other individual in the history of the university had an impact upon it comparable to that of Seashore. This was the more remarkable in that he did not occupy a position of strength in the administrative hierarchy. The historical circumstance in which graduate education in the United States emerged out of the liberal arts colleges resulted in graduate colleges without formal authority over the appointment, promotion, or salaries of the graduate faculty. At best, the graduate dean would be "consulted" on such matters. At Iowa, however, thanks to Seashore's unique combination of personal qualities, scholarly interests, and institutional opportunities, there was a burst of creative activity which shaped the course of university development for nearly half a century. Only after the Second World War did the forces of institutional inertia reassert themselves as the university resumed its normal patterns of activity.

Carl Emil Sjöstrand was born in Sweden in 1866 and at the age of three came to the United States with his family, settling on a farm in Boone County, northwest of Des Moines. The translation of the family name into its English form, Seashore, epitomized the determination of the family to assimilate itself to the dominant Anglo-American culture. Carl learned to read and write Swedish at home and studied no English until he went to the local school at the age of eight. His father, who was head of the local school board, insisted that nothing but English be spoken at school—so much for bilingual education. The four Seashore sons all went on to earn doctorates. The immigrant farm boy growing up on the rich Iowa prairie was dominated by a sense of rising expectations. "Sowing and reaping, feeding and breeding, branding and butchering, breaking horses and opening markets, planting trees and grafting them, knitting and candle dipping, music and handicrafts in family, social, educational and religious life—all calling for initiative, forethought, ingenuity, and economy. A great school."[3] Although he wrote of his childhood in idyllic terms he was at pains to represent it as a meticulous and comprehensive preparation for

Carl Seashore (right) with George Stoddard.
Courtesy of the University of Iowa Photographic Service.

a life of strenuous endeavor. The rural life was not something which he looked back upon with nostalgia, but an experience to be prized for its value as preparation for the creative struggle of life. It instilled the invaluable qualities of self-reliance, positive thinking, and pride of tangible accomplishment.

At Gustavus Adolphus, the Lutheran college in St. Peter, Minnesota, Seashore cultivated his love for music, singing in the choir and playing the organ. Music was to play a role of major importance in his life, furnishing the material for his scholarly interests, which in turn led to the development of research techniques applicable to a broad range of subjects. At Yale, where he went for graduate work in psychology, he encountered the emerging conflict between the older philosophical psychology represented by George Trumbull Ladd and the newer experimental psychology represented by Edward W. Scripture. Seashore threw in his lot with the experimentalists, but, unlike Scripture, was careful to maintain amicable relations with the philosophers. He later remarked that he had come into psychology "on the ground floor," in the 1890s, visiting the pioneer laboratories in Berlin, Leipzig, and Göttingen, and meeting personally all of the leaders of the new scientific discipline. When he came to the university in 1897 as assistant professor of philosophy and psychology he found a rift comparable to that at Yale between his predecessor, the experimentalist J. Allen Gilbert, and the head of the department, G. T. W. Patrick. He was determined to work harmoniously with the older man, however, and always spoke appreciatively of the assistance and encouragement he had received. Patrick, who was neurasthenic, was happy to turn over management of the department to his energetic younger colleague, who became its head in 1905.[4]

Although Patrick's principal interest was in philosophy he had been trained in psychology as well and had also visited the European laboratories. The Iowa laboratory which he opened in 1890 was one of the first in the United States. It was equipped with such instruments as tuning forks, rotating disks for mixing colors, acoustical devices for testing hearing, instruments for measuring reaction times, and exhibits of the brain and nervous system. But the course he offered in experimental psychology was demonstrative rather than a laboratory course. His psychological interests were always colored by his ethical and social concerns. Thus while the next generation of educational psychologists would make meticulous studies of reading skills, Patrick was content to declare that children read too much and let it go at that. His major contribution was as a philosopher. His *Introduction to Philosophy*, which was published in 1924, was said to have been the most widely used textbook of its time in that field. Its principal theme was the idea of the evolutionary emergence of both material forms and spiritual values. This was the dominant idea among Iowa's intellectuals down to the mid-twentieth century. Patrick skillfully combined an optimistic and purposive view of the universe with Darwinian natural selection, freedom of the will, and a pragmatic theory of knowledge and truth. Held in a generalized, nondogmatic form the idea of emergence permitted scholars to do their work without coming into conflict with the conventional religious piety of the Iowa public. It allowed professors to retain their connections with the churches to which they belonged, while permitting university spokesmen to gloss over the increasing secularization of the institution.

Seashore's psychology was much more narrowly focused on topics amenable to experimental investigation. His laboratory contained instruments he had designed himself for the measurement of sound: audiometer, tonoscope, spark chronoscope, tone generators, and phono-photographic cameras.[5] Central to his work was the concept of individual differences. The European pioneers had worked with a generalized theory of mind, whereas the Americans were concerned with the differences between individual minds. Seashore declared that the outstanding contribution of modern psychology was "the discovery of the individual." His instruments were used to measure individual differences. These were expressed most importantly as differences of capacity. He spoke of "the law of distribution of capacity for academic work," a law which functioned automatically to punish those who defied it. He was contemptuous of those educators who cherished the uniqueness of each individual and thus attempted to circumvent the competitive dimension.[6]

A pivotal event in Seashore's career as an educational administrator occurred in 1909, in the first year of his deanship, when he visited H. H. Goddard's famous school for "feeble-minded" children at Vineland, New Jersey. There he found some 465 children with various degrees of retardation who had been unmanageable burdens to their families and communities. Goddard, however, had achieved a transformation which Seashore declared to be "a masterpiece of basic and enduring significance in applied psychology." Goddard had first determined whatever capacity each child possessed. The various tasks necessary for the maintenance of the institution were carefully analyzed for the degree of complexity involved. Individuals then were assigned to the jobs calculated to engage them to the full extent of their abilities. The result was a community of functioning and

happy individuals. Seashore was enormously impressed with this achievement, to which he referred repeatedly for the remainder of his life. He
formulated what might be called the Vineland Principle: "Keep each individual busy at his highest normal level of successful achievement that
he may be happy, useful, and good." Returning to the university, he informed the liberal arts faculty that the principle was relevant not only to
children but also to the average college sophomore and to the learned full
professor.[7]

As an educational policy the Vineland Principle required the careful determination of the academic capacities of each student, as well as an educational program sufficiently flexible to provide precisely the challenge necessary to elicit the maximum effort from each. During the First World
War Seashore had been involved in the development of the famous—or
infamous—Army Alpha intelligence tests. In the summer of 1923, probably on the dean's suggestion, Jessup without consulting the faculty ordered
that such a test be administered to incoming freshmen. Students and faculty were not yet hardened to such ordeals, and the experience shocked
many students and outraged the faculty. Seashore reported that he was
threatened with burning at the stake! At the end of the following semester,
however, he claimed that there had been found to be a striking correlation
between the test scores of the top and bottom ten percent and performance in course work. The faculty, he claimed, was persuaded of the diag-
nostic value of the tests, which were thereafter administered "judiciously,
sympathetically, and confidentially."

George Stoddard, who at the time was a research assistant in psychology and much closer than his mentor to the administration of the tests,
reported very different results. He found that correlations of intelligence
test scores with reading comprehension scores were too low to have
predictive value. In any event, in view of the hostility to the practice
among parents and public the dean found it expedient to substitute for a
projected radio talk on "Who Should Go to College?" the less controversial "Dreams." Out of his proposal that high schools institute such tests
emerged Everet Lindquist's academic "brain derby," the statewide competition to measure achievement in high school subjects. Measurement of
achievement in a particular subject was, of course, not the same thing as a
test purporting to measure an abstraction called intelligence. To identify
and measure an all-purpose capacity presumably possessed in varying degrees seemed more threatening than to measure the student's success in,
say, mathematics.[8]

THE GRADUATE COLLEGE

President Jessup noted a tendency in American education for curricular elements to filter down from higher to lower grades with the passage of time. Modern elementary schools had taken over most of the curriculum of the older New England grammar schools. The modern high school had taken over much of the curriculum of the nineteenth-century liberal arts college. In his own day he estimated that high school and college curricula overlapped by as much as twenty to thirty percent. The anticipated growth of junior colleges could be expected to increase the overlap. At the same time the techniques of the graduate school had filtered down to the undergraduate college and even to the lower schools with their "projects" and "problems" approach to learning. In his complacence Jessup failed to note that, in filtering down, the subject matter was often diluted and trivialized, while the student was not laying the foundation skills for more advanced work. But he did see the need for more rigorous standards of graduate work, and he invariably supported Seashore in his efforts to strengthen the bond between the graduate program and the scholarly work of the faculty.[9]

The "university principle"—teaching, research, and service—the formula which specified the duties and expectations of the university professor, was never embraced with enthusiasm by the entire faculty. It always remained a goal to be sought with varying degrees of enthusiasm by certain administrators and faculty members and achieved by those programs and departments where rigorous criteria of appointment and promotion were implemented. The first element, teaching, was the least controversial. Given its origins in liberal arts colleges no one questioned the responsibility of the American university to welcome students and provide them with the means of formal instruction. Although the seminar and individual research supervision became the distinctive forms of instruction in the Graduate School, most graduate faculty members continued to function as members of the liberal arts faculty and to offer courses for undergraduates. The heavy teaching loads during the early years of the university were mute testimony to the fact that teaching might justifiably occupy the full time of the faculty. It was only in more recent years that the modern emphasis on research began to encroach on the time allotted to teaching, resulting in reduced teaching loads, and occasionally in complaints from students that they were being neglected by faculty members preoccupied with their research. Nevertheless, although research made its demands, teaching still retained its primacy to the extent that faculty members were expected to hold their classes whatever their scholarly preoccupations. Eventually the practice of formal student evaluation of teaching effectiveness was introduced as a means of keeping teachers on their toes.

The growing recognition of the proper role of research provided one practical measure of the spread of the university principle. When President Schaeffer insisted that the faculty member should be a specialist he was paving the way for the research scholar. The time had passed when, for instance, it was deemed appropriate for Dr. James Grant Gilchrist, professor of homeopathic medicine, to offer a course in the English department on literary monuments. Later, when President MacLean identified the university as one of the major state universities of the Midwest, he knew that such a position implied a scholarly faculty whose research activity would compare favorably with that of neighboring institutions.

Under Seashore's guidance research became the distinctive feature of the Graduate College program. Only scholars actively engaged in research were to supervise the work of graduate students, many of whom would be employed as teaching assistants. Seashore insisted that graduate study properly conceived meant the full fusion of teaching and research as student and professor focused their attention on the common problems of laboratory and seminar. There teaching ceased to be instruction and became joint exploration and discovery. When the physicist George W. Stewart, acting dean of the Graduate College during Seashore's absences and one of the principal scholars of the faculty, enumerated the reasons why the faculty should be engaged in research he justified it largely in terms of its relationship to teaching. Active involvement in research, he noted, assured the presentation to students of the most advanced knowledge. It also cultivated in their minds the idea of constructive or creative work. Research made the professors students themselves, having their own difficulties, and consequently curbing their arrogance and increasing their sympathy for students. Only as an apparent afterthought did Stewart add that research training provided the experts needed for various public and private purposes.[10]

In stressing the intimate relationship of teaching and creative work—the term he preferred to research—Stewart was undoubtedly aware of the passive resistance of certain faculty members to engaging in research. One of these was the head of Romance languages, Stephen Bush. In 1920 a committee of which Bush was a member was charged with recommending measures to improve the quality of graduate work. It proposed the erection of a library building, a sabbatical leave policy, and reduced teaching loads for researchers. Doubtless reflecting Bush's views, it also proposed that a distinction be made between a graduate faculty engaged in research and an undergraduate teaching faculty. Both faculties would enjoy the same pay scale and the same expectations of promotion. Nothing came of this proposal.[11] Stewart's attempt to fuse creative work with learning obviously left Bush unimpressed. To the humanist, forming the minds of students was more important than training them in methods of research. To assume as he did, however, that a teaching faculty whose merits could not be known beyond the walls of the classroom could for long hold its own against a research faculty known across the land for the published results of its labors was wholly unrealistic. The teaching faculty would inevitably become second-class citizens. If the university were to hold a place among the leading state universities it had no choice but to conform to the scholarly expectations of those institutions. Those among the faculty who believed that effective teaching was sufficient to justify continuing tenure had reason to fear Seashore, who urged that the able and productive scholars should be rapidly promoted, while unproductive teachers should be weeded out.[12]

"Service" was the most elusive of the three components of the university principle. In the professional colleges it meant service to the public. Professors of medicine and dentistry combined their teaching with the care of patients in hospital wards and dental clinics; professors of law might provide legal services or expert advice to public agencies. Elsewhere service meant "academic good citizenship"—service on university committees and peer-review panels, journal editorships, off-campus speaking engagements, or even participation in community activities. Faculty members who felt threatened by the expectation of research sometimes claimed that service was a legitimate substitute for research.

Although never fully achieved, Seashore's conception of the university principle represented an intimate union of the three elements of teaching, research, and service. Teaching at its best elicited from students the full development of their critical and creative powers. These powers appropriately focused upon the investigation of outstanding problems of a practical nature whose solution would be of benefit to society. As early as 1876, when he opened the doors of the new Johns Hopkins University, Daniel Coit Gilman had emphasized the practical character of the university as a service institution. The university, he said, "means a wish for less misery among the poor, less ignorance in the schools, less bigotry in the Temple, less suffering in the hospital, less fraud in business, less folly in politics; and among other things it means . . . more security in property, more health in cities, more virtue in the country, more wisdom in legislation, more intelligence, more happiness, more religion."[13] Seashore promised a similar cornucopia of good things, all flowing from the practical application of research to problems in a variety of fields. His university was to be no ivory tower but a service station dedicated among other things to child welfare, stutterers, the mentally ill, and the refinement of musical and artistic skills.

The Graduate College as Seashore conceived it was to be the institutional center and sponsor of research. He did not pursue MacLean's notion of graduate study beginning in the upperclass years of the liberal arts program, being content to say that graduate work begins where undergraduate work leaves off, that is, with the attainment of the bachelor's degree. The Graduate College was the capstone of the other colleges, both liberal and professional. Its functions were to train advanced students at the postgraduate level and to foster research and creative work. The graduate faculty consisted of all members of the university faculty above the rank of assistant professor who participated in graduate-level instruction. A Graduate Council originally appointed by the president and later elected by the faculty exercised a broad range of functions, including approval of dissertation topics, awarding of degrees, and review of the budget. Seashore found, however, that election did not always produce council members whom he considered to be valuable; with characteristic forcefulness he introduced a nominating committee over which he presided in order to be certain that only approved candidates would be offered for election. With the passage of time the council's original functions were reduced to administrative routines handled by the dean's office, and the council was left with a general advisory role.[14]

Although by temperament a man inclined to seize and exercise power, Seashore gracefully accepted the weak position of the graduate dean in the administrative hierarchy, professing to be content with whatever influence he could exert through persuasion and professional eminence. He extolled the virtues of what he called "the Vertical Plan," the arrangement whereby departments, schools, and colleges provided both undergraduate and graduate instruction. Matters of appointment, promotion, and budget were determined within these respective units after "informal" consultation with the graduate dean. This was, of course, no "plan" at all; it was merely the traditional way of doing things with a gesture of good will to the newcomer. The dean insisted that where good will and cooperation did not exist the president should remove one dean or the other, but there is no evidence that Jessup or his successor, Eugene Gilmore, entertained any such expectation.[15] The plan assured the autonomy of each instructional unit, which Seashore professed to approve, although it resulted in the wide diversity of policies and standards that the Capen Commission deplored. It seems probable that the dean was content with the existing situation because it afforded him the latitude to approach each program with whatever plans for instruction and research he had in mind for it. Beyond the existing departments and colleges he envisioned an elaborate structure of research institutes in such diverse areas as public affairs, business, education, dramatics, music, public health, criminology, and orthopedics. The Graduate College would coordinate the activities and administer the funds to operate these agencies, thus assuring the proper concentration of effort on fields where the most useful accomplishments could be expected.[16]

Such formal powers as the dean possessed related to the programs of graduate students, over which he exercised a measure of control difficult for a later generation of students or faculty to comprehend. The Graduate College was only eight years old in 1908 when Seashore became dean, enrolling 173 students in the fall and spring semesters and 111 in the summer session. He interviewed all applicants for admission, accepting only those found to be qualified. He also reviewed and passed upon all proposed thesis and dissertation topics, not hesitating to reject those felt to be inappropriate. Faculty members sometimes complained that he ruled upon matters of which he knew little. (Craig Baird, the speech professor, taunted the dean for confusing George Fox, the seventeenth-century Quaker, with Charles James Fox, the eighteenth-century politician.) Nor did he restrict his oversight narrowly to academic subjects. He declared that the roles of intelligence and formal preparation as factors making for academic success were grossly overestimated. Educators were only beginning to recognize the large part played by personality, health, moral character, and supply and demand in determining the chances of success in a given field. The dean did not hesitate to evaluate such elusive criteria in his counseling of students. "Personnel work of an intimate, frank, and aggressive character has come to be the main function of the office of the dean."[17]

Never a man to conceal his opinions, Seashore expressed reservations about the graduate training of women which may well have been shared if not so openly stated by other men of his academic generation. If he did not hold the conventional view of the time that women's place was in the home he at least believed that homemaking was "a career in itself, the most universal, the most laudable, and the most desirable career for a normal woman."[18] It did not occur to him that any appreciable number of women could manage to combine homemaking with academic careers. Near the end of his life he reported that in the beginning he had awarded graduate stipends to qualified students without regard to sex. A survey made in 1920, however, showed that some forty of the male graduate students of the previous fifteen years had achieved marked distinction in their respective academic fields, whereas among the women only one had even advanced to the rank of assistant professor. There was a strong implication that thereafter stipends for women were awarded only after searching scrutiny. The dean recognized three classes of women in the Graduate College. First, those preparing for certain occupations such as secondary school teaching for which one year of graduate study was necessary. Second, those who anticipated marriage to men in learned occupations and who wished to prepare themselves intellectually to be fitting spouses— some careful distinctions would have to be made here since the dean had no use for mere husband hunters. The most troublesome category consisted of career-minded women who persisted in seeking scholarly careers in spite of all the handicaps. These women were most in need of counseling and guidance since they were prone to ill-health from overwork and lack of exercise. The dean recognized the value of the independence assured by a career, but at the same time he advised that the choice of subject be made with a view to its value should the woman subsequently marry.[19] It was during his long tenure as dean that women made steady advances in most academic fields, a circumstance which he never recognized. An institution which had prided itself on having from the beginning opened its doors to women continued to treat them as second-class academic citizens.

THE INTERDISCIPLINARY THRUST

Academic psychology in the United States had originally been a branch of philosophy. In 1906, the year following Seashore's appointment as head of the department of philosophy, its name was changed to "department of philosophy and psychology," reflecting the growing importance of the latter. Under Seashore's forceful leadership work in the new field quickly came to overshadow that of its parent. By 1921 nine full-time faculty members were offering twenty-one courses in psychology, while only two were offering nine philosophy courses.[20] Intellectually the two subjects were drifting apart as the psychologists committed themselves to laboratory research, while the philosophers became impatient with what they considered to be narrow technical work. With Patrick's semiretirement and frequent leaves of absence the senior position in philosophy was occupied by Edwin D. Starbuck, who became increasingly isolated.

It was Starbuck's misfortune to work in the psychology of religion without employing methods which Seashore considered sufficiently rigorous. The dean was a strict experimentalist who resolved his research problems into component elements which could be studied with laboratory techniques, a method which he called fractionation. Starbuck, on the other hand, believed that the nature of the problem determined the method of investigation and that such a subjective phenomenon as religious experience could hardly be investigated with laboratory methods. The two men came into open conflict over the supervision of graduate students. As dean and head of the department Seashore did not hesitate to use his authority to discourage students from working with Starbuck, advising several of them to switch to his brand of psychology. Following a confrontation in 1923 Seashore agreed not to criticize Starbuck to his students, a pledge which the latter maintained was not kept. The dean continued to offer assistantships and promises of employment as "certified psychologists" to students who would come over to his brand of psychology, while warning Starbuck not to be "unreasonably obstinate in defending an unjust cause." He reaffirmed his right to approve or disapprove the choice of dissertation topics while blandly assuring Starbuck that criticism of student choices was no reflection on their professor. Poor Starbuck could only take his grievances to President Jessup, with the recommendation that philosophy and psychology be reorganized as separate departments. Seashore resisted separation, but Jessup was persuaded of its necessity; in 1927 Starbuck was named head of the department of philosophy, while Seashore continued as head of psychology.[21]

The Iowa psychological laboratory—located successively in the Old Capitol, in a sound- and shock-proof room in Schaeffer Hall, and finally, after removal of the hospital to the west side, in East Hall (now Seashore Hall)—was modeled on those at Yale and Leipzig. Here Seashore assembled the equipment, much of it of his own design, used to translate musical sounds into visual and measurable images. Beginning in 1899 he and his students published a continuing flow of books, papers, and monographs in which the principles of acoustics were applied to a variety of practical problems in fields ranging from musical aptitude and speech to otology and art education. In all of this work there was a common emphasis upon the use of scientific methods to resolve problems into elements which could be attacked with precision. Seashore emphasized the psychological aspects of work in child welfare, psychiatry, education, physiology, zoology, physical education, music, art, speech pathology, physics, anatomy, journalism, and philosophy. The range of his professional interests coincided nicely with the broad scope of his academic responsibilities as graduate dean. Together, they enabled him to move with remarkable forcefulness into fields of learning seemingly far removed from his own. He constantly emphasized the fruitful results of collaboration between the academic specialists in a given subject and the psychologists who brought their distinctive techniques to the solution of its problems.[22]

These activities supported the dean's persistent complaint about the isolation and sterility of departmentalized knowledge in the modern university. The disciplines which had constituted the core of the nineteenth-century liberal arts colleges emerged as organized departments in the new university. Newer subjects also assumed departmental status as the university grew. The curricular requirements of major and minor specialization generated student specialists who went on to graduate work and eventually took their places as teachers and scholars in their respective disciplines. Departmental organization came to enjoy some measure of autonomy as administrators consulted the members on such matters as appointment, promotion, salaries, and curricular offerings. As the commitment to scholarly research became more firmly fixed the members of a department formed ever closer relationships with their disciplinary colleagues in other institutions, sustaining their specialized organizations and journals, reviewing one another's work, and forming schools of thought in what often approached the dimensions of a vast collaborative enterprise. Thus university department and academic discipline became closely identified with each other; for many faculty members the department was the most tangible reality of university life. To resist this trend was to set one's face against one of the strongest currents in the modern university.

Some measure of dissatisfaction with the situation was expressed from time to time in proposals to create schools or divisions embracing departments with common features. The advantage to be gained by such combinations was not always clearly specified. It was sometimes rumored that the object was nothing more important than to salve someone's ego, or to impose another administrative layer between an abrasive subordinate and a harassed superior. Seashore, however, was much more explicit about the reasons for his sustained attack upon departmentalism. He believed that the intellectual life of many areas of the university was moribund because the life-giving light of science was being shut out by departmental barriers. He made it his mission to revivify these areas by inserting his own brand of applied psychology.[23]

If he had some alternative plan of university organization in mind he never indicated what it was. Critical though he was of departmentalism and the consequent disciplinary sterility he did not propose that departments be replaced by some more comprehensive form of organization. He was content to use applied psychology as an entering wedge to break down departmental barriers by introducing a research technique which would revivify the discipline. His procedure was to train one or more students in the laboratory methods appropriate to the subject in question then persuade the department to require or advise its students to take work with the psychological specialist in addition to the regular departmental curriculum. In this way a fresh understanding of the discipline would result. An enumeration of research projects underway in the psychological laboratory in 1929–30, when the plan was in high gear, illustrated the dean's ambitions: seven studies in the psychology of music, dealing with vibrato, rhythm, tempo, and the musical development of children; four studies in the psychology of emotion, dealing with fatigue, and the effects of motion pictures on children; six projects in speech, including reading problems, speech rhythms, vision problems, and muscular contractions; four studies in the psychology of art, dealing with composition, aesthetics, and color discriminations; five studies in social psychology, including personality traits, public opinion, superstition, and racial attitudes; and five projects in child psychology, including infant reactions, motivation, and problem solving.[24] Students and faculty members involved in research of this kind were prepared to hold full or joint appointments in relevant departments.

While he did not envision significant reorganization Seashore did contemplate the addition of a new group of extradepartmental research institutes. As previously noted, there would be an Iowa Life Institute and Iowa institutes for educational research, dramatic art, the science of music, orthopedic research, public health, social research, and criminology, as well as bureaus of legislative and business research. Taking a long view into the future he foresaw the day when a much larger share of the university budget would be allocated to research, with the Graduate College acting as the central administrator for the allocation of research funds.[25]

At the turn of the century, when there was a recognition that the advancement of the university depended upon a scholarly faculty, but when there were still relatively few scholars around, the president had to take the initiative in seeking them out. Faculty recruitment had been a major challenge for MacLean and Jessup. To the extent that they were successful, strong departments emerged which were staffed by experts in a position to do their own recruiting and thus perpetuate themselves. The president then ceased to be a recruiting officer. The departmental and disciplinary thrust was one of the strongest forces in the new university. It had scarcely begun to make itself felt when Seashore challenged it in the name of inter-disciplinary study, and it is clear that he failed to appreciate its strength and timeliness. One even suspects that he confused his own proprietary concern to pursue the applications of acoustics in the particular disciplines that interested him with a more grandiose conception of the virtues of in-terdisciplinary study. In any event he confused the fruitful results of par-ticular combinations of expertise in attacking specified problems with a general declaration of the sterility of disciplinary specialization. It was not the time to challenge departmentalism, and it was inevitable that, although he might momentarily bend the structure, he could not break it.

CREATIVE WORK

The principle of research as fostered by the modern university had originated in the physical and biological sciences. From this source it had spread to the social sciences and humanities, dictating the criteria and methods which gave legitimacy to academic work. Establishing facts, clas-sifying the data, tracing derivations, and analyzing forms of expression or behavior became acceptable modes of activity for the humanist or social scientist, resulting in the staffing of academic departments with scholars adept in the use of these methods. It was the genius of George W. Stewart to see that behind the ability of the scientist to accumulate and manipulate data lay a deeper factor, namely, the insight, hunch, or inspiration which prompted the investigator to see a problem in a new light, possibly result-ing in a fruitful approach or solution. To this factor Stewart attached the term "creativity." Research conceived as a creative act thus became the bridge which permitted the educator to pass over, so to speak, from scien-tific research to imaginative work in the arts and letters. In a university dominated intellectually and institutionally by the scientists as the Univer-sity of Iowa was in the early decades of this century it was crucial that the scientists should share in the initiative to accept creative work in the hu-manities in order to avoid what would otherwise have undoubtedly been a deeply divisive issue.

Creative work in the form of courses in verse and prose writing taught by George Cram Cook had been offered in the English department as early as 1896. Ten years later the affiliated School of Music, which com-bined elements of a conservatory with an academic department, provided instruction in vocal performance, piano, organ, and string instruments. Likewise, the department of fine arts offered courses in drawing and painting as well as conventional work in art history and appreciation. The existence on the campus of these opportunities for creative work undoubtedly made it easier for scholars and administrators to take the next step and recognize such work as a legitimate alternative to the research theses or dissertations hitherto required of graduate degree recipients.

One of those who was instrumental in persuading the faculty to accept creative work was the English professor Edwin Ford Piper. A student of Ansley's at Nebraska, in 1905 Piper had come to the university, where he introduced a seminar in creative writing. He was one of the midwestern regionalists in literature and painting. On the occasion of the celebration of the university's Diamond Jubilee, February 24 and 25, 1922, he wrote a masque, or dramatic performance, "The Land of the Aiouwas," dealing with the coming of Marquette and Joliet to Iowa, with music by Philip Greeley Clapp and direction by Edward C. Mabie, one of the rare occasions of collaboration between those two doughty antagonists.[26] In that same year, Piper and Stewart, then acting dean of the Graduate College, met with Jessup to sound him out on the recognition of creative work. Seashore was absent from the campus at that time, but there is no doubt that he was heartily in favor of the proposed innovation. The president was receptive, and on February 21 a faculty conference was convened at which Piper, Dean Chester Phillips of the College of Commerce, and Jessup spoke, followed by discussion. The faculty response must have been largely favorable, for the agenda of the Graduate Council meeting of October 24, 1922, contained the item: "The thesis requirement may be interpreted broadly so as to include artistic production, e.g., in literature, art, or music; the performance of a project, e.g., in education or sociology." As originally drafted the provision was intended to apply to both master's and doctoral degrees, but the provision for the latter degree was at some point stricken out.[27] The catalog announcements for 1922–23 stipulate that master's theses show "independent scholarship and creative ability." The first master of arts degrees based upon creative work in the arts were awarded in 1925 and 1926, when degree requirements were satisfied by two symphonic compositions in music and a painting in fine arts. The first degree in literature for a thesis in the form of poems was awarded in 1931. All of these pioneers were women.[28]

In view of the later publicity enjoyed by the Writers' Workshop it is worth noting that in spite of Piper's efforts the English department lagged behind art and music in taking up the new option. There was in fact substantial opposition to creative work within the department itself. John T. Frederick, another of the literary regionalists, complained to Jessup that the graduate program of the department was dominated by philologists who clung to the old Germanic conception of the research degree and who resisted the new frivolity. The coming of Norman Foerster in 1930 as professor of English and director of the new School of Letters proved to be the decisive factor in persuading the department to endorse the new option, which it did in 1931. The first creative doctoral dissertation in English, in the form of a group of essays, was accepted in 1935.[29] Foerster made a sharp distinction between the critical study of literature as the expression of the human experience and the study of literature as science, as in literary history and philology. He did not conceal his condescension toward the historians and philologists, and when they resisted his efforts on behalf of creative work he attacked them bitterly. In later years he extolled Seashore for his championing of creative work, but he failed to appreciate the dean's conception of creativity as an integral part of scientific method. It was Seashore's dream, however fatuous, that the introduction of scientific methods in the analysis and criticism of literary productions would enhance the creative process. But Foerster, when he drove his wedge between the science of literature and creative work, was unwittingly making certain that Seashore's dream would come to nothing.

CLINICAL PSYCHOLOGY

When Seashore came to the university in 1897 there was no practicing psychiatrist in the state, and no courses in psychiatry or clinical psychology in the Medical College. The state hospitals for the insane were merely places of detention. As a member of a committee appointed by MacLean to address the problem of mental illness Seashore attended the famous meeting at Clark University in 1909 where he met Freud, Jung, and other pioneers in psychoanalysis. There is no evidence, however, that he became tainted with Freudianism. He resolved to attack the problem of mental illness in Iowa at the beginning, so to speak, by establishing a psychological clinic for the treatment of mental disorders in children. After a pattern which was to become characteristic he selected a bright student, R. H. Sylvester, put him through the master's degree program in psychology, and then sent him to the University of Pennsylvania for the doctorate in its pioneer program in clinical psychology. In due time Sylvester returned to the university and in 1911 introduced a course on the mental defects of schoolchildren.[30] He also opened the university's first psychological clinic for children.

Since there was at that time no corresponding interest in the treatment of mental illness among the medical profession in Iowa it was necessary for Seashore to carry on an educational campaign to persuade the public of its importance. Eventually the board and legislature were induced to act, and the Psychopathic Hospital was opened in 1919 with Dr. Samuel Orton as director. A collaborative attack upon common problems by psychiatrists and clinical psychologists was deemed essential to Seashore's research program, and an outpatient psychological clinic was established in the new hospital. But the jurisdictional battle between medically trained psychiatrists and clinical psychologists put an end to the dean's hopes for fruitful collaboration. Tension between the two groups was aggravated by an unfortunate dispute between Seashore and Dr. Orton. The latter charged the dean with failing to acknowledge his authorship of material Seashore had incorporated in a journal article. Seashore had attributed the disputed material to his own student, Lee Travis. Whatever the merits of the complaint, the episode became one of the factors leading to Dr. Orton's resignation in 1927. Undeterred by these difficulties, Seashore persisted in his efforts to bring psychology and psychiatry together in fruitful collaboration. He projected an Iowa Institute of Mental Hygiene drawing its staff from child welfare, speech, and education as well as psychology and psychiatry. Unfortunately, the Depression of 1929 prevented the Julius Rosenwald Fund from providing the necessary funding, and the institute failed to materialize.[31]

MUSIC AND SPEECH

Seashore's publications on the psychology of music began in 1899, two years after he came to the university, with papers on pitch discrimination, rhythm, and time sense. Thereafter, for the remainder of his life, came a steady flow of papers and books on those aspects of music that could be measured and analyzed in the laboratory with scientific rigor. Studies showed that the ability to make pitch discriminations varied greatly among individuals and that it was a native gift which could not be changed by training. Sensory and motor capacity for the production of musical tones could also be tested. This work was not an end in itself, however, but a means to assist students in determining their musical aptitudes and to improve the quality of performance. Instruments to measure pitch and tone quality were of little value if they were not used by students and teachers to discover and cultivate musical aptitude. Seashore developed a test for "Measures of Musical Talents" which he promoted for use in the public schools. It caught the attention of George Eastman, the Kodak man, who was instrumental in introducing it in the public schools of Rochester, New York, and in the Eastman School of Music. In later years Seashore acknowledged that his instruments and tests had not been as widely used as he had hoped, but he remained optimistic that eventually their value would be properly appreciated.[32]

Given his zeal to overcome departmental barriers one might have expected that Seashore would have established an effective working relationship with the university's School of Music. In fact, however, the obvious lack of enthusiasm for his projects among the musicians must have been discouraging to him. In 1911–12 he introduced a course on the psychology of music in his own department, but the catalog gave no indication that the affiliated School of Music either required or recommended it. Five years later private instruction in "voice culture" was introduced, with the notation that students who wished to make tone tests or measurements of musical talent were free to use the psychological laboratory. After the study of music was made an integral part of the university and Philip Greeley Clapp came in 1919 to provide vigorous leadership no further reference to the psychology of music was made in the school's curriculum. Publicly Clapp supported Seashore's work, but privately he dismissed it as of little consequence. Trained musicians did not need laboratory equipment to tell whether or not they were playing in tune. Clapp was an able composer, pianist, and conductor who had come from Harvard where he had been a protégé of Dr. Karl Muck, conductor of the Boston Symphony Orchestra. Under his leadership the School of Music inaugurated a graduate program in 1924 and developed a symphony orchestra which *New York Times* music critic Olin Downes praised as the best student orchestra he had heard.[33] But Clapp was a difficult person—even his friends acknowledged him to be conceited and egotistical. He fought bitterly with Edward C. Mabie, making any collaboration between music and theater impossible. It was a major irony of Seashore's career as an educational reformer that his campaign to break down departmental barriers should have encountered the formidable resistance of the very people he had counted upon for support.

It was in the study of speech that Seashore's brand of applied psychology registered its principal impact. He found that the laws of acoustics used in the analysis of music applied equally well to speech sounds. The production and hearing of tones, whether musical or verbal, involved a common set of phenomena. Both were expressed wholly or in part by the voice, and both were intimately associated as media of communication and social intercourse. The reduction of speech sounds to visual graphic representations made possible the same kind of analysis and refinement that had been demonstrated for musical sounds. Norms of performance for intonation, control, rhythmic effectiveness, and tone quality could be established. Traditional aesthetic principles which had been largely intuitive could now be given a firm scientific foundation. Beginning about 1915 Seashore moved vigorously to reorganize the speech field in accordance with this objective.[34]

Speech, or rhetoric as it was then called, had originally been taught in the English department, where Harry Evarts Gordon had held the first appointment in that field, in 1900. Courses were offered in public speaking, debate, Expression in Voice and Action, and drama. Gordon was succeeded in 1912 by an assistant professor, Glenn Merry, and three years later a separate department of public speaking (later renamed speech) was created. Seashore persuaded Merry to take a Ph.D. in psychology, which he completed in 1921 with a dissertation on "Voice Inflection in Speech." Merry also served as assistant research director for Dr. Lee W. Dean, head of otolaryngology, studying X-rays of head cavities and the physiology of voice inflection.

Seashore's interest in the physiology and psychology of normal speech led to an investigation of speech defects, a field which had as yet received little attention. A cooperative appointment with the Child Welfare Research Station was made in 1920 to provide speech training for normal children together with correction of speech defects. This was only a stopgap arrangement. What was needed was a comprehensive speech clinic in which psychology, psychiatry, otology, and normal speech would cooperate, exemplifying Seashore's conception of a fruitful interdisciplinary attack upon a common problem. Since no properly trained person was available to direct such a clinic the dean was determined to train one. He selected a likely-looking undergraduate, Lee Travis, and laid strong hands upon him. Half a century later Travis recalled: "My original interest in this area was practically an order from the Dean. He had chosen me and would not be denied."[35] Travis received his B.A. from the Liberal Arts College in 1922. A year later he received the M.A. in clinical psychology and biology, and two years after that the Ph.D. in abnormal psychology. There was nothing like a push from the dean to propel a young man expeditiously through the graduate program. It was a prime example of "inbreeding," a practice which Seashore stoutly defended against those who condemned it as perpetuating local mediocrities. After all, when one was inaugurating something that had not been done before, what better method was there than to select promising students and see that they received the necessary training?[36] The clinic Travis founded fully justified Seashore's confidence in him. A succession of able speech pathologists brought national renown to the speech program.

In the meanwhile the dean exercised considerable influence in developing the program of the speech department along the desired interdisciplinary lines. In a series of conferences with Glenn Merry Seashore proposed that the required freshman course in public speaking identify students with speech defects and refer them to the clinic for corrective treatment. The departmental program should consist of two divisions: the art of speaking and the science of speaking. The former would consist of conventional courses in rhetoric, public address, and drama; the latter, of laboratory work in the fields relevant to the problems of speech. But when in 1923 Merry proposed a doctoral program in speech the dean emphatically rejected the idea, saying that speech was an "art," and as such was not to be allowed a doctoral program. Students desiring a doctorate in speech should take it in one of the cooperating scientific fields, just as Travis was doing. Merry, who felt that he was being bludgeoned, appealed in vain to Jessup and then promptly resigned.[37]

Merry's successor as head of the speech department, Edward C. Mabie, was a man of very different stripe. Outwardly he professed enthusiasm for Seashore's approach, but inwardly he was determined to run his own show and was prepared to bide his time. His principal interest was in the theater, and it must have galled him to hear Seashore boast that "the university has done notable pioneer work in reducing play writing to a laboratory procedure."[38] The procedure involved three steps. First, play writing, admittedly a creative act uncontained by rules. Second, laboratory analysis and criticism by specialists in the writing laboratory who subjected the play to the "well-developed psychology of item analysis" for the selection, distribution, weighing, and balancing of items and techniques. Experiments might be conducted to consider rejections and possible alternatives or refinements. Laboratory technicians would apply principles of acoustics, lighting, scenery design, and emotional appeal. "It is gratifying," wrote the dean, "to see how adequately the University Theater laboratory can simulate and parallel the best scientific laboratories in dealing with hypotheses, invention, and interpretation." Third, production under the student's direction served as the ultimate test of fitness in costuming, lighting, acoustics, and music. "In the theater as a writing laboratory," the dean triumphantly concluded, "we have one of the most clear cut and rigorous demonstrations of the possibility and necessity of a scientific approach to an art." [39] Since most of these activities would go on in any well-run student theater one may assume that Mabie put up with the jargon and went about his business.

Although he continued to support Seashore's interdisciplinary objectives Mabie was determined to develop the speech program as an independent departmental unit. Craig Baird was brought in to teach public address in historical and cultural terms. Graduate students continued to take the prescribed courses in acoustics, anatomy of the ear and vocal organs, statistics, phonetics, and experimental psychology, but unless their dissertations were in the field of speech pathology there is no evidence that their research involved the interdisciplinary work Seashore had prescribed, thus defeating the purpose of his plan. The prohibition upon the doctoral program in the "art" of speech was lifted prior to 1930, when the department awarded its first two doctorates, both in the field of public address under Baird's supervision. The first dissertation in the form of an original play was accepted in 1936. [40] With the passage of time the tension within the department between the "artists" and "scientists" of speech reached the point where a separation became necessary, and in 1956 an independent department of speech pathology was created. The date may signify the point where Seashore's assault upon the autonomy of departmentalized disciplines finally failed, the departments resuming their traditional control over the work of their graduate students.

In a closely related field Seashore was instrumental in inaugurating work in audiology. He devised an instrument for the testing of hearing capable of distinguishing forty steps or decibels on a logarithmic scale of intensity. A program for testing the hearing of schoolchildren aroused some opposition from the medical profession, but in the long run the administration of such tests came to be accepted as a suitable function for school psychologists. [41]

THE CHILD WELFARE RESEARCH STATION

The "discovery" of childhood as a distinct portion of the life cycle with its own rights and claims to autonomy was a product of the nineteenth-century romantic movement. Evolutionary science with its emphasis upon growth and development endowed childhood with a new importance as the seed ground from which the mature adult would emerge. During the later years of the nineteenth century educators assisted by the

newly developing science of psychology began to reshape their conceptions of primary education in terms of the distinctive needs of childhood.
As John Dewey, the prophet of the new movement, put it, if the needs of
the child are properly served, all other good things will follow in due sea-
son. G. Stanley Hall, one of the pioneer American psychologists, called for
a scientific pedagogy based on knowledge of that portion of child behavior
which was the result of learning as distinct from the portion determined
by "original nature." [42]

Cora Bussey Hillis may not have known specifically of these intellectual
currents, but she was thoroughly imbued with the modern solicitude for
the welfare of children. A prominent Des Moines woman active in community affairs, Hillis had herself known the anguish occasioned by the
death of two of her children, and she dedicated herself to the promotion of
a program designed to work for child welfare. "Give the normal child,"
she wrote, "the same scientific study by research methods that we give to
crops and cattle. Study his inheritance, racially, physically, temperamentally, and socially; his prenatal development, infancy, childhood, adoles-
cence, and youth. Learn how the normal child develops in body, mind, and
spirit and gradually evolve a science of child rearing by accumulative, comparative data and by intensive study of selected groups carried on through
the years under natural conditions and in a controlled environment." [43]
The breathless quality of her prose was equaled by the stubborn determination with which she pursued her goal. She took her plan to the nearby
Iowa State College in 1901 and again in 1904, only to be informed by
presidents Beardshear and Storms that such a program did not fall within
the scope of the institution's mission.

She brought her project in 1909 to President MacLean and in a series of
impassioned letters depicted the tragic waste of human lives resulting
from the ignorance and neglect of child nurture. She recognized that it
was a dual problem of training men and women for enlightened parent-
hood as well as realizing the full potential of the children. "We equip expensive laboratories to study the angle-worm etc., why not the little child,
made in the image of God, the citizen of tomorrow, the hope of the
race." [44] She shrewdly appealed to MacLean's zeal to advance the status of
the university by predicting the prestige that would accrue to the pioneer
in this field. MacLean responded enthusiastically to these overtures, assuring her that the proposal would be pursued vigorously. He envisioned a
"laboratory for the scientific care and study of childhood" to be organized
under the School of Education and the Extension Division. She was urged
to use her political influence to secure a special appropriation from the

legislature. A faculty committee with Seashore as chairman was appointed to study the establishment of the laboratory.[45]

Opposition to the plan, surprisingly enough, came from Seashore himself. He was already interested in the establishment of the psychological clinic for the treatment of childhood problems, and he urged Hillis to reconsider her plan and begin first with the study of abnormal children. But she stubbornly refused to alter her program, insisting that the world first needed to know the nature of normal child development. She pointed out that there were already hospitals and special schools for handicapped children, whereas "the great majority of normal children are misdirected, badly cared for, and only half developed." Owing to Seashore's opposition and MacLean's troubles with the new Board of Education nothing came of the laboratory project.[46] Following MacLean's departure Hillis approached President Bowman, only to find that he was uninterested. Her persistence was finally rewarded when Macbride proved to be receptive, Seashore abandoned his opposition, and the legislature was persuaded in 1917 after intense lobbying to appropriate $25,000 to finance a Child Welfare Research Station employing "the best scientific methods of conserving and developing the normal child."[47] It was certainly ironic that one of the most important research developments during the long period of his deanship should have come about in spite of Seashore's initial opposition.

The term "Research Station" was coined to emphasize the interdisciplinary and nonpedagogical character of the new organization. Six divisions were contemplated: Heredity and Prenatal Care, studying the conditions which resulted in "well-born" and "ill-born" children, including heritable diseases, alcoholism, degeneracy, and parental intelligence or ignorance; Child Nutrition; Preventive Medicine and Dentistry; Social Surveys and Social Policy, gathering vital statistics and data on public health, hygiene, and recreation; Education and Morals, studying the home as the most important center for early childhood education for its influence on the development of character and morals; and Applied Psychology. The scientific study of childhood contemplated by this division came closest to Seashore's interest in helping children to unfold their fullest possibilities. The measurement of mental capacities would support a program in vocational counseling.[48] As the work of the station developed it realized only in part the original plans projected for it. But in other respects, notably its preschool laboratory and its work on intelligence, it achieved successes that had not been contemplated.

The work of the station was ably guided by its first two directors, Bird T. Baldwin and George D. Stoddard. Under Baldwin's leadership the broad scope of research was established through joint projects with psychology, speech, sociology, home economics, education, medicine, and dentistry. Not the least of the station's accomplishments was the opportunity it afforded to women to make outstanding contributions to scholarship. Amy Daniels in nutrition, Beth Wellman in child learning, and Ruth Updegraff in child psychology were the first Iowa faculty women to achieve national stature in their respective fields. Baldwin's work on the physical growth of children noted the close correlation between physical and mental growth. He also staked out the general position of the station when he stressed the intimate interaction of heredity and environmental influences in child development.[49]

Although research remained the primary function of the station, its commitment to child "welfare" obligated it to bring its research findings to the public by direct means of communication not usually employed by university programs. Information was disseminated through conferences, publications, lectures, radio talks, and exhibits. Parent study groups on child care were organized in 1924, with centers in Des Moines and Council Bluffs. Annual conferences on Child Development and Parent Education were well attended, with 715 registering for the 1932 conference. By 1939 some two and a half million pieces of literature had been distributed.[50]

Perhaps the most important achievement of the station was its contribution to the heredity-environment controversy. The hereditarian belief that each individual possessed a fixed amount of intelligence which could be measured by a test was associated with the famous tests devised by the French psychologists Binet and Simon and promoted in the United States by Lewis Terman and his associates at Stanford University. The army tests during the First World War had given intelligence testing wide publicity, and in the 1920s and 1930s such tests were often used in schools to identify the learning potential of students. As already noted, Seashore was a firm believer in the fixed IQ, a position which he never abandoned. In 1926 he had proclaimed in his characteristically dogmatic fashion that IQs of 25, 100, or 125 tended to remain fixed throughout life, with or without extensive education, and he was prepared to make decisive educational decisions on such evidence. Ironically enough, Iowa's own Child Welfare Research Station was to be the principal locus of the attack on hereditarianism in learning. During the 1930s Beth Wellman and Harold Skeels, supported by director Stoddard, accumulated data from IQ testing of preschool children which showed substantial improvement in scores resulting presumably from the advantageous learning environment. Foster children from an orphanage who were transferred to an institution for the retarded where they received more attention gained 27.5 IQ points over a two-year period, while others who remained at the orphanage lost 26.2 points. These findings were highly controversial, the hereditarians attacking the Iowans for alleged methodological faults which vitiated their results. In the long run, however, there could be no doubt that the hereditarian position in educational theory and practice had been severely weakened. The Iowa position as summarized by Stoddard in his 1943 book, *The Meaning of Intelligence*, held that nature and nurture were intimately intertwined and could not be artificially separated.[51]

The history of the Child Welfare Research Station illustrated both the strengths and the weaknesses of Seashore's vision of the university. Its success in initiating fruitful interdisciplinary projects with such diverse fields as physiology, physical education, sociology, psychology, and education was certainly impressive. Although originally projected as a research and service organization the station enrolled a substantial number of graduate students who took master's and doctoral degrees. But it was never incorporated in the collegiate structure, the director reporting directly to the president. Its budget came primarily from foundation grants, notably the Laura Spelman Rockefeller Memorial, and in the long run the dependence upon outside support proved a fatal weakness. Seashore always prided himself on accomplishing great things on a shoestring, which may have been appropriate to specific projects but not for maintaining an ongoing program. By the time that Robert Sears came as director in 1942, he found that each staff member was working in isolation, with little sense of involvement in a cooperative enterprise. Moreover, the College of Education under Dean Paul Packer and the department of psychology under its new head, Kenneth Spence, programs which might have been expected to be supportive of the station, were indifferent or hostile to it.[52] But in its heyday the station realized as close an approximation to the ideal of combined teaching, research, and service as any university program ever achieved.

THE PSYCHOLOGY OF ART

S eashore believed that much of the work done in the psychology of music and speech had a direct bearing on the graphic and plastic arts, especially in the analysis and interpretation of artistic talent. The psychology of individual differences suggested that means be found to measure degrees of artistic talent. Norman Meier, who came to the university in

1922 for graduate work with Seashore, had a background in drawing and an interest in applying the dean's ideas in the graphic arts. He declared that all great works of art exhibited harmony, balance, rhythm, and their variations. Each element could be isolated and measured as a variable, thus establishing a psychological basis for aesthetics. The "Meier-Seashore Measures of Artistic Judgment" was a test designed to reveal the extent to which the student possessed these aesthetic qualities.[53]

When the School of Fine Arts was established in 1929, consisting of the graphic and plastic arts, theater, music, and museum, it was Seashore's expectation that work in applied psychology would be the common intellectual bond which would unify the school. He expected that graduate students would receive a good grounding in acoustics, anatomy, and experimental psychology. Rufus Fitzgerald, the first director, was sympathetic to Seashore's objectives, but his successor, Earl Harper, was not, and when the dean sought to represent his testing programs as furnishing the foundation of the work of the school Harper tersely informed him that "we teach art as art."[54] Moreover, the director no longer exercised direct authority over the departmental budgets and personnel of the school. Department heads insisted upon reporting directly to the dean of liberal arts. Thus in the end autonomous departments emerged the victors in the struggle to subordinate them to the unified purposes of the school.

Undeterred by the resistance to his plans for music and the visual arts Seashore moved boldly to impose his program on literature. Verse forms, even more than the rhetoric of speech, lent themselves to acoustical analysis. The metrics of poetry must be heard to be fully appreciated. Wilbur Schramm, a young instructor in English, was persuaded to accept a year's fellowship in the psychological laboratory in order to learn Seashore's acoustical techniques. The result was a monograph published in 1935, *Approaches to a Science of English Verse*,[55] in which Schramm studied the scientific characteristics of syllables, stress, accent, rhyme, and meter in spoken verse. Two years later, when he became the first director of the Writers' Workshop, it might have been expected that these techniques would have been fruitfully applied to the analysis of student verse. But Schramm worked with prose writers, not with the poets, during his brief tenure in the workshop. Unlike Lee Travis or Scott Reger, men whose lives were permanently shaped by Seashore's influence, Schramm moved off into the field of journalism, leaving no evidence that quantitative methods of analysis were ever employed in the workshop.[56]

Seashore's efforts to promote research were confined for the most part to the academic subjects represented in the Liberal Arts College and the

Graduate College. But he was also concerned about the professional colleges, where prior to the Second World War little emphasis was placed on research. The professional degree programs in medicine, law, and commerce were designed to train practitioners rather than researchers. The dean's ambition was to integrate the professional colleges with the Graduate College by introducing research degree programs which would parallel or follow the professional degree work. In this he was only marginally successful during his tenure as dean.[57]

Medical faculty members were generally cool to his overtures. In the clinical fields, where the faculty divided its time between teaching and practice, there was little opportunity or incentive to engage in research. Seashore thought he detected signs of research interest in the traditionally strong departments of orthopedics, otolaryngology, and ophthalmology, but little came of it until after the Second World War. So long as the basic medical science departments continued to be staffed by M.D. degree holders the work in those programs was oriented toward practice rather than research. It was not until physicians lost interest in teaching the basic medical sciences and were replaced by doctors of philosophy in those fields and research funding became available that research became an integral part of training in anatomy, physiology, biochemistry, and pharmacology. But Seashore played no part in this transformation.

A comparable situation existed in law. The three-year law course leading to the J.D. degree was a professional program for practitioners. There was, however, a research tradition in law sustained by the nature of the Anglo-American legal system, with its central concern for legal precedents. The preparation of legal briefs and judicial opinions was in some sense an exercise in historical research, however partisan in accordance with the adversarial system. The law reviews maintained by most law schools provided opportunity for the publication of research papers by students and faculty. Seashore nevertheless felt that formal research programs in law would be desirable, and in 1933 he suggested to Dean Eugene Gilmore that three alternative graduate degree programs be considered: an S.J.D. degree requiring a fourth year in law with emphasis on research; an M.A. for law graduates with a major outside of law but related to it through a thesis; and a doctoral degree in a nonprofessional subject with a minor in law and a dissertation relating major and minor. It was Seashore's hope that a graduate degree such as these would become a requirement for teachers of law. But the law faculty was content to recruit its members from among those with the standard professional degree, and nothing came of the dean's proposals.[58]

A CRITIQUE OF LIBERAL EDUCATION

As a professor and department head Seashore was a member of the liberal arts faculty and was by no means inclined to restrict his activities to matters of graduate education. Apart from the normal involvement in undergraduate education entailed by his position he served for five years, 1922–27, on the "Gifted Student Project" of the National Research Council, a program designed to identify and encourage outstanding undergraduates to pursue scholarly careers. The council had been created during the First World War to assist in identifying and recruiting scientific personnel for the war effort. After the war it noted that the ablest college students were entering the professions and business, creating a justifiable concern for the future of science and scholarship. Work on the project, which involved visits to a number of college campuses, served to focus Seashore's attention on means of improving undergraduate education. Rather than concentrate narrowly on methods of recruitment the council wisely decided to take a broad approach based on the assumption that an educational program which challenged every student to perform up to the limits of capability would inevitably uncover the talents needed to satisfy every social need.[59]

It would be difficult to exaggerate the severity of Seashore's indictment of the prevailing pattern of undergraduate education. While he was unwilling to abandon the ideal of mass education, he was convinced that drastic reforms were necessary. The signs of the problem were obvious: the indifference and childishness of the vast majority of undergraduates, their preoccupation with sports and social life, the fact that half of them dropped out without having found direction or vocation. The cause of the problem lay in the misguided attempt of the college to cater to the needs of everyone. The elective system which had been introduced as a means of motivating students had proved in fact to be simply a shelter for the lazy and unmotivated and was perpetuated by a faculty competing for students and corrupted by jealousy, cynicism, and resignation. Much of the instruction was being provided by cheap labor in the form of graduate student teaching assistants. Low academic standards generally prevailed. On a wider scale the indiscriminate encouragement of young people to attend college created social imbalances in the form of an excessive supply of professionals, frustrated ambitions among those encouraged to seek goals beyond their capacities, and desertion of useful but less prestigious occupations like farming which were being left to be filled by "trash." Terminal junior college programs of a practical nature should help to raise the dignity of skilled labor. In the 1920s only Robert M. Hutchins among senior university administrative officials penned an equally damning critique of higher education.

The solution to these problems was nothing less than to seek salvation with the "feeble-minded" at Vineland. The college program must be so rearranged as to keep every student busy at studies which exacted the last ounce of ability and determination. An extensive testing program based on the psychology of individual differences would determine abilities and aptitudes and in conjunction with intensive counseling would direct students to the programs calculated to elicit their best efforts. College admission should be restricted to about five percent of the college-age population, the others to receive a terminal junior college training which would emphasize what Seashore called "euthenics," the art of right living.

The dean was contemptuous of progressive educators whose zeal for the salvaging of every student resulted in an equalized routine of mediocrity. His college would be intensely competitive, with regular testing and elimination of the unfit. Qualities of personality and character were as important as intelligence, although admittedly changeable and difficult to measure. The gifted students should be identified as early as possible and pushed ahead as rapidly as they completed their assigned tasks. The introductory departmental courses should be taught by the ablest teachers, with sectioning of students on the basis of ability. Advanced courses should employ the project method of instruction, with each student assigned a project which would challenge and cultivate scholarly resourcefulness. In laboratory courses the assignments should be flexible so as to provide a challenge to each student. Honors courses and other forms of recognition for outstanding accomplishment should be instituted.[60]

By setting his face against the dominant trend of the state university as it entered the great period of its growth Seashore could hardly be expected to have had much success in persuading his colleagues to alter course. A special committee of the Liberal Arts College appointed to consider his recommendations deliberated for some two years before the faculty in 1926 adopted a proposal to experiment with sectioning courses on the basis of ability, but on an optional basis only.[61] Thereafter honors sections in various introductory courses were occasionally designated, but it cannot be said that Seashore's proposals for the reform of undergraduate education had any appreciable effect upon his own university.

When Seashore reached the age of sixty-eight in 1934 he offered his resignation as dean. Knowing that Jessup was also resigning the board declined to accept the resignation, apparently in the interest of administrative continuity.[62] It would have been appropriate had both men left the scene of their labors together, since theirs had been an effective working partnership in which the president appreciated the dean's energetic promotion of innovative projects and usually gave him firm support. By staying on into the Gilmore administration Seashore found himself in a less supportive environment. The most conservative of all of Iowa's presidents in the twentieth century, Gilmore had little interest in educational innovation or scholarly research. When the dean again offered his resignation two years later Gilmore recommended that the board accept it, thus terminating an administrative tenure of twenty-six years.[63] When his successor as dean, George Stoddard, departed for wartime government service Seashore returned as acting dean for two years. But the days of his usefulness were over, and he was content to rest on his laurels as the revered "Dean of Deans."

CHAPTER FOUR

Virgil Hancher and
the Inertial University

There was a sense in which the presidency of Virgil M. Hancher (1940–1964) represented the intrusion of the alumni into the management of the university. Previously the governing board had chosen its presidents from within the academic community, acting on the implicit assumption that appropriate candidates were to be found among those already experienced in teaching and educational administration. Upon the retirement of President Gilmore the initial impulse of the board was to turn again to the academics, and it is likely that a traditional type of appointment would have been made but for the fact that a deadlock developed between the principal on-campus candidates: Paul Packer, dean of education, and the graduate dean, George Stoddard. Fearing that the choice of either man would entail a legacy of bitterness, the board sought someone not identified with local factions. At that moment W. Earl Hall, an energetic board member long active in alumni affairs, vigorously promoted the candidacy of his classmate Virgil M. Hancher.[1]

A fourth-generation Iowan who had grown up in the agricultural village of Rolfe, in the northwestern part of the state, Hancher had entered the university as a freshman in 1914. He proved to be a good student and a natural leader, graduating in 1918, a member of Phi Beta Kappa and president of the senior class. In the following year he went to Oxford as a Rhodes Scholar, an experience which had a profound effect upon the shaping of his mind and outlook. After receiving the B.A. degree from Oxford in 1922 he returned to the Iowa Law College, where he received the J.D. degree in 1924. While completing his legal studies he had held a part-time appointment as lecturer in political science, his only academic appointment. For the following sixteen years, 1924–40, he practiced law in a large Chicago law firm. During that period he maintained an active interest in university affairs, assisting in fund raising for the Memorial Union and serving as president of the Alumni Association, in 1938. Earl Hall, a former editor of the *Daily Iowan* and now editor of the *Mason City Globe-Gazette*, together with another close friend, Professor John Briggs of the political science department, had for some time fixed upon Hancher as an ideal man for the presidency; when Gilmore announced his forthcoming retirement they at once began to urge Hancher to give serious thought to becoming a candidate for the position.[2]

Hancher was understandably hesitant over changing careers, although he had no doubt of his ability to handle the job. He had on three previous occasions considered an academic appointment. Now his love for his alma mater, the urging of his friends, and the opportunity the position would afford to develop and expound his educational ideas proved to be an irresistible attraction. If he overlooked anything it was his lack of scholarly credentials, which in his mind would come to impose a permanent barrier between president and faculty. He never felt comfortable with the faculty, a fact which served to distance him and to accentuate his preference for authoritarian methods of administration. Although he understood the importance of research and publicly supported it, privately he seems to have harbored some resentment against an activity which gave faculty members a measure of independence in their institutional relationships. Earl Hall anticipated that one with Hancher's background of experience with corporate types would know how to deal effectively with legislators. In fact, the president proved to be singularly ineffective in his legislative relationships. He felt most comfortable in the small circle of friends which included Allin Dakin, the administrative dean; Elwin Joliffe, business manager; Robert Ray, dean of extension; John Weaver, graduate dean; and Robert Hardin, medical dean.[3]

Both by personal preference and as a consequence of his alienation from the faculty Hancher reoriented the presidency toward the community which the university served. More than any of his predecessors he addressed himself to the general public, becoming an ambassador and spokesman for higher education. He loved to make speeches and spent much time revising and polishing them. Alumni gatherings were of course frequent occasions on which to keep friends of the university abreast of campus developments and to expound his philosophy of education. The university had lagged behind other midwestern state universities in the systematic cultivation of direct alumni financial support, having previously used its alumni organizations to seek more adequate legislative appropriations. Now, under the able leadership of Loren Hickerson, the alumni sec-

Virgil Hancher. Courtesy of the University of Iowa Photographic Service.

retary, the foundations were laid for a program of alumni giving which was to become an ever more important source of support in the later decades of the century.

A CONSERVATIVE OUTLOOK

Virgil Hancher was a profoundly conservative man. As he explained to a member of his faculty, "temperamentally, I'm an evolutionist, content to make changes within the traditional pattern." But in an age of rapid educational expansion following the Second World War, when such energetic and aggressive educational leaders as presidents James Hilton of Iowa State, John Hannah of Michigan State, and Herman Wells of Indiana were seizing the opportunities to thrust their institutions into new fields and programs, Hancher's evolutionism seemed conservatism incarnate. It was no accident that he hated each of those doughty captains of erudition. When he heard of proposals to "reform" postwar Oxford and Cambridge by admitting larger numbers of students he warned a British friend that "there is danger in innovation." On his own campus, when the liberal arts faculty proposed to adopt a manual of procedure for the college he informed Dean Stuit that "it seems to me that good morale and democratic relationships must be achieved by mutual trust and confidence based on customs and experience rather than on written documents. . . . It is the spirit rather than the letter that matters." Hancher's public statements displayed none of the optimism which his predecessors seem to have accepted as part of their official obligation. He spoke frequently of unsolved problems and looming dangers. A man of prudence and caution, he refused to celebrate science as offering solutions to current problems.[4]

It was appropriate that as a native Iowan Hancher should extol the virtues of his state: its balanced agricultural and manufacturing base, its favorable climate and physical environment, and its happy blend of "sound racial stocks, English, German, Czech, Scandinavian, Dutch, and Irish." But unlike that of his fellow Iowan, Carl Seashore, Hancher's pride in the Iowa heritage was wholly nostalgic. The university must train its students to understand and appreciate their heritage in order to perpetuate its values. The Iowa pioneers had been home-makers, people of vision who had never lost sight of spiritual values. "Many, perhaps most, of the tensions of our society arise because we know what is right and we don't do it. We have set up false gods and we worship them and they do not satisfy." The old nineteenth-century complacence had given way to "a fear that we may be the unredeemed victims of a perverse and malignant universe."[5]

As the custodian of a great civilization the university could not ignore religion. Continuing the practice of his predecessors Hancher declared the university to be religious but nonsectarian. Belief in the sanctity of the individual, a central value of Western civilization, was a heritage from the Jews and the Christians. In our own day Christianity was the third choice between capitalism and communism. Properly tempered by Christianity, capitalism could remake the world.[6]

The prevailing anti-intellectualism of the McCarthy era seemed to Hancher to be an endemic feature of American life. Americans celebrated the average, melting everything down into a dead level of conformity and mediocrity. They disliked the expert unless he was engaged in the production of new gadgets. While they professed to believe in education they resented its critical and creative functions. He noted with approval the observation of Geoffrey Gorer that Americans rejected authority in all its forms, including the authority of intellect. In the nineteenth century the phrase "the two nations" had been used to designate the rich and the poor; now it could more appropriately refer on the one hand to those who knew the modern world, understood scientific advances, and knew that all men are brothers and on the other to those who lived in an atmosphere of economic fatalism, scientific ignorance, and political parochialism. It was not surprising to Hancher that educators should be singled out for attack since they professed to live the life of reason. In this gloomy mood he defined optimism as the triumph of hope over experience.[7]

A lifelong Republican, "one of few" who had never voted for Franklin Roosevelt, Hancher spent much time preaching to the converted. While he was not a radical Republican of the George Norris stripe, he was not a provincial reactionary either. His Oxford training and his long residence in a metropolitan center had given him a sophistication and breadth of outlook that set him apart from many of the auditors in the service clubs and alumni gatherings he frequently addressed. He often found it necessary to remind his hearers that problems of unemployment, sickness, and old age would not go away and that the New Deal programs, however flawed, which attempted to address these problems were necessary and inevitable. It depressed him greatly to realize that Iowa had reached the peak of its influence in national affairs at the turn of the century and that subsequently it had steadily declined. "Somehow, the solid, dependable, progressive world of fifty years ago had slipped away from us." As young people in increasing numbers had left the state the population had become stagnant and its leadership narrow, fearful, insular, and disgruntled. Iowans had developed a preference for mediocrity.[8]

The depth of Hancher's pessimism was apparent in his characterizations of his own times. It was an age of anarchy, of "hard roads and soft thinking," when individuals refused to accept decisions in which they had not themselves participated. There was a general failure to understand that the successful management of the increasingly complex institutions of the modern world required a large measure of cooperation and good will. Buffeted about in his biennial struggles with a narrow-minded and self-serving legislature he lost all faith in the legislative process. Noting that in the presidential election of 1948 less than sixty percent of the eligible voters went to the polls, he questioned whether the American people had the will, the self-confidence, and the ability to be self-governing.[9]

One of the greatest tragedies of the age, in Hancher's opinion, was the loss by Americans of their cultural past, their connection with the best of European civilization. When he spoke of anarchy he meant in part that a distinctive American culture had not yet formed and that when it did emerge it would no longer be a European culture. Every cultural element from Europe was being destroyed. Immigrants quickly lost their former national cultural identity. Symptomatic of the prevailing nihilism was the sordid and obsessive self-preoccupation of modern literature and art. Instead of portraying great themes the modern artist looked to the gutters and the slums. "The curse which has been laid upon the American is not that he fails to believe in God, but that he fails to believe in anything. Never has a great nation been thrust into world leadership with less assurance of the worth of its contribution to world civilization or greater grounds for its misgivings." The restlessness and casual informalities of the age were symptomatic of an underlying insecurity. Himself a man of invariable courtliness of manner, Hancher found in personal etiquette a clue to an important social characteristic of the age: "where the rules of etiquette are clearly established and faithfully observed, one knows what one's social obligations are and when they have been discharged. There is neither danger of the tyranny of excessive demands on the one hand nor of unintentional discourtesy on the other. Security lies in certainty, and the establishment and observance of strict forms gives certainty." [10]

Thanks no doubt to his Oxford experience Hancher had a lifelong interest in international relations and often used his off-campus speeches as occasions to discuss America's role in world affairs. No midwestern isolationist, he viewed the rise of Hitler with alarm and well before Pearl Harbor was thinking about the problems involved in putting the university on a wartime footing. After the war he recurred frequently to his conviction that America was woefully unprepared for its role as a world leader. It was appropriate that these concerns should be recognized by his appointment in 1959 as an alternate delegate to the General Assembly of the United Nations.

America's deficiencies as a world leader had first become apparent, Hancher found, following the First World War, when the nation declined to accept the responsibilities entailed by its role in achieving victory and refused to join the League of Nations or to support the peace settlement it had been instrumental in making. By 1950, five years after the end of the Second World War, from which America had emerged as the dominant world power, it presented the "astounding" spectacle of "a great nation unsure of itself, and aware that its unsureness is of its own making." It was intellectually unprepared for leadership. Confronted by the great Asiatic communist powers which now surpassed it in material resources, America's weakness lay primarily in its inability to define its position as the heir to the historic values of Western civilization. Forgetting for the moment that he had previously found that America had cut itself off from that tradition Hancher invoked its central elements: the Judeo-Christian religion, the intellectual inquiry of the Greeks, Roman law, British liberty, and American judicial review, mass production, and mass education. It was his fear that the tradition would be destroyed from within by ignorance and inertia.[11]

Hancher faced the future with unrelieved pessimism. For the first time in its history the nation confronted the hatred and destructive intent of the great communist powers. While the communists confidently believed that they rode the wave of the future, Americans were mired in bewilderment and self-doubt. Although they were themselves the descendants of revolutionaries and possessed a heritage of freedom, exploration, and creativity, they had little understanding or appreciation of their own traditions and consequently were unable to capitalize on their advantages. Instead, they celebrated the virtues of their political system, which was in fact the weakest element in their national life. Impressed with what the nation had been able to accomplish in the wartime emergency Hancher toyed with the idea of a "Universal Classified Service" in which a General Staff for Peace would make an inventory of the nation's brain power to be employed in solving national problems.[12]

LIBERAL EDUCATION

As an academic layman preoccupied with the social life of his times, Hancher located his educational thinking in a broad public context. His sense of estrangement from academe was both a strength and a weakness. It was a strength insofar as he never lost sight of the fact that education was not an end in itself, but must always serve a desirable social purpose. It was a weakness in that, although he held firm views on educational matters and frequently expressed them publicly, he rarely made any effort to influence the university's curricular decisions or even to communicate his ideas formally or informally to the faculty. During the first years of his presidency the Liberal Arts College deliberated an ambitious plan for general education. It proved to be a highly controversial affair, and a president with distinctive ideas on the subject who felt secure in his relationships with the faculty might well have exercised a significant influence on the outcome. Characteristically, Hancher was willing to discuss his ideas with the dean and other administrative officers, but he rejected a request to become involved with the faculty, fearing that his involvement would be counterproductive. Throughout the years of his presidency his discussions of educational ideas had little connection with the institution over which he presided.[13]

Like most educational administrators of his generation Hancher was a firm believer in general education. In addition to providing the necessary knowledge and tools for specialized training, undergraduate education should acquaint the students with the fundamental principles of their cultural heritage. While admitting that the precise content of the general education curriculum was controversial, he was prepared to specify that it should include knowledge of the physical and biological worlds, of the principal social institutions, of the fundamental ideas of Western civilization, and perhaps some knowledge of Oriental civilizations, of great literature, and of the foundations of moral behavior as well. He was certain that one could understand current events only in the light of knowledge of the past. Faced with an uncertain future, students would need to think independently and be adaptable.[14] He knew from his experience at Oxford that a good general education was not necessarily dependent upon courses specifically designated for that purpose. In the Oxford Honors School of Jurisprudence a third of his time had been devoted to technical legal subjects, a third to international law and jurisprudence, and a third to Roman law and legal history, yet from this seemingly specialized curriculum he concluded that he had received an excellent liberal education. The benefit lay not in the subject matter as such but in the breadth and sophistication with which it was presented.[15]

The distinction between undergraduate and graduate and liberal and professional education was more clearly marked in American than in English universities. Although Hancher was familiar with both systems and had firsthand experience of an American professional school, he always retained a primary interest in undergraduate education. He insisted that no university could achieve greatness if it divorced itself from undergraduates, a conclusion which he thought was confirmed by wartime experience when the vast majority of students were drawn off into military service. Graduate and professional training focused on specialized knowledge and research skills. Undergraduate education, on the other hand, was designed to produce great men and women, not just great scientists and scholars. Hancher attached supreme value to the social and moral qualities displayed by the cultivated and ethically responsible individuals trained in the liberal arts tradition.[16] Such views hardly conformed with the realities of his own university, where the liberal arts and graduate faculties were—with the exception of teaching assistants—one and the same. Thanks largely to the influence of Jessup and Seashore and to the competitive pressures from other major public universities, the combined faculty was increasingly research oriented. Many of the courses offered to upperclass undergraduates were also open to graduate students. These combined courses inevitably reflected the specialized scholarly interests of their teachers rather than the general values Hancher associated with liberal education at its best. The struggle over the core curriculum of the Liberal Arts College was in a real sense a struggle between proponents of general education as Hancher conceived it and those who attached primary value to specialized knowledge.

At the moment Hancher acknowledged that graduate education and professional education were superior to undergraduate training, and that the Liberal Arts College would do well to adopt the approach and methods of the graduate and professional colleges. Their programs were characterized by clearly delimited subject matter; the acquisition of skills in managing and adding to it; cultivation of the capacity to think and act in novel situations; and the inculcation of ethical attitudes toward the uses to which knowledge is put. The fusing of liberal and professional education would give focus to the undergraduate program while enabling specialists to understand their specialty in its broader cultural context. Pertinent though these proposals may have been, they pointed precisely in the opposite direction to that in which the university programs were then moving.[17]

In Hancher's mind the general education movement was in part an expression of dissatisfaction with the fragmentation of the university into specialized, unrelated bodies of subject matter. But knowledge was a seamless web which cried out for integration. This fact was acknowledged both in earliest childhood education and at the ultimate borders of inquiry where physics, chemistry, and biology merged. It was in the collegiate years that rigid departmentalization sustained an unnatural disciplinary isolation. It seemed ironical to Hancher that centrifugal forces in college teaching should be driving the students away from general principles toward specialized, fragmented knowledge while at the same time the faculty members as researchers were pursuing inquiries across departmental lines toward the unity of knowledge.[18]

THE UNIVERSITY PRINCIPLE

It was a major shortcoming that Hancher should have failed to understand the central assumption of the modern university—namely, that teaching and research are mutually supporting and enriching activities. He persisted in thinking of them as conflicting functions. He told Dean Stuit that as an undergraduate he had seen only an inverse correlation between teaching and research. His best teachers had not been researchers, and he suspected that they had been superior as teachers to the present-day faculty, given the modern emphasis on research. He considered student opinion to be the best criterion of good teaching, undergraduates, of course, knowing nothing of research. Stuit, who alone of Hancher's administrative officers told the president what he needed to hear, replied that the best test of good teaching was not student opinion but student performance in the largest sense and that the best performance was found in the prestige research universities.[19]

Although Hancher did not openly reject the appropriateness of the university principle of teaching, research, and service as criteria for faculty appointments and promotions, several of his administrative officers did. Stuit complained that the Liberal Arts College was the only unit of the university which adhered to the principle. Following a discussion of the matter among the collegiate deans Stuit reported that the deans were hostile to applying the principle to educational and personnel decisions in their respective colleges. They preferred that each college be a law unto itself. The professional college deans would subordinate research to exemplary teaching and service as the basis for faculty promotions. The law dean, Mason Ladd, was particularly emphatic about this. It seemed to Stuit that they were less concerned about the national or regional standing of their colleges than with the satisfactory provision of local services. When he complained to the provost, Harvey Davis, the latter replied that diversity of standards among the colleges was inevitable. Undoubtedly reflecting Hancher's views, the provost held that, while ideally everyone should be outstanding in research, teaching, and service, in fact some would excel in two areas or even only one. Some promotions would always be based on good teaching or service alone. It was not surprising that the provost was never known to have rejected a promotion recommended by a collegiate dean.[20]

Hancher often chided his fellow Iowans for their contentment with mediocrity, but there is little evidence that he felt any necessity to advance the standing of his own university. Presidents MacLean and Jessup had been acutely conscious of the low standing of the institution among the universities of the region and had been determined to elevate it. Hancher never made such comparisons and was content to celebrate the distinctive programs and services offered by the university. He seems to have been oblivious of the competitive relationship, whether out of complacence or from an underlying sense of the hopelessness of the situation. He was unwilling to make the unqualified commitment to scholarship which would have been an essential feature of any program to enhance the standing of the university. Indeed, he complained that the criteria for faculty appointments were too narrowly focused on academic credentials. Search committees should also consider integrity, academic responsibility, and personal appearance. Much of what passed for research was, in Hancher's opinion, of relatively little value. "Indeed, it is a grave question whether some who are engaged in research would not make a greater contribution to their respective universities and to society if they were engaged in the interpretation and utilization of existing knowledge rather than ineffectual and minuscule efforts for the advancement of knowledge."[21]

In the face of the McCarthyite hysteria over radicalism in academe Hancher took a sound position on the vexed question of academic freedom. He was careful to distinguish academic freedom from freedom of speech, of which it was a special case with features peculiar to the academic context. He understood correctly that academic freedom concerned the freedom to engage in research and the transmission of knowledge, as distinct from the expression of opinion on topics of current interest. Academic freedom pertained to professional competence and was justified by the benefit society derived from the advancement of learning. He was aware of the difficulty of discovering new truth, and he knew that most research was unproductive. There was a sense in which academic freedom was the right to be wrong. In some fields the public was indifferent; but in others, such as economics, highly sensitive issues might be at stake. Hancher held that economists had the right to teach and publicize their views, however controversial. But however correct his stand in principle, he seems to have been determined to avoid the initial appointment of potential troublemakers, and in at least one instance he rejected the recommended appointment of an individual alleged to support radical causes.[22]

Hancher's conservatism was apparent in his traditional attitude toward the education of women. As late as 1963 he observed that most women would marry and have children and that their education should ideally equip them for motherhood and family life. Similarly, after the Second World War, when the federal government became the principal patron of university research, Hancher warned that federally sponsored research jeopardized the survival of higher education. But he had no qualms about accepting federal money for the support of teaching. Iowa, he said, was a have-not state, exporting its young people to the rich industrial states. Education was a national resource which should be supported nationally.[23]

The ultimate task of education as Hancher understood it was to transmit the culture through the development of free men and women who were vigorous, courageous, and of good character and moral integrity. He acknowledged sadly that the latter was a casualty of our time, too often neglected in the educational process. The other essential dimension of a liberal education was social. He often spoke of the "ease and grace of outlook" that was the mark of a well-educated man. In his mind, education was inseparable from a certain social style, the courtliness of the gentleman which was the embodiment of the cosmopolitan ideal. He was himself an excellent exemplar of the type, with his abiding interest in world affairs, his devotion to the British tradition, his service to the United Nations, and, following his retirement from the university, his final dedication to education in India, where he died.[24]

THE ADMINISTRATIVE STRUCTURE

Hancher took seriously his administrative responsibilities and gave much thought to devising the organization best suited to carrying out the educational mission of the university. When he became president he found that he had inherited an administrative structure little changed from the small-college days when the president had been personally involved in virtually all aspects of daily operations. It was apparent that if he were to have time to think about important matters he would have to be relieved of the immense burden of routine administration. The nature of a public educational institution being what it was, he could not hope to isolate himself to the degree possible for a corporation executive, but it should be possible to diffuse administrative functions through a more elaborate structure of authority. Contrary to the usual perception of faculty members, the university was underadministered, and Hancher noted with approval the opinion of the Princeton president, Harold Dodds, that those universities that spent money on administration made the most rapid progress. Hancher believed that not more than eight officers should report directly to the president, whereas at Iowa he found thirty-two reporting to him, eighteen of them very actively.[25]

Any intention he may have had of moving promptly on reorganization was frustrated by the coming of the war. Much of his time during the first four years of his presidency was taken up with military programs and other exceptional issues. It was also necessary to find a liberal arts dean, a search which he conducted himself. When he assumed office there was no central administrative officer with university-wide academic responsibilities other than himself, unless one counted the graduate dean, an officer with little formal authority. Given his academic isolation, both real and perceived, Hancher needed an associate with whom he could interact intimately. For this purpose he summoned a friend from his student days, Allin Dakin, comptroller of the Claremont Colleges, and installed him in 1944 as administrative dean. Dakin's status was peculiar. He was not a line officer to whom anyone reported. In retrospect he had some difficulty in specifying precisely what his duties had been. Finance was his specialty, and in practice he gradually took charge of budget matters, even to the extent of intervening in the internal operations of the colleges. This provoked protests from the collegiate deans, who resented intrusions upon their jurisdictions. They also complained about unclear channels of communication and the absence of a functioning Board of Deans to provide direct contact with the president. In the absence of a centralized administrative structure the colleges had become accustomed to a large degree of autonomy which they were reluctant to surrender.[26]

At the end of 1946 Hancher projected a university organization consisting of four executive deans and a business manager each reporting directly to him. The deans would be responsible respectively for health affairs, graduate and professional education, student life and public relations, and undergraduate education. The latter would include the colleges of Liberal Arts and Commerce, with five assistant deans responsible for the major subdivisions of those colleges. The plan was implemented only in part. In the following spring the president announced the creation of a Division of Health Sciences consisting of the colleges of Medicine, Dentistry, and Pharmacy, the University Hospital and Psychopathic Hospital, the State Bacteriological Laboratory, the Hospital School for Handicapped Children, and the Oakdale Tuberculosis Sanatorium. The executive dean of the new division was to be Dr. Carlyle F. Jacobsen, who had come to the university a year earlier as dean of the Graduate College.[27] Rather than carrying out the 1946 plan by creating the other proposed academic divisions Hancher now announced the formation of a new Division of Research and Teaching, which would include the Graduate College and the colleges of Liberal Arts, Law, Commerce, Engineering, and Education. The executive dean of this division would be Elmer T. Peterson, currently dean of education and acting dean of the Graduate College. Clearly, Peterson, in whom Hancher had great confidence, would be a busy man, even when relieved of his collegiate duties.[28] Peterson, however, was promptly replaced as executive dean by the new graduate dean, Harvey Davis, and for two years the academic structure of the university consisted of the two divisions of Health Affairs and Research and Teaching. Jacobsen left the university in 1950; rather than replace him Hancher combined the divisions under a single officer, the provost. The first provost was Harvey Davis, who had come to Iowa from Ohio State, where he had been vice-president for academic affairs. He was a man of imposing appearance and equable disposition with whom Hancher felt comfortable. The academic programs of the university were now for the first time brought within the jurisdiction of a single administrative officer under the president, an arrangement which was to persist to the present day.[29]

That the president was not entirely satisfied with the evolution of his administrative structure is evidenced by the fact that he continued to speculate about the ideal organization. He envisioned three distinct functions, each represented by an officer with an appropriate title. The first was external relations, including fund raising, legislative liaison, alumni affairs, and public relations. It was appropriate that as a nonacademic, alumnus president Hancher should consider elevating the public relations function to a status coequal with that of the educational functions. The officer in charge of public relations need not necessarily have academic credentials.

The second function would be the formulation of educational policy and programs. Hancher acknowledged that within limits this should be the responsibility of the faculty, although he quickly added that many faculty members were unsuited to the task. While educational policy must be generally acceptable to the faculty and the governing board it should be the responsibility of one officer, working with a faculty group. The third function would be that of executive officer charged with the carrying out of educational policy. No attempt was ever made to implement these ideas.[30]

The proper role of the faculty, if any, in the management of the university remained a vexed problem for Hancher. He acknowledged that in principle university administration was simply an aid to the central function of teaching and research. But his image of the faculty member, with a few individual exceptions, was of a somewhat scruffy impractical specialist who knew little of the real world and who could not be expected to devote the time and effort necessary to reach balanced and responsible positions on policy matters. Hancher remained fearful of faculty encroachments on his prerogatives. Because of his high regard for the English universities with their largely self-governing faculties he was at special pains to emphasize the distinctive conditions on this side of the Atlantic which in his opinion justified the American type of full-time administration. In stressing the broad range of routine functions which he performed he unwittingly diminished the importance of his role by leaving to the faculty the creative educational tasks. He insisted that it was his concern for the academic program that had led him to accept the presidency, but there is no evidence that he ever involved himself actively in academic matters, for which his inability to relate effectively to the faculty was undoubtedly the root cause. He observed that "the proportion of those [faculty members] vitally interested in the university and its concerns tends to diminish, and the presidency increasingly becomes a lonely eminence from which to view the university as a whole." This was a self-fulfilling prophecy. What he professed to observe was what he really wanted: a faculty which would mind its own business and leave the management of the university to him. Near the end of his tenure he remarked that "the president of a university—like the conductor of a great orchestra—may be less of an artist than those over whom he presides. Many in the orchestra—many in a faculty—may be supremely greater than he. Yet his task, too, is a challenging, even a noble one—not the achievement of unison (futile goal in any university!) but the achievement of harmony out of diversity, so that members will perform better than they know, so that the whole may be greater than the sum of all its parts!" This pleasing figure was an apt one in that Hancher could not bear the sound of discordant voices, but the critic would have to say that the conductor singularly failed to elicit a spirited performance from his musicians.[31]

In many universities a formal means of communication between faculty and administration was provided by a university Senate. Such an organization had been created at Iowa as early as 1887. It had originated in a recommendation by the collegiate faculty and was designed to achieve closer relations between faculty and administration through the discussion of matters of common interest. The president presided, and membership originally included the entire faculty and administrative officers. Subsequent modifications restricted the faculty component to department heads and full professors. However constituted, the ultimate purpose of the Senate was to advise the president on matters of interest to him, and for this purpose MacLean and his successors found that the Board of Deans, created in 1899, was better suited to their needs. Senate meetings were held infrequently until President Jessup allowed them to lapse.[32]

For twenty years the university faculty existed in name only, without formal organization. Each of the colleges was a law unto itself with regard to faculty organization. The liberal arts faculty had for many years functioned actively in the management of college affairs. At the other extreme, the education faculty never met, the dean conducting the business of the college by personal consultation.[33] The professional college faculties were likewise slow to develop a collegial sense. The Medical College was dominated by the department heads. Dentistry and engineering were oriented toward their respective professions and were largely indifferent to university affairs. Without any formal means of expressing its views on institutional policies the faculty sank into a mood of apathy and cynicism.

Hancher was quite content to let sleeping dogs lie; it was ironic that the first stirrings of discontent should occur in his administration and that after expressing his reservations as to the wisdom of it he should grudgingly consent to the formation of an organization designed to give the faculty a voice of its own in university affairs. An important role in this innovation was played by the director of libraries, Ralph Ellsworth. An energetic library planner with innovative ideas about the educational potential of the library, Ellsworth came to Iowa from the University of Colorado in 1943. Administrative officers serve at the pleasure of the president, but they enjoy security of tenure by virtue of a professorial appointment in an appropriate college or department. In Ellsworth's case his status as professor of library science was more than a nominal assurance of security. He thought of himself as both faculty member and administrator, and he refused to recognize the tacitly accepted barrier that had always separated the two groups at Iowa. He interacted freely and effectively with faculty colleagues throughout the university while at the same time taking for granted his ready access to the president.

It was at an informal gathering at Ellsworth's home in December 1943, which the president attended, that the low state of faculty morale was discussed. Hancher was urged to authorize the formation of a representative body which could give voice to faculty concerns and begin the process of cultivating a more positive sense of participation in the institutional life of the university. All of the president's instincts were opposed to such a step, and it seems unlikely that he would have acted were it not for the fact that the initiative had been taken by one of his own administrative officers. Hancher believed firmly that any transfer of authority from an administrative officer to a faculty body would be a gross mistake. A dean could be held responsible for decisions, whereas a committee whose members could melt back into the faculty could not. He knew of no evidence that a faculty committee would be wiser, fairer, or more disinterested than a single administrative officer. Virtue was not found in individuals in direct ratio to their distance from administration, as sentimentalists like Ellsworth seemed to think.[34] Nevertheless, at the librarian's prompting Hancher agreed to appoint a committee to draft a plan for such a body. Allin Dakin, who generally reinforced the president's authoritarian impulses, warned him against this, pointing out that disaffection was confined to the liberal arts faculty and that the pressure would be relieved if that faculty met more frequently and involved itself in educational planning. But under Ellsworth's prodding a strong committee was appointed which proposed a representative faculty council (officially named the University Council). A faculty referendum overwhelmingly approved the creation of the council, which held its first meeting on May 26, 1948.[35]

The function of the council was of course to be advisory only, without legislative or administrative authority. It would serve as a medium of communication between faculty and president. While the latter was not a member, he frequently attended meetings, either on his own initiative or by invitation. The council promptly went to work and within the following two years took up a wide range of issues on which the administration had previously been accustomed to act without appreciable outside input. Inadequate faculty salaries were of course an object of earnest attention. Improved fringe benefits, including a pension plan, health insurance, and university hospital privileges, were explored. The shortage of faculty housing was noted. Sabbatical leaves of absence, travel grants for attendance at professional meetings, athletic ticket policy, and automobile parking facilities were practical matters of interest to the faculty. The council also took up the need to increase the library book fund, the desirability of a university press, a staff newsletter, and a procedure for ascertaining the reasons for resignations from the faculty. Especially annoying to Hancher was the designation of a council committee to study faculty participation in the selection of administrative officers. He informed the council tartly that circumstances in the various colleges varied so widely that he could not consider a common procedure for the selection of collegiate deans.[36]

The president complained that the council was involving itself in administrative matters, such as salary scales and library needs, about which the administration was better informed and in a position to act responsibly. He pointed out that sabbatical leaves of absence were illegal in Iowa; the council should either withdraw its recommendation on that subject or present a brief showing that such leaves were in fact legal. It did not occur to him to enlist faculty support in an effort to change the law. Instead, he chided the council for taking up matters "impossible of accomplishment" and thus embarrassing him. He even went so far as to request that agenda items be cleared with him in advance of meetings in order to determine whether any of them had already been considered by him. When this step proved to be ineffective he demanded that minutes of council meetings be submitted to him for approval prior to distribution in order to delete matter which might reflect adversely on his administration or suggest an undesirable adversarial relationship. In acquiescing to this demand the council went far toward conceding the right of censorship over its minutes. In at least one instance a council resolution on campus planning which the president found to be offensive was expunged from the minutes.[37] In order to dissociate himself from council activities Hancher recommended that its name be changed from University Council to University Faculty Council, a change which was effected in 1953.[38]

Undeterred by the president's hostility the council continued to press for needed reforms. It endorsed a proposal of the Graduate Council to establish a Research Council, research professorships, and the funding of research grants for summer and semester-long research projects. It recommended a review of teaching loads and a study of needed classroom space. The need for an auditorium was emphasized. A formula for salary scales based upon achieving and maintaining third place among seventeen public institutions in an eleven-state area of the upper Midwest was endorsed. In the event of failure to attain this objective the council favored limiting enrollments rather than jeopardizing educational quality by increasing class size. And in an action particularly annoying to Hancher the council proposed term appointments for members of university standing committees. It had been the president's practice to staff committees with faculty members in whom he had confidence and to continue them in office indefinitely.[39]

After a decade of mounting annoyance with the council Hancher resolved to take positive steps to remove this source of irritation. He ordered his administrative assistant, Charles B. Righter, to prepare an analysis of council actions which might be considered to be intrusions on his administrative prerogatives.[40] Armed with Righter's findings he appointed a special committee of deans under the chairmanship of the law dean, Mason Ladd, to draft a constitution for a university senate to replace the Faculty Council. In the meanwhile the council, sensing the president's hostile intent, appointed its own committee to consider ways in which the council could more effectively represent faculty opinion and at the same time satisfy the president's concerns. Under the leadership of law professor Allan Vestal the council's committee proposed the creation of a university senate of sixty-six members, sixteen of them to be appointed by the president, who would preside. A council of sixteen elected faculty members would serve as executive committee.[41] These concessions did not satisfy Hancher, and the council committee worked through seven successive modifications of its plan in a vain effort to preserve some vestige of faculty autonomy. Eventually the president took the matter out of the hands of his own committee and drafted a constitution for a University Council which the Faculty Council's committee agreed to cosponsor. A university senate in all but name, Hancher's plan provided for a council whose function was to provide a forum for the exchange of ideas and the formulation of recommendations to the president on educational policies and goals. The membership was to include the president and all of his administrative officers, ten faculty members appointed by the president, ten elected by the council, and forty elected by the college faculties distributed in proportion to faculty size. A Steering Committee composed of the provost or vice-president, four council members appointed by the president, and ten council members each representing one of the colleges would function as a study group to screen matters to be presented to the full council. To tighten the president's control further there would also be an Agenda Committee over which he would preside in order to determine a priority order of items for consideration. It was clear that the president was determined to restore the traditional type of university senate in which the business would be limited to those matters on which he desired to have advice.[42]

The plan was sent to the council in May 1962, with the suggestion that it be submitted to the faculty as a joint recommendation of the president and council for faculty approval. During the summer the faculty digested the plan and gathered on October 30 to discuss it in an open meeting at which the president presided. It quickly became apparent that there was widespread opposition to its adoption. A group of twenty-two faculty members signed an open letter prepared by Professor Jerry Kolross of zoology pointing out that the faculty's own elected council would be replaced by a body in which approximately half the members would be appointed by the president, including ex officio administrative officers and faculty members chosen by him. It was also noted that the president's control of the Agenda Committee would permit him to suppress discussion of issues distasteful to him. Others pointed out that, although the intended purpose of the plan was to provide an all-university forum in which the divisiveness inherent in a faculty council would be overcome, in fact the resulting organization in which the president could determine topics for discussion would have precisely the opposite effect; there would be constant complaints that the faculty was being muzzled. Following the meeting there was substantial opposition in the council to carrying the matter further, especially since the president indicated that he was unwilling to consider concessions. But by a vote of eight to four it decided to refer the plan to the faculty, with the proviso that sixty percent approval would be required for adoption. The result of the mail ballot, reported on December 20, 1962, indicated that seventy-seven percent of the 646 faculty members who returned their ballots had voted against the president's plan.[43]

Thus ended Hancher's attempt to suppress a distinctive faculty voice on university affairs. He continued to assert—in spite of all the evidence to the contrary—that scholarly specialists had neither the time nor the inclination to devote themselves to university affairs beyond their narrow specialties. "Consequently the percentage of faculty with a university-wide point of view and in possession of the basic data necessary for such a view tends to diminish." He attributed this unfortunate state of affairs to research. Scholarly preoccupation increased academic mobility and eroded traditional faculty loyalty to teaching and to the institution by which one was employed. It never occurred to him that loyalty to the institution might be cultivated—even among scholars—by vigorously pursuing the ideal of a university committed to scholarship and welcoming faculty interest in the management of its affairs as evidence of pride in and loyalty to the institution.[44]

On a smaller scale Hancher was confronted with challenges to administrative authority in the Liberal Arts College and Medical College. In the former college, with its long tradition of organized faculty activity, there was felt to be a need for a manual of rules and regulations in which the organization and functions of the college faculty and its committees would be codified. Dean Earl McGrath was sympathetic, and upon authorization by the faculty he appointed a strong committee under the chairmanship of the philosopher Everett Hall to draft such a manual. Ralph Ellsworth, now wearing his hat as professor of library science, was one of the members. Hall and Ellsworth held advanced ideas about the powers of the faculty, and the draft which they authored in the fall of 1947 declared that the liberal arts faculty possessed the authority to legislate on educational matters. It also provided for Executive and Educational Policy Committees and a Committee on Professional Welfare. The latter was charged with a wide range of functions, including the analysis of the professional standing of the college and its various units, the promotion of professional activities, and the mediation of differences between the dean and the faculty on such matters as promotions, dismissals, salaries, teaching loads, and research policies. Each department would be at liberty to specify whether its executive officer should be a head with indefinite tenure or a chairman with a limited term of office. The ultimate governing power of the Board of Education was acknowledged.[45]

A minority of the committee refused to endorse the proposal, finding that although the faculty may have customarily enjoyed the delegated power to manage its own affairs it did not possess the formal authority claimed by the majority. Since all power resided in the board, the minority feared that a direct claim of faculty power would provoke the board to withdraw the customary delegation. Dean McGrath, who might have been expected to find the functions assigned to the proposed Welfare Committee to be an objectionable encroachment on his powers, in fact told Hancher that the plan had great merits and that in his judgment it did not improperly usurp the functions of administrative officers. He reported that the plan was comparable to those in operation at the universities of Minnesota, Illinois, and Michigan. He informed the president that he intended to submit it to the faculty for approval.[46]

Hancher asked that the dean hold the plan in abeyance while he studied it. As might have been expected, he found both general and specific provisions to be objectionable. In general the plan was faulty in that it combined regulations governing the business of the college with a constitution vesting governmental powers in the faculty. He agreed with the committee minority that any such claim was inadmissible. He doubted that a college manual was necessary, telling Dean Dewey B. Stuit, who had succeeded McGrath, that "good morale and democratic relationships must be achieved by mutual trust and confidence based on customs and experience rather than on written documents." [47] He questioned the value of voting as a means of determining college policy, and he was distressed by what appeared to be encroachments on the authority of the dean and department heads in the name of faculty control. At the president's insistence the manual went through several revisions during which the Professional Welfare Committee disappeared. Although he knew of no evidence to justify the substitution of an elected chairman for a permanent department head Hancher allowed the provision for the exercise of choice when a vacancy occurred to stand. [48]

The *Manual of Procedure* which was eventually adopted by the faculty and approved by Hancher in 1950 provided that the faculty should have "such powers and duties as may have been lawfully delegated to it and which it has been accustomed to exercise." In fact, the only powers and duties enumerated, in addition to teaching and research, were consultation and recommendation on matters of educational policy and professional welfare. At the departmental level broad authority was vested in the executive officer, whether head or chairman, to manage departmental affairs. Although it was stipulated that each department should hold regular meetings, no powers were specifically vested in the departments. In practice wide differences in procedure grew up among some thirty departments of the college. By insisting that the departmental executive officer concur in any decision brought to him Dean Stuit greatly strengthened the authority of the executive in dealing with departmental colleagues. He remarked that it made no difference to him whether a department preferred a head or a chairman, since in his eyes both functioned in the same manner. But it made a substantial difference to the departments, since those choosing a chairmanship invariably involved their members more actively in the management of departmental affairs. [49]

SALARIES AND FRINGE BENEFITS

Given the determination to hold a place among the major state universities, the inadequate financial support which the state government was able or willing to provide was always a prime concern to the university and its leaders. The relative success or failure in the biennial struggle for appropriations was inevitably a major factor in reaching a judgment as to the effectiveness of each successive university administration. By this criterion the presidency of Virgil Hancher could not be considered to have been successful. Iowa salaries ranked at the bottom of the Big Ten throughout his administration, and major building needs remained unmet. Under prodding from his administrative officers and the Faculty Council Hancher agreed to adopt the formula of third place in the Big Ten as his salary objective. The board considered this to be unrealistic and substituted for it third place among state universities in an eleven-state area of the upper Midwest which included the Dakotas, Kansas, and Nebraska, a formula proposed by a State Tax Study Commission. To achieve this more modest position in 1956 would have required an eighteen percent increase in the salary budget. No allowance was made for current salary increases at neighboring institutions, and two years later the university found that it had not improved its competitive position.[50]

Hancher was more successful in his efforts to institute a package of fringe benefits for the faculty. When he took office in 1940 the university had no firmly stated rule as to the age of retirement, no pension plan, and no life or disability insurance. It had been generally understood that faculty members would retire at the age of seventy, but in the absence of pensions many of them lacked the means to support themselves in retirement, and the university was obliged in all decency to continue them on a part-time basis well beyond that age. In some instances individuals continued to receive small stipends for nominal teaching duties which they were no longer capable of performing. For some years, the Teachers Insurance and Annuity Association (TIAA) had offered a solution to the problem in the form of a pension plan to which both the faculty member and the employing institution would make regular payments. In consultation with TIAA the university in 1939 drafted a plan for mandatory retirement at seventy to be financed by a contribution of five percent of the individual's base salary, matched by an equal university contribution. The objective would be an annual income in retirement of thirty to thirty-five percent of maximum salary. But when the plan was presented to the board for approval President Charles E. Friley of Iowa State objected that it would be politically unwise to adopt such a plan when the legislature had recently rejected a proposed pension plan for public school teachers. The board was so impressed with the force of Friley's objection that it not only rejected the proposal, but it also expunged from its records all reference to the subject.[51]

With his characteristic caution Hancher was as much concerned with the legal as with the humanitarian implications of a situation in which a few individuals were receiving compensation without rendering service. Fortunately, the coming of the Second World War changed thinking on many subjects. The board's timidity was overcome, and in 1944 a contract with TIAA was signed which provided for a modest pension plan to which the individual faculty member and the university both contributed. This was shortly followed by the inauguration of group life and permanent disability insurance plans to which the university also contributed. Hancher and Dakin concurred in the belief that these measures were among the major accomplishments of a long administration.[52]

THE LIBRARY

For forty years after President George MacLean proposed in 1900 to elevate the university to a place among the major institutions of the region the continuing lack of a library building served as a constant reminder of the unrealized aspirations of the university's friends and supporters. It was to Virgil Hancher's credit that he made the erection of a library building a major objective of his administration. Within six months of his inauguration he secured from the legislature an appropriation of $300,000 with which to construct the first unit of the long-awaited building. The Second World War then intervened, and when Hancher retired in 1964 after twenty-four years in office the library was still less than half completed.[53]

On assuming office Hancher moved promptly to appoint a strong library planning committee, of which Elmer T. Peterson of education was the moving spirit. The committee was determined to strengthen the educational functions of the library, both by securing a senior library staff with academic qualifications and by nurturing a closer integration of library services with instructional needs. It found in the University of Colorado librarian, Ralph E. Ellsworth, a man whose thinking paralleled its own. Ellsworth had recently planned and built a library at Colorado designed to function as a teaching instrument. Three specialized reading rooms with open shelves for books, periodicals, and reference works served the needs of upperclass undergraduate and graduate students in the sciences, social sciences, and humanities, respectively. Each academic department assigned instructors or assistants to work with students in the library, while the library itself appointed staff members with appropriate subject matter as well as technical library training.[54] Ellsworth also had innovative ideas about library construction. In place of the traditional monumental library building with its fixed allocation of spaces for books, readers, and services Ellsworth proposed a strictly functional building of the commercial type based upon a rectangular spatial unit or module of ten by twenty feet, with artificial light and forced ventilation. Any number of modules could be assembled to constitute a building of the desired shape and size. Movable partitions would permit the rearrangement of functional spaces as needs might change with time. At Iowa, where the library was to be built in four installments over a long period of years entailing extensive reallocations of space, the modular principle proved to be a godsend. Unfortunately, W. T. Proudfoot, the architect of the Pentacrest buildings, was no longer alive to take up the aesthetic challenge of the new functionalism, and the first unit of the library turned out to be an eyesore.[55]

The Iowa committee enthusiastically endorsed Ellsworth's principles, which were incorporated in its own plan for the "Library and Instructional Center," drafted by Peterson. The prime objective was to integrate the educational program with the library facilities in order to bring students, books, and professors into a vital relationship. Prominent in the thinking of the planners was the analogy of the laboratory where students confronted problems directly. In addition to stack space for 1,250,000 volumes, three divisional reading rooms, or "instructional laboratories," were planned for lower division undergraduates, for the School of Letters (languages and literature), and for the social studies. Each reading room would accommodate 160 readers and house some 15,000 volumes. Conference rooms, small classrooms, carrels for graduate students, and offices for faculty and staff would be located nearby. Benjamin Shambaugh's popular Campus Course provided something of a model. That course had been offered in a large room in Schaeffer Hall which combined the informality of a library browsing room with the seating of a lecture hall. The committee hoped to commemorate Shambaugh's achievements and possibly perpetuate the Campus Course as well by making provision for a large auditorium where courses making appropriate use of library materials might meet.[56]

Colorado had embraced Ellsworth's educational theories, but it had refused to build a modular library. The Iowa committee assured him that if he would come to the university as director of libraries it would firmly support both his educational ideas and his plan of construction. He indicated that he would accept an Iowa offer subject to three conditions: first, that as director of libraries he would have the rank of dean with the administrative relationships necessary to execute his responsibilities; second, that his role be recognized as that of a "library statesman" and not merely a technician; and, third, that he be allowed to use his summers as he thought proper. A prudent executive—which Hancher certainly was— might well have requested a clarification of each of these conditions, but in any event the committee chairman, W. T. Root, reported that they were acceptable to Hancher, whose offer of appointment was made and accepted in September 1943.[57]

Planning the new building and refining his ideas about the role of the library in the educational program fully occupied Ellsworth during the war and postwar years when defense and other pressing needs forced delays in the construction program. Obstacles and frustration marked the project from the beginning. The Board of Education had selected an architectural firm for political reasons, ignoring the objections of the Planning Committee. The senior member of the firm stubbornly refused to employ the modular method of construction. It was only after much wrangling and costly delays that a junior member took charge and proceeded with modular construction. The original allocation of $300,000 was a mere pittance in terms of postwar prices, and three additional appropriations totaling just under two million dollars were necessary to build the first unit.[58] It was not until 1949 that ground was broken for the new building.

In the meanwhile, Ellsworth was perfecting his plans for the library as a teaching instrument. His ideas supplemented and amplified those of the committee. He continued to emphasize the analogy of the properly conducted library to the scientific laboratory. Progress in science, he believed, had been achieved because of the fruitful meeting of professor and student in the laboratory. Comparable success would be achieved in the humanities and social sciences when library facilities permitted students and teachers to work together in the presence of their study and research materials. The sterile distinction between classroom learning and library research would be submerged in a vital and creative joint experience. Professional library staff members fully qualified in the relevant subject matter areas would work closely with the students. Each of these specialists would teach as well as work informally as research advisers. As Ellsworth put it: "The creation of a natural working relationship in which the instructor and the student use the library as a laboratory is thus the first foundation stone of the Iowa program."[59] The laboratory analogy served to obscure the fact that one form of learning experience would be substituted for another. It was a proposal undoubtedly congenial to Hancher and E. T. Peterson, but it remained to be seen whether it would appeal to the liberal arts faculty, which was committed to the conventional classroom method of instruction.

Special facilities were to be provided for the newly adopted core curriculum. The College Library (later renamed the Heritage Library), a large area on the main floor with space for 700 readers, but broken up into small spaces to provide the atmosphere "of a fine home library," would house the materials to be used in the core courses. These materials would include not only books but also pictures, maps, cultural artifacts, slides, recordings, and audiovisual materials, and would be organized in eight chronological periods. In the Shambaugh Auditorium adjacent to the College Library a lecture series on contemporary problems would be offered by a lecturer selected by Ellsworth. The academic counseling service would also be located in the library. There would be seminar rooms for graduate courses as well as graduate student and faculty lounges. The basement would contain a bookstore, a newspaper room, and possibly a soda fountain.[60]

More conventional library functions which had previously been neglected were to be vigorously promoted. Now that appropriate facilities would be available, plans were made for the collection of rare books and manuscripts. Deposits of the papers of prominent Iowans were solicited, and an Iowa authors library was assembled. A collection of "right-wing" political material was begun. These and other collecting activities were to be supported by the organization of a Friends of the Library group, a membership organization composed of patrons interested in enriching the library's holdings of rare and valuable materials. The model was found in similar organizations at the private universities of the eastern seaboard, where wealthy alumni and other patrons made generous gifts to their respective institutions. It quickly became apparent that the University of Iowa lacked a comparable constituency of bibliophiles. Ellsworth too readily became discouraged, and the organization was allowed to lapse. It remained for his successor to revive it on the assumption that an ongoing group, however modest its accomplishments, could eventually demonstrate its value to the university. And in anticipation of the day in the not too distant future when even the largest libraries would be overcrowded,

Ellsworth was an active promoter of the Midwest Interlibrary Center, a cooperative storage library where participating institutions could deposit little-used materials.

As the librarian unfolded his ambitious plans it became apparent why he had stipulated that he have a dean's status, for he was determined to be an educational officer with an important role in the instructional program. His criticism of the sterility of the traditional classroom lecturing, if taken to heart, would have a significant effect on the university. Over the collegiate faculties he would have only the power of persuasion, although he reported that the faculty in political science, English, economics, sociology, and history had enthusiastically approved his ideas.[61] He would of course have direct control over those of his own staff who might be engaged in teaching. Nevertheless, his position was an awkward one. Although Hancher approved of his ideas and gave him encouragement, the president was unwilling to intervene in college affairs. Within the faculty the principal support for Ellsworth's educational program came from the College of Education. Peterson, later dean of that college, had drafted the original proposals of the Library Planning Committee. Harry Newburn, who had come to the liberal arts deanship from that college, was a firm supporter. Earl McGrath, who had succeeded Newburn and was also an educationist, was sympathetic. Dewey B. Stuit, who became liberal arts dean in 1948, was a psychologist and the popular choice of the liberal arts faculty. He was determined to keep control of the liberal arts program and insisted that the teaching faculty hold departmental appointments.

The projected library was to be a large building with 427,188 square feet of usable space. The first unit consisting of three floors fronting on Washington Street contained only 137,532 square feet, less than a third of the projected total. As soon as it was completed and occupied in 1951 Ellsworth began to press Hancher for funds with which to add a second unit. The president responded that there were other urgent needs; the library would have to wait its turn. In addition to its library functions Ellsworth and the Planning Committee had hoped to locate the offices of all of the social science and humanities departments in the new building. But without space in the first unit for some 60,000 volumes of the existing collection it was obviously impossible to implement their ambitious plans. Only the geography and philosophy departments were housed in the new building. When Ellsworth complained that his educational program would be jeopardized by lack of space Hancher assured him that his plans were not to be abandoned; space would be saved for the teaching function. Nevertheless, as the years passed without further funding Ellsworth became increasingly pessimistic.[62]

An integral part of the plan to use the library as a teaching instrument had entailed the conferring of faculty status on those professional staff members involved in teaching. Ellsworth had not received a specific commitment from Hancher, but he apparently took it for granted that such appointments would be made. When in 1950 he appealed to the president on the matter he was told that it would be "held in abeyance." He was referred to the Faculty Council, to which he reported that thirty-two of the seventy-three library staff members were professionally qualified for faculty status. He assured the council that although these people were qualified for teaching appointments in the academic departments he preferred to have them on the library staff. Council members were critical of the plan and voted against it. Hancher was content to allow this representative faculty group to decide the matter. It was a bitter defeat for Ellsworth. By 1953 he had concluded that space limitations and policy disagreements made it futile to continue to press for his program.[63]

Ellsworth's third condition of appointment had been that he be permitted to use his summers as he saw fit. His Colorado mountain cabin was a valued place for relaxation and uninterrupted thinking. He had requested the standard faculty nine-month or two-semester appointment rather than the eleven-month appointment with one month off held by administrative officers. He had been assured by the Library Planning Committee that his terms were acceptable to Hancher, but it eventually transpired that the committee had not in fact mentioned the conditions to the president. When certain administrators, presumably jealous of his extended "vacation," complained, Ellsworth was called to account by Dean Dakin, and an unhappy exchange of communications revealed something of the tensions within the administration. After considerable vacillation Hancher agreed to Ellsworth's terms and assured him of his high regard. Coming on top of lagging construction and the frustration of his educational objectives, this unhappy episode further alienated Ellsworth from the university. He welcomed an opportunity to return to the University of Colorado, leaving a library which was innovative in form but conventional in function. Small additions to the building were made in 1961 and in 1965. It was not until 1972 that the library was completed with a fourth addition equal in size to the first three units. The extensive rearrangement of functions in the completed building was facilitated by the flexibility of the modular principle, a fitting monument to the departed planner.[64]

INTERINSTITUTIONAL RIVALRY

The competitive struggle among the state's public higher educational institutions which came to a head in the closing years of the Hancher administration was precipitated by state government itself with its perennial insistence on eliminating duplicating programs in the interests of economy. The inability of the board to control duplication left it to the institutions to fight it out among themselves. The struggle in Iowa was not unique. In the postwar era the land grant colleges and the teachers' colleges were everywhere demanding university status, entailing the prospect of costly duplicating programs in the arts and sciences. To the University of Iowa with its Liberal Arts College and Graduate College fell the thankless task of resisting encroachments by its sister institutions on its cherished monopoly. Hancher was not well adapted to shoulder this burden successfully. He was temperamentally a complainer who, although he could analyze the situation clearly, was incapable of moving forcefully and effectively to resolve the problem.

The frequent surveys by outside experts mandated by the legislature or board were of little help. Another study by the ubiquitous Capen made in the year before Hancher took office reported that duplicating programs were nationwide. Some of these were said to be inevitable, and Capen blithely ignored duplications between the university and the State College in English, mathematics, economics, chemistry, and physics, although these were now at the heart of the problem in Iowa. He found that the principle of allocation according to the distinction between major and service lines was not being fully applied, but that the situation had improved since 1925. The old struggle over engineering no longer carried a positive charge; each school had as much business as it could manage. Extensive duplications in the arts and sciences between the university and the Teachers' College were shrugged off as inevitable. In fact, the depressed economic conditions of the 1930s had so weakened the institutions that they had little strength with which to compete. Each was wholly preoccupied with the struggle for its own existence.

A decade later, at the outset of the great period of postwar expansion, George Strayer of Columbia conducted another survey. Reflecting the optimism of the period, Strayer sought in a positive fashion to shift the emphasis from competition to a collaborative management of growth. Instead of finding fault with interinstitutional competition he focused attention on the failure of the board to provide educational leadership. It had failed to observe the distinction between policy making and administration and had not established an effective working relationship with the institutional officers. While it was giving close attention to financial matters, educational policy was being neglected. The inauguration or abandonment of degree programs, the relationship of teaching and research, and the allocation of resources ought to be matters of major importance to the board, not left to others. Strayer recommended that each president be required to submit to the board an annual report dealing exclusively with educational programs. The interinstitutional committee established by the board in 1947 and charged with the responsibility of controlling duplication should take a positive approach to the coordinated development of programs in all three institutions. On the subject of duplication Strayer conceded that duplication in the arts and sciences at the undergraduate and master's degree levels was inevitable. In advanced fields he could only advise that the interinstitutional committee should maintain close surveillance and encourage constructive cooperation.[65]

Hancher was unwilling to accept the advice of the outside experts and to reconcile himself to the competition for excellence which was implied in their recommendations. His attention remained fixed on the financial consequences of the traditional competition among duplicating programs. Iowa State had always been more generously financed in terms of its limited mission, and Hancher feared that as its programs expanded it would gain further ground on the university. James Hilton, who in 1953 succeeded Charles Friley as president of Iowa State College, was an alumnus of the college and a specialist in animal husbandry. He was determined to elevate the college to university status in substance as well as in name. Hancher bitterly complained of the "cancerous urge" of the state colleges to be what they were not. If the traditional arrays of specialized institutions were to be abandoned and all were to offer duplicating programs in the arts and sciences resources would be spread too thinly, and a common debasement of quality would result.[66]

In resisting the demand of the State College for university status Hancher pointed out that the Morrill Act which created the state college system had contemplated the teaching of agriculture and the mechanic arts in a liberal and practical spirit. His own English education had demonstrated that technical and professional subjects could be taught in this manner by teachers who understood their specialties in the context of modern learning and culture. Instead, the land grant colleges were choosing to develop traditional liberal arts programs largely unrelated to their original mission.[67] The board, fearing that open conflict would jeopardize legislative good will to the detriment of both institutions, pressured Hancher not to resist Hilton's drive to change the name of the college to Iowa State University. Hancher reluctantly agreed, despite the resulting confusion between Iowa State University and the State University of Iowa. The Iowa City institution, which had once been known as "the Iowa State University," was once again obliged to find a new identification for itself, settling upon "the University of Iowa," the name which for simplicity's sake has been employed throughout the present history.[68]

Worsted in his struggle to prevent the elevation of the State College to university status Hancher blamed the board for its failure to maintain the proper differentiation among the institutions under its nominal control. He repeated Strayer's criticism that the board spent some ninety-five percent of its time on internal matters properly left to the local administrators, thus neglecting its proper role of long-range planning and policy making.[69] In the absence of a board able or willing to control duplication Hancher at the end of his administration arrived at the conviction that there should be one consolidated state university with three campuses. He was persuaded that a president presiding over three chancellors would be able to coordinate programs and to prevent the costly duplication which he anticipated would flourish under present board policies. The "One for Iowa" plan which he proposed to the board some three months prior to his retirement remained his legacy to the problem of coordinated higher education in Iowa. It was stillborn.[70]

FOUR SUCCESSFUL PROGRAMS

In characterizing the Hancher years as inertial I am mindful of the fact that the law of inertia refers to movement as well as to immobility. The university was steadily growing, and without forceful leadership the law of inertia was, so to speak, free to achieve its effects without executive direction. Increasing student enrollments made possible additions to the faculty, and in the absence of an overall plan of university development these opportunities were seized by departmental and program leaders who sensed the vacuum and moved forcefully to fill it. In the professional colleges, where growth was usually curtailed by limited instructional facilities as well as by advanced qualification for admission, enrollments remained relatively stable. But in the liberal arts, at both the undergraduate and graduate levels, there was virtually unlimited opportunity for growth, and the incidence of enrollment increases among the various disciplines had a significant potential for strengthening academic quality.

Hancher acknowledged that the standing of a university was determined by the quality of its faculty, but unlike his predecessors he did not actively involve himself in recruitment, being content to leave this to the deans and faculty. This was just as well, for in addition to scholarly accomplishment and teaching ability he believed that prospective faculty appointees should be of acceptable nationality, religion, marital status, and other "more intimate personal details." [71] These specifications underscored the president's ultimate conception of the faculty as a family, preferably a happy one, in which amiable personal associations among colleagues of similar backgrounds and outlook were highly desirable. Given these principles, had the president had a significant role in faculty recruitment it is likely that improvement of the academic standing of the university would have been even more difficult than it was. Larger was not necessarily better. But growth offered an opportunity to strengthen the institution that would scarcely have presented itself had enrollments remained static.

A University of Pennsylvania study of the comparative standing of academic departments made in 1960 clearly demonstrated the catastrophic effect of prolonged economic depression and ineffectual administration on the University of Iowa. In 1925 ten of the university's departments were rated among the top fifteen nationally. By 1957 only five enjoyed a similar ranking. Overall ten departments had gone down in the ratings, while only three had improved their standing. Hancher noted, appropriately enough, that these were comparative ratings and that several Iowa departments which had fallen were still superior to what they had been earlier. Nevertheless, it was obvious that if the university were to hold its own in the national competition there would have to be a substantial increase in its financial support as well as more rigorous scrutiny of prospective faculty appointees. [72]

Hancher repeatedly stressed the central role of the Liberal Arts College as the foundation on which the university rested. The advanced and specialized programs prepared students for careers, but the liberal arts prepared them to live in and understand a complex civilization. The goals toward which specialized knowledge pointed were determined by one's philosophy of life, which was the ultimate concern of liberal education. [73] Nevertheless, Dean Stuit complained that the Liberal Arts College did not receive the financial support relative to that provided for the health sciences, the University Hospital School for handicapped children, the extension services, or the College of Nursing. He believed that the university had been too generous in its promotion policy, tying up too much of its salary budget in unproductive senior faculty members. He agreed with Hancher that the university must of necessity limit the number of programs in which it sought to achieve excellence. He directed each department to select certain fields in which it would strive to be outstanding, while settling for mere competence in others. Iowa should not attempt to compete in every field with stronger institutions such as the universities of Michigan or Illinois.[74]

Lengthy as it was, Hancher's tenure in office was exceeded by that of Dewey B. Stuit, who was dean of liberal arts for thirty years, from 1948 to 1977. A specialist in testing and counseling, Stuit had affiliations with both psychology and education. He had been one of the advocates of a stronger faculty voice in university affairs, and his selection as dean was favorably received by his colleagues. The interrelationship of the Liberal Arts College and Graduate College was a particularly intimate one in which the accidents of personality could have a significant influence. Seashore and Stoddard had been forceful administrators who were able to offset in considerable measure the inherently weak position of the Graduate College. But Stoddard's successor, Walter Loehwing, was not a strong personality, and the balance of power shifted abruptly to the Liberal Arts College.[75] Relations between the two deans were always cordial, but Stuit got what he wanted. During his tenure new departments were organized in anthropology, computer science, East Asian languages, library science, linguistics, recreation education, Russian, statistics, social work, and speech pathology and audiology. Stuit knew that in order to get and keep a high-quality faculty there would have to be suitable salaries and fringe benefits. The rapid growth of colleges and universities in the postwar period generated intense competition for capable faculty members which the university had great difficulty in meeting. Departments like history which used great care in the recruitment of promising young scholars were regularly "raided" by institutions with greater resources and prestige. Stuit repeatedly pressed Hancher for more vigorous promotion of the university's cause in the legislature. At his suggestion a legislative contact program was inaugurated in 1956. Members of a team of administrators and faculty met individually with legislators and candidates in order to familiarize them with the financial needs of the university. These efforts supplemented and perhaps strengthened the relatively ineffectual efforts of Hancher and the Board of Education.[76]

Nevertheless, in spite of all the constraints, several notable achievements were recorded by programs in which capable leadership was able to expand the offerings and recruit outstanding teachers and scholars. One of the most successful of these was the program in art. A department of fine arts had been organized as early as 1906, offering a limited amount of work in drawing and painting as well as art history and appreciation. In the older eastern universities the study of art history was well established, but creative work, if available at all, was offered only on an extracurricular basis. The Iowa program for creative work in the arts and letters represented a major innovation in higher educational theory and practice. Its establishment on a permanent footing required forceful leadership capable of binding together the often discordant interests and temperaments of the creative and scholarly people. The initial program in fine arts failed in this respect, and two separate departments of graphic and plastic arts and history of art emerged. The former was led by Charles A. Cumming, a well-known artist who recruited his faculty from his own proprietary art school in Des Moines. The History and Appreciation of Art was taught by members of the classics department, with major emphasis on ancient art and archaeology. These programs grew slowly through the 1920s. The Cumming group worked in the traditional French academic style of painting. Nevertheless, in 1934 they found a place in their faculty for Grant Wood, who had achieved sudden fame in 1930 with his *American Gothic*, a painting which combined a regional theme with a technique derived from German medieval primitive painting.[77]

The organization of the School of Fine Arts in 1929 may not have achieved the hoped-for integration of work in the full range of the arts of music, theater, and graphic and plastic arts, but it led to important developments in the narrower field of the visual arts. The moving spirits behind the effort, Fitzgerald, Seashore, and Jessup, were determined to combine the programs in creative art and art history. A new art building financed jointly by alumni, the Carnegie Corporation, and the Works Progress Administration was constructed on the west bank of the river in 1935. Frederick Keppel, president of the Carnegie Corporation, recommended Lester D. Longman, an art historian trained at Princeton, to head the combined program.[78] An able and energetic organizer, Longman brought the two programs together and launched the new department of art on a course of rapid expansion. Graduate programs leading to the master of fine arts and doctor of philosophy degrees were added to the traditional B.A. and M.A. programs. The faculty was greatly enlarged and strengthened by the appointment of a succession of talented creative artists, among them Philip Guston, Byron Burford, Mauricio Lasansky, James Lechay, and the art historians William Hecksher and William Burke. Printmaking, metalsmithing, ceramics, and design were added to the traditional fields. The new program rested on the presumption that creative and historical work were mutually beneficial and that all art students should have experience of both. Longman found that most creative artists were "uneducated," by which he meant that they had had no training in the liberal arts. A major objective of the program was to prepare college teachers of art, and for this a traditional liberal arts experience was essential.[79]

As Iowa director of the Civil Works Administration art project Grant Wood was involved in the production of large-scale mural paintings for public buildings. Students who worked closely with him on these projects were paid from public funds while receiving university credit for their work. Artists who were unaccustomed to the constraints of the academic setting were often uninhibited in the expression of their opinions of one another's work. The academic painters within the department complained that to compensate for his deficiencies in drawing Wood projected photographs onto canvas and painted over them, requiring students to work in his own manner. As a painter widely known to the general public Wood was considered by administrative officers to be a highly prized public relations asset to the university, and Longman was ordered to "make Wood happy."[80] The two men each possessed a powerful ego, and the animosity which developed between them was both personal and professional. Longman was determined to assemble a group of artists who worked in the contemporary idiom, several of whom considered Wood's popular regionalism to be little more than poster art, a view that Longman came to share. Wood's critics liked to point out that except for the Chicago Art Institute's purchase of *American Gothic* no reputable museum had acquired any of Wood's paintings. Longman's official position was that the painters should represent all schools, and that if Wood were to have his way a one-man academy type of painting would be imposed upon the department.[81] For his part, Wood complained that Longman's policies put so much emphasis on the historical and critical side of the program as to stifle the creative side. He also charged that the disparagement of his work within the department factionalized the students and hampered his teaching.[82]

The conflict remained an internal matter until the end of 1940, when news of it reached *Time* magazine, a journal which was favorably disposed toward Wood and had occasionally featured his work. Harper and Dean Kay were alarmed at the prospect of unfavorable publicity for the university and did what they could to persuade the *Time* reporter that the rumors of dissension were unfounded. Others were less discreet, and two of

Wood's critics, Emil Ganso and Fletcher Martin, allowed their names to be identified with the criticism of Wood as a painter and teacher. It was also erroneously reported that Wood, who was on leave of absence for the academic year 1940–41, had been fired. Wood now publicly identified Longman as the source of his troubles and demanded that the creative work be separated from the historical and be placed under his own direction. Longman in turn responded that Wood represented an obstacle to achieving "world standards of art quality" at the university.[83] Seashore and his successor George Stoddard were supportive of Wood, while Harper and Kay backed Longman. In response to Wood's threats to resign Harper offered to organize the creative artists as a semi-autonomous "panel" within the department, with direct access to the director of the School of Fine Arts. Wood rejected this, as he also rejected an offer to be artist in residence under the director and free from all teaching duties. It was clear that he was determined to oust Longman and control the department.[84]

When Hancher became president at the end of 1940, one of his first tasks was to settle the Wood controversy. Following a long conference with the painter he concluded that Wood would not be a suitable administrative officer and informed him that he could not accept Wood's proposal to separate the two branches of the department. He accepted Harper's opinion that the department would suffer more from Longman's removal as head than from Wood's resignation. He asked Wood to take no action until a successor to Dean Kay was appointed. The new dean, Harry Newburn, won Wood's confidence and persuaded him to accept a new position as professor of fine arts directly under Newburn's jurisdiction. He would now be in effect a one-man department. Although this solution did not address Wood's complaints about the art department he was assured that the dean would "put the house in order." Before Newburn could make good on this promise, whatever it meant, Wood fell victim to a rapidly developing cancer. From his hospital bed he offered his resignation, in January 1942, which the university in all decency refused to accept. He died a month later.[85] But as is often the case, the artist had the last word. *Honorary Degree*, a lithograph executed with characteristic lighthearted satire, depicted Seashore and Foerster with fawning obsequiousness draping the academic hood over the shoulders of a rather bewildered little fellow who is, of course, Wood himself.

Longman survived the Wood affair and went on to preside successfully over a rapidly developing program. The academic painters and the regionalists had departed, and modernism in its various forms reigned supreme. Distinguished artists whose work was widely exhibited accommodated themselves to the requirements of an academic program within the Liberal Arts College and Graduate College. Any possibility that these constraints might have generated a new "academicism" was dissipated by the prevailing principle that each student should develop his or her own style. Longman was also successful in securing a place for the arts in the new undergraduate core curriculum. By the time of his resignation in 1958 the art faculty had nearly tripled in size, and the number of students enrolled in art courses had increased from 386 in 1936 to 1,400.[86]

A distinctive feature of the modern American university has been the emergence of the study of English and American literature as the most popular subject in the undergraduate and graduate curricula. With the steady growth in enrollments in the decades following the Second World War, the influx of students into English department courses permitted an able departmental leadership to expand its programs and to enlarge the faculty with a succession of capable appointees. The leader principally responsible for these accomplishments was John Gerber. Originally brought to the university in 1944 to organize the new skills program in rhetoric, Gerber became chairman of the English department in 1961. Within a decade he was able to increase the size of the faculty from twenty-six to sixty-three and to add several new programs. A conflict precipitated by Norman Foerster between the literary critics and historians was healed with the assurance of a place for both schools. The Writers' Workshop flourished thanks to aggressive promotion by Paul Engle, and new programs were added in comparative literature, linguistics, American studies, printing and bookmaking, a Translation Workshop, and an International Writers' Program.[87]

Undoubtedly the most productive of Iowa departments in terms of contributions to its discipline was psychology. Building on the foundations laid by Seashore, his successor, Kenneth Spence, who was head of the department from 1942 to 1964, introduced animal psychology and made the department a major center of behavioristic psychology. The tightly controlled experimental work undertaken by doctoral students in that field permitted rapid completion of degree requirements. By 1978 some 770 doctoral degrees in psychology had been conferred, 176 of them on women. Spence had supervised 75 of these dissertations, Seashore 52, Arthur Benton 46, and Lee Travis 35. Seventy-three percent of the dissertations were subsequently published. Among the graduates were 22 editors of scholarly journals, 72 presidents of scientific or professional organizations, and 4 members of the National Academy of Sciences. These accomplishments include those of the closely affiliated Child Welfare Research Station (later the Institute of Child Behavior and Development), as well as clinical psychology and speech pathology.[88]

As a strict experimentalist Spence was not particularly sympathetic to social psychology. At the opposite pole was Kurt Lewin, a gestalt psychologist trained in Germany, who joined the staff of the Child Welfare Research Station in 1935. Lewin held psychology to be an independent discipline not reducible to physiology or neurology. Perceptions were said to depend upon their forms as organized wholes. These assumptions led him from child psychology to a broad range of topics in social psychology such as ethnic psychology, the psychology of authoritarian leadership, and industrial psychology. Increasingly constrained by his obligations to work in child behavior, Lewin left Iowa in 1944 to organize his own Research Center for Group Dynamics at MIT.[89]

The foundations for a strong program in physics had been laid by George W. Stewart, the second Iowa faculty member to be elected to the National Academy of Sciences. A dedicated educator as well as research scientist, Stewart initiated graduate work in physics. By the time of his retirement in 1946, 70 Ph.D.s and 150 M.A.s had been conferred. Among the graduate students was James Van Allen, who received the Ph.D. in 1939 and became head of the department in 1950. His research on cosmic rays using rockets and satellites to place instruments in space led to the discovery of the Van Allen radiation belts in 1958. An important role in instrument design and interpretation of data was in turn played by his graduate students, notably George Ludwig and Carl McIllwain, thus laying the foundation for an Iowa school of magnetospheric physics.[90]

CHAPTER FIVE

The Bowen Revival

T he fourteenth president of the university, Howard R. Bowen, was installed with traditional academic pomp and circumstance on December 5, 1964. The dissonant chords of Professor Richard Hervig's "Presidential Fanfare" ringing out through the rafters of the Field House symbolized the awakening of the university from the fitful slumber of the Hancher administration. In the brief five years of his tenure (1964–1969) Bowen was to raise the university to a higher level of excellence than it had yet achieved in the twentieth century.

Like that of his predecessor, Bowen's candidacy originated within the Board of Regents. As president of Grinnell College he was well known to several of the regents, and while he did not actively seek the university position he was willing to be considered. Other candidates were deans Robert Hardin, John Weaver, Dewey Stuit, and Robert Ray, dean of the Extension Division.[1] Bowen was eminently qualified for the position. Following graduation from the State College of Washington he had come to Iowa for graduate work in economics, receiving the Ph.D. in 1935. For seven years he was a member of the economics faculty, resigning in 1942 to accept a wartime position in the Department of Commerce. He then served briefly as chief economist for the Irving Trust Company in New York before becoming dean of the College of Commerce and Business Administration at the University of Illinois. Here he had his first instructive if painful experience in academic administration. George Stoddard, then president at Illinois, brought Bowen to Urbana in order to strengthen the program in economics. The new dean's vigorous pursuit of excellence alienated and frightened senior faculty members, who organized a vigorous counterattack which resulted in his ouster. Then followed three years as professor of economics at Williams College and nine years (1955–1964) as president at Grinnell. Any doubts of his administrative abilities that might have arisen from the Illinois experience were laid to rest by his success at Grinnell. He found the college in a deteriorated condition both

Howard Bowen. Courtesy of the University of Iowa Photographic Service.

financially and academically, but was able to revive and strengthen it while winning the respect and affection of its students, faculty, and alumni. Thus he came to the university case-hardened by his difficult experience at Illinois and self-confident as a result of his outstanding success at Grinnell.[2]

Bowen's scholarly career as an economist was marked by his continuing concern with social issues. As a liberal thinker of the type that came to maturity during the Depression and New Deal era, he consistently approached economic problems from the point of view of human welfare. He published books on such topics as the social responsibilities of businessmen and Christian values in economic life. He had written one of the first postwar monographs on poverty in the United States, as well as a national commission report on poverty, unemployment, and education for minorities. As a student he had had pacifist leanings and had "flirted" with democratic socialism on the Swedish model. He had found the university campus in the 1930s a lively and stimulating place for the discussion of such issues. Iowans in general had impressed him as being sensible middle-of-the-roaders, tolerant of both the moderate right and the moderate left. A man of fundamentally positive and optimistic temperament, he was prepared to overlook the hostility of the conservative Iowans in the legislature who deplored his appointment and who contemplated with aversion the demands he would make for more generous support of the university.[3]

The medical dean, Robert Hardin, who held senior administrative positions under both Hancher and Bowen, compared their administrative styles. He reported that Hancher liked a straight-line organization with final authority held in his own hands, while Bowen preferred to be aloof. The new president expected his top executive officers to make and implement their own decisions. One of his first acts was to appoint law professor Willard L. Boyd vice-president for instruction and dean of faculties with full responsibility for academic affairs. Duane Spriestersbach, a speech pathologist, was appointed graduate dean and later vice-president for research. Merritt Ludwig, who came with Bowen from Grinnell, was to be in charge of buildings and grounds. Max Hawkins was to handle legislative relations. The president wanted to be informed but not involved. Nevertheless, he did not hesitate to intervene at any point if he felt that the occasion warranted, sometimes to the distress of his subordinates. His own role was to establish the overall goals and policies of the institution. Like his predecessor he was a fluent speaker, although he wasted no time in polishing his speeches for oratorical effect. He took seriously his role as an educational administrator, studying national demographic and economic trends and analyzing the place of the university in the network of state educational institutions.[4]

The gulf separating the administrator from the scholar-teacher which always loomed before Hancher was easily bridged by Bowen. He had abundant experience in both capacities, and he did not share Hancher's belief in their incompatibility. He knew the functions of both, and he knew that each prospered to the extent that they were mutually support-ive. He recalled from his earlier experience at Iowa that there had been a virtually complete separation of faculty and administration, a condition which Hancher had been content to perpetuate. At Grinnell, on the other hand, Bowen had seen the advantages of working with a vocal and power-ful faculty, and he had vivid recollections of the consequences of his failure to consult effectively with the faculty at Illinois. In his inaugural address he remarked that "the work of a university is teaching and research. The basic policies must be shaped primarily by academic considerations. If this is to happen, the faculty must take part in the policy-making of each col-lege and of the university at large."[5]

The "somewhat dispirited" condition in which Bowen found the Iowa faculty was attributed to low salaries, inadequate facilities and equipment, weak participation of the faculty in the government of the institution, and heavy teaching loads. In the absence of adequate incentive to identify with the university as a whole, collegiate and departmental faculties were con-cerned primarily with their own affairs and had little sense of institutional responsibilities. Salaries and facilities would have to await legislative ac-tion, but the improvement of faculty morale was a matter on which some steps could be taken immediately. The president announced that he and Dean Boyd would work closely with the Faculty Council and that a Fac-ulty Senate would be organized. Faculty membership on university stand-ing committees would be increased, and the Faculty Council rather than the president would designate the faculty members for these positions.[6]

The new president's first report to the faculty breathed the positive and optimistic spirit which was to characterize his administration. He sensed that the tide was running with the university, which had the potential for great advancement. The prospect of rapid growth presented the oppor-tunity to strengthen the university with many new faculty appointments. Indeed, there was much catching up to be done, since the student-faculty ratio of 14.2 to one in 1939–40 had increased to 19.0 in 1966–67. Faculty recruitment was thus the most important immediate problem. Bowen es-timated that 150 new faculty members would be needed annually for five years in order to reduce the student-faculty ratio, offset enrollment increases, and provide replacements for retirements and resignations. This would amount to a fifty percent faculty turnover in five years, an extraordinary opportunity to affect faculty quality. Aggressive recruitment should be a constant obligation of every department. It would not be enough to commence a search when a vacancy occurred. There should be an ongoing evaluation of current work in each field, with particular attention to younger scholars. To finance these positions the board agreed to request of the legislature a thirty-three percent increase in the operating budget of the university, amounting to $18,000,000, with an even larger amount for capital expenditures.

As frosting on the cake, so to speak, the president promised that in addition to the normal recruitment activities he would authorize the appointment each year of five new professors of outstanding distinction, as well as five visiting professors. He was setting aside $100,000 to finance these appointments wherever quick action might be necessary. Members of the faculty were reminded that in their recruitment efforts they should emphasize Iowa's favorable salaries, improved fringe benefits and facilities, research support, moving expenses, housing assistance, and favorable living environment. Among Bowen's predecessors only Jessup and MacLean had a similar determination to attempt a quantum leap into the front rank of American universities. It remained to be seen whether the state and, indeed, the university itself would sustain such an effort.[7]

The recruitment of a distinguished faculty should go hand in hand with comprehensive educational planning at all levels of the university. Bowen urged each unit to engage in systematic long-range planning, to be implemented in sequential stages. The dean of faculties was to work with selected units on the implementation of their plans. Matters to be considered included appropriate course offerings, possible off-campus programs, research institutes, and service agencies. Staff needs, including size of the faculty, qualifications and duties, research expectations, criteria for appointment and promotion, and the appropriate use of teaching assistants, should also be analyzed. The most effective teaching methods, whether in large or small classes, opportunities for independent study, the use of television, and separate courses for undergraduate and graduate students should be examined too. Extra funds to implement these plans would be available, depending on the merits of the proposals.[8]

It was taken for granted that the faculty was committed to research. Bowen decisively dismissed the old bugaboo of the presumed incompatibility of teaching and research. At a major university this could no longer be an open question. Research was essential to good teaching at the university level. The occasional exception merely proved the rule. Professors were expected to divide their time between the two functions and were culpable if they neglected either. The university had always made specific provision for teaching assignments, while it had left research time to be claimed by the faculty members from what was left after the discharge of teaching duties. Bowen proposed to integrate research more closely into the academic schedule by making specific provision for research time. A faculty committee which he appointed to study the matter recommended that leaves of absence for research in the order of one hundred per semester be granted to those presenting promising research proposals. While he was sympathetic to the committee's objective the president believed that a "leave of absence" connoted a departure from the regular routine, whereas he preferred a procedure which would locate research in the regular schedule of academic work.[9]

The university traditionally offered both nine-month (two semesters) and eleven-month (two semesters and summer session) appointments. Administrators and certain faculty members held eleven-month appointments; the remainder served for nine months, although they were eligible for optional summer-session appointments whenever enrollments justified them. Bowen proposed the radical innovation of abandoning nine-month appointments and placing the entire faculty on an eleven-month basis with provision for research time free of teaching. All faculty members would be considered full-time workers and would be treated alike, sharing summer-session teaching and research assignments in rotation. The goal to be achieved within three or four years, and at a cost of about $1,250,000, would be a research assignment for each faculty member of one and one-half semesters (summer session equaling one-half) every three years. Research time would thus be integrated into the regular full-time appointment. Bowen did not, however, propose to make this arrangement mandatory. Those who chose to do so might have a nine-month appointment, which would now be considered to be a part-time appointment without eligibility for summer teaching. He suggested that the plan could be implemented voluntarily by colleges or by departments. The response to this proposal, made within a few months of his inauguration, was the first hint of the disagreements within the administration which were to frustrate him in his efforts for reform. Although the Faculty Council reacted favorably to the proposal the two most powerful deans, Hardin in medicine and Stuit in liberal arts, opposed it on the ground that a majority of the faculty favored a nine-month appointment with the prospect of an optional summer-session appointment. In other words, they opposed the integration of research time into the standard faculty appointment.[10] Without support of the deans Bowen preferred not to pursue the matter.

Closely associated with the emphasis on research was Bowen's determination to strengthen the university's library facilities and holdings. The main library which had been under construction for nearly twenty years was to be completed, with a final addition doubling its existing size. Over a five-year period the allocation of funds for the acquisition of books and other library materials would be doubled. Plans were announced for a health sciences library serving the medical, dental, pharmacy, and nursing colleges, speech pathology, and their associated hospitals and clinics on the west-side campus. Enlargements were to be made in the engineering, law, and education libraries. These added facilities would permit the doubling of library holdings within a decade and would require a substantial increase in the library staff.[11]

It seemed only appropriate that the revitalized spirit of the university should be symbolized by the adoption of a new name. The word "state" had always played a confusing role in the designation of the institution as the State University of Iowa, since it was the word commonly used throughout the country to designate the land grant institution. In earlier times the university itself had often been referred to as "the Iowa State University." The confusion was compounded in 1959 when Iowa State College became Iowa State University. In October 1964 the regents adopted Bowen's proposal that while keeping the traditional name for legal purposes the university thereafter be known in current usage as the University of Iowa.[12]

The growth of the university, which had faltered briefly in the early 1950s with the graduation of veterans of the Second World War, resumed its steady pace in the 1960s. During the five years of the Bowen administration on-campus enrollments increased from 14,500 in 1964–65 to 19,500 in 1968–69. These figures do not include large annual enrollments in off-campus, correspondence, and short courses. With the postwar baby boomers now of college age, the steady increase in disposable family income, the availability of more student aid, and the growing demand for professional and technical people, Bowen anticipated that the university would double in size between 1965 and 1980, a projection which proved to be roughly accurate. Growth of this magnitude would require a much larger faculty, new instructional facilities and housing, and reshaped educational and research programs. Much of the president's time was devoted to planning the means for coping with these anticipated increases.[13]

He did not, however, regard growth as an unmixed blessing. It had the potential for transforming the university into a vast impersonal bureaucracy which could stifle the very qualities that the university should be most concerned to cultivate. Growth should be controlled by raising admissions standards, especially in the Liberal Arts College where most of the larger enrollments were expected to occur. More rigorous admissions standards in mathematics, English, and foreign languages would reduce the number of freshman admissions, minimize remedial work, and shift the emphasis in liberal arts to the upperclass years.[14]

Bowen was also concerned to increase the enrollment of women and minority students. In the academic year 1929–30 women had constituted forty-six percent of the student body, while in 1964–65 the proportion had shrunk to thirty-five percent. In the latter year only one woman was enrolled in engineering. Of the 692 students in medicine 40 were women, but that number included interns, residents, and postdoctoral students. Most of the women were in liberal arts, where they numbered 3,682, or forty-five percent of the 8,111 students in that college. The president urged that positive steps be taken to increase the number of women students. It would be more difficult to increase the number of minority students. The small black communities of the state had not traditionally sent students to the university, and no effort had been made to recruit them. Bowen emphatically affirmed the university's commitment to human rights. Passive nondiscrimination would not be enough; there must be an active effort to recruit, finance, counsel, and assist underprivileged students, although he did not propose that academic standards be relaxed in their favor. A university Committee on Human Rights was established, and a counselor to minority students was appointed. Bowen personally solicited the faculty and alumni for contributions to a Martin Luther King, Jr., Scholarship Fund. Exchanges of faculty members on visiting appointments were arranged with LeMoyne-Owen and Rust colleges. An Afro-American Studies Program was established and an Afro-American Center opened.[15]

Housing the expected influx of students was a matter which required immediate attention. The university was predominantly a residential institution and Bowen was determined to keep it that way. Good residential conditions were an essential element of a quality education. Dormitories for single students and apartments for married students should be available for approximately a third of the student body. Another substantial fraction would find quarters in fraternities and sororities. A fraternity man himself, Bowen was favorably disposed toward these self-selected groups. He thought it desirable that a large student body should be divided into small groups where the individual would have congenial associates and a sense of belonging. There must of course be no racial or ethnic discrimination. Later in the decade, when the campus was rocked by disturbances, it did not escape the president's notice that certain of the dormitories were centers of unrest, while the fraternities and sororities remained largely unaffected. The gradual removal of wartime "temporary" Quonset hut housing for married students necessitated the building of the Hawkeye Village apartments and the purchase of the Mayflower apartments. In general Bowen believed that no class of students should be required to live in university housing, although he acknowledged that debt servicing for the new dormitories might make it obligatory for freshmen. But he also believed that dormitories should be more than merely facilities for sleeping and eating. They should play an important role in the intellectual and social life of the university. He encouraged departments to schedule classes in the dormitories and at least toyed with the idea of introducing an "academic college" or house plan.[16]

Dormitory construction proceeded rapidly. Kate Daum Hall on Clinton Street was already being built when Bowen arrived. It was followed by Carrie Stanley, Rienow, Slater, and the Hawkeye Village. Plans were drawn for Melrose Towers, a cluster of three dormitories for men and women which would house 2,090 students. Revised estimates of future enrollments failed to justify the need for this facility, plans for which were shortly abandoned. The same fate overtook the projected Harrison Hall, a minimum-cost coeducational dormitory for 1,134 students. Housing in town had traditionally been provided in private homes, but now the beginning of a boom in apartment building in Iowa City and Coralville promised a substantial supplement to university housing.[17]

Bowen's administration was indisputably the university's greatest era of building. At the end of a forty-year "dry spell" in which virtually no construction had taken place he found the campus run down and shabby, littered with temporary structures and cheap additions. He believed that in important if intangible ways the style and appearance of a campus had an effect on the spirit of its activities, and he was determined to provide the physical facilities appropriate to the renewed intellectual vitality which he hoped to stimulate. He succeeded in persuading the regents and the legislature to abandon the tradition of employing local architects, and he was able to incorporate landscaping costs into the building budgets. The firm of Sasaki and Associates was retained to develop a campus plan. The arts campus on the west side of the river adjacent to the Art Building and Theatre Building, consisting of the museum, Music Building, Hancher Auditorium, and an addition to the Art Building, was designed by Harrison and Abramovitz. The equally distinguished firm of Skidmore, Owings, and Merrill designed the new buildings of the health sciences complex.[18] Other new construction included the English-Philosophy Building, the Spence Psychological Laboratory, Phillips Hall, Van Allen Hall, the Wendell Johnson Speech and Hearing Center, a South Wing of the General Hospital, and additions to the Biology Building and the main library. Projects under construction or funded at the time of Bowen's departure included the Art Museum, Dental Science Building, Hancher Auditorium, Music Building, Recreation Building, Basic Medical Science Building, Nursing Building, and further additions to the library, hospital, Biology Building, and Chemistry-Botany Building. A building program of this magnitude would not have been possible without a very substantial increase in the capital budget. Bowen estimated the total cost of the program to be some $125,000,000, financed by state appropriations, revenue bonds, federal grants, and private gifts.

The increase in capital expenditures was paralleled by the growth of the operating budget, which doubled during the Bowen years, from $54,000,000 in 1963–64 to $104,000,000 in 1968–69. An ever growing portion of the operating budget was borne by students in the form of tuition increases. In 1952–53 students had paid eight percent of the cost of their university education; by 1967–68 the students' share had risen to twenty-five percent. The regents were disturbed by the mounting burden on the students in a public university, but when the legislature refused to provide what the regents considered to be their minimum needs there was little choice but to raise tuition. Bowen proposed to offset the burden with a national program of outright grants for needy students and loans for which no means test would be required. Resentment over tuition increases was one of the issues which fueled the campus unrest of 1968–71.[19]

The state of Iowa participated in the nationwide trend to transform agricultural and mechanical colleges and teachers' colleges into universities. It was more than a mere change of designation, for many of these institutions sought to be universities in fact as well as name. Locally the proliferation of specialized graduate degree programs at Iowa State and the University of Northern Iowa imposed added burdens on scarce resources and intensified the perennial rivalry for public financial support. The Committee on Educational Coordination which the board had established in 1951, consisting of representatives of each of the three institutions, was expected to control duplication. But the intent of the board was easily circumvented by subdividing fields of study in order to introduce new subspecialties not being offered at one of the other institutions. Thus while graduate work in history had always been within the province of the University of Iowa, Iowa State felt justified in introducing graduate programs in agricultural history and the history of science.

Bowen was resolved not to repeat what he believed to have been Hancher's mistake of resenting encroachments on the university's mission. He was determined to maintain friendly relations with his rivals and proposed that the three presidents work together in formulating legislative askings, presenting a united front to regents, governor, and legislature. He found, however, that cordiality did not mitigate the power struggle, and that the university was at a disadvantage. Statements of mission drafted by the three presidents in January 1967 indicated extensive overlapping of programs in the arts and sciences. While the University of Iowa was seeking only to strengthen its existing programs, the other two institutions were introducing new graduate degree programs in the arts and sciences and in business administration, all of which fell within the mission of the university. Rather than oppose these innovations Bowen took the position that the university's need to improve its existing programs should have equal priority with the proposals of the other institutions to establish new programs.[20] The inability or unwillingness of the regents to control duplication meant that none of the universities was adequately supported.

LIBERAL ARTS PROBLEMS

After a year in office in which he had an opportunity to study the university in all its aspects Bowen issued a comprehensive book-length report which quickly became known as "the Green Book."[21] Although the report took up the full range of topics, from admissions policies to extension programs and financial matters, its central concern was undergraduate education. In contrast to the generally positive tone of his discussion of university affairs in general, Bowen was highly critical of current trends in liberal education. He found that disciplinary specialization and a strong preprofessional emphasis had undermined the traditional pursuit of a liberal education as a unifying intellectual experience. The faculty was oriented toward research and the training of graduate students. Without in any way weakening or undermining graduate study the problem as he saw it was to revivify undergraduate education by strengthening the unity of the Liberal Arts College.

In the report he addressed himself not to the substance of a liberal education but to the instructional methods currently in use. In general he found that the routine of frequent classes, textbooks, and examinations resulted in the passive absorption of information rather than the active pursuit of learning which should launch the student on a lifelong course of intellectual activity. Bowen would reduce the number of courses offered and the number elected by students by eliminating many of the one-, two-, and three-hour courses and by offering four credit hours for three-hour courses. These reductions would free the faculty from hours in the classroom and allow time for individual guidance of students in independent study. Lecturing should preferably be restricted to a few large courses taught by senior professors of proven skill and authority. Students should spend less time in the classroom and more time in the library, and Bowen proposed to double the library budget in anticipation of the heavier library use which would result from a greater emphasis on independent projects.[22]

Major attention was paid to the extensive use of graduate students as teaching assistants (TAs). It was, in Bowen's opinion, the aspect of undergraduate education most in need of improvement. About a quarter of all undergraduate instruction was being provided by TAs, while for freshmen the proportion was as high as forty percent. The university was a leading center for the training of college teachers. Between 1953 and 1963 it had awarded 1,592 Ph.D. degrees, and eighty-three percent of the recipients had entered the teaching profession. But these graduates had received no training designed specifically to prepare them for teaching. Many of them had been TAs, in which capacity they may or may not have had the benefit of guidance and supervision by experienced senior faculty members. The graduate faculty in the liberal arts had always held the view that prospective teachers should know the subject and beyond that could safely be left to their own devices. In practice beginners looked back to their own teachers as models, counting themselves lucky if they were capable, but all too often perpetuating sloppy or counterproductive techniques.

Bowen was fully aware that the university was vulnerable in its extensive reliance on TAs. He knew that the private colleges often boasted that their students were taught exclusively by full-time experienced teachers. He proposed, therefore, to reform the use of TAs by upgrading their status as four-year "honor" appointees, to raise their stipends, to provide for annual advancement in teaching responsibility and independence, and to require all to participate in symposia and lectures on teaching methods. He urged the faculty to give serious thought to ways in which to improve the preparation of college teachers, even going so far as to raise the vexed question of a special degree program for college teachers. The Graduate College was ordered to develop specific proposals to implement the plan.[23]

The faculty response to this aspect of the report was not long in forthcoming. At a meeting with Bowen the Faculty Council welcomed the proposed increase in stipends for TAs as well as the annual increments based on experience and performance, but it objected strongly to other aspects of the proposal. Teaching assistants had always been appointed by the departments and paid from the departmental budgets in the Liberal Arts College or other undergraduate colleges (Business Administration, Engineering, Nursing). Council members objected strongly to the proposal of a Graduate College role in the appointment and administration of teaching assistantships. They insisted that the departments retain full control over the use of TAs. They also pointed out that because the utilization of TAs varied widely from one department to another it would be inappropriate to require participation by all of them in a teaching tutorial program. Dissatisfaction with the president's proposals arose in part from the fact that in the science departments research assistantships paid from research grants carried more money and prestige than did teaching assistantships. Scientists objected to the proposed subordination of research appointments to teaching.[24]

This was Bowen's first encounter with the conservatism of a complacent faculty. He was forced to agree that the departments were free to appoint, promote, or discharge TAs without the approval of the Graduate College. Nevertheless, he ordered Dean Spriestersbach to proceed with the planning of a program for the more effective use of TAs. The dean and his staff labored for two years to produce a plan which would be acceptable to the departments. In its final form the plan provided for teaching-research fellowships, four-year appointments for which departments choosing to participate could nominate superior candidates. One year of the fellowship was to be devoted to the fellow's own research. Although the Graduate College would make the appointments from among candidates recommended by the departments the latter were assured that they would have full control of their fellows. Supervision of performance and provision for pedagogical instruction, if any, were to be left to the discretion of the departments. The number of teaching-research fellows amounted to only a fraction of the total number of TAs. In the end Bowen's hope for a plan to enhance teaching effectiveness boiled down to a new category of TA to which a year for personal research was added.[25]

Another problem in liberal arts which distressed Bowen was presented by the School of Religion, one of the units of the college. Over the years the school's sponsors had been successful in transferring an increasing proportion of the cost of its program to the university budget. By 1965 some sixty-five percent of its expenditures came from the university appropriation, with the remainder from denominational, foundation, and private sources. The school's trustees welcomed the trend while acknowledging that faculty members should be selected "primarily" for their scholarly competence without "primary" attention to religious affiliation. But at the same time the trustees reaffirmed the historic affiliation of the school with its Catholic, Protestant, and Jewish constituencies and expressed the desire that faculty appointees continue to have the support of their respective religious groups.[26]

The conflicting objectives inherent in the relationship were exposed by the B'nai B'rith and Hillel foundations, which informed Dean Stuit that Professor Frederick Bargebuhr, whose salary they furnished, was no longer acceptable as professor of Jewish studies. The dean was told that the foundations would fund the appointment of a professor of Jewish studies if Bargebuhr were relieved of this responsibility and transferred to the university budget. These proposals were approved by the school's Jewish trustees and by its director, Robert Michaelsen. Over his protest, Bargebuhr was relieved of his course in Old Testament and another Jewish scholar was added to the faculty. Dean Stuit saw nothing wrong with these arrangements so long as the scholarly expectations of faculty appointees were maintained.[27] Not everyone shared the dean's complacency. A candidate to succeed Michaelsen as director of the school raised the same disturbing questions that the AAUP had earlier raised concerning the dismissal of Moses Jung. If the study of religion was academically legitimate and necessary, should not the state take full responsibility for its staffing and financing? Could there be complete freedom of inquiry and teaching unless it was wholly clear that the scholar's loyalty was unconditionally defined by the objectives and standards of the university? And, most pertinently, was it clear that the university alone had final authority to hire and assign duties to its faculty? The questioner did not ask whether the university might willingly surrender these rights, but the possibility may have occurred to him, for he withdrew his candidacy for the directorship.[28]

President Bowen also was disturbed by the dependence of the school upon its sectarian patrons. He realized that the tendency of donors to intrude upon university decisions constituted a potential or actual threat to academic freedom. He proposed to the regents that the constitution of the school be changed "gradually and tactfully" so that its faculty would be appointed by the university and be subject to the same conditions of salary, tenure, and assignment of duties as other faculty members. Denominational contributions should be made to the school as a whole and not for specific faculty positions. For its part the school would assure its patrons that the three traditional faiths would continue to be represented in the curriculum and that the study of Buddhism, Hinduism, and Islam would also be available.[29]

Thanks to Bowen's initiative, the university was better prepared to deal with the next challenge to the autonomy of the School of Religion. Fr. Robert Stenger, assistant professor of Catholic theology, announced in 1970 that he was resigning from the priesthood, although he intended to remain in the Catholic church as a layman. His salary was furnished by the Diocese of Davenport, and Bishop Gerald O'Keefe demanded that he be dismissed from the faculty. This time the university did not bow to the pressure as it had earlier in the case of Moses Jung; nor did it reassign Stenger as it had Bargebuhr. Dean Stuit informed the bishop that university regulations required that a year's notice of intention not to reappoint an assistant professor was necessary. Stenger's salary for the remainder of his term of appointment was paid from university funds. The bishop was also informed that henceforward faculty appointments in the School of Religion would be made by the university and would conform as to salary, promotion, and tenure with other university appointments. The bishop gave some thought to withdrawing Catholic support from the school, but finally agreed to maintain it provided that he would have the privilege of "presenting" candidates for the Catholic chair, it being understood that such candidates would possess the credentials expected of all faculty appointees. Under these terms he presented Fr. John Boyle, which proved to be an eminently successful appointment.[30]

ADMINISTRATIVE ORGANIZATION

B owen found administrative understaffing to be one of the more serious problems facing the university. The staff was essentially unchanged since the day when there were less than 10,000 students and a limited research program. The percentage of the budget allocated to administration was steadily declining. Additional staff positions were especially needed in view of the rapid rate of growth. He believed that the recruitment of new faculty was lagging at least in part for want of administrative support. Several colleges and departments needed associate or assistant deans and administrative or technical assistants. In his first year he authorized the appointment of associate and assistant deans in medicine, dentistry, and the Graduate College.[31]

Understaffing was only part of the problem in the Liberal Arts College and Medical College, which Bowen found to be in need of general reorganization. In medicine he was able to move decisively, while in liberal arts the dean and faculty effectively resisted his proposals for reform. A statement drafted by Dean Stuit and endorsed by the elected college committees and departmental executive officers served notice on the president that the Liberal Arts College was not in a mood to tamper with its administrative organization. Dean and faculty were agreed on the virtues of a "lean" administration in which each of some forty executive officers enjoyed direct access to the dean. Responsibility for decisions was thus kept close to the operational level. Schools or divisions within the college should not be imposed arbitrarily, but should emerge spontaneously in response to felt needs. Under this system much responsibility remained in the hands of the departmental executive officer, who was relied upon by the dean to initiate decisions concerning curriculum, appointments, promotions, and salary increments. The dean acknowledged that he could not personally oversee or evaluate the work of each member of the large faculty under his jurisdiction. He relied upon the departmental executive, whom he regarded as occupying the primary level of administration.[32] The system presumably worked well as long as there was general satisfaction with the status quo, but it was ill-suited to the needs of a reform-minded administration.

Composed of more than forty schools and departments, the College of Liberal Arts was so large and diversified that there was little or no feeling of collegiality among its faculty. Many of them were wholly absorbed in their own departmental programs. The diversity of interests and academic backgrounds, ranging from traditional liberal arts subjects to occupational and practical fields, was so great that there was a mutual lack of respect and trust which prevented the faculty from agreeing upon common standards to be implemented by college-wide committees. Individual departments preferred to establish their own goals and priorities in direct negotiations with the dean. The periodic occasions when revision of the core curriculum was being considered brought the tensions to the surface.

Following Bowen's call for a review of the administrative structure Dean Stuit appointed a special committee to review the organization of the college and to bring to the faculty such recommendations as it thought desirable. It consisted of three members of the Educational Policy Committee, three from the Executive Committee, and three present or former directors of schools. The dean was presumably confident that these individuals shared his views, which proved to be substantially the case. The committee prepared a questionnaire soliciting faculty opinion on administrative matters to which only a third of the faculty bothered to respond, a fact which reflected either indifference or satisfaction with the status quo. Those who did respond preferred the existing organization to such alternatives as subject-matter divisions, parallel colleges, undergraduate/graduate divisions, or underclass/upperclass divisions. The humanities and social science faculties in particular favored the existing arrangement most strongly. The faculty was largely indifferent to the work of its elected committees, but it strongly opposed any involvement of these committees in faculty appointments, promotions, or curricular decisions above the core level. The low repute in which the faculty held its own elected committees doubtless reflected its satisfaction with a system in which departmental executive officers had direct access to the dean. Practice had shown that this was an effective means of preserving departmental autonomy.[33]

In its formal report the committee was content to be guided by prevailing faculty sentiment, although it recognized several weaknesses which should be addressed. It endorsed the existing organizational structure of the college while recommending the appointment of an associate dean whose functions were unspecified. It acknowledged wide divergencies in the quality of departments and proposed regular periodic reviews of departmental performance. It reported some feeling that undergraduate teaching was in need of improvement and that more effective counseling of underclassmen would be desirable. In the main, however, the report failed to convey a sense of urgency, and, save for the inauguration of departmental reviews, which was to become a university-wide policy, no significant action resulted.[34]

RESEARCH SUPPORT

An important development during the Bowen administration was the beginning of an attempt to rationalize the financial support of research. This was to be the work of Duane Spriestersbach, graduate dean and vice-president for research. The Graduate College faculty, consisting of those of all professorial ranks in each of the colleges, was the closest thing to a functioning university-wide faculty, although its activities were of course confined to graduate education. While professional college fac-

ulties were also members of the graduate faculty, the supervision of professional degree programs did not fall within the province of the Graduate
College; consequently the affairs of that college were peripheral to their
concerns. The liberal arts faculty was the principal constituency of the
Graduate College, and the relationships between the two entities were intimately intertwined. Since the days of Seashore, Graduate College functions had been allowed to atrophy, the management of graduate programs
being taken over for all practical purposes by the instructional colleges and
departments. John Weaver, who came from Nebraska as graduate dean in
1961, stipulated that he should also hold the title of vice-president for research. Weaver began the process of strengthening the office of the graduate dean by obtaining Hancher's consent to adding a line for the graduate
dean's signature on professorial appointment forms, over the strenuous
objection of Dean Stuit. These appointees were, after all, members of the
graduate faculty.

Following Hancher's retirement and Weaver's resignation, Bowen appointed Spriestersbach, a professor of speech pathology, graduate dean.[35]
Although a wide search had been conducted, Dean Stuit complained that
he had not been consulted and accused Bowen of "throwing his weight
around." Strained personal relations simply accentuated the problems
arising from the overlapping of the Graduate College with the other instructional colleges. In theory the Graduate College was in charge of the
graduate degree programs of the university. In practice the other colleges,
by virtue of their control of salary budgets and the appointment process,
virtually ignored the Graduate College in making decisions on programs
and personnel. Spriestersbach protested to Bowen that appointments of
faculty members and department executives were being made without
consulting him, even though consideration of graduate education and research was involved. He discovered that the reorganization of the Medical
College had been underway without his knowledge of it. Proposals to establish separate liberal arts departments of linguistics, sociology, and anthropology were presented to the regents without consulting the graduate
dean, even though a prime purpose was to offer new graduate degree programs in these fields which would eventually come to the Graduate College for approval.[36]

While he was frustrated in his efforts to strengthen the role of the
Graduate College in its nominal function of supervising graduate education, Spriestersbach found an outlet for his energies in developing machinery for obtaining financial support for research. He requested and received the title of vice-president for research. In order to make a major

effort in fund raising he needed to add sixteen persons to his staff and triple the size of his budget. When Bowen replied that he expected to receive ten dollars for every dollar invested in fund raising, Spriestersbach assured him that with a budget of $165,000 he could raise $16,500,000 and that a major university should not hesitate to spend that amount. When Stuit objected to what he considered to be a wasteful and unnecessary duplication of services Spriestersbach pointed out that the $4,337,396 received for research projects in liberal arts in 1968 had involved the development of more than one hundred grant applications with the assistance of his staff. Over three million dollars in construction funds had also been received under the Higher Education Facilities Act. Income in these amounts clearly justified the expansion of his office. A major achievement was the receipt in 1967 of a National Science Foundation grant of $5,101,000 to establish a Center of Excellence in the Biological Sciences. Eight departments in medicine and liberal arts would receive support for research in genetics, endocrinology, and neurobiology. The grant would help to support forty new faculty positions and thirty additional graduate assistants. In order to house these activities a portion of the grant would aid in the construction of a basic medical science building and an addition to the zoology building. The former of these buildings would appropriately be named for Bowen.[37]

THE CAMPUS UPRISING

As it became increasingly apparent during the first two years of his administration that the implementation of reforms would require a sustained and concerted effort on Bowen's part, his attention was diverted in ever increasing measure by the campus uprising precipitated by the Vietnam War. Turmoil came to the Iowa campus relatively late, and it never attained the degree of violence or destructiveness that occurred on several other campuses. Much of the activity was imitative in character, as though the students felt that they must do what was being done elsewhere in order to keep their self-respect. Bowen noted that several of the ringleaders were non-Iowans, confirming his assessment of Iowans as a moderate and sensible people. Nevertheless, a succession of demonstrations over a period of more than three years generated mounting tension which came to a head in the spring of 1970 with the Cambodian incursion, the Kent State tragedy, and the burning of the rhetoric building. The atmosphere of frenzy which then gripped the campus certainly represented the failure of education to develop the qualities of mind which should have resisted the spread of crowd psychology. The frenzy also elevated to prominence some of the less attractive among the campus population—unstable types, drug pushers, opportunists—as well as a few dedicated radicals.

Local demonstrations against the Vietnam intervention began in October 1965 with a march around the business district, draft card burning, and Student Senate recognition of the local chapter of Students for a Democratic Society (SDS). Bowen remarked that he believed strongly "that the campus environment should scintillate as a forum for the discussion of contemporary issues." His hopes were to be realized in a measure doubtless greater than he would have preferred.[38] In order to quell fears that the academic standing of students would be taken into account by draft boards when considering student deferments he announced that no information would be released other than the fact of registration and degree status without the consent of the student. Assurances of this sort did not mollify students who were persuaded that the university was in complicity with the military-industrial complex. The major event of the year was the announcement by assistant professor of sociology and anthropology Donald Barnett that he would not submit student course grades as a protest against the government's Vietnam policy. Barnett had been appointed to a three-year term in 1965 and had just been notified that the appointment would not be renewed; he had little to lose by failing to comply with university regulations. His announcement received widespread press publicity damaging to the university, whose scrupulous adherence to disciplinary procedures angered patriots like state representative Charles Grassley, who demanded summary dismissal. Perhaps more important was the signal it sent to the students that a faculty member was seemingly prepared to sacrifice his career in the cause. From this point onward campus demonstrations were not simply student affairs; there were always a small number of faculty supporters who either openly or covertly encouraged the demonstrators.[39]

Sit-ins and the blocking of access to recruiters for such hated employers as the CIA, the Marines, and Dow Chemical Company became the principal forms of protest during 1967. The first large-scale confrontation occurred on the first of November, when an organized attempt was made to block access to Marine recruiters in the Memorial Union. A flier circulated by SDS announced the intention to "stop the Marines" and to support the Vietnamese people in their struggle for liberation. Bowen declared that the right of student access to recruiters would be assured, that local and state police would be called upon if necessary, and that students violating university regulations would be subject to disciplinary action. Thus forewarned, some 200 well-organized demonstrators blocked the east entrance to the Union, where a large crowd of counterdemonstrators and observers gathered. Following refusal of the demonstrators to disperse, local and state police arrested 101 persons for disturbing the peace. Seventy students were subsequently placed on probation. Twenty-two of those arrested were nonstudents. None of the counterdemonstrators was arrested, a fact which was made much of by the demonstrators. Two days later blood was spilled on the Union steps and a large crowd marched to Old Capitol to present Bowen with blood-stained petitions denouncing the Vietnam War.[40]

The appearance on campus of local and state police represented the failure of the university to keep order in its own house. The university security forces were not police officers in the usual sense, lacking authority to carry arms or make arrests. The idea that the university should require a law enforcement agency was repugnant to the traditional image of a peaceful community of students and scholars. Accordingly, when violence erupted, demonstrators attempted to exploit the idea that the campus was a privileged sanctuary where they were immune from pursuit. On the other hand, if they were indeed adults it seemed reasonable to assume that they were subject to the same constraints as other citizens, on or off campus.[41] Contrary to carefully nurtured claims of police brutality the behavior of the law enforcement units was for the most part commendably restrained and professional in the face of calculated provocations. In Iowa City, unlike certain other university towns where the police were accustomed to look upon students as their natural enemies, there was happily no tradition of town-gown hostility. An observer of the uglier disruptions at Cornell University remarked that the most chilling aspect of the situation there was the widespread feeling that no one was in control. While the presence of the law enforcement officers at Iowa probably had little deterrent effect on the small hard core of radicals it did help to reassure the large number of students among whom fear of violence was rapidly growing.

During the spring of 1968 the mounting tension was expressed not so much in overt demonstrations as in individual acts of lawlessness. In March alone there were thirty-seven "fire incidents" in the men's dormitories, seventy-five acts of vandalism, thirty-eight grand larcenies, and fifty-six petty larcenies, all representing a great increase over the previous year. At the annual spring Governor's Day ROTC review, protesters presented petitions to Governor Hughes demanding the abolition of ROTC. Formerly mandatory for all male undergraduates, the ROTC requirement had gradually been reduced to a prescribed series of up to five lectures. Bowen now proposed to the regents—over the protest of Dean Stuit—that this requirement be abandoned, leaving only a voluntary program.[42] Such a concession did not, of course, placate the radicals. A local chapter of the New University Conference (NUC), a national organization of radical faculty and graduate students, was organized in September 1968, under the leadership of Professor Howard Ehrlich. Its announced purpose was to oppose the Vietnam War, end the draft, promote black liberation, fight discrimination against women, and introduce radical ideas into the university curriculum. Its recruiting brochure declared that it was dedicated to the creation of a democratic university in which faculty, students, and staff would all have a voice in its management. Bowen's conception of the university as a house of intellect was roundly denounced as a subterfuge for an institution subservient to the military-industrial complex.[43]

In the spring of 1969 the demonstrators enlarged the areas of their concern to include reform of the university. "Student Power" became a battle cry, forcing Bowen to attempt to instruct student leaders in the principle of delegation of authority. He admitted that the university could no longer stand *in loco parentis*, but so long as its various constituencies laid claim to powers not legally theirs he had no choice but to assert his own authority as the local representative of the regents in order to maintain an orderly campus.[44] The ultimate difference between Bowen and his campus critics turned upon their conception of the university as a political institution. An SDS brochure attacking the Code of Student Life put the radical position succinctly:

> The University is a major institution in this society. It is the prime supplier of the "specialized" manpower which keeps the other institutions running, the corporations, the military, the economic and political institutions. The University even supplies itself with the personnel necessary to train the next generation of students. Without trained manpower the key institutions would collapse; i.e., the University keeps the whole system running smoothly. In this context, the placement center, ROTC, and courses that are little more than apologies for the present economic and political systems, hold a central place in the *raison d'être* of the University.[45]

Nothing could be more remote from Bowen's traditional conception of the university as a house of intellect, "a place which is open to the truth and in which the truth is found through reason, discussion, and experiment, not through pressure, threats, and violence," a place where friendly rapport and mutual trust among students, faculty, and administration exist. Thinking in political terms, radical students conceived of themselves as a majority constituency deprived of the rights of participation in a democratic society. Bowen would go with them only so far as to concede that the political rights of freedom of thought and speech lay at the heart of the university, while also insisting that free speech entailed the obligation to listen and to observe the restraints of rational discussion. Time would test the limits of the radicals' tolerance.[46]

A more promising radical tactic, and one which appealed to a broader spectrum of the student body, was a proposal to offer a range of student services which had always been provided by Iowa City businesses. The Student Senate voted to organize a corporation which would sell life insurance, sponsor foreign travel, establish a bookstore, provide student cooperative housing, publish student manuscripts, and, of course, conduct and publish course and teacher evaluations. These activities would be financed by an allocation from student activity fees. Sympathetic though he was to this proposal as representing a more constructive form of student activism, Bowen was obliged to point out that student fees could not be used for these purposes. A symposium on student power sponsored by the Student Union Board in February 1969 was addressed by the nationally known radicals Tom Hayden and Harry Edwards. A delegation of conservative legislators attended the meeting and subsequently complained to the regents about the obscene language and inflammatory rhetoric of the speakers. State senator Francis Messerly demanded that the regents bar from the campus anyone who advocated the overthrow of the democratic form of government, apparently overlooking the fact that the radicals were among its most ardent advocates. The regents found the discussion with the legislators "rather unproductive." But they might well have been concerned for the loss of good will among a large sector of the public which had no sympathy for the more boisterous forms of campus protest.[47]

The demand for student power was also focused on the structure and curriculum of the university. The student body president, Jim Sutton, claimed that student participation in policy making was a matter of right and that their exclusion was one of the major causes of campus disruption. He demanded that student members be added to all university committees and that a Student-Faculty Senate with policy-making powers be created. On the academic side he proposed the creation of a College of General Education and a College of Fine and Applied Arts offering a bachelor's degree without a language requirement. He would also institute a new grading system which would "guarantee students the right to fail without penalty." Bowen responded that, while each of these proposals should be considered on its merits by an appropriate university agency, there was no student "right" to any arrangements. SDS took the next step by declaring that the only way to force the administration to accede to student demands was to shut down the university with a student strike. Students who continued to go to class were denounced as scabs who supported the administration and the ruling class.[48]

President Bowen unexpectedly resigned in the spring of 1969 to accept a professorship of economics at the Claremont Graduate School. He explained that he had done what he could to strengthen the university and that to remain longer would result in diminishing returns. He was sixty years old and was eager to resume his scholarly work in economics. He also acknowledged increasing fatigue and noted the adverse effects of the rigorous Iowa climate on the health of his wife; he had considered but rejected an invitation to return to Williams College in favor of the milder climate of Claremont. Neither publicly nor privately did he concede that the campus turmoil had been a factor in reaching the decision to depart. Nevertheless, there could be little doubt that the events of the previous three years bore heavily upon him. Apart from the general stress generated by the campus uprising he had been subjected to repeated acts of personal harassment. He had been confronted in his office by intruders who threatened him physically, obstructed his movements at home and on the campus, subjected him to citizen's arrest, and vandalized his office. His determination to maintain orderly university activities while defending full freedom of expression simply brought down upon him a torrent of abuse. Only a person less sensitive than Bowen could have willingly tolerated these additions to the normal burdens of the presidency.[49]

His successor, Willard L. Boyd, had been the academic vice-president and was closely identified with Bowen's administration. He continued the same moderate policies as his predecessor, maintaining the rights of freedom of speech and assembly while refusing to permit encroachment upon students' right of access to university facilities and services. Thus he refused to suspend classes on Vietnam Moratorium Day, October 15, 1969, although he encouraged students and faculty to participate in the protest activities of that day. Unlike Bowen, who refrained from publicly expressing his views on controversial public issues because he felt that they could not be separated from his official obligation to remain impartial, Boyd did not hesitate to express his personal opposition to the government's Vietnam policy. His sympathy for the demonstrator's position on public issues did not, however, deflect them from their attack on the university, which continued in a mounting crescendo through 1969 and 1970.[50]

One of the first tangible consequences of the campus turmoil was the ending of the generous budget increases which Bowen had been able to secure from the legislature. Faced with the prospect of an "unrealistic" cut in appropriations for the 1969–71 biennium, Bowen warned the students that a substantial tuition increase was inevitable. The Student Senate called for a boycott of classes; when the president summoned a meeting of faculty, student, and staff representatives to discuss the situation the Student Senate refused to send a delegation. Instead, student leaders confronted Bowen in his office and threatened him with citizen's arrest and subpoena of records. Inadequate appropriations during the 1970s was to be a continuing burden for the Boyd administration.[51]

In December 1969 a Labor Department employment interviewer was physically harassed and prevented from conducting interviews at the Union. The joint student-faculty Committee on Student Conduct which met to hear charges of misconduct in the matter was disrupted by friends of those charged and the Student Senate then withdrew the student members of the committee, rendering it inoperative. The Senate also declared the section of the Code of Student Life under which the committee functioned to be invalid. If it thought that it could force President Boyd to consult it on the creation of acceptable judicial machinery it misjudged the new president's resourcefulness. With his lawyer's sense of the importance of judicial continuity he invited a retired chief justice of the Iowa Supreme Court, Theodore Garfield, to act as hearing officer on charges of violation of the code and to recommend appropriate action to the president. The judge accepted the assignment, however distasteful it must have been to him, conducting quasi-judicial hearings resulting in several recommendations of probation or suspension which were carried out by the president.[52]

The protest movement came to a head in the spring of 1970, in reaction to the Cambodia incursion and the Kent State shootings. As President Boyd grimly remarked, before Cambodia the protesters numbered in hundreds—now they numbered in thousands. As tension on campus rapidly mounted the president moved his office from the Old Capitol to a less accessible secret location at Oakdale. On May 1 demonstrators forcibly occupied the Recreation Building, resulting in the cancellation of an ROTC awards ceremony. Four days later protestors marched to the National Guard Armory south of town, then back through the business district, trashing store windows. The New University Conference called for the cancellation of classes and the resignations of Boyd and Provost Heffner. On the evening of May 7 a peaceful sitdown of protestors on the east steps of Old Capitol resulted in the arrest on presidential order of over 200, following their refusal to disperse. Boyd was out of town on that day and had received information which led him to overestimate the seriousness of the situation.[53]

The annual Governor's Day exercises scheduled for May 9 were canceled by Boyd, who announced that he did so reluctantly in order to avoid the possibility of violence. Governor Robert Ray, who had come to Oakdale to lend Boyd his moral support, ordered the State Highway Patrol to patrol the campus, while a National Guard unit, the 34th Military Police battalion, was deployed at the fairgrounds, south of the town. On the same night, the rhetoric building, a "temporary" wartime wooden structure, burned to the ground, and a small fire also occurred in the old electrical engineering building at the corner of Iowa Avenue and Dubuque Street. The fact that the arsonists had shown commendable discrimination in choosing for the torch edifices which should long since have been torn down did not at the time relieve the mounting feeling of insecurity among the student body. Faculty monitors patrolled campus buildings, while the Student Senate voted to close the university. On Sunday, May 10, Boyd announced that, while the university would remain open, students who feared for their safety were free to withdraw without penalty. Such students were offered the options of taking incomplete grades, accepting a pass or withdrawal grade, or accepting a grade based on course work through May 3. Those who chose to withdraw must vacate their university housing within twenty-four hours. Some 11,796, nearly two-thirds of the student body, including 4,095 of the 4,750 who lived in dormitories, chose to withdraw. The remainder finished the semester, which ended on May 26.[54]

Whether or not he had foreseen it, the president's options succeeded in dividing his tormentors. Some declared that they had shut down the university and went home in triumph. Others, particularly the teaching assistants in the humanities core courses, angrily denounced the options as a strike-breaking tactic and went on strike. The *Daily Iowan* reported, however, that the strike, although it was supported by the Student Senate, had little deterrent effect on those who chose to remain in the university. Still others had second thoughts, realizing that if they had succeeded in shutting down the university they would have jeopardized their status as students, possibly exposing themselves to the scrutiny of their draft boards.

At least a few began to wonder whether attacking the university was the most appropriate tactic.

In the following week the Faculty Senate took up the controversial question of ROTC. Formerly a compulsory obligation for all male undergraduates, ROTC had become a voluntary program in the Liberal Arts College. A few faculty members had always questioned its appropriateness on educational grounds, but it had not been a divisive issue prior to the Vietnam era. Now, however, it became one of the principal targets of the campus protest movement, and it was the first issue to involve large numbers of faculty members. A Faculty Senate resolution recommended that with the expiration of the present contract ROTC be discontinued as an on-campus activity. Its sponsors were not deterred by the fact that it represented the incursion of an all-university body into the curriculum of the Liberal Arts College, something which would have been unthinkable in other circumstances. ROTC had become a political rather than an educational issue. By the narrow margin of thirty-one to thirty the Senate voted to adopt the resolution. It was a smashing victory in the eyes of the demonstrators, although the action was promptly repudiated by the president and summarily rejected by the regents.[55] In a subsequent straw poll of the faculty some seventy percent of those responding voted to retain ROTC, indicating that the Senate had not accurately reflected faculty opinion. It had been a carefully engineered triumph for the radicals, marking the high-water mark of the attack on the administration. Boyd was deeply distressed by the Senate vote. He thought of himself as the faculty's man, expecting that on a matter such as this it would support him. It seems unlikely that those who voted against ROTC thought that in doing so they were voting to overthrow his administration. They simply did not share his sense of the precariousness of the situation. President Bowen had felt that it was important to encourage more active involvement of the faculty in university affairs. While this was most immediately a matter of improving faculty morale it was also a strategy for inculcating in the faculty a more positive sense of joint responsibility for the welfare of the institution. Traditionally the faculty had regarded the administration as an alien entity. But in the face of the first serious challenge in the university's history to the continuity of its administrative authority such a simplistic attitude would have to be abandoned if faculty and administration were to make common cause against those who would disrupt it. As heir to the Bowen policies and as the faculty's choice Boyd could reasonably expect faculty members' support, especially on such an issue as ROTC, over which neither he nor they had effective control. For behind the university stood the regents and the legislature, and on this matter the ultimate authorities were adamantly opposed to concession.

Other evidence of the failure of a faculty group to perceive the turmoil as a crisis situation was furnished by the capture of the *Daily Iowan* by the New University Conference. The campus newspaper was controlled by Student Publications, Inc. (SPI), a faculty-student board which appointed a student editor annually as well as a publisher and a professional operating staff. In the spring of 1970 the board chose as its editor Leona Durham, a graduate student in English who was also a member of NUC and a well-known campus radical. The editor was privileged to appoint her own staff, and she selected several radicals for key editorial positions. The chairman of the SPI board naively said that he didn't care about Durham's political views, although he was favorably disposed toward her because of her "political awareness." Conflict immediately erupted between the new editorial board and the operating staff, who reported that they had been subjected to harassment and intimidation and who threatened to resign. The SPI board thereupon reversed itself and within a month of her appointment removed Durham from office, accusing her of threats, insults, and intimidation. Her lawyer claimed that the real reason for her dismissal was her radicalism and charged the board with political censorship. Sensitive to the charge of infringing upon the freedom of the press, the board appointed a fact-finding commission which recommended that Durham be restored as editor. The board now reversed itself again, and for the following year the *Daily Iowan* covered the news from the radical point of view. Reflecting her hostility to the business community the editor remarked that in trashing store fronts the demonstrators had chosen those establishments that had gouged students most mercilessly. Enraged businessowners withdrew their advertising from the paper, which quickly ran up a large deficit. Board members now came to the editor's defense, one of them characterizing the merchants as "boobs." The Durham episode illustrated the inability of a representative faculty group to define and adhere to a consistent conception of the university's best interest and of the responsibility to defend it.[56]

The events of May 1970 marked the high tide of the campus protest. Sporadic acts of violence continued throughout the academic year 1970–71, but they were the work of a small number of dissidents, some of them nonstudents, who were no longer able to mobilize mass student support. During the summer of 1970 the regents finally moved to assert a firmer control of campus affairs, announcing that they would not tolerate disruption of university functions or permit interference with the right of student access to university services. The use of injunctions was authorized, and students were warned that they would be disciplined for off-campus as well as on-campus infractions. Qualified members of the campus security force were given police officer status, with the power of arrest. Perhaps most important of all was the appearance on campus of the State Highway Patrolmen, whose presence had an immediate stabilizing effect. The demonstrations and rioting had frightened many students who saw that the university had no effective means of defending itself against determined demonstrators capable of acts of arson, destruction of business property, and harassment of university officials. The firm but calm and friendly demeanor of the patrolmen as they walked the campus conveyed to the vast majority of students a reassuring sense that disorder and violence would no longer ravage the campus unchecked. From that day the radicals lost control of the campus.[57] Following the Laos invasion of February 1971, when radicals called for a strike against the university, the Student Senate refused to support the strike call, and even Leona Durham pointed out that a strike would only deprive the protestors of their own base as students.

Faculty support of the demonstrators gradually dried up. Several of the senior faculty who had at first openly supported it quietly distanced themselves from the protest movement. Some of the younger radicals and teaching assistants left the university. By 1971 only Ehrlich and history professor Peter Larmour were still active in the NUC, and both of them shortly resigned from the university. The NUC chapter itself reorganized as a "collective" and passed its last days solemnly debating the role of violence in the revolution. The protest movement was dead even before the draft expired in July 1971.[58] Reflecting on the campus turmoil, Loren Hickerson, the university's director of community relations and former alumni secretary, remarked sadly that young people needed "to learn all over again, the hard way, in a new world, that discipline, and standards, and taste, and human dignity, and tolerance, and order are imperative for any freedom worthy of the name."[59]

The final event of that unhappy time, and perhaps the most ominous one, occurred on February 25, 1972, when Richard Herrnstein, a Harvard psychologist, was prevented by demonstrators organized by SDS from presenting a "research seminar" on the effects of rewards and punishments on the behavior of pigeons. This was the only occasion when an academic exercise at the university was actually disrupted, constituting a gross violation of academic freedom. Subsequent to his acceptance of the invitation from the psychology department but before coming to Iowa City Herrnstein published in the *Atlantic Monthly* an article entitled "IQ." In this article he traced the history of intelligence testing, discussed the interaction of the genetic and environmental factors involved, and summarized the correlations which had been established between IQ and occupational and ethnic groups. He had taken no personal position on this explosive issue; he had only laid out the pertinent findings on the subject. Nevertheless, even to discuss the topic gave great offense to radical fanatics whose movement was crumbling and who were desperately casting about for allies and supporters. Radicals in Cambridge denounced Herrnstein as a racist and resolved to hound him wherever he might appear. When it was announced by the psychology department that he would present a public seminar local SDSers began at once to plan a confrontation at which the visitor would be "questioned" about his IQ article.[60] The university authorities were aware of these plans and kept out-of-town demonstrators under surveillance. When the seminar hour came, however, the demonstrators easily outwitted the security officers who were to have prevented them from entering the lecture hall by infiltrating the room during the previous class period. When they were discovered in possession of the room a decision was made not to attempt to evict them. Posters denouncing Herrnstein as a racist and sexist decorated the walls, and some 300 people chanted slogans and delivered impromptu harangues. No effort was made to remove the signs or restore order. Knowing from previous experience what would happen if he attempted to speak, Herrnstein begged off and was taken to the Faculty Club in the Union for a reception, the demonstrators dogging his footsteps and literally driving him out of town.[61]

The response of university officials to this disgraceful episode left little doubt that they were woefully unprepared to make a vigorous defense of academic freedom. President Boyd was out of town, and his administrative assistant was quoted in the press as saying that departments "will think twice" before again inviting a controversial speaker.[62] Provost Ray Heffner, acting president in Boyd's absence, said nothing. In all probability nothing more would have been said publicly by anyone had not members of the Faculty Senate, astounded by the lack of response, challenged the administration and persuaded the Senate to launch an investigation. Provost Heffner then acknowledged that he had been remiss in not expressing his concern, and Boyd issued a memorandum in which he set forth his understanding of the issues involved in the episode, and indicated the way in which the university would deal with such matters in the future.

The president's memorandum made it clear that he failed to appreciate the difference between academic freedom and freedom of speech. He viewed the Herrnstein affair as a free speech issue. He insisted that an "open market place of ideas" was essential both for an educational institution and for a free society. He noted the university's long-established commitment to freedom of speech, and he acknowledged with regret its failure to sustain the commitment in Herrnstein's case. He pledged that in the future the university would adhere rigorously to the regents' rule on controversial speakers. This rule required that arrangements for such events should assure that the speaker be "subjected to questions from the audience" and that the meeting be presided over by a tenured faculty member, presumably as a means of assuring order and a balanced discussion.[63] There was nothing very reassuring about this, since the arrangements for Herrnstein's appearance had satisfied these requirements. The regents' rule was designed to permit students and staff members to hear diverse points of view from speakers sponsored by recognized student, faculty, and staff organizations. It was clearly intended to apply to public, extracurricular events, rather than to formal academic exercises, but the president appeared to apply it to any campus event in which the public might choose to show an interest. Freedom of speech is a public and political right, the right to persuade, and all free government rests upon it. Academic freedom, on the other hand, is a much narrower and more specialized right. It is the freedom to teach and to learn. It presupposes the presence of an expert, someone who possesses the best current information on the subject at hand, and it assumes the presence of a student who wants to acquire that information and perhaps even to learn to improve upon it. If the expert is "subjected to questions" these are hardly the challenges to moral sensitivity or political acumen characteristic of debate on public issues. They are either requests for clarification or critical inquiries into the methods and hypotheses which have led the expert to the conclusions. If academic freedom were to survive at the University of Iowa challenges to it would have to be met with a clearer understanding of its requirements than was evident in the response to the Herrnstein affair. The psychologist himself summed it up when he wrote to the chairman of the Iowa psychology department that "the universities have yet to recognize that their professed commitment to free speech or freedom of assembly has muzzled me."[64]

In attempting to understand the campus upheaval it is well to bear in mind that as an outgrowth of the liberal arts college the modern American university inherited many of the values and attitudes of its predecessor. The college had been a place for learning, of preparation for adult life. Its students were not yet adults, and the occasional riots and demonstrations which had punctuated college life were adolescent expressions of rebellion against restraints imposed upon the young and immature. Although there was still some vestige of this in the student unrest of the 1960s and 1970s, as evidenced in panty raids and dining hall riots, the situation had changed significantly. University attitudes had generally replaced college attitudes. The greater impersonality of the university left the students with a feeling of being on their own, which was certainly an element of adulthood. In the public universities, with their intermixing of undergraduate and graduate students, the feeling was accentuated.

At the same time the inability of the liberal arts faculty at Iowa to reconcile the claims of general and specialized education symbolized the ambivalent intent of the university with respect to its students. Its strong vocational emphasis oriented many students toward specific careers. For career-minded students the university had a definite role in their plans and was important to them in the achievement of their objectives. This was particularly the case for students in the professional colleges and for graduate students in the sciences. These students were relatively impervious to the appeals of the campus rebels. But there were many other students whose objectives were not so clearly focused. These tended to be concentrated in the less exact subjects such as literature, history, and sociology. For many of these students the university functioned as a kind of holding pattern while they struggled to define their objectives. They were exposed to events in the world outside the university without the kind of involvement in a disciplinary training process which would have insulated them. These students brought contemporary public issues into the university for the first time and furnished the core of the student movement.

What was distinctive about the campus uprising of the 1960s was the fact that it was precipitated by events external to the campus itself, notably the civil rights movement and the Vietnam War. The specific issues on campus—the prospect of compulsory military service, ROTC, CIA and Dow recruiters, and defense-related research—drew their animus from larger public issues. The old idea of the university as a place of preparation for life had begun to fade, at least for those whose vocational objectives were vague. For many students the university was becoming life itself, a regular part of the adult world. They became conscious of their identity as citizens and of their political role as student activists. As adults they demanded release from parietal rules and a share in the government of the university. They made it their institutional base and proceeded to exploit it for their own purposes. As adults they could make common cause with those faculty members and outsiders who shared their concerns. That many of them continued to display juvenile traits was a sorry commentary on the inadequate education to which they had been exposed.

In his effort to mold public response to the campus disturbances and to deflect hostile criticism Bowen repeatedly emphasized the mild and relatively peripheral character of the disorder. Following the Placement Office demonstrations of November and December 1967 he criticized the press for exaggerating the seriousness of the events, pointing out that no classroom or campus speaker had been disrupted and that only a tiny fraction of the student body had been involved. The disturbances at Iowa, he noted, did not begin to compare with those at Berkeley, Columbia, Ohio State, Northwestern, or Stanford.[65] In order to improve the public's understanding of the situation the president called attention to the remarkable change which had come over student attitudes in recent years. The former mood of apathy had given way to an active concern with such public issues as the Vietnam War, nuclear armaments, civil rights, and the urban ghetto. Aroused by these external problems it was not surprising that students should also discover a new interest in internal university affairs and demand a voice in curricular reform, abolition of parietal rules, and a share in university government. Critics often failed to credit the positive forms of public service rendered by students through such activities as legal aid, health care, the Peace Corps, and VISTA. "Without question," the president concluded, "because of the new student activism, the universities are intellectually and socially more aware and awake than they were a decade ago, though they are less orderly."[66]

Internally, however, when he addressed the university community, Bowen took a far more serious view of the situation. When the demonstrators had attempted to block access to the placement facilities the good order of the university had been breached, and it had been necessary to summon external law enforcement agencies to restore order. The integrity and independence of the institution were threatened by external as well as internal forces. Editors and legislators demanded stern reprisal against the disrupters. Under attack from either side, Bowen was obliged to define the place of the university as an independent entity.[67]

He declared:

A university is partly ivory tower, and it must be so. If faculty and students are to have the detachment and the objectivity needed in the search for truth, they must not be too directly immersed in public issues or too emotionally identified with particular causes or interests.

They must be open to ideas of all kinds. They must be able to weigh the pros and cons—to stand aside and look at things as they *are*, not as they want them to be. That is why a university must guard its freedom and must avoid entangling involvements with parties and causes and programs. The university is a house of intellect, not a house of propaganda or of political action.

To those who assailed the university for its indifference to the sins of an immoral world Bowen responded that the university had its own ethic which came first in its scale of values and which it must be prepared to defend at all costs. It affirmed the right of free thought and speech, the right to seek the truth and report it regardless of the consequences, the obligation to evaluate people according to their merits, to respect the judgment of peers, to avoid plagiarism, and to practice high standards of performance. The highest morality of the academic community, he insisted, was the thoughtful search for truth, free expression of views, tolerance of differing opinions, and rational discourse. No appeal to a higher morality was justified in the university context, and anyone who would not accept the university code should get out.[68]

The university was confronted with a situation in which both external and internal forces were seeking a share in its control. Federal and state legislatures, federal granting agencies, accrediting bodies, foundations, and private donors all threatened its autonomy. Internally, the governing board, administration, faculty, students, and staff demanded a voice in its management. Each group emphasized its rights rather than the soundness of decisions arrived at. The university itself could be faulted for its educational conservatism, inefficiency, disorderliness, and indecisiveness. Higher education and health care were, in Bowen's opinion, among the most backward areas of the economy. What was needed was a system of government which would harmonize the claims of each constituency with institutional responsibility. He toyed with the idea of a council representing each interest which would be advisory to the president and deal with the full range of issues confronting the university. But the most pressing challenge came from the students, and here the president had no alternative but to assert his authority.[69]

Sympathetic though he was with the student critique of militarism, colonialism, racism, and hypocrisy Bowen could not consent to the use of the university as an agency to attack these evils. Then how could students play an effective role in public life and still adhere to the basic principles of the university? He gave some thought to creating a University Parliament, a membership organization open to all full-time students in which current social and political issues could be discussed and action taken. The Parliament could provide a forum for guest speakers and discussion groups. Although it would be independent of the university Bowen was prepared to offer limited academic credit for participation. It would be financed by dues, gifts, grants, and even by a university contribution. For whatever reason, the president did not pursue this idea either, and nothing came of it. In its place, he proposed to the deans a "Contemporary Issues" program, a less formal means of providing for seminars, guest speakers, and social service activities. Out of this came in turn the "Free University," or Action Studies Program. Organized in February 1968, Action Studies offered courses, several of them for credit, on such topics of current interest as History of Vietnam, Literature and Theology, The New Industrial State and the Question of Peace, and Practical Creativity for Poets, Writers, and Other People. Action Studies continued for three or four semesters before fading from view in the general exhaustion which followed the turmoil of the Vietnam era.[70]

CHAPTER SIX

The Rise of the
Medical College

The rise of the university's College of Medicine properly dates from the visit of Abraham Flexner, in 1909. The college at that time was housed in a group of small buildings with a ninety-bed hospital on the north side of Iowa Avenue. It boasted a faculty of 15 professors. The students, of whom there were 267 in that year, were admitted after one year of work in a liberal arts college. The preclinical faculty who taught the basic medical sciences of anatomy, physiology, biochemistry, and pharmacology held full-time appointments. The clinical members in the various specialties of medicine proper served part-time while devoting much of their time and energies to private practice. Iowa City could not itself support so large a concentration of medical skills. It had always been necessary to draw several of the clinical faculty members from surrounding communities where they continued to maintain regular practice. Five of the faculty also served as the medical staff of Mercy Hospital, a community hospital operated by the Sisters of Mercy.[1]

THE FLEXNER REPORT

The everyday practice of medicine at the turn of the century was of poor quality owing primarily to the generally low standards of medical education. There were over 150 medical schools in the United States and Canada, many of them small proprietary schools operated for profit and wholly incapable of providing training commensurate with the current state of medical science. Although the American Medical Association had established a program for the evaluation of medical schools, the standards were so generously applied that many weak schools were rated acceptable. Progressive elements in the medical profession, apparently despairing of reform from within, asked the Carnegie Foundation for the Advancement of Teaching to make an independent investigation of stan-

210

dards in medical education. The president of the foundation, Henry S. Pritchett, chose as his investigator a layman, Abraham Flexner, a Louisville schoolmaster who had taken a Ph.D. in classical languages at Johns Hopkins and who had recently published a critique of American college education. In selecting a man not trained as a physician Pritchett assumed that the problems of medical education at that time could be identified by an intelligent and well-informed layman.

The reformer had a strong sense of the proper status of medicine as a science built upon the basic medical sciences. Wherever he went his first concern was with the competence of the faculty and the quality of the facilities for instruction and research in these basic preclinical fields. There is little doubt that the severity of his overall criticism of the Iowa medical program was mitigated by his satisfaction with the quality of the instruction being offered in the basic medical sciences.

Prior to visiting the college in April Flexner had requested various categories of data and had notified President MacLean that he would spend eight hours in Iowa City, visiting the various departments of the college and inspecting student records. MacLean accompanied him on his tour of inspection, but no member of the clinical faculty was present, although they had been notified of the visit. Absorbed in their own private practice and insensitive to the antiquated character of their teaching, the clinical professors failed totally to appreciate the potentially explosive consequences of this visit by a mere layman. In spite of the apparently cursory nature of the inspection MacLean was nervous.[2] He knew that behind Flexner stood the Carnegie Foundation, whose financial resources were important to his plans for the development of the university. A favorable report from Flexner would undoubtedly strengthen the university's claims to future benefactions.

Flexner's preliminary report to the foundation, a copy of which Mac-Lean received early in July, was highly critical of the Iowa medical program. To be sure, the instruction and equipment in the preclinical fields were "generally good and at some points excellent." Flexner had high praise for Dr. Henry J. Prentiss, whose work in anatomy was as good as could be found anywhere. The same was to some extent true also of the work of Dr. John T. McClintock in physiology, and of Dr. Henry Albert in pathology and bacteriology. Unfortunately, the clinical situation left much to be desired. The dean, Dr. James R. Guthrie, professor of obstetrics and gynecology, lived in Dubuque and came to the college twice weekly. The professor of surgery, Dr. William Jepson, lived in Sioux City and traveled all night for his weekly visit to the hospital. Under these circumstances it was not surprising to Flexner that the clinical work lacked close integration with the preclinical fields. He found at Iowa precisely the fault he professed to see in American medical practice in general—namely, a failure on the part of medical practitioners to keep abreast of the work in the basic medical sciences.

The clinical instruction given in a hospital with fewer than ninety beds available for clinical purposes was, in Flexner's opinion, wholly inadequate. Disorganization was apparent in the fact that the visitor could find no one, neither physician nor nurse, who could describe the system of bedside teaching. There were no hospital records worthy of the name. No hospital reports were compiled. It was impossible to determine what ground the clinical teaching had actually covered. While the eye and ear clinic was large, the medical clinic was small, and there were no clinics at all in surgery, gynecology, or urology. The conclusion was inescapable to Flexner that the clinical teaching methods were disorganized and antiquated.

The clinical opportunities could not be fully realized, in the visitor's opinion, without a resident dean, resident clinical faculty, and a hospital superintendent familiar with modern medical teaching. Apart from deficiencies in personnel a major handicap was a hospital inadequate for clinical teaching. Even with one of adequate size it remained a serious question whether a small community could furnish the necessary number of patients.

Beyond all of these deficiencies of personnel and facilities Flexner directed the regents' attention to the larger question of whether a modern medical center in Iowa City could be justified in view of the national need to reduce the total number of schools and the great cost of making the necessary improvements. Would it be a wise use of limited financial resources to put into medical education funds better used in fields that were not handicapped by local conditions? The regents might well consider the experience of adjoining states. Chicago and Minneapolis provided the large populations to justify major medical centers. Michigan already had a highly developed medical school at Ann Arbor, yet even there the competition from the larger centers was keenly felt. The University of Wisconsin, with opportunities at Madison superior to those of Iowa City, had nevertheless decided to limit its medical school to the two preclinical years. Missouri had recently come to the same decision. Flexner warned in conclusion that as soon as an additional year of undergraduate work was required for admission to the Iowa school the better-trained and more mature students would perceive the inadequate quality of their instruction, with the result that the competition from Chicago and Minneapolis would become ever more severe.[3]

In consternation MacLean sent copies of the report to the heads of the medical departments with a request for the strongest possible positive response to Flexner's criticisms. He told the department heads bluntly that "the University is being held back on account of the College of Medicine."[4] But if he expected constructive proposals to strengthen the program he was disappointed. The professors in the preclinical fields, who had received generally favorable notice, tactfully observed that fault had not been found with them. The clinical professors were not prepared to acknowledge any shortcomings. Either Flexner's data were faulty or his complaints were without merit. Dr. William Jepson, writing from his residence in remote Sioux City, was openly contemptuous of "a certain Abraham Flexner" who was apparently "'drumming up trade,' (as the Jew would say) for Minneapolis and Chicago." Jepson saw no need to respond to the report in specific terms since he found the facts as stated to be so far from the truth.[5]

The complaints of the medical faculty were loud enough to be heard in the Carnegie offices in New York, and President Pritchett asked Flexner to take another look, accompanied this time by Dr. R. H. Whitehead, dean of the University of Virginia College of Medicine. Charlottesville was also a small community, and the dean could be expected to be familiar with the problems of operating a medical school under conditions similar to those in Iowa City.[6]

In the six-month interval between visits the university experienced a change in management. Its own Board of Regents was replaced by the new Board of Education which also had jurisdiction over the State College and the Normal School. The most immediate consequence of the change was the appearance of William R. Boyd as the board's representative. For thirty years Boyd was to exercise a dominating influence over public higher education in Iowa. Formulating a response to Flexner was to be the first challenge to the new board, and there can be no doubt that Boyd played a crucial part in determining its policy.

When Flexner notified MacLean of his return visit in October the president begged Boyd to accompany the visitor on his rounds. After the inspection the two men returned to the St. James Hotel on Clinton Street where they had a long talk. The details of the conversation are not recorded, but it is apparent that Boyd succeeded in persuading Flexner that the Board of Education took his criticisms with the utmost seriousness and that it was determined to maintain a medical school of the first rank. Boyd kept up his contacts with Flexner, who later left the Carnegie Foundation to become an officer of the Rockefeller Foundation. Many years afterward Flexner penned a striking tribute to Boyd as "the highest type of American citizen: absolutely correct, candid and straightforward; absolutely without personal ambition; absolutely devoted to the welfare of his State and particularly to the upbuilding of the State University." [7]

In the report on his second visit, addressed to board president James H. Trewin, Flexner noted that while some improvements had been made since his first visit, presumably in the matter of record keeping and plans for hospital enlargement, there was still no clear understanding of what needed to be done to bring the college up to modern standards. The principal problem was the inadequate clinical departments. The nonresidence of important senior faculty members was a partial explanation, but ultimately the members of the clinical faculty were not in all respects up-to-date medical men. The prime need was a resident dean who would be the chief clinician with full authority over his faculty, able to insist upon residence in Iowa City, and determined to eliminate in-breeding. But it is important to note that, in contrast to his first impressions, Flexner was now persuaded that it was feasible to develop a strong medical faculty in a small town. He was impressed with the determination of the board to deal vigorously with the matter. [8] This significant change undoubtedly reflected the influence of W. R. Boyd.

Dr. Whitehead was even more pointed in his criticisms. The facilities for clinical instruction, he noted, were entirely inadequate. The hospital was too small, and the number of patients too few for proper clinical instruction, with the exception of the eye/ear/nose/and throat department. The internal medicine department was most deficient. The instruction in this department was too didactic and demonstrative, both outmoded and old-fashioned, the students not being sufficiently involved with the patients. With the professors of gynecology and surgery not in residence it was inevitable that there should be inadequate clinical supervision of students. [9]

The most imperative need, in Dr. Whitehead's opinion, was a new dean of sufficient energy and ability to institute the necessary reforms. He should be thoroughly conversant with modern methods, possessed of the authority to clean house, and free to devote full time to the job. His most important task would be to reform the methods of clinical instruction. Without saying so directly Whitehead clearly implied that the present clinical faculty would have to be replaced. The dean himself should be an internist of sufficient standing to attract difficult cases by referral, thus increasing the supply of clinical material.[10]

In his published report Flexner's criticisms of the Iowa medical program were muted. He noted that the state had two to three times as many physicians as were needed for a stable population. There was no justification for training more doctors unless it were to improve the quality of medical care. None of the four existing schools—Drake and the osteopathic school in Des Moines and the two colleges in Iowa City—was up to this challenge, although the regular medical college at the university was clearly the most promising candidate. Apart from the antiquated training in the clinical fields the chief deficiency was the hospital, which provided inadequate facilities for clinical training and insufficient numbers of patients for the clinics. On the positive side the report noted the capable preclinical faculty and laboratory facilities. Plans to enlarge the hospital were noted with approval. In conclusion Flexner believed that a strong resident faculty and the wise use of state patients would permit the University of Iowa medical school to duplicate what Michigan had achieved at Ann Arbor.[11]

There is no evidence that Flexner visited the university's Homeopathic Medical College, although he received data on the program and included it in his published report. Instruction in homeopathic medicine had been introduced in 1876 by legislative fiat and was maintained by the continuing political pressure of state and county homeopathic medical societies. Flexner had no use for homeopathic medicine, which by that time was clearly waning in public patronage. There still remained fifteen homeopathic medical colleges in the United States, none of them requiring more than a high school education for admission. With an enrollment of only forty-two students, a budget of $5,453, income from fees a mere $1,864, and a hospital budget of $7,847, the Iowa Homeopathic Medical College was surviving thanks only to the reluctance of the legislature to offend a vocal constituency. Flexner pointed out that the homeopathic college was only half of a school—the clinical half. Instruction in the preclinical subjects was provided by members of the regular medical faculty, none of whom was in sympathy with homeopathy. Work in the preclinical fields was premised on one or two years of college science, which must have put the homeopathic students at a further disadvantage. Flexner found that in general, although homeopaths agreed that medicine was a science, they had contributed nothing to its development during the century of the sect's existence. Their fundamental assumption was sacred, and no science could flourish where dogmas were exempt from critical inspection. The sacred dogma of homeopathy was the "Law of Similars," the belief that a substance was of therapeutic value for a given disease if it produced in a healthy person the symptoms exhibited by the sick person. Homeopathy was little more than a theory of therapeutics, and its identification of the disease with its symptoms was an idea long since abandoned by scientific medicine. In his published report Flexner recommended that the two university medical colleges be combined, with optional courses in homeopathic materia medica and therapeutics for those students desiring a homeopathic diploma. Given the long-standing professional and social barriers that separated the two medical traditions he must have known that any such union would be impracticable.[12]

Following the receipt of Flexner's and Whitehead's reports it quickly became apparent that the medical faculty acknowledged neither shortcomings nor need for reform. The only action by the medical faculty was the unanimous adoption of a resolution introduced by Dr. Jepson affirming full confidence in Dean Guthrie and dismissing as unjust the charge that he was in any way responsible for the condition of the college.[13] Since the faculty could hardly have intended to imply that the dean had no responsibilities this curious resolution was presumably intended simply to affirm support of his administration. If there was to be a positive response it would have to come from the initiative of President MacLean and the Board of Education.

The board's response was not long in forthcoming. Its initial impulse was to adopt the suggestion in Flexner's preliminary report and abandon the clinical part of the medical program. But Boyd was determined to preserve and develop the college in Iowa City, and he persuaded the board to refer the matter to the legislature, in the meanwhile proceeding as though the legislature would support his position by shifting current funds from other parts of the university budget to the Medical College. He addressed a letter to alumni of the college assuring them that contrary to rumors of abandonment the board intended to ask the next legislature to do more for the college than it had ever done before.[14] He then met with the university faculty, several of whom, he noted, were his former teachers, and asked them to forego budgeted salary increases in order to save the Medical College. He must have been a singularly persuasive man, for members of the faculty consented to freeze their own salaries, while the legislature subsequently agreed to a much larger medical appropriation.[15]

In its *First Biennial Report*, issued in 1910, the board formally announced its intention to strengthen the Medical College and to secure its position among the leading institutions of the region. Eminent resident professors would be appointed to the faculty, the hospital would be enlarged, and more clinical material would be provided by arranging for the treatment of indigent patients at public expense. The announced object of the board was to improve the quality of medical education, not to increase the number of practicing physicians.[16]

If any one individual bore the brunt of the Flexner-Whitehead criticism it was the professor of the theory and practice of medicine and clinical medicine, Dr. Walter L. Bierring, who was also vice-dean of the college and hospital director. In the absence of Dean Guthrie the daily management of the college was his responsibility. The complaints of antiquated clinical teaching and inadequate hospital record keeping pointed directly at him, as did the recommendation that the key to improvement would be the appointment of a competent and respected internist. A prolific publisher of medical papers, Dr. Bierring went on to a long and successful career in organized medicine, culminating in the presidency of the American Medical Association. The board wanted him to give up his large private practice and devote full time to the college.[17] This he was unwilling to do; bowing to the pressure he resigned from the medical faculty to accept appointment in the Drake Medical School, which collapsed three years later, in 1913.

Dr. Bierring's resignation presented the first opportunity to make the strong appointments that the board had promised. A national and indeed international search was immediately inaugurated to find the most promising available teacher and research scientist in the field of internal medicine. Although Dean Guthrie participated in the search, the initiative was taken by President MacLean and W. R. Boyd. The most eminent teachers in the field were consulted, among them Drs. William Osler, William Welch, and Frank Billings. The applications of Iowa alumni were politely but firmly set aside. Choice finally settled upon a former student of Osler's, Dr. Campbell P. Howard, of McGill University. Boyd hastened to Montreal to assure Dr. Howard that the board would provide the additional staff member and research funds and facilities he had stipulated as conditions for acceptance. The Howard appointment represented a new concept at Iowa—namely, the emergence in the clinical fields of a teacher–research scientist, one who devoted most of his time and energies to those activities, carried on in a hospital and clinical setting, but without a major commitment to the care of private patients.[18]

President MacLean's successor, John G. Bowman, came to the university in 1911 from the position of secretary to the Carnegie Foundation. As a friend and associate of Flexner's he was even more determined than his predecessor to carry out the proposed reforms. The physiologist Dr. John T. McClintock replaced Bierring as junior dean, and Dr. Lee W. Dean succeeded Bierring as hospital director. Dr. Dean, the professor of ophthalmology and otology, maintained a large and efficiently organized eye/ear/nose/and throat clinic at Mercy Hospital. His managerial skills appealed to Bowman, who appointed him dean of the college in 1914. Dr. Guthrie, who had refused to move to Iowa City, became dean emeritus. Under Dr. Dean's aggressive management the college was to undergo rapid expansion. Protracted negotiations to bring Dr. Jepson into residence finally collapsed, and he resigned in 1913, to be succeeded as head of surgery by Dr. Charles J. Rowan, of the Rush Medical College.[19]

The appointment of outsiders brought to the fore the problem of inbreeding. One aspect of the professionalization of knowledge during the nineteenth century was a growing conviction of the undesirable consequences of inbreeding. Professional training should involve an awareness of the latest advances in the field wherever made, to which exclusive localisms seemed to present a standing challenge. In support of his criticism of inbreeding Flexner noted that eighty-seven percent of the medical students were Iowa residents and that of the fifteen faculty members in 1909 eleven held their medical degrees from the university. No doubt it appeared to the investigator that these were the makings of a self-perpetuating provincialism that could fall behind the general medical advance. One of the undesirable aspects of inbreeding was the jealous possessiveness that resented what was felt to be outsider incursion into a cherished monopoly. The state medical community, which included many alumni of the college, was inclined to look upon the college as its own possession. It expected to supply the faculty as a matter of right. There was apparently no opposition to the appointment of Dr. Howard, but the appointment of Dr. Rowan aroused widespread opposition. Sensitive to local sentiment, board president Trewin reprimanded Bowman sharply for having appointed Rowan without consulting Dean Guthrie, and he insisted that junior appointments in surgery be made without awaiting the appointment of a department head.[20] Bowman's aggressive approach to medical reforms was one of the factors leading to his forced resignation in 1914.

In the meanwhile the implementation of Flexner's recommendations concerning the College of Homeopathic Medicine proved to be unexpectedly difficult. As a first step the board equalized the entrance requirements of the two colleges: two years of undergraduate work, including a year each of physics, chemistry, biology, and a foreign language, would now be required. The homeopaths were understandably unhappy with the new requirements because enrollments would be curtailed, and homeopathic students, now on an academic par with regular students, would be exposed to enticements to transfer to the regular college.[21] Although President MacLean considered homeopathy to be a delusion he felt it his duty to support what the legislature had mandated, and members of the homeopathic faculty believed that he treated them fairly. President Bowman was also unsympathetic, but armed with Flexner's opinion and the board's keen desire for economy and the elimination of duplicating programs he moved forcefully against homeopathy. On his recommendation the board determined to consolidate all work in surgery, obstetrics, gynecology, and eye/ear/nose/and throat in the regular college, leaving to the homeopathic college only its distinctive chairs in materia medica and therapeutics. The homeopaths objected strenuously, maintaining that homeopathic therapy permeated all branches of medical practice and that the medical specialties could not be successfully separated from it. The board assured them that its intention was merely to achieve economies of operation and that patients desiring it would be provided with homeopathic care before and after treatment in the regular departments. Bowman reluctantly agreed to this concession, although homeopathic dean George Royal later complained that the pledge was not kept. Despairing of support within the university the homeopaths turned to the legislature, where their well-organized state and regional medical societies could bring pressure. The 35th General Assembly in 1913 obligingly established in the homeopathic college chairs in surgery, eye/ear/nose/and throat, and obstetrics and gynecology, thus prolonging the life of a dying institution.[22]

Neither Flexner nor Whitehead had referred to the practice of fee-splitting, an abuse firmly established in Iowa medical practice at that time. The *Journal of the Iowa State Medical Society* reported that there was abundant evidence that "some of the most prominent members of the clinical faculty" engaged in the practice of remitting to outside physicians a portion of the fees charged to patients referred to them. Both MacLean and Bowman publicly condemned fee-splitting as unprofessional and unethical. Upon Bowman's insistence the medical faculty unanimously repudiated the practice, and the board subsequently confirmed the action, although only by majority vote. The *Des Moines Register* reported that Dr. William R. Whiteis, professor of obstetrics, used his influence with certain board members in an attempt to obtain a reversal of the decision. After considerable vacillation the board finally decided to reaffirm its condemnation of fee-splitting.[23]

The year 1915 may be taken as marking the full response of the university to the Flexner investigation. The vexed problem of private practice versus public service was by no means settled in that year, but a principle was adopted that would eventually furnish the framework for achieving a satisfactory relationship. The issue was precipitated by a curiously archaic complaint. Certain physicians complained to the board that the University Hospital, a public institution, was being monopolized by faculty physicians for the treatment of their private patients to their own profit. Should not a public hospital be available to any physician who might wish to use it? The complaint reminds us of the early days of railroading when certain entrepreneurs argued that anyone should have the right to operate a train on tracks laid by right of eminent domain. Nevertheless, Bowman was obliged to take the matter seriously. He consulted law dean Henry W. Dunn, who submitted a lengthy explanation of why such a practice would be both unwise and impracticable.[24]

But the deeper question as to the proper allocation of a faculty member's time and energies was thus brought to the surface. On June 7, 1915, the medical faculty unanimously adopted a regulation affirming that only those physicians willing to make private practice "wholly secondary" to teaching were to be appointed to faculty positions. "An extensive, time-consuming private practice is not permissible." Each clinical teacher must spend an average of at least three hours daily in the hospital during the college year. Clinical patients were to have precedence over private patients wherever hospital space was limited. Private patients were to be available for clinical teaching wherever the head of department considered it appropriate.[25] Controversy and ill-feeling arising out of private practice were by no means settled by these regulations, but they at least staked out principles by which private practice would eventually be successfully integrated into a teaching and research institution.

Also in 1915 Dean Lee W. Dean called the attention of the faculty to the fact that although the college had acquired an excellent reputation as a teaching institution it was not known for its contributions to medical research. The faculty thereupon voted unanimously to inform the Board of Education that it would thereafter be the policy of the college to expect that every member of the instructional staff would engage actively in research.[26]

In his original report Flexner had expressed grave doubt of the ability of the small Iowa City community to provide the necessary volume of clinical material to support an adequate teaching hospital. Boyd and others had subsequently persuaded him that the state could be prevailed upon to furnish patients at public expense. Such assurance could more readily be given than actually realized. It took five years of hard work to persuade the legislature, in 1915, to provide medical care for the children of indigent parents, as well as care for inmates of correctional institutions under the Board of Control. A Children's Hospital was authorized two years later. And in 1919 provision was made for the treatment of all indigent adults.[27] The problem of clinical material was now solved. Thus within a decade of his first visit Flexner could have had the undoubted satisfaction of seeing a feeble institution of merely local usefulness begin the process of transformation that would eventually establish its position as a major medical center.

STAFF PROBLEMS

The relocation of the college on the west side of the Iowa River had been first proposed by President MacLean, but it remained for President Jessup to inaugurate what would eventually become the most massive building program in the university's history. The first units of the new medical complex, the Children's Hospital and Westlawn Nurses' Dormitory, were opened in 1919, and the third, the Psychopathic Hospital, in 1922. The Rockefeller Foundation in 1920 granted $20 million to the General Education Board for the advancement of medical education. Ever on the alert to promote the interests of the university, Boyd proposed to Jessup that funds to build a new medical laboratory be requested. It was a happy coincidence that Boyd's good friend Flexner was now secretary of the General Education Board. Flexner had been pleased with the vigorous response at Iowa to his critical evaluation of the medical program, and he was now favorably disposed to providing material assistance. He urged Boyd and Jessup to think big and estimate the cost not merely of a new laboratory but of transferring the entire Medical College to the west side. An estimate of $4.5 million was presented, of which the Rockefeller Foundation and the General Education Board each agreed to furnish $1,125,000 provided that the state would furnish the remaining half. Governor Nathan E. Kendall and legislative leaders were persuaded to support the proposal, and in 1923 the 40th General Assembly pledged $450,000 annually for five years. The completion of the new hospital and laboratory building in 1928 marked a major turning point in the history of the Medical College.[28]

Although the professional colleges were located on campus in space adjacent to the undergraduate colleges they had always stood somewhat apart institutionally. The Medical College in particular fostered a tradition of authoritarianism which was unique to medical education, arising out of hospital routines. The college had been organized, at least in its clinical departments, on the German model, in which the head of department chose his own staff and insisted on the prerogative of hiring and firing at will. Dr. Lee W. Dean, who was dean from 1914 to 1927, readily acknowledged that he would not intervene when a department head treated a member of his staff in a particularly arbitrary or inhumane manner. "The only way to run a college of medicine," declared the dean, "is to select heads of departments and have each one administer his own department." When Dr. O. H. Plant, head of the department of pharmacology, notified Associate Professor H. V. Atkinson that his appointment was being terminated, Atkinson challenged his authority to dismiss an associate professor. Plant informed Jessup that Atkinson was incompetent and that no rank should protect a professor who was incompetent. So much for tenure rights.[29] The price of authoritarianism was the fostering of a spirit of protest and rebellion; every twenty years the Medical College was rocked by controversies in which arbitrary administration provided a persistent theme.

The question of full- versus part-time appointments was also a recurrent source of conflict in medicine. The reforms stemming from the Flexner report had established the principle of a resident medical faculty, but it was still taken for granted that members of the clinical faculty would hold part-time appointments and supplement their salaries with fees from the care of private patients. These doctors conducted their practice in the university hospitals, where a portion of the beds was set aside for their patients. Flexner himself did not approve of this practice, believing that teaching and research formed a full-time occupation for the medical faculty as for other faculties of the university. While the west-side hospital plans were still under discussion he advised Jessup that the heads of the clinical departments should be on a full-time basis in order to limit the amount of private practice. He understood that the payment of full-time salaries in medicine would be a burden beyond the immediate capacity of the university budget, and he offered assurance that the General Education Board would provide a generous five-year grant to ease the transition to full-time salaries. Between 1924 and 1928 five of the clinical departments—obstetrics and gynecology, pediatrics, ophthalmology, otolaryngology, and psychiatry—were placed on a full-time basis.[30]

Other clinical departments, however, were strongly opposed to full-time appointments and strenuously resisted the plan of Jessup and the dean to convert the entire college to a full-time basis. The heads of surgery, internal medicine, orthopedics, and urology received substantial incomes from private patient fees which they were understandably reluctant to forgo. These incomes had a significant impact on the college budget. Dr. Arthur Steindler, the widely known surgeon who was the head of orthopedics, was said to run his department out of his own pocket. He himself acknowledged that he contributed twice the amount of his part-time state salary to the salaries of his junior staff members. He was able to do this because of his extensive private practice, his patients occupying about a quarter of all the hospital beds reserved for private patients.[31] Some attempt was made to adjust base salaries to the range of earnings from fees, but this did not allay the jealousies and hard feelings among the medical specialists who depended upon one another for referrals. Nor was it surprising that a widening gap opened between the full-timers content to work as medical scientists within their university salaries and the part-timers who were perceived as money-makers.[32]

The tensions within the medical faculty were compounded by the animosity which developed between the dean and his faculty colleagues. Dr. Lee W. Dean was an able and forceful otolaryngologist who had implemented the reforms proposed by Flexner and had been instrumental in strengthening the college with several strong appointments. He was, however, arbitrary and secretive in his management of the college, alienating several of his senior colleagues. In the spring of 1927 five senior members of the faculty resigned, together with the superintendent of the hospitals and the director of nurses. It was rumored within the faculty that the dean suffered from a cocaine addiction and that Jessup demanded his resignation. In any event he resigned the deanship on May 6 and left town, taking his files with him.[33]

Members of the medical "faculty," which at that time consisted solely of heads of departments, demanded fundamental reforms in administrative procedures. They asked that Jessup appoint a dean in whom they had full confidence, thus in effect proposing consultation, a significant limitation on the president's freedom of action. They also demanded faculty approval of all future faculty appointments in medicine and the right to deliberate on the college budget and educational policy. Before responding Jessup consulted the board, which issued an emphatic assertion of its authority to appoint deans and faculty and to determine policy. To yield such powers to the faculty would result in "hopeless confusion." Board president Baker was firmly opposed to "letting down the bars in any way in the permitting of faculty control or even approval" of institutional policies. He thought that he could detect behind the medical faculty the malign influence of the American Association of University Professors, which he perceived to be intent upon taking control of the institution. Jessup did his best to soften the board's harsh assertion of administrative authority by assuring medical faculty members that, while under the law they had no "rights," he would consult with them on all matters of appointment and policy, promising to furnish all relevant information on which decisions would be made. Faculty opinion would always be considered.[34]

Although on its face the board's position appeared to be a bald assertion of its unlimited power, in fact the episode contributed an important element in the gradual development of the practice of delegation of authority. The board denied the right of the medical faculty to govern the college because it held the president fully responsible: all recommendations must come to the board through him and with his approval. The president in turn must impose a similar obligation on the medical dean. Although the right of appeal through regular channels was inherent at each administrative level it was not to be confused with the power to act. Nevertheless, it is important to note that the board no longer asserted its right to intervene at will in the administrative structure. By holding its subordinate officers responsible it distanced itself from daily operations and granted them a new measure of discretionary authority.[35]

The departure of the dean together with Jessup's assurances that the faculty would be consulted on the choice of his successor largely relieved the tensions. The new dean, Dr. Henry S. Houghton, was the first to devote full time to administration without being simultaneously a department head. He had been director of the Peking Union Medical College in China, a Rockefeller philanthropy, and had come to Iowa on the recommendation of Flexner.[36] Dr. Houghton moved promptly to reorganize the college so as to give the staff a greater measure of involvement in its management. Formal faculty membership was enlarged to include all in the several professorial ranks. Three stated faculty meetings were to be held annually for the consideration of college policies. Standing committees on admissions, curriculum, hospitals, library, nursing, and standards and scholarship were created. A faculty council consisting of heads of departments and full professors was to advise the dean on all matters of administration.[37] Houghton understood what the president and board seemed not to recognize—namely, that a faculty cut off from the administrative process and discouraged from developing a sense of shared responsibility for the management of the institution easily developed attitudes of cynicism and hostility which furnished fertile soil in which to nurture the kind of rebellion that had rocked the medical college. Having done what he could to develop a wholesome atmosphere Dr. Houghton resigned in 1932 to return to China.

THE MEDICAL SERVICE PLAN

Flexner's report of 1910 had brought an end to proprietary medical schools and had placed medical education with a few exceptions under the auspices of the universities. But it was not easy to reconcile a professional school for the training of doctors with the idea of a medical college as a unit of a university. The university principle of teaching, research, and service as a full-time occupation came into conflict with private practice for fees. The conflict was intensified by potentially high earnings and by the strong sense of self-importance often found in the healer of the sick in an affluent society increasingly preoccupied with good health.

Flexner was a strong proponent of the university principle. When discussing with Jessup the proposed west-side medical campus he advised the president that the college should have more full-time heads of the clinical departments and that limitations on private practice should go hand in hand with planning for the new hospital. His access to the deep pockets of Carnegie and Rockefeller lent his opinions an authority to be reckoned with. By 1941, with the coming of the Second World War, the entire medical faculty save for the heads of eight of the clinical departments held full-time appointments. This was a silent revolution, the implications of which became apparent only in the controversies of the postwar period.[38]

The growth of programs and increase of services which might have been expected to flow from the new west-side facilities were steady but less than spectacular. From 1923 to 1943 college and hospital expenditures less than doubled, from $1,313,319 to $2,113,793. Student enrollment increased by only 19, from 385 to 404. The number of indigent patients less than doubled, from 6,988 to 12,125; while the number of private patients nearly tripled, from 1,177 to 2,996.[39] The faculty increased in size from 53 in 1923 to 82 in 1943. But the change in distribution by faculty rank revealed a clue to impending troubles. The number of heads of departments and full professors remained virtually constant—24 in 1923 and 26 in 1943—while those in the lower ranks increased from 29 to 56. In most of the clinical departments the department head monopolized the private practice, leaving the care of indigent patients to the junior members, who received no compensation beyond their salaries. The resulting discrepancies in income generated tensions to be considered below. The consequence to be noted here was the obstacle to growth presented by a senior clinical faculty preoccupied with the care of private patients and consciously or unconsciously intent upon preserving its monopoly of the income, which in individual cases amounted to several times the maximum full-time salaries of the college.

The problems resulting from part-time appointments plagued many American medical schools and were by no means peculiar to the Iowa Medical College. In a national survey of the situation made in 1945 Dean A. C. Furstenberg of the University of Michigan Medical School found that four different plans had been devised to cope with the problems arising from the prevailing mixture of full- and part-time appointments. The first, found only at the University of Chicago, was to place the entire medical faculty on a full-time salaried basis. This represented the triumph of the university principle and could be defended on idealistic grounds of teaching, research, and service. But although it was extremely expensive it was still vulnerable to competition from private practice. The second plan, more widely in use, was called "geographic full time." Members of the faculty held full-time appointments but were permitted a limited amount of private practice. The plan was said to be difficult to regulate and subject to abuse. The third plan placed department heads on full-time with substantial salaries and other staff members on part-time. Fees from patients were placed in a fund from which supplements to part-time salaries were drawn. This plan was found to be unsuited to state-supported schools and to arouse resentment in the medical profession against what was perceived to be group practice. The fourth plan permitted the senior clinical professors to retain fees from private patients up to a stipulated limit, with further income being distributed to junior members of the department. Under this plan departments were found to profit inequitably according to the varying demand for their specialties. It was also said to result in overemphasis on private practice. While each of these plans had its shortcomings, together they furnished elements which could be combined to form an acceptable solution.[40]

In the fall of 1941, within a year of his inauguration, the problems in the Medical College were brought forcibly to Hancher's attention. Having as yet no provost or academic dean he was obliged to deal with the matter himself, with whatever help he could get from the medical dean, Ewen M. MacEwen. An anatomist whose sympathies lay with the full-time faculty members, most of whom were in the preclinical departments, MacEwen was subjected to the importunate demands of the part-time heads of the clinical departments. A sensitive and discriminating man, he lacked both the forcefulness and the faculty confidence that the situation required, and the turmoil of the ensuing five years eventually destroyed him.

For many years the salaries of certain clinical faculty members had been supplemented by fees received from private patients. In the departments of internal medicine, urology, surgery, and orthopedics the fees were received directly by part-time senior staff members and were not accounted for to the university. In the absence of reliable information, rumors, no doubt inflated, of incomes in six figures circulated. In other clinical departments the fees earned by full-time staff members were deposited in fee funds administered by the university and originally used to support research. MacEwen, who had become dean in 1935, decided to use the fee funds to supplement the salaries of the full-time faculty. By 1941–42 these supplements amounted to about a third of the salaries drawn from the state appropriation.[41] In spite of the supplements, however, the full-time base salaries remained extremely modest, and the resulting discrepancies between the incomes of part-time heads of departments and their full-time colleagues resulted in deep dissatisfaction and unrest.

The leader and spokesman for the part-time department heads was the urologist Dr. Nathaniel G. Alcock. An able surgeon who introduced new operative techniques and who was widely known and respected in the profession, Alcock built up a large private practice from which he was reputed to receive a very substantial income. He was an extremely aggressive and domineering man who ran his department with quasi-military discipline, claiming the authority to hire and fire at will. One of the last of the academic anarchists, a veritable *Tyrannosaurus rex*, he insisted that all university regulations yield to the single objective of retaining the most capable staff possible. He regarded the trend toward full-time appointments for the clinical faculty as a colossal mistake, and he bent every effort to reverse the trend.[42]

The second man in urology, Dr. Rubin Flocks, was also an able physician. Alcock informed Dean MacEwen that in order to keep Flocks it would be necessary to change his appointment from full- to part-time, and that he was prepared to share his private practice with Flocks. In fact, Flocks was already caring for Alcock's patients during the latter's frequent absences from the hospital and was receiving additional income from Alcock. Alcock considered all of the private patients in urology to be his own regardless of which doctor cared for them, collecting all of the fees himself. MacEwen found this to be intolerable and complained bitterly to Hancher, who instructed the dean to draft the necessary regulations to prohibit the practice.[43]

The number of private patients was restricted by an agreement of 1928 with the State Medical Society limiting the practice to five percent of the bed capacity of the university hospitals, or about forty-eight beds, provided that the remaining beds were occupied by indigent patients. But the indigent quota was often unfilled, releasing as many as eighty-nine beds for private patients. Alcock acknowledged that on occasion he had admitted private patients as "indigent" when no beds for private patients were available. On the prompting of Drs. Alcock and Lierle the faculty voted on May 19, 1941, to request an increase of thirteen beds in the allocation for private patients. Tax-paying patients allegedly complained that they were denied care while beds for indigents remained unoccupied. Hancher and W. R. Boyd were adamantly opposed to increasing the number of private patients and refused to take the faculty's request to the board. Boyd declared that the tendency toward money-making should be strenuously resisted.[44]

The policy statement drafted by Dean MacEwen, on December 11, 1941, reaffirmed the primary purpose of the university hospitals to be the care of indigent patients and the furthering of the education of medical students and nurses. There should be no increase in the number of beds for private patients. To increase the number of part-time faculty members would lead to dissatisfaction within the college and to competition with the physicians of the state. Specifically, to change Dr. Flocks's status to part-time implied extension of the option to all full-time faculty, reversing the desirable trend of recent years. MacEwen was persuaded that the college received more favorable recognition under its present policy than it had enjoyed under the old part-time system. If funds were available he would place the entire faculty on a full-time university basis, which he believed would eliminate much of the present dissatisfaction. Hancher endorsed these principles and notified Alcock that he could not approve the proposed change in Dr. Flocks's status. Alcock continued to insist upon the need for part-time appointments as a means of getting and keeping a first-rate faculty. He declared that the best years of the Medical College had been 1915 to 1923, when all of the principal clinical men had held part-time appointments. He told Hancher that his friend Dr. Campbell Howard had resigned because of his fear of the coming of full-time appointments.[45]

Although the part-time issue was a matter of concern chiefly to the heads of the clinical departments, involvement in private practice concerned everyone in those departments. MacEwen reported to Hancher that the pressure for more private practice was becoming very great and that some way must be found to accommodate the demands of the junior faculty. In a conversation with the president on January 31, 1942, the dean suggested that private practice on a limited scale be made available at least to the second or third member of a department. Thus an individual who received a salary of $4,000 might be allowed an additional $4,000 in fees, any further income going to a fee fund. All billings and collections would be handled by the university. The dean considered this arrangement preferable to the alternatives of a general increase in salaries or part-time status for the entire clinical faculty. This was the first local suggestion of the principle which was to become the foundation of the Medical Service Plan.[46]

By 1943 Hancher realized that he would have to involve himself more directly with the problems of the college. His views largely coincided with those of the dean, but it was apparent that MacEwen was incapable of furnishing the forceful leadership the situation required. During the war years federal policy required faculty members to remain in their positions or accept immediate assignment to military hospitals. But Hancher realized that as soon as the war was over there would be a mass exodus to other medical schools or to private practice unless drastic reforms were introduced. He began a series of private conferences with individuals both within and outside the university on the proper course to be pursued. Given his strong sense of the importance of rank and seniority, all of his conferences were with heads of departments and other senior faculty members. He nevertheless received clear indications of unrest and frustration among the junior faculty. Dr. James A. Greene, who was leaving to become head of internal medicine at Baylor University, believed that if part-time appointments were to be made they should be restricted to the junior ranks. Heads of departments should be full-timers in a position to curb excesses of private practice. He considered an extensive private practice to be a corrupting influence. Dr. Everett D. Plass, head of obstetrics and gynecology, supported the dean's earlier proposal of a modified fee plan to supplement base salaries from a fee fund. The head of internal medicine, Dr. Fred Smith, one of the principal beneficiaries of private practice, nevertheless agreed that it should be restricted. Dr. Clarence Van Epps, head of neurology, was strongly opposed to extensive private practice and urged that those who desired it should resign. On the other hand, an influential consultant on medical matters, Dr. Alan Gregg, of the Rockefeller Foundation, advised Hancher that full-time appointments were not the answer, however attractive in theory. He recommended part-time appointments with limited private practice and salary supplements up to a specified maximum drawn from a fee fund. Further conferences with staff members following the end of the war in 1945 gave Hancher a detailed picture of the tensions within the faculty. He realized that the time had come for decisive action.[47]

Dean MacEwen was ordered to recommend policies for a college whose principal functions were teaching, research, and care of the indigent. Private practice was to be "definitely secondary." The agreement with the State Medical Society limiting the number of beds for private patients was to be strictly observed. Policy with respect to full- and part-time appointments should be defined so as to address the dissatisfactions of the faculty. Appropriate limitations should be placed on the activities of the part-time faculty with respect to the number of private patients seen and fees received. Limitations on out-patient practice should also be considered. A formula for faculty incomes was suggested: department heads should receive a base salary plus fees up to a stated maximum such as $20,000. Earnings in excess of that amount should be divided between a departmental fee fund (sixty percent) and a college fee fund (forty percent). The same formula could be applied with appropriate lesser maximums to the second and third men in the various departments. MacEwen was reluctant to undertake this assignment. He knew that a movement was underway in the faculty to oust him from the deanship, and he informed Hancher that reforms such as the president had in mind would have a more favorable reception if they came in the form of committee recommendations which the medical faculty could act upon.[48]

Hancher adopted this suggestion and, in January 1946, authorized the dean to appoint such a committee. Five of its seven members, Alcock among them, were department heads, although the urologist complained that five of the members were full-timers. The guidelines which the president set for the committee noted the general agreement that the college was in need of reforms. The disparities in income among the faculty were greater than their respective abilities would warrant. Certain senior members were too absorbed in private practice, throwing the care of indigent patients on the junior members. The principal assignment of the committee was to provide adequate compensation for all without placing undue emphasis on private practice at the expense of teaching and research. Full-time appointments for all, although perhaps the ideal arrangement, were not feasible under existing conditions. On the other hand, to extend the privilege of unlimited private practice to additional staff members would be to retreat from the ideal.

Some kind of compromise between the two positions was clearly in order. Hancher proposed to retain both full- and part-time appointments, allowing each faculty member to choose the type preferred. Full-timers would receive a full salary from the university while engaging in teaching, research, and the care of patients within limits to be set by the Board of Education. Fees from private patients seen by full-timers would be deposited in a college fee fund to be used for research and support services. Part-time appointees would devote at least half of their time to teaching, research, and the care of patients, both indigent and private. They would receive a base salary to be supplemented by fees up to a specified maximum according to rank. Hancher suggested $20,000 for department heads. Excess fees would be deposited in the college fee fund administered by an elected committee under the dean. All fees from private practice must be accounted for to the university, but part-time faculty would be allowed to practice outside the university. Both classes of appointees would enjoy the same tenure rights, retirement rules, and participation in the TIAA pension plan. Save for restraints upon the earning power of the part-timers these proposals made little change in the existing situation.[49]

The president then summoned the committee on January 18 and modified his guidelines in a crucially important respect. He now abandoned the distinction between full- and part-time appointments, while recognizing that salary supplements from fees were essential for all. The committee was instructed to formulate the terms of a uniform faculty appointment in order to achieve the closest possible approximation to full-time. This clearly implied limited and closely regulated private practice for all members of the clinical faculty who desired it. The president gave the committee a polite but firm ultimatum: if it failed to agree upon an acceptable plan he would institute one of his own.[50]

The committee went promptly to work, but in spite of Hancher's ultimatum it found itself hopelessly deadlocked, owing presumably to the insistence of Dr. Alcock upon preserving his part-time status and extensive private practice. In any event, it was Alcock who suggested that the committee seek the assistance of Dr. Henry S. Houghton, the former dean of the college, as a mediator. Houghton had been closely identified with the medical philanthropies of the Rockefeller Foundation, having spent much of his life in China. During his brief tenure as the first full-time dean of the college, 1928–33, his administrative skills and attractive personality had made him universally admired and respected. When President Jessup resigned in 1934 the Board of Education had offered the university presidency to Houghton, who, however, chose to return to China where he remained until captured by the Japanese and imprisoned for the duration of the war. He had recently returned to the United States when he received and accepted Hancher's invitation to assist the committee in devising a plan for medical compensation.[51]

Dr. Houghton met with the committee on April 17, 18, and 19, and then departed, leaving with it a proposal which it adopted by a vote of five to two. "The Houghton Plan," as Dr. Alcock called it, provided for "a near full-time plan of medical practice and teaching." Basic salaries were fixed for each faculty rank: $4,000 to $6,000 for assistant professors, $5,000 to $8,000 for associate professors, $7,000 to $9,500 for full professors, and $8,000 to $10,000 for department heads. Assistant professors would be allowed to supplement their basic salaries by fifty percent from private practice funds up to a maximum of $9,000; associate professors, by seventy-five percent up to a maximum of $15,000; and professors and heads, by one-hundred percent up to a maximum of $18,000 for professors and $20,000 for heads. As a special concession, the current part-time heads would be allowed a maximum of $25,000. Fees in excess of departmental needs would be deposited in a central scientific fund. Retired professors would be eligible for part-time teaching duties. It should be noted, however, that the anticipated income from fees would not be sufficient to finance the new salary scale. Dr. Houghton estimated that the cost of implementing the plan would require an increase of $175,000 in the annual legislative appropriation for salaries.[52]

The plan was promptly approved by the Medical Council, composed of department heads, by the medical faculty, and by the Board of Education, and became fully operative on July 1, 1947, for a two-year trial period. Dr. Houghton's contribution in formulating the plan and forging the committee majority in its support was properly acknowledged by those who were familiar with his role. But as he himself told the committee, the president had set the bounds within which the committee must work and had furnished the elements which Houghton had put together in a coherent plan. Insofar as the plan had made possible a successful resolution of the compensation problem the ultimate credit properly belongs to Virgil Hancher.

A minority committee report drafted by Alcock and signed by him and by Dr. Frank R. Peterson, head of surgery, professed to endorse the plan but in fact rejected its principal feature. The minority would retain part-time appointments and extend them to those junior faculty members who desired them. The majority had not presented any evidence of the alleged evils of private practice, and in any event the plan would actually increase it in order to raise the money needed to finance the full-time salary supplements. In view of the difficulty of obtaining increased legislative appropriations the added cost of the new plan would in all likelihood have to be borne by patient fees. Finally, the minority raised the bogy of socialized medicine. It was predicted that the medical profession of the state would be alienated. Alcock had in fact done what he could to stir up opposition to the plan in the State Medical Society, which instructed its Standing Committee on Medical Education and Hospitals to investigate the situation and report. After holding several meetings and interviewing President Hancher the committee reported that no action was indicated.[53]

Forty members of the clinical departments accepted the plan, while the two senior surgeons, Drs. Peterson and Dulin, resigned. Hancher noted that prior to the adoption of the plan five had resigned out of dissatisfaction with their incomes, while ten more would have departed had drastic action not been taken. Dr. Peterson testified to the depth of feeling that divided the faculty when he informed Hancher that his resignation was motivated less by financial considerations than by the deterioration of relations with many of his colleagues.[54]

Dr. Alcock chose to remain at the university and fight the plan from within. It quickly became apparent how extensively he had integrated his private practice with university operations. He was paying about $5,000 annually out of his own pocket for secretarial help and about $1,000 for telephone and telegraph charges. He admitted to Hancher that he was paying $12,000 annually in additional compensation to full-time staff members in urology, in violation of university regulations. He defended these practices on grounds of economy, claiming that it would cost the university much more to provide the same services under the new plan. A crucial element in his opposition concerned control of the departmental fee fund established under the new plan. Alcock believed that he should control disbursements from this fund, which would enable him to manage his department much as he had in the past. The dean and the president, on the other hand, held that its use was subject to policies to be determined by the college administration. Alcock considered this ruling to be in violation of the plan, absolving him from his pledge to support it. He thereupon went public, airing his complaints in the *Iowa City Press-Citizen* and *Des Moines Register* and stirring up the medical profession with the threat of socialized medicine.[55]

Hancher was outraged by what he considered to be Alcock's "recalcitrance and insubordination." The president distinguished between a professor's right to express opinions of university regulations and the obligation of a department executive to implement and abide by those regulations. Drs. Peterson, Lierle, and Steindler had expressed their opposition within the bounds of accuracy and fairness, while Alcock had used the headship to undermine and sabotage the plan. Hancher believed that Alcock's defiant conduct justified the president in relieving him of his headship, but in view of his long service to the university the president was content to demote him to acting head of department until such time as it should become clear that Alcock was willing to administer the plan fairly and desist from seeking to involve the State Medical Society in the affairs of the college. If he continued to insist that he would not be bound by the plan he would have to leave the faculty. No publicity was given to the demotion, which lasted some six months. Alcock at first protested the action and requested a public hearing, apparently in the hope of generating outside support. Hancher persuaded him that a hearing would not be in his best interest; he then resigned himself to the inevitable and was restored to favor. Dr. Alcock retired in 1949 and continued part-time as emeritus professor.[56]

The durability of the Medical Service Plan is attested to by the fact that it survived with modifications for more than forty years to the present time. Successive changes in subsequent years resulted in the abandonment of the original fixed differentials in percentages of compensation according to rank. The base salary of each individual as well as the additional fraction from practice fees were now fixed by the dean in consultation with the department head. In 1967 the "commutation fraction" for all faculty members was fixed at not more than 150 percent of base salary. Income from fees not allocated to salaries remained in a departmental fund, and each department contributed to a college trust fund. By 1977 the plan was earning some $10 million annually, much of it going to salaries. In 1985–86 it amounted to some $49 million. In the opinion of a later dean, Dr. Robert Hardin, the plan saved the Medical College.[57]

By providing a reasonable formula for compensation the plan removed the threat of a mass exodus of junior faculty members. In placing everyone on a near full-time basis with limits on maximum earnings it broke the monopoly of private practice by certain senior faculty members. The consequence was to reorient the faculty toward teaching and research. The reforms happily coincided with the organization of the National Institutes of Health and the Public Health Service, resulting in the rapidly growing influx of federal research money.

Having successfully dealt with the problem of compensation, the committee went on to address the larger question of faculty participation in the management of the college. It believed that the low morale of the faculty reflected more than dissatisfaction with salaries and disparities in income. It recommended that, while recognizing the authority of the dean, the president, and the board, the medical faculty be accorded the right to discuss the policies of the college in a democratic fashion and to make recommendations through established channels. It proposed that an annual meeting of the faculty be devoted to reports from the dean and from newly created standing committees on curricula, research, hospital affairs, admissions, and student achievement. It also recommended the creation of an executive committee of seven elected members, four of them to be heads of departments, to advise with the dean on matters of policy, budget, the selection of department heads, and determination of the size of departments.[58]

It may come as a surprise to realize that as recently as the 1940s the medical faculty did not have even an advisory role in the determination of the policies of the college. In any event, the authoritarian tradition in medical education conformed completely to Virgil Hancher's personal conception of the proper centralization of authority in the administration. He insisted that this portion of the committee report be deleted on the ground that it was irrelevant to the committee's charge to deal with the compensation problem. He believed that the objectionable proposal was intended to curb the authority of Dean MacEwen, although he also acknowledged his more fundamental concern that it would authorize faculty control of the College of Medicine.

As previously noted, Hancher in 1947 had created the Division of Health Sciences and Services, with Dr. Jacobsen as executive dean. In May of that year Dean MacEwen suffered a heart attack and died a month later. Jacobsen thereupon moved in to take closer control of Medical College affairs. As a means of improving morale he perceived the need for better channels of communication between faculty and administration. Undeterred by Hancher's mistrust of the faculty, he summoned a faculty meeting to consider "provision for wider participation in the affairs of the college by the general faculty." This would be the first of a series of meetings in which the faculty would begin to function as a corporate body. Had the initiative come from the faculty Hancher would in all probability have suppressed it as a threat to administration, but because it came from a senior administrative officer he kept hands off.[59]

ADMINISTRATIVE REORGANIZATION

In contrast to the frustration which he experienced in his attempt to reform the Liberal Arts College, Bowen's success in reforming the administration of the Medical College was achieved in collaboration with the medical faculty, which was determined to carry out such a reform. Only half the size of the liberal arts faculty, the medical faculty was bound together by its involvement with a common subject matter. Overcoming considerable internal resistance, it was able to draft and secure the adoption of a constitution for the college which provided for substantial faculty involvement in its management.

Traditionally, the medical faculty had consisted of the department heads only, among whom the dean was "first among equals." But while the reformers had been able to enlarge the voting faculty to include professors of all ranks, virtually unlimited power remained in the hands of the dean and department heads. Robert Hardin, who became dean in 1962, revised a proposed constitution submitted the following year by a faculty committee so as to give to the faculty only the power to recommend.[60]

Bowen was concerned both with the internal distribution of power in the college and with what he felt to be the inadequacy of its administrative organization. He found a dean attempting to administer a $25 million program with a staff and organization appropriate to an operation only a fifth of that size. He told the medical faculty that it should not want or need a military type of line organization such as had been traditional in medical colleges. Every line function should be delegated, which would leave the dean free to plan and to consult with the faculty and students. The problem as he saw it was to find an organizational structure compatible with academic traditions yet adequate to the peculiar needs of medical education.[61]

Medicine was only one of the related group of health sciences which included dentistry, pharmacy, nursing, and the State Hygienic Laboratory. It was important to Bowen that these programs should occupy adjacent spaces, and thought was given to relocating them at Oakdale, a few miles to the west. It was finally decided, however, that they should not be isolated from the rest of the campus, but should remain on the west bank of the river, where they would be near the Veterans Administration Hospital and be served by a common health sciences library. Pharmacy was already located east of the general hospital, and space would be found nearby for the colleges of Nursing and Dentistry and for a basic medical science building. Bowen decided that these colleges and programs should report to a vice-president for health services and that the paramount position of the Medical College should be reflected in the fact that the vice-president and the medical dean should be the same person.[62]

Within the Medical College Bowen relieved Dean Hardin of the daily management of administrative affairs, assigning these responsibilities to a newly created position of associate executive dean. Dr. Hardin was not happy with these arrangements. He preferred Hancher's style of administration and grumbled that Bowen was afraid of the faculty. The new associate executive dean, Dr. Daniel Stone, took up his duties energetically, pushing Hardin out of the dean's office into peripheral space at Westlawn, the nurses' dormitory. In practice it proved to be difficult to disentangle the duties of the two offices, and there came to be general agreement that the arrangement was not a success.[63]

The medical faculty members who were determined to have an effective voice in shaping the policies and standards of the college were supported by Bowen, who rejected the traditional authoritarianism in medical education when he observed that "administrators are really only faculty members who are freed of teaching and research duties so they can help the active faculty members achieve their goals."[64] With the president's encouragement the medical faculty elected an ad hoc committee to draft a manual of procedure for the college. Reformers within the faculty were determined that the manual should not simply codify existing practices, but should establish the faculty as the governing body of the college. The concentration of power in the hands of the department heads was perceived to be the principal obstacle to the elevation of standards as determined by a college-wide consensus.

Since the composition of the seven-member committee was crucial to the hopes of the reformers there was intense electioneering in order to assure the election of members who shared the sense of a need for reform. Several of the department heads were disgusted with the political activity, which they correctly perceived to be a threat to their own power. The committee, which represented both the clinical and preclinical fields, informed the faculty at the outset of its deliberations, in October 1967, that in order to build a great medical school all of its departments must be strong. "The faculty," it declared, "cannot permit departmental autonomy, parochialism, or provincialism to drag down the total potential of the college." One of the principal means of achieving this objective would be to conduct periodic faculty reviews of the performance of the various departments and programs of the college. Thus the medical faculty was asked to adopt the principle of college-wide faculty responsibility for the standards observed by its various departments, a principle which the liberal arts faculty emphatically rejected.[65]

The "Manual of Procedure" which the committee drafted was in effect a constitution for the College of Medicine. It specified the functions of the faculty, Executive Committee, departments, Medical Council, and dean. Its most notable features—which were indeed revolutionary—were to provide for a five-year term of office for the dean and a four-year renewable term for department heads, periodic reviews of the performance of departments and the dean, and an elected executive committee with a wide range of powers and responsibilities.[66] A preliminary draft of the manual was circulated to the dean and department heads for their comments, and the responses quickly revealed the depth of feeling aroused by the proposed changes. Several of the department heads objected strongly to term appointments on the ground that it would be impossible to recruit capable heads without security of tenure in office. Term appointments would make the head a political officer, which they regarded as a deplorable prospect. The same objection pertained to a term appointment for the dean. Critics of the plan failed to recognize that politics in one form or another was an integral part of institutional life. Term appointments would merely substitute ongoing institutional politics for the sporadic revolutionary politics of which the Medical College had a rich experience, the ad hoc committee itself being only the latest example.[67]

Provision of periodic reviews of performance was the most important of the proposed innovations. In order to raise the standards of the college the reformers believed it necessary to improve weak departments, and for this purpose a critical examination of each department by a committee of colleagues and outside experts was essential. Although several department heads objected to such reviews deans Hardin and Stone approved of them. The committee was warned that reviews could be a "hornet's nest" and that only a strong administrative body could be expected to implement remedies of perceived weaknesses. That body was to be the Executive Committee of the college. The plan provided for a strong committee of elected faculty members who would choose their own officers. To the objection that the dean should preside the ad hoc committee maintained that the election of its own officers was the best way of assuring that the Executive Committee would remain a faculty body independent of the dean's influence. (The reformers may well have studied experience in the Liberal Arts College, where the elected committees were presided over and dominated by the dean.)

In addition to its principal function as adviser to the dean on policy matters the Executive Committee was to initiate departmental reviews. Dr. Tidrick, head of surgery, objected to what he called government by committee, the most inefficient and time-consuming form of management. Others perceived that the Executive Committee would replace the Medical Council, the assembly of department heads, as the principal advisory body to the dean. The new plan retained the council but confined the scope of its functions to administrative as distinct from policy matters.[68]

Following numerous meetings and after several revisions a "Manual of Procedure of the College of Medicine" was presented to the faculty for approval and was adopted on December 15, 1967, by eighty-one percent of those voting. In its final form the manual dropped the earlier provision of terms of office for deans and department heads, the provision for periodic five-year reviews being felt to be sufficient to assure acceptable performance by administrative officers. The eleven-member Executive Committee was to be representative of all professorial ranks, thus introducing assistant and associate professors into a management system previously monopolized by a few senior members of the college, and over the objection of those who complained that assistant professors lacked both experience and security of tenure.[69] The objectors appealed to past experience; the innovators, to the need for an informed and involved faculty.

The new Executive Committee was designed to be the active voice of the faculty, meeting weekly and advising the dean on appointments, promotions, and educational policy. The traditional independence of department heads was curtailed by the stipulations that regular meetings should be held for the transaction of departmental business and that appointments and promotions should be made only after consultation with members senior to the rank in question. If the recommendation of the head differed from that of a majority of the department the reasons should be indicated to them and to the dean. The autonomy of departments was also significantly curtailed by the provision that whenever the headship became vacant the dean should appoint an ad hoc search committee from the faculty at large and that before acting on the committee's recommendation he should consult the Executive Committee and the Medical Council as well as the department concerned. These provisions represented the principle that the college as a whole shared with its various departments a concern for their professional and scientific welfare and standing.[70]

Although Bowen was supportive of the determination to involve the faculty in the management of Medical College affairs he was also concerned to preserve the administrative authority of the dean. The new manual came to his desk for approval early in 1968, when demonstrators aroused by Vietnam and other public issues were already challenging him to maintain order on campus. He believed that he had no choice but to assert his authority. Where the manual stipulated that the Executive Committee should "initiate" departmental reviews it appeared to the president that the fine line between delegation of authority and the improper arrogation of authority had been breached. He suggested that the Executive Committee should "cooperate" with the dean in initiating reviews. The ad hoc committee objected strenuously to making this concession, and Bowen backed off, saying that he was only concerned over the prospect of some "busy body" initiating a vindictive review. He approved the manual without revision, and a new era in the history of the Medical College began.[71]

The initiation of a program of periodic departmental reviews was the first and perhaps most significant fruit of the new constitution. Within a year of its adoption four reviews were completed. These were by no means perfunctory exercises. Sharp criticism was directed at inadequate performance. Of the four, only the department of biochemistry received a generally favorable review. Pathology, psychiatry, and surgery were found to have serious deficiencies. The surgery review in particular could only be described as devastating. Of the three conventional functions of the faculty—teaching, research, and service—service in surgery was found to be fair, teaching poor, and research largely nonexistent. The department enjoyed little status either locally or nationally. In view of the inadequate departmental leadership the reviewers recommended that an outsider be brought in as head of the department.[72]

A problem common to the clinical departments was the uncertain status of research. "Service" may have been a somewhat ambiguous obligation in the liberal arts, but there was no question as to what it meant in medicine. Several of the clinical departments bore a heavy burden of patient care, and it was not surprising that many members of those departments should consider service more important than research. That opinion was reinforced by the Iowa chapter of the American College of Surgeons, which reminded Dean Hardin that the purpose of the Medical College was to train physicians for practice and that this consideration should be paramount in choosing a new head for surgery.[73] After the other colleges had accepted the research obligation at least formally several faculty members in the clinical departments still resisted it. There was considerable sentiment in favor of promoting good teachers and able clinicians regardless of their research records. In Executive Committee discussions of the issue there was considerable support for promotions on the basis of superior performance in teaching or service without regard to research. The possibility of promotion without tenure or tenure without promotion was considered for such individuals. A direct confrontation with university regulations was avoided by acceptance of the Delphic opinion of Vice-President Boyd that while the research requirement should not be waived completely each individual should be evaluated on the basis of credentials. It would clearly take some time before the higher expectations could be realized in fact.[74]

RESEARCH AND SERVICE

The institutional evolution of the Medical College provided the necessary foundation for the enormous growth of programs and services in the postwar period. While the number of medical students in each class remained relatively constant, the faculty increased from 86 in 1945 to 488 in 1980, not including some 500 resident physicians and dentists.

The tradition of dominant personalities so distinctive in medical education continued into the recent period. Arthur Steindler built the distinguished department of orthopedics. Rubin Flocks strengthened the program in urology which Alcock had initiated. Adolph Sahs developed the program in neurology from a faculty of three in 1948 to a staff of some sixty in 1976. Alson Braley disregarded Dean Norman Nelson's advice to limit the work in ophthalmology and recruited a distinguished faculty in that field. Work in psychiatry, which had languished following the departure of Orton, was reinvigorated by Paul Huston. The department of internal medicine—or theory and practice of medicine, as it was then called—grew from a faculty of nine in 1945 to eighty-four, together with numerous clinical professors, in 1980. This growth resulted from the leadership of William B. Bean, who found the college dominated by its medical specialties and who was determined to strengthen the position of internal medicine as its central function.

One of the most striking features of the postwar medical program was its emphasis on service. Elmer DeGowin had pioneered before the war in developing methods of preserving blood from deterioration during storage. Robert Hardin, who had assisted him, introduced these methods to the armed forces and became head of the Blood Transfusion Services for the European Theater of Operations. In psychiatry, while Huston enlarged the staff and emphasized research, he also vigorously promoted outreach activities. Ignoring Hancher's admonitions of caution, he went directly to the citizens of the state on behalf of mental health promotion. Appealing to interested local groups, he organized some thirty mental health centers. Within the university he encouraged closer relations with neurology and speech pathology. In ophthalmology, in order to obtain eyes for corneal transplants, Braley organized an Eye Bank. The public was educated to the need for this service through work with service clubs, beginning with the Lions Club of Fort Dodge. The Eye Bank Association of America was organized in 1962, with an emergency network of ham radio operators to coordinate activities. Funeral directors were trained in the removal of eyes for transplantation. The ophthalmology clinic was enlarged to the point where it was treating over 30,000 patients annually.[75]

Following the Flexner investigation the Medical College had secured its future as part of the university complex in Iowa City by developing its program for the hospital care of the indigent at state expense, thus securing the necessary patients for its hospitals. With the coming of Medicare and Medicaid this service was now provided by local hospitals, and the university hospitals transformed themselves into a tertiary care facility, receiving difficult cases by referral from local hospitals. This transformation reinforced the increasing specialization of the Medical College departments. Specialization in this college, however, unlike specialization in the Liberal Arts College, did not result in increasing isolation of the various specialties. Rather, it led to the development of a number of interdisciplinary medical centers and to a new integrated curriculum which represented collegiate rather than narrowly departmental objectives. The Clinical Research Center, Cardiovascular Research Center, Diabetes and Endocrinology Research Center, Cancer Center, Digestive Disease Center, and Alzheimer's Disease Research Center brought together the resources of relevant departments to bear upon particular medical problems.

Following an accreditation report of 1960 on the educational program which had been critical of the traditional "bloc time" curriculum in which each department had been assigned a portion of a student's time to be used as it saw fit, a new integrated curriculum was adopted. It rested on the assumption that medical education was the responsibility of the whole college and not simply of its respective departments. An interdepartmental committee planned a basic course in clinical medicine to be team-taught by teachers from each of the participating departments. This course followed three semesters devoted to the preclinical medical sciences and was followed by a third year of clinical clerkships consisting of nine weeks of internal medicine; six weeks each of surgery, pediatrics, psychiatry, and obstetrics and gynecology; and two weeks each of anesthesia, dermatology, neurology, otology, urology, and family practice. The fourth year consisted of more intensive work in selected medical specialties.[76]

President Bowen estimated that half of his time was spent on medical matters. He found a great shortage of medical personnel and was determined to increase the size of the college, build additional facilities, and obtain the necessary financial support. He was able to enlarge the faculty by twenty-five percent and triple the amount of grants and gifts for medical purposes. The rapid growth of the college continued through the Boyd and Freedman administrations. By 1984–85 the medical budget totaled $119,074,606, of which only fourteen percent represented state-appropriated funds. The largest portion, thirty-eight percent, came from grants, contracts, and gifts, followed closely by income from the Medical Service Plan.[77] The Medical College was leading the way toward the new mixed type of university.

CHAPTER SEVEN

General Education

The general education movement of the 1930s and 1940s reflected the changes that had overtaken the American educational scene since the turn of the century. The number of students enrolled in colleges and universities increased more than fourfold between 1900 and 1930. It was inevitable that these students should bring a much greater diversity of preparation for college than had been provided by the high schools and academies of the past. The increased enrollments accompanied a subtle but pervasive shift toward vocationalism as the colleges greatly enlarged the number and variety of courses offered. Freedom of choice of a major subject from among an increasing number of departmental options together with the principle of elective freedom replaced the nineteenth-century consensus as to the content of a liberal education. The disintegration of the old liberal arts curriculum went hand in hand with increasing specialization of courses taught by scholars who sought to accommodate their teaching to their research interests. The result of these changes was a collegiate experience which in many instances lacked coherence and a common body of knowledge.

The economic depression of the 1930s and the following war years created the abnormal conditions in which educators were encouraged to reconsider theories and practices long taken for granted. The demand for general education took several forms, often reflecting little more than a vague desire for reform. The "great books" movement of which Robert M. Hutchins of the University of Chicago was the best known proponent sought to acquaint students directly with the writings of the seminal minds which had shaped Western culture. A related concern was represented by those who favored a common "core" of basic subjects with which all students should be familiar. Still others, who counted themselves disciples of John Dewey, emphasized the importance of recognizing and serving the needs of students who varied greatly in their aptitudes and interests. Each of these forms of the general education movement received some support from Iowa faculty members. Nevertheless, it remained a significant fact that at this university it was the administrative officers rather than the faculty who were the principal advocates of general education.

The nineteenth-century liberal arts curriculum with its prescribed work in the classical, philosophical, or scientific course during the underclass years was replaced at Iowa in 1905 with the twentieth-century curriculum built around an upperclass major with prescribed underclass work in English, foreign languages, social science, and natural science. Sensitive to the potential imbalance of enrollments among the various departments the faculty also required the student to elect courses in a wide range of fields outside the major subject. Departments were arranged in three groups corresponding roughly to humanities, natural sciences, and social sciences. The student was required to elect at least twelve hours of course work in each of the two groups in which the major was not located. One virtue of the distribution requirement was that it forced students to sample work in different disciplines without infringing on the freedom of departments to specialize their courses. The curriculum requirements thus adapted themselves conveniently to the pedagogical preferences of a faculty becoming ever more specialized in its scholarly activities. Nevertheless, it was a more tightly controlled and traditional curriculum than was to be found in many colleges in the early decades of the twentieth century and might have posed as a not unrespectable program in general education. In later years the physicist G. W. Stewart characterized it as "a statistical way of liberalizing education—forced liberalization without specification" of particular courses. He remarked that it had worked well for thirty years, and he strongly implied that would-be reformers would do well to leave it alone.[1]

DEAN HARRY NEWBURN

One of Virgil Hancher's first important tasks was to appoint a liberal arts dean to succeed George F. Kay. Kay, who had been dean for twenty-five years, had given the affairs of the college only a portion of his time, for he continued to serve as head of the geology department as well as state geologist. In the absence of an academic vice-president or provost Hancher conducted the search for a dean himself. He consulted widely, both within and outside the faculty. Some thought was given to offering the post to Milton Lord, librarian of the Boston Public Library and former Iowa librarian, who would serve as both dean and librarian. But the president finally decided to choose the appointee from within the faculty.

Among those recommended were Earl Harper, director of the School of Fine Arts; Kirk Porter, political science; Cornelius deKieweit, history; Frank Luther Mott, journalism; Henning Larsen, English; and Harry K. Newburn, education.[2]

The appointment of Newburn had been urged upon Hancher by Paul Packer, dean of the College of Education. The president was warned that the choice of a professor of education would be highly unpopular with the liberal arts faculty and that a protégé of Packer's would be particularly unacceptable. Newburn had no very obvious qualifications for the position. A graduate of Western Illinois State Teachers College with a Ph.D. in secondary education from the university, he was currently serving as director of the University High School. He was an imposing man with an attractive personality, qualities important to Hancher. More pertinent was the fact that the president was determined to appoint a full-time dean who would not be diverted by teaching or research interests. Newburn satisfied these requirements and was appointed dean on September 1, 1941.[3]

Despite the less than wholly auspicious circumstances of his appointment Newburn was determined to begin at once the difficult process of review and revision of the undergraduate curriculum in liberal arts. He was supported by Hancher, who had his own ideas about undergraduate education. In his inaugural address the president had stressed that in addition to the necessary work in the sciences, social sciences, and humanities the college should provide its students with a proper appreciation of the Judeo-Christian and classical bases of Western culture. He justly observed that too many young people suffered from historical amnesia, facing the future without comprehension of past achievements and failures. He was concerned about narrowly specialized courses and asked Kirk Porter about the possibility of offering an integrated social science course. Influenced no doubt by his Oxford experience, he questioned the wisdom of packaging education in credit-hour units, suggesting instead that each department prepare a syllabus indicating material to be covered in a comprehensive examination for which the student would assume the responsibility of preparation. Such a plan would permit elimination of a substantial number of courses. It apparently did not occur to him that Iowa students might not be prepared for such a measure of independence. Impressed by his friend Frank Aydelotte's honors program at Swarthmore he proposed to Newburn that Iowa institute an honors program for seniors, with emphasis on the major field rather than course work.[4]

Newburn's educational philosophy reflected the progressivism that was particularly influential among teachers of social studies. He believed that liberal education was concerned with the purposes and goals of human be-ings rather than with prescribed subject matter. It addressed itself to total personal growth and was concerned with the richness and effectiveness with which we live. It could be obtained in many environments, formal and informal. Because of the wide range of student ability and interest the only valid standard of achievement was performance at the highest level possible for each individual. Although skills in communicating and cal-culating as well as physical fitness were necessary for all, subject matter as such was not the object of liberal education, but only a means of achieving personal goals. Citing with approval a report of the Association of Ameri-can Colleges on the nature and aims of liberal education, Newburn de-clared that the liberally educated person was literate and verbally articu-late; informed about the physical and social environment; sensitive to values; able to understand the present in terms of the past and the future; and capable of deciding and acting as a responsible moral being. In more specific terms, the dean believed that the choice of an academic spe-cialty should be made as soon as possible and that the entire academic pro-gram should be built around it. It should be defined broadly as an area of knowledge rather than a narrow departmental specialty. Elective courses chosen arbitrarily to round out a requirement should disappear. There should be less emphasis on formal classroom activities, especially the lec-ture, and more on conferences, seminars, and other methods of individual instruction. Newburn's conception of general education was essentially social in character. He sought the fullest possible development of indi-viduals both as persons and as citizens in order to realize the potentialities of a democratic society.[5]

As the country dedicated itself to wartime activities and young men left the campuses, which instituted a variety of military training programs, it was an appropriate time to review the nature and purposes of liberal education. The demand for specialized technical training in many areas seemed to pose a threat to the liberal, nonvocational subjects which lay at the heart of traditional conceptions of liberal education. Many educators were disturbed and sought to reinvigorate the traditional disciplines. Pro-gressive educators like Newburn were uncomfortable on finding them-selves in such conservative company. Progressives were dedicated to demo-cratic ideals, the realization of which provided them with a large agenda of unfinished business. They thought of themselves as forward-looking rather than conservative. The social studies education movement with which Newburn was identified was a center for such thinking. It traced its roots in part to John Dewey's progressivism and in part to the distinctively

American differential psychology of individual differences. The latter had close affiliations with the University of Iowa. Seashore's emphasis on fractionation and measurements, the Child Welfare Research Station work on individual growth, and the College of Education's involvement with testing all furnished a congenial soil for educational theories which placed central emphasis on the achievement of individual goals.

On assuming the office of dean, Newburn began at once to plan for a major revision of the curriculum looking toward a general education requirement in liberal arts. Letters of inquiry were sent to foundations and to institutions known to have such programs, and a shelf of books on general education was assembled. The elected faculty Committee on Curriculum and Instruction was informed that students, faculty, and administration were all agreed that fundamental reforms were in order. The dean proposed that the committee authorize the appointment of a small Steering Committee to study and make such recommendations as seemed desirable. On February 13, 1942, the committee authorized him to appoint such a committee together with subcommittees as needed. Thereafter the elected faculty Committee on Curriculum played no part in the discussions or decision-making process other than to transmit to the faculty the recommendations of the Steering Committee.[6] Designating himself chairman of the new committee, the dean appointed Joseph Bodine (zoology), Howard Bowen (economics), Alan Craig (mathematics), Norman Foerster (English), Edward C. Mabie (speech), and Kirk Porter (political science) to serve with him. Bowen and Craig soon left for wartime service, to be replaced by Paul Olson (economics) and Arthur K. Miller (geology). It was a strong committee, although several of its members, notably Bodine, Mabie, Miller, and Porter, were closely identified with their respective disciplines and not known for their interest in general education. Subcommittees were subsequently appointed for social sciences, history, natural science, foreign languages, fine arts, literature, and skills. Members of the subcommittees sometimes complained that the Steering Committee ignored their recommendations. No Steering Committee secretary was designated, the dean keeping only informal minutes. Faculty members complained that they were not informed of the committee's deliberations.

NORMAN FOERSTER

The presence of Norman Foerster on the Steering Committee made it certain, however, that the issues of general education would be discussed by a man who had thought about them intensively and who held deep convictions about them. But as would become increasingly apparent, his convictions were fatally compromised by institutional self-interest. Foerster had come to Iowa in 1930 as professor of English and director of the School of Letters. A Harvard graduate who had studied and taught at Wisconsin and North Carolina, he was a member of the humanist school of literary criticism. His mentor, Irving Babbitt, had rejected behavioristic naturalism by insisting that humans were unique among nature's creatures in possessing imagination, analytical reason, and powers of self-control. While Babbitt was not hostile to science as such, he deplored the tendency to glorify science and the scientific method as holding the solution to all problems. Although the human spirit did not operate according to the laws of physical science, Babbitt was reluctant to invoke divine agency. His humanism was compatible with but independent of many of the orthodox religious formulations. He appealed to the authority of Western cultural traditions, maintaining that the function of humanism was to uphold cultural standards in an age of sentimental humanitarianism.[7]

Foerster's special contribution to the humanist movement was to bring its principles to bear on the problems of public higher education. In holding that everyone was possessed of a dual nature, part animal and part spiritual, he set himself against the naturalistic monism that dominated the modern university. He believed that naturalism denied humanity's relation to an order of ultimate values, although many who held this view were unaware of its ultimate dangers, living as they did off the capital of their classical and Christian heritage.[8] It was ironic but not surprising that bitter enmity should develop between Foerster and Newburn, both of whom professed to be advocates of general education.

A liberal education as Foerster conceived it made a whole person and not a narrow specialist. It was peculiarly appropriate to a democratic society in which the welfare of the individual citizen was the ultimate object, and where the rapid tempo of change demanded adaptability and broad training. The cultivation of critical intelligence could best be achieved through direct contact with the great minds of the past as displayed in mathematics and science, historical writings, literature, philosophy, and religion. The student should also have a reading knowledge of French and German. Foerster would devote half of the liberal arts course to this common subject matter and half to a specialty of the student's choice. He insisted that a proper liberal education would place primary stress on the humanities, with lesser attention to the sciences, since values were the special concern of the humanities. "An education largely in the sciences, natural and social, conducted as it usually is from a scientistic and naturalistic point of view, is simply unthinkable in a college that bears the proud name of liberal." Special importance was attached to the basic course in literature for it was here that Foerster would introduce the study of values which was to be the central preoccupation of his version of a liberal education. Selections from Greek and biblical writings together with English and American classics were to bear the burden of introducing the student to the fundamental values of Western culture.[9]

Foerster shared Hancher's concern over the encroachment of graduate study on the Liberal Arts College. As scholarly productivity became the most important criterion for academic advancement the faculty, which was shared by the Liberal Arts College and Graduate College, was becoming a company of research scholars who preferred to offer specialized advanced courses. Yet, in the absence of a sound foundation in the liberal arts, the quality of graduate education was inevitably declining. Foerster perceived the Liberal Arts College as being ground between a lower millstone composed of studies of high school grade in the first two years and an upper millstone of undergraduate-graduate level courses in the last two years. The upper millstone should be removed at once by eliminating graduate-level courses and replacing the graduate faculty with a liberal arts faculty engaged exclusively in teaching undergraduates from the liberal point of view. Curricular reform without faculty reform would be fruitless. So long as academic specialists were privileged to appoint people of their own kind the undergraduate faculty would be staffed by pedants, dilettantes, and career-builders. Responsibility for faculty appointments should rest with an administrative officer who, with the advice of the department head, would of course choose teachers with a humanistic orientation.[10]

As director of the School of Letters and professor of English, Foerster worked diligently to implement his ideas. When he came to the university he found a two-year requirement in English consisting of freshman composition and a sophomore survey of English literature. He was able to transform these courses into an integrated two-year requirement called Literature and the Art of Writing based on a study of Greek, biblical, Renaissance, and modern writers in which the study of values was the principal focus. Believing as he did that the teacher was as important as the subject matter he used his forceful influence in the English department to secure the appointment of men with the proper humanistic orientation. Seymour Pitcher, René Wellek, Joseph Baker, and John MacGalliard joined the faculty in junior positions, although Austin Warren was the only senior appointee Foerster was able to secure. His influence was by no means restricted to the introductory course. The doctoral program in English was substantially modified in order to introduce work in literary criticism, aesthetics, and the option of creative writing. Courses in poetry and prose writing had been offered for some years, but Foerster was one of those who persuaded the department and the Graduate College to recognize creative work as a legitimate alternative to the conventional literary-historical doctoral dissertation.[11]

For the further support of creative work outside of the degree-granting programs of the department Foerster endorsed the organization of the Writers' Workshop. He found that many writers were lamentably uneducated, and it was his hope that the workshop would bring writers and scholars together. Over the years, however, the workshop drifted away from the academic program of the department while retaining its nominal institutional affiliation. Within the department Foerster's strong views and domineering personality factionalized the faculty and created enduring animosities. He was outspoken in his disapproval of the traditional branches of literary scholarship. He complained that linguistics, properly a branch of anthropology, had begun in Germany under the influence of science and had resulted in neglect of the literary aspects of language. Similarly, the historical study of literature as practiced by several of his colleagues revealed the impact of science in its taxonomic tendency to describe and classify, to the neglect of quality and value. What was needed was a critical interpretation of literature as an affirmation of human values. His complaints of antiquarianism and pedantry did little to smooth relationships with his colleagues.[12] Whether Newburn was fully aware of Foerster's views and his quarrels when he asked him to serve on the Steering Committee cannot be determined, but it seemed certain that the appointment would precipitate controversy and create personal animosities.[13]

THE PLANNING COMMITTEES

The liberal arts program deemed to be in need of revision consisted of the required two-year course in English, a one-year course in the principles of speech, eight special freshman lectures on School Problems, physical education in the underclass years, two years of military science for men, and a foreign language "when specified in the curriculum undertaken," which usually meant two years of college-level work. Twelve hours were also required in mathematics and natural science, and twelve hours chosen from a group of subjects including commerce, economics, education, history, home economics, philosophy, political science, psychology, religion, and sociology. There was no similar requirement in the humanities group because the English, speech, and language requirements were presumed to represent that group. Consequently, the departments of philosophy, religion, art, and music were excluded from participation in the distribution requirements. In the ensuing discussions of curriculum revision it became evident that these departments were determined to be included as well. The program culminated in a major departmental concentration of from twenty-four to forty hours.[14]

The Steering Committee met weekly and by April 1942 produced a statement listing the inadequacies of the existing program, a set of purposes for the college, and a pattern by which the purposes were to be realized. The objective of liberal education was defined as the fullest possible development of the intellectual, spiritual, physical, emotional, and aesthetic capabilities. Provision should be made for the cultivation of speaking, reading, writing, and the computing skills as well as for physical fitness. The student should be guided toward a mastery of the leading ideas, significant facts, habit of thought, and methods of work in the sciences, social studies, languages and literature, fine arts, history, and philosophy. Resourcefulness, independence of mind, and strength of character were the objectives of liberal education.[15]

It was apparently assumed that the appointment of subcommittees in various areas indicated the intention of the Steering Committee to designate required general education courses in those areas, although no statement to this effect was made. The subcommittee for history found itself in a peculiarly uncertain position. Foerster and other advocates of general education were agreed that history should have a central place in any general education requirement. Newburn, however, would subordinate history to the social studies. One of the most vigorous and articulate members of the history subcommittee was Lester D. Longman, head of the art department, who insisted that there was no such thing as history by itself. There was history of economic life, of politics, or of art, each of which should be taught in its respective discipline. Longman's apparent intention was to strengthen the claim of art history to a place in the basic requirements by eliminating general history. His obstructive tactics prevented the subcommittee from accomplishing anything for several months. Eventually the subcommittee chairman, W. T. Root, head of the history department, rallied the group behind a proposed course in Western Civilization, and Longman resigned from the subcommittee in a huff.[16]

The subcommittee on literature was firmly controlled by Foerster and his allies, Pitcher and Baker. They saw their task as reaffirming the central role of the two-year course in literature in the general education program. As described by Pitcher, the professor in charge of the course, it traced the sources of Western culture in the parallel traditions of Greece and Palestine as found in both original texts and later commentaries. It introduced the student to humanistic and religious values. Chaucer and Shakespeare were studied for their intrinsic merits, while modern literature was largely ignored. Pitcher defended the neglect of much of English literature because he favored a definitely ideological approach. He acknowledged that training in composition was carried on separately, contrary to Foerster's later insistence that the two could not be separated. This was to become a crucial issue since a proposal to offer a separate program in basic skills would be used as one of the justifications for cutting back the literature course to one year. The subcommittee was adamant that the course must carry twelve credit hours and extend through two years.[17]

The fine arts subcommittee moved aggressively to enlarge the position of the fine arts in the undergraduate curriculum. Its members in addition to Longman included Philip G. Clapp and E. C. Mabie. It urged the adoption of a general education core curriculum and recommended that the fine arts be represented in it. Rather than attempt to fashion a general course in art it proposed that an introductory course in each of the three arts then being taught at Iowa—music, plastic arts, and theater—be offered as core courses, with students free to choose one of them. The subcommittee appeared to take it for granted that a core curriculum should represent a judicious balance of the various fields of study offered by the college rather than prescribe certain subjects chosen for their general educational value. The core program should rectify existing imbalances in enrollment by admitting the arts as a core area. The implication of this position was that the college was doing the right thing; all that was needed was a program to present courses in a balanced fashion so as not to exclude essential elements. If this line of thinking were to prevail it would be unlikely that significant changes in the curriculum would be enacted.[18]

The social science subcommittee was unable to agree on the formulation of a general course integrating the social sciences. It was willing to attempt an experimental course, Man in Society, under carefully controlled conditions with limited enrollment. It would be essentially sociological in character, and Kirk Porter, the political scientist, was outspoken in his opposition to it. As a compromise, the subcommittee recommended that in addition to the experimental course the departments of political science, economics, sociology, and psychology should each offer an introductory course.[19]

Comparable differences of opinion divided the members of the science subcommittee. The botanists and zoologists were able to agree upon a core course in biology which would, however, be a conventional introductory course using "the text by Stanford." The physical scientists, apparently feeling obliged to offer something in the area of general education, proposed a course which would give equal coverage to mathematics, astronomy, physics, chemistry, and geology, each department being responsible for its share of the instruction. Each instructor would be expected to hear all of the lectures, and one of them should be trained in all five fields. The proposed course closely resembled a course that was currently being offered called Group Science, but would presumably be better integrated. Having made its gesture of cooperation the subcommittee proceeded to condemn general education in the sciences in scathing terms. It did not attempt to conceal its low opinion of its own proposed course, recommending that students intending to major in one of the physical sciences be excluded from "a high school level course." As for the other students, the purposes of general education would be better served if they were required to work in a single science rather than receive a smattering of several. In any event, if a core course in physical science were to be offered, enrollment should be restricted to those who had never taken a science course and who intended never to take another. Foerster and his allies proposed a course in scientific theory and methods as appropriate to general education, but the subcommittee did not address itself to that suggestion.[20]

The Steering Committee also created a subcommittee to address students' problems with written and spoken English. The work of this subcommittee related directly to the existing required courses in English and speech. Perennial faculty complaints of students' inability to communicate effectively in writing and speech indicated the need for a special program directed specifically at these skills. The subcommittee proposed special courses to be required of students found to be deficient in reading, writing, and speaking.[21] The creation of such a skills program would weaken the position of the two-year required course in English by detaching from it the work in these areas. Some faculty members complained that the skills were being neglected by English department instructors who preferred to emphasize the literary part of the course.

Taken as a whole, the discussions in the subcommittees showed substantial disagreements as to the nature and content of a general education program. The departmentalists among the faculty, those who were primarily concerned with advanced teaching in their respective fields, considered general education courses to be unsatisfactory substitutes for the introductory courses which they preferred to admit to the core. So far as their views were to prevail it would be impossible to maintain a clear distinction between general education and disciplinary specialization. It was also apparent that there was no agreement on the question whether a core should consist of a small number of required courses or a larger number among which choices could be made. Some felt that it was sufficient to require a course in a single art or science. It was not clear whether the skills program would require college-level performance or would be remedial. The uncertain status of history and the controversial two-year course in English remained problems to be resolved if possible by the Steering Committee.

DEPARTMENTALISTS VERSUS GENERALISTS

By the end of September 1942 that committee had agreed that the reformed liberal arts curriculum should consist of basic skills, a core of general education courses, a departmental major concentration, and electives. Before the end of the year it distributed to the faculty a statement on the function of the College of Liberal Arts, a proposed curricular pattern, and a recommendation concerning the foreign language requirement. The faculty approved the curricular pattern on December 9 and thereafter all discussion and actions took place within the context of that pattern (see accompanying chart).

The chart distributed to the faculty indicated clearly enough the dominant influence of the departmentalists on the Steering Committee. In the face of the thrust for general education their object was to preserve the major concentration and to minimize the number of hours allocated to general education. Although the hours allocated to the major subject were not specified, it is apparent that as many as sixty-two hours or more might be available, depending on other requirements. While work in the common core would presumably begin in the freshman year the choice of a major subject by freshmen was to be encouraged as a motivational influence, and course work in the major could begin at the outset. In view of the importance attached by general educationists to the advisory function it was significant that as soon as a student chose the major subject the adviser would represent that department, and there was no reason to assume that departmental advisers would always be sympathetic to general educa-

Proposed Curricular Pattern
College of Liberal Arts

FREE ELECTIVES
(0–30 s.h.)

Selected from any subjects available in the university, including courses in other colleges, such as Nursing, Medicine, Law, Dentistry, and Engineering. Not more than 30 permitted, in many cases less will be available.

BASIC SKILLS
(0–15 s.h.)

Required of all who have not reached a minimum standard of performance in writing, reading, speaking, mathematics, etc. Credit for the first year's work—thereafter the work will be taken without credit.

COMMON CORE
(Approximately 30–40 s.h.)

Selected from courses designed specifically to provide general experiences for all students. Certain courses will be taken by all but a degree of flexibility will be retained. Common core work will be heaviest in the first two years but will not be confined to this period. Certain students will be encouraged to secure more than the usual amount of this type of experience. Different combinations of core courses will be arranged to meet variations in student needs.

AREA OF CONCENTRATION

Normally one course in the area of concentration will be selected in the first year though in some cases for sufficient reason two such courses will be permitted. This portion of the program will be developed by the student and his adviser (a member of the staff in the area concerned) in close cooperation and will involve a continuous study of the student's interests, aptitudes, and goals. Designed to provide an *integrated* educational program for the individual giving breadth as well as depth of educational experience, the area of concentration will be used to include related courses outside the major field and even outside the area itself. It is expected that many different combinations of subject matter, some of them unique, will be used in each area to provide "tailor-made" educational programs for individual students. This does not mean, however, that certain courses may not be required of all students in a given area or for majors in departments within the area.

4th Year

3rd Year

2nd Year

1st Year

tion. The influence of Newburn was apparent in the flexibility and options built into the program. Much would be left to the discretion of the student and adviser. Even within the major area the requirements would be "tailor-made" to the needs of the individual student. Certain courses in the core would be taken by all, "but a degree of flexibility will be retained." "Different combinations of core courses will be arranged to meet variations in student needs." This was the committee's answer to those who believed that the core should consist of a limited number of courses required of all students. There was no mention of a foreign language requirement in the proposed curricular pattern, although the Steering Committee had voted that four years' study of a language (three in high school and one in college) be required.[22]

Throughout 1943 the various committees wrestled with the content of the core area, and with the number of hours to be allotted to the core and the various elements within it. The departmentalists wanted to minimize the hours in the core and to make introductory departmental courses eligible for core credit. Foerster and his followers wanted to maximize the core to forty hours or more and to constitute it so far as possible of general education as distinct from departmental courses. Newburn's sense of the importance of freedom to accommodate individual needs was more readily adapted to the position of the departmentalists than to that of their opponents, with the result that an alliance—probably unspoken rather than explicit—began to emerge between the dean and the departmentalists.

Foerster moved first, persuading the Steering Committee in January 1943 to endorse unanimously his proposal of a thirty-two hour core consisting of five hours of biological science, five of physical science, five of social science, five of history including fine arts, and twelve hours of humanities distributed over four semesters. Although the content of the humanities hours was not specified it was understood by all that it was Foerster's intention to perpetuate the two-year English course. All of the courses designed to satisfy these requirements should meet general educational rather than introductory departmental criteria. The adoption of these proposals represented the high-water mark of Foerster's influence in the Steering Committee. From this date forward the object of his opponents was to bring about a reversal of the Steering Committee's action.[23]

Although the general educationists considered the study of foreign languages to be an integral part of a sound general education, the Steering Committee preferred to deal with it as a separate issue. The ancient languages had long since yielded to the modern in the college requirements. The command of at least one foreign language up to the second year of college-level work remained a requirement for the bachelor's degree. The Steering Committee on November 21, 1942, reaffirmed this traditional requirement. Within the following two weeks, however, a significant change in its thinking occurred. Cognizant, perhaps, of the notorious fact that students who satisfied the requirement remained for the most part unable to make effective use of the language studied, the committee now recommended that each department should determine its own requirement in order that it might graduate "an adequate proportion" of its students possessed of a working command of a foreign language. No effective means of implementing this curious requirement was proposed, and the faculty at its meeting on December 9, 1942, voted to table the proposal. Three months later it was reintroduced, with the added provision of an interarea committee to review the results. Porter's motion to adopt the plan was now approved by a vote of fifty-five to twenty-one. For all practical purposes the college would now be without a foreign language requirement. Furthermore, to leave the determination to individual departments would introduce destabilizing elements into the distribution of curricular elections quite apart from educational considerations, and many faculty members must have become uneasy about the decision. Foerster, who had at first supported the proposal, now charged that Newburn was determined to dump the language requirement.[24] The issue enabled him to rally the humanistic departments to a more lively sense of the threat to general education as traditionally conceived. Consideration of the language requirement became intertwined with other general education matters, and the Steering Committee was forced to consider how faculty sentiment could be used to secure support for its other objectives.

During the spring of 1943 the Steering Committee turned its attention to the size and composition of the common core. A group of sixteen faculty members proposed a core of fifty-four hours, a plan which would accommodate all of those departments that wished to be represented, including foreign languages. At the other extreme, the Steering Committee offered for discussion a minimal core of thirty-two hours in which literature would be limited to ten hours, with no provision for foreign languages. Only the social science subcommittee endorsed the latter alternative, believing that neither English literature nor history merited places as requirements by themselves. The sociologist Edward B. Reuter represented the social science point of view in an open letter to the dean in which he contemptuously dismissed history as unscientific and relegated literature to the status of one option among the several arts. As a compromise Foerster proposed a forty-two hour core—or forty-eight if one year of foreign language were to be included. His plan would preserve the two-year English requirement and allocate twelve hours to science, preferably the method and philosophy of science; six hours each for history and the social sciences; and six hours for a choice among the fine arts, philosophy, and religion. Foerster's plan was approved by the Steering Committee and transmitted to the faculty for consideration at its meeting on June 9, 1943.[25]

At this point Kirk Porter intervened to rally the departmentalists behind a plan to sidetrack action on Foerster's plan and gain time in which to substitute a plan more acceptable to them. In a private letter to Newburn dated the day before the June 9 faculty meeting Porter listed his objections to the Foerster plan. It was too heavily weighted, he believed, on the side of the humanities. Furthermore, the proposed core was so large as to jeopardize the proper place in the curriculum for introductory departmental courses. For these reasons Porter urged that no action on the core be taken until the entire set of degree requirements was laid out. There was no need for immediate action; the faculty should have more time in which to consider alternatives.[26]

THE STEERING COMMITTEE

When the faculty met on June 9 it was presumably prepared to act on the Steering Committee's recommendation. But after it transacted some routine business Dean Newburn suggested that it would be desirable if the faculty were to adjourn the meeting in order to have a "free and informal" discussion of general education. Bodine then moved adjournment, which was seconded and carried. During the informal discussion that followed Porter moved and the faculty unanimously agreed it to be the sense of the meeting that the Steering Committee be requested to submit during the following year a comprehensive plan for curricular reform. Thus the plan Foerster had so laboriously maneuvered through the Steering Committee was shunted aside, never to be acted upon. There was little doubt that the tactic had been carefully prepared in advance of the meeting and that Porter and Bodine at least were privy to it. Newburn later explained that action had been averted because of the growing realization that a forty-two hour core together with language and skills requirements could total as many as sixty-two hours for some students, thus encroaching on the hours necessary for the major, a matter of vital importance to the departmentalists. Foerster had not been informed of this concern, and he was understandably infuriated at what he took to be a deliberate sabotaging of his plan, which indeed it was. He offered to resign from the Steering Committee, but allowed himself to be dissuaded by Newburn, although he thereafter absented himself from most of its meetings.[27]

Although the tide had now clearly turned against him and the type of general education he represented, Foerster and his allies continued the struggle in an attempt to swing faculty opinion toward their views. His colleague Seymour Pitcher proposed the most radical reform yet presented: a three-year plan for the B.A. degree without major specialization. Pitcher believed that a liberal education properly conceived required a fairly definite curriculum of prescribed studies. He did not believe that the Steering Committee's pattern provided for a true liberal education. He would allot sixty of the ninety hours in a three-year curriculum to six elements: knowledge of the history of civilization from ancient times to the present; familiarity with the chief systems of political thought; familiarity with the best literature; an understanding of the significance of science; the capacity for articulate expression of one's opinion; and a thorough knowledge of one foreign language. Twelve hours would be allocated to work in two of the following subjects: philosophy, religion, fine arts, or mathematics. Eighteen hours would thus be left for concentration in a subject of the student's choice. Throughout the fall of 1943 the Steering Committee seemed to wander aimlessly, but it was unanimously agreed upon rejection of Pitcher's proposals.[28]

Following the June 9 meeting Hancher in a letter to Newburn offered his own suggestions for a liberal arts curriculum. His thinking was closer to that of Foerster than to that of the departmentalists. He proposed a full freshman-year curriculum of general education courses in verbal and quantitative skills, literature, history and social science, the history and methods of natural science, and appreciation of the various arts. In the sophomore year the student would elect introductory departmental courses. Although major concentration might begin in that year it was apparent that most of the student's time in the first two years would be preempted by general and distribution requirements. Whether Newburn transmitted Hancher's suggestions to the committee cannot be determined, but it is apparent that if he did so the committee brushed them aside. This was the president's only attempt to influence curricular decisions.[29]

As bitter animosity developed between Foerster and Newburn the former charged that the dean manipulated the Steering Committee in order to impose his progressive educationist philosophy on the college. But the surviving evidence hardly supports the charge. As late as December 1943 the committee was still discussing matters that a determined dean would have settled at the outset. What was the nature of the common core, and how much of it should consist of prescribed courses? Should a group of courses representing a specific theory of general education be adopted, or should a compromise among divergent points of view be sought? To what extent should responsibility for general education be left to the departments? The committee's inability to reach agreement on these questions after nearly two years of discussion suggests not so much the manipulations of the dean as the stubborn resistance of the departmentalists— Porter, Miller, Bodine, and Mabie—to the adoption of a substantial core of courses representing a coherent philosophy of general education.[30]

In spite of its continuing uncertainties the committee felt by the end of the year that the time had come to conclude its deliberations and to formulate a proposal for faculty action. Porter was now the dominant figure. In a series of December meetings in Foerster's absence the committee fixed upon a thirty-two hour core to consist of courses in science, social science, literature, and a group including fine arts, philosophy, religion, and history. The key to this arrangement was the detachment of history from its association with the social sciences and its assignment to an optional status in what was to be designated as "historical and cultural studies." It was assumed that each of the four areas would be allotted eight hours. This would cut four hours from the current twelve-hour, two-year requirement in English, reducing that course to a two-semester sequence of four hours each. The committee justified the reduction by proposing a basic skills requirement in reading and writing, thus separating elements which were combined in the existing English course. Foerster and his colleagues in the English department protested bitterly that such a separation was educationally unsound; effective instruction in writing could not be separated from a specific subject matter. The dean replied that faculty members had complained that the teaching of writing had been neglected by instructors who were interested primarily in literature.[31]

As it became increasingly apparent to Foerster that he had lost his influence in the Steering Committee and that he would lose the battle both for a viable general education program and for the continuation of the two-year English course his anger and frustration overflowed. Believing that Hancher shared his general educational philosophy he wrote a bitter letter to the president in which he pinned responsibility for his defeat on Newburn. "Is a solitary high-school type of mind to be suffered to prevail against the national as well as local consensus of the college teaching profession?" In such a situation Hancher's instinct was to support his administrative officer. He conferred with Newburn, who told him, no doubt accurately, that Foerster had alienated the Steering Committee by his stubborn insistence upon preserving the two-year English requirement. They discussed the possible damage to the reputation of the university should a scholar of Foerster's national standing resign in protest. Hancher decided to keep hands off, thus in effect supporting the dean and the committee.[32]

Realizing that he would get no support from the president, Foerster resigned from the Steering Committee on March 17, 1944. In justification he cited the committee's dishonesty in failing to present the forty-two hour core to the faculty; the inadequacy of the proposed student advisory system; and the omission from the plan of a mandatory course in the history of Western civilization.[33] He then took his grievances to the student body, the press, and the Board of Education. This gave great offense to Hancher, who felt strongly that such matters should not be aired in public. A group of student supporters organized a magazine, *Perspectives*, in which to promote Foerster's educational ideas. The first issue—which also proved to be the last—contained a slashing attack on Newburn and the Steering Committee written by Melvin Peete, an undergraduate English major. Obviously primed by Foerster, the author showed how a committee composed of disciplinary specialists led by a dean committed to fostering individual differences rendered a true general education impossible. Although the committee paid lip service to general education it did not know what it was. In fact, there were only three faculty members who did—Bush, Bergmann, and Foerster. Peete's lively paper was undergraduate journalism at its best, although as usual it had no discernible influence on the course of events. Nor did an article in the *Des Moines Register* inspired by Foerster. It noted that there was substantial opposition in the faculty to the proposed thirty-two hour core as inadequate for general educational purposes.[34]

There was more reason to hope that Foerster might gain support from the Board of Education. Following his resignation from the Steering Committee he wrote to his friend W. R. Boyd that he was contemplating resigning from the university. Although he believed that Hancher was "on the side of the angels" he realized that the president could not intervene without seeming to be authoritarian. Boyd was strongly supportive, urging Foerster not to resign, but to stay on and keep up the fight. He expressed great concern for the future of liberal education threatened by specialization, vocationalism, and triviality and promised to take up the matter with Hancher. Although the board should respect the distinction between policy making and administration, Boyd nevertheless believed that a fundamental educational issue was certainly a policy matter and therefore proper matter for the board. Foerster warned that should the committee's plan be adopted he would in any event have to resign the directorship of the School of Letters since as an administrative officer he could not in good conscience take part in implementing the plan. With his usual good sense Boyd counseled Foerster not to insist upon everything he wanted, but to be content with modest gains while continuing to work for improvements. If he did in fact intercede with Hancher and the board he was unable to affect the course of events.[35]

It was at this juncture that the National Association of State Universities published a report on postwar educational problems of which Virgil Hancher was the principal author. Foerster was shocked to discover how far the president's views diverged from his own. Hancher emphasized that "we need a frank recognition that we are dealing with two types of students." For those who would not go beyond two years of college—in effect, the junior college students—a common core of general education courses would be desirable. But for those who would take the full four-year program for the bachelor's degree introductory departmental courses leading to the major concentration were appropriate. He saw no differences between the objectives of liberal and of professional education. Both required a minimum body of fundamental knowledge, skill in handling and adding to relevant information, ability to think and act in novel situations, and the cultivation of an ethical attitude toward the uses of knowledge. Two years later, looking back on the struggle from his retreat in North Carolina, Foerster poured out his bitterness in a vitriolic attack on the report as a model of futility, devoid of intellectual virility and abounding in the old claptrap of progressive education. Without mentioning Hancher by name he identified him as one of a type of state university president that was helpless, bewildered, devoid of critical and creative thought, and unable to imagine a revitalized university.[36]

THE CORE PROGRAM

In the meanwhile the Steering Committee moved quickly to secure acceptance of its plan by the faculty. The report which it adopted on March 11 was approved by the faculty Committee on Curricula on March 18 with only cursory discussion and forwarded to the faculty for action at its April 5 meeting. The dean made careful preparations to guide the measure to adoption, reviewing the rules of order in case of obstructive tactics and preparing to meet anticipated objections. His precautions proved unnecessary, the faculty adopting the committee's plan after an hour and a half of debate, by a vote of 108 to 50. In reporting on the meeting to the Board of Education Hancher (who had not been present) expressed surprise that Foerster had not presented his own plan as an alternative. In fact, the botanist G. W. Martin had proposed an alternative acceptable to Foerster which provided for a thirty-six hour core in which literature and history would both have secure positions. The Martin substitute was rejected *viva voce*.[37]

The new liberal arts curriculum of 126 semester hours provided for proficiency in the basic skills of reading, writing, and speaking. Four semesters of physical education for all students and of military science for males would be required. Faculty pressure had resulted in the restoration of the foreign language requirement: students must be able to read or speak a foreign language with the degree of proficiency to be determined by the staff. The thirty-two hour core requirement on which the protracted struggle had centered consisted of eight hours each in natural science, social science, literature, and historical-cultural studies. The major departmental concentration allowed a maximum of fifty hours in one department, although in deference to Newburn's preference for an "area" of concentration additional hours in related departments were to be permitted. Finally, elective credits up to thirty hours would permit combined programs for degrees in the professional colleges. Although Newburn hailed the new program with enthusiasm Hancher informed the board that it represented relatively little change.[38]

As Foerster became aware of the divergence of Hancher's views from his own, relations between the two men rapidly deteriorated. At Boyd's suggestion Foerster requested permission of Hancher to speak to the board, but the president refused, saying that he would present the new curriculum according to "the usual procedure." Realizing that further struggle was futile Foerster on July 27, 1944, submitted his letter of resignation as director of the School of Letters and professor of English, effective September 1, 1944. The letter focused on the alleged dictatorial behavior of the administration in ramming through its curricular reforms. The dean had informed him that further opposition to the new program would be considered insubordination; he must either acquiesce or get out. Accusing the administration of "intolerance, deceit, and abuse of power," he sent a copy of his resignation to the press. Hancher promptly fired him as director of the School of Letters, saying that Foerster had rendered himself ineffective as an administrator.[39]

It is difficult to accept Foerster's persistent charge that Newburn dominated the Steering Committee. A forceful dean who knew what he wanted would have achieved more in the way of innovation. Although reduced to one year the course in English literature remained the only required course in the core curriculum. The work in writing which had been an integral part of the old course survived in a new form as part of the basic skills requirement which all students must satisfy. While the humanists failed to secure a mandatory course in Western Civilization, such a course became the most popular option in the historical-cultural area. The foreign language requirement which Newburn would have abandoned was retained. Far from being a dominating influence it appears more likely that the dean with his belief in the importance of serving individual differences played into the hands of the departmentalists who were determined to minimize general education requirements and to protect the major concentration as the prime focus of undergraduate education. Two years of discussion of general education finally broke down in a scramble for enrollments among a faculty largely oriented toward departmental specialties.

IMPLEMENTING THE PROGRAM

No sooner had the general education program of 1944 been adopted than debate began as to how instruction in the various core areas should be provided. Dean Newburn believed strongly in comprehensive area courses and urged the faculties in each of the four core areas— literature, social science, natural science, and historical-cultural studies—to offer such courses. This was no problem for English and American literature, where such a course, now reduced to two semesters and shorn of its writing component, was already in place. The social sciences were divided between those who supported an Introduction to Social Science and the departmentalists led by Kirk Porter who favored the introductory departmental courses offered by each of the disciplines in the area. Similarly, the natural scientists were split between the physical scientists who preferred to offer introductory departmental courses and the biological scientists who devised a course called Biology of Man drawing upon material from botany, zoology, home economics, hygiene, and psychology. In the historical-cultural area the history department proposed a new course to be called The Development of Modern Civilization, a comprehensive survey of the political, economic, religious, and artistic aspects of Western culture. Postdoctoral teaching fellows would be recruited from the social science, philosophy, and art departments as well as from history. Although such a course would have appeared to satisfy the historical-cultural area requirement, it was impossible to exclude optional departmental courses offered by the philosophy, religion, art, music, and theater programs. In offering these various options the college was in effect acknowledging that it could not agree upon the character of basic instruction in the various areas. But it was difficult to say whether the disagreement reflected educational theories or the desire of departments for a share of student enrollments.[40]

The concept of the core area as an integrated entity was further weakened by introducing options within core courses designed to appeal to the special interests of different groups of students. The core literature course which originally assigned a common group of readings for all students extended the list greatly, thus permitting instructors to offer a variety of literary options according to their individual interests. Similarly, the history department supplemented the course on Modern Civilization with a number of Problems in Human History courses of a highly specialized character. Eventually it introduced an optional core course in Asian Civilization, thus repudiating the idea that all students should have a common introduction to the history of their own culture.

Dean Newburn resigned in 1945 to accept the presidency of the University of Oregon. His successor was Earl J. McGrath, who came from the University of Buffalo, where he had been administrative dean and professor of education. The new dean assured Hancher that he was strongly committed to general education. With the president's blessing he founded and edited the *Journal of General Education*, in the first number of which he threw down the gauntlet to the departmentalists, saying that the salient feature of the movement was a revolt against specialism. General education undertook to prepare young people for the common life of their time by integrating the subject matter of related disciplines. In order to achieve this objective a substantial portion of the undergraduate program should consist of prescribed courses designed to serve vital needs. The newly adopted Iowa program did not, in McGrath's opinion, give sufficient prominence to general education. The core courses remained under the exclusive control of the departments, several of which were not sympathetic to its objectives. He believed that control of these courses should be placed under the management of a special agency which would have the interests of general education at heart.[41]

McGrath moved aggressively to strengthen the core program. On his urging the Executive Committee summoned the college faculty to discuss the issue, while a group of some dozen supporters met privately with him for several meetings at which a manifesto was drafted and subsequently published, entitled *Toward General Education*. The faculty approved the creation of a small committee to function in the dean's office as an administrative agency charged with strengthening the general education program. Assurance was given that it was not the intention to divide the college into upper and lower divisions, nor to create a separate faculty for general studies, although on occasion a temporary appointment for this purpose might be made. The faculty also resolved that more should be done to strengthen honors courses, independent study, and tutorials, and to provide senior fellowships for superior students.[42]

E. C. Mabie was appointed director of general studies, to be assisted by a faculty committee of seven. McGrath announced that while the pledge not to create a separate general education faculty would be respected, he would take control of the salaries of those teaching general education courses out of the hands of their respective departments in order to reward effective teachers. Mabie took up his new duties with enthusiasm. With the consent of Dean Dakin, but without consulting McGrath or the botany and zoology departments, he proposed to appoint a new teacher for the core course on the Biology of Man to be paid from the collegiate rather than from the departmental budgets. A similar appointment was to be made in the social sciences. McGrath was alarmed when he learned of Mabie's actions, since they appeared to contradict his pledge not to create a separate faculty for general studies. He knew of the hostility of the departmentalists, and he could not risk alienating his supporters in the biological and social sciences. His concern was well taken, since Kirk Porter complained bitterly of the new dean's domineering behavior. Going directly to the central administration, Porter pointed out that there had been no meeting of Mabie's advisory committee and that it had been the Executive Committee rather than the Curriculum Committee which had sponsored McGrath's proposed reforms. There had in fact been no meeting of the latter committee since McGrath took office. Realizing that he was in danger of alienating the faculty, the dean repudiated Mabie, who promptly resigned his directorship.[43]

Porter then went on the offensive, assembling the committee of departmentalists which recommended that students have the option of fulfilling core requirements in each area by substituting two departmental courses for the general course in that area. By substituting what would in effect be a departmental distribution requirement for core courses the proposal would destroy any pretense of general education. McGrath persuaded the faculty to refer the recommendation to its elected committees, where it quietly expired. By the summer of 1948 it was apparent to the dean that far from leading the faculty to adopt a stronger general education program he must struggle to defend the existing program. He acknowledged that, while there was widespread dissatisfaction with it, there was no faculty consensus as to what should be done. He could only counsel further discussion in the hope that eventually a consensus would emerge. At that juncture the University of Chicago offered him an opportunity to develop a new program for the training of college teachers. As he told Hancher, it was an opportunity "hand-tailored" for him, since he had become convinced that professors trained exclusively as researchers were rarely able or willing to confront the challenge of general education. He resigned in 1948, after a tenure of only three years, taking the *Journal of General Education* with him.[44]

Two deans had now sought with but mixed success to persuade the faculty to adopt a meaningful general education program. Hancher remained dissatisfied with the lack of cohesiveness or "scatteration" of the liberal arts curriculum, but he rightly sensed the faculty's weariness and desire for a period of tranquillity. McGrath's successor, Dewey B. Stuit, was not an ardent advocate of general education, at least in the sense in which his predecessors had understood the term. He believed strongly that the academic standing of the university was determined primarily by the scholarly accomplishments of the faculty members in their respective disciplines, and that the general education program, however desirable it might be, should accommodate itself to that fact. He recognized that general education had not become an integral part of liberal education in the United States, in part because of the conservatism of the departmentalists and in part because it had not yet been thought through as it related to disciplinary specialization. At his suggestion the faculty authorized the appointment of seven interdepartmental staff seminars representing the major divisions of the college. The object of these seminars was to determine whether departmental and general educational objectives could be reconciled. Each was to consider whether divisional courses in its area could be organized in such a way as to serve simultaneously as introductory departmental courses for students majoring in the subject.[45] After a year of deliberation the seminars concluded that integrated interdepartmental or area courses were impracticable. The dean and the Educational Policy Committee then for all practical purposes gave up on general education. They agreed that departmental courses "which stress the aims of general education"—whatever that might be—should qualify for core credit. After a series of acrimonious faculty meetings it was apparent by 1953 that inability to agree upon the meaning of general education together with jealous protection of departmental interests meant that the core program was little more than a distribution requirement.[46]

During the remaining years of the Hancher administration the steady drift toward departmentalism continued. In the sciences, the Introduction to Physical Science was dropped, leaving only the course in Life Science as an alternative to the introductory departmental courses in the various sciences. In the social science area, the two core courses, Introduction to Social Science and Man and Society, were combined, leaving the integrated course to compete with six departmental courses.[47] The objective of general education had gradually come to be defined in terms of the discipline-interdisciplinary dichotomy. Thinking in these terms was congenial to the departmentalists, who could focus attention on the problems of integrated courses. Any concern with the question whether particular subjects were of general educational value was forgotten.

REFORM PROPOSALS

Invigorated by the fresh breeze which accompanied the coming of the Bowen administration the liberal arts faculty once again turned its attention to general education. An ad hoc faculty committee proposed significant modifications in the core course requirements which had now been in place for more than twenty years. A new definition of general education was proposed—namely, an understanding of the nature of analysis in a discipline, what was meant by "knowing" in that discipline, and the kinds of questions it asked. Each student should be acquainted with four types of discipline: scientific, social-scientific, historical, and critical. The committee proposed to abandon the quasi-fiction that existing core courses were collegiate rather than departmental courses. It would assign each course to a relevant department with the understanding that it address the topics indicated above. It also recommended that the core course in English be grouped with art, music, and drama as one of the courses in the "critical" type of discipline. History, philosophy, and religion would constitute the historical group. The committee justified the regrouping with the observation that "art" in its various forms should not be used as an aid to the understanding of history.[48]

It was a statesmanlike attempt to address and overcome the conflict between the departmentalists and general educationists which had frustrated every effort to achieve a consensus on general education. The departmentalists would retain their introductory courses with the understanding that in them they would address the kinds of questions which would enable the student to integrate the information from the different types of discipline in a common web of understanding—an important expectation of the general educationists. Another innovative proposal was to introduce upper-level courses of an integrative or interdisciplinary nature. The committee observed that many students would profit more from general education courses in the senior rather than freshman year. These would be optional courses of a short-lived, experimental nature, such as the course on world affairs in which Virgil Hancher had participated some years earlier. Again the faculty failed to respond positively to an opportunity to revitalize its general education program. It was doubtless a mistake for the committee to have proposed the regrouping of courses in the critical and historical areas, since the departments concerned strongly opposed any change in their associations. The Educational Policy Committee was content to bestow its blessing on the creation of upper-level interdisciplinary courses, but declined to act on other aspects of the recommendations.[49]

In a series of public addresses Bowen complained of the failure of the faculty to come to grips with the problem of general education. The curriculum, he said, should be less scientific-rational and more aesthetic-intuitive-emotional. There were too many shallow surveys and courses which conveyed bodies of knowledge without cultivating a sense of values, purposes, or attitudes toward life. The core curriculum had failed to integrate the undergraduate experience. He found the faculty incorrigibly conservative and concluded that reform would have to come from outside its ranks, by which he presumably meant the administration.[50] Here, however, he was confronted by the stubborn resistance of Dean Stuit. Thoroughly entrenched after many years in office, the dean had molded a program which incorporated his preferences. A strong believer in departmental autonomy, he cultivated a close working relationship with the departmental executive officers, and he shared the view that core courses should be departmental rather than interdisciplinary in nature. He did not share Bowen's concern over the deterioration of liberal education—nor did the two men see eye-to-eye on several other policy matters. The dean was content to allow departmental preferences to prevail.[51]

The general education program had been in place for over thirty years when Dean Stuit retired in 1977. A thorn in the flesh of three presidents, Stuit had survived thanks to his sturdy integrity and his unquestioned devotion to the welfare of the university. During his tenure as dean he had guided the successive modifications in which departmentalism had steadily encroached upon the original conception of general education as consisting of distinctive "core" courses of a broad character. His successor as dean was Howard Laster, a physicist trained at Harvard and Cambridge University, who came to Iowa from the University of Maryland. A man of broad learning, familiar with the humanities as well as the sciences, Laster seemed ideally qualified to preside over the first major reassessment of the general education program. One of his first acts was to appoint a strong faculty committee on general education requirements under the leadership of Professor Marleigh Ryan, chair of the department of East Asian languages and literature. Consisting of nine faculty members and three students, the committee was instructed to hold hearings and submit recommendations to the Educational Policy Committee and eventually to the faculty.[52]

After eight months of deliberations the committee submitted, in October 1979, a preliminary report to serve as a basis for discussion and action in a series of faculty meetings. The report was notable for its subordination of practical departmental interests to general educational objectives. It spoke well for the existing program that the committee conceived its function to be remedial rather than revolutionary. It accepted the basic premises of the skills and core program of 1944 and sought only to strengthen and improve their implementation. It conceived of general education in traditional "Eurocentric" terms as gaining an understanding of the world through work in the arts and sciences. Emphasis was placed on the principle that general education—the term which should replace the traditional "skills and core courses"—was a college-wide program stressing ideas and concepts rather than facts. The program should not be left to the mercies of individual faculty members or departments, for the committee reported that it could find no rationale for certain existing courses. The college in its official capacity should exercise direct supervision of these courses in order to assure that the objectives of the program be kept clearly in view. This had always been one of the official functions of the elected Educational Policy Committee, and the Ryan committee was in effect condemning the EPC for its failure to monitor the program effectively. It proposed the establishment of a Steering Committee for each of the seven general education areas: English language, mathematics, foreign languages, natural science, social science, historical perspectives, and art and ethics. These committees would define the educational purposes of their respective areas and exercise a supervisory role, considering proposals for new general education courses, reviewing existing courses, and recommending appropriate actions to the EPC. The committees should also monitor the use of teaching assistants, take steps to improve their preparation, and establish annual prizes for the best teaching performance in each area. These prescriptions were, of course, in the nature of exhortations, rather than enforceable regulations.

Impressed with the parochial interests and outlook of the average undergraduate, the Ryan committee proposed that every student be required to take a course in international studies, a requirement which could be met in a variety of ways, including courses which might satisfy other requirements simultaneously. Just as in 1944, the required work in English received critical scrutiny. The chairman of the art department, Wallace Tomasini, held that English was no more deserving of favored status than any other art, and the historian Sydney James noted that the proponents of the English requirement were not agreed as to the reasons why English should be required. The Foerster emphasis on the study of values in literature had gradually dried up. The committee recommended that the English requirement be reduced to three hours.[53]

The rhetoric requirement was also carefully examined. There was widespread faculty complaint that students could not write, a deficiency for which the committee held the rhetoric staff only in part responsible. It recommended that one required semester of rhetoric should emphasize writing and that an upper-level colloquium in the student's major field should involve both written and oral reports. The existing mathematics requirement was found to be "shockingly deficient." The committee recommended that if suitable proficiency were not demonstrated within twelve months of initial registration the student should be required to pass the introductory mathematics course. It also proposed a new requirement in "analytical thinking" as represented by a specified course in logic, mathematics, statistics, or computer science. Elements of the faculty had always been critical of the physical education requirement, which was felt to be without educational merit. The committee recommended that the requirement be abandoned, thus assuring a lively contest when the issue would ultimately come to the faculty.

The moderate and accommodating spirit of the Ryan committee was most apparent in its discussion of general education in the areas of the natural and social sciences. These areas had always preferred introductory departmental courses to broader area or interdisciplinary courses, and the committee showed no disposition to impose specially designated general education courses on them. Similarly, in the area of historical perspectives, where the committee specified that courses should familiarize students with the chronological dimension of human experience, it nevertheless approved the existing courses in art, drama, music, philosophy, and problems in human history as well as the general courses in Western and Asian civilizations.[54] In order to strengthen work in the arts a new area in art and ethics was introduced. Altogether, the revised general education requirements totaled fifty to sixty-four hours for B.A. candidates, and thirty-eight to forty-eight hours for the B.S., B.M., and B.F.A. degrees.

The Educational Policy Committee adopted the committee's report and referred it to the faculty for action. In a series of meetings during April 1980 the faculty rejected the recommendation that the physical education requirement be dropped, but approved the remainder of the report.[55] The strengthening of the general education program would depend in large part upon the functioning of the area "Coordinating Committees," as the proposed Steering Committees were now to be called. It remained to be seen whether they would actively involve themselves to ensure the realization of general educational objectives. The Liberal Arts College was so large, embracing such a wide variety of subjects, that there was little feeling of collegiality among its faculty. Some departments had little respect for others, with a consequent lack of trust which prevented the faculty from consenting to the adoption of standards to be implemented by college-wide committees. Departments preferred to establish their goals and priorities through direct negotiations with the dean. Under the circumstances the Ryan committee had done what it could to strengthen the commitment of the college to its general education program.

Beneath the overt struggle between departmentalists and generalists was a deeper distinction between knowing and understanding. The nineteenth-century liberal arts curriculum had consisted of subjects which it was believed that the student should know. Familiarity with them was taken to be the mark of an educated person. What these subjects were might be a matter of dispute over the years, but that it was essential that certain things should be known was taken for granted. The student was commonly required to "recite" as evidence of having mastered the required material. In the twentieth century a subtle but pervasive shift began. The subjects which it was now necessary to know assumed a distinct form as technical or occupational specialties. One needed precise information for some practical purpose. The professional and technical fields extended their roots into the undergraduate years in the form of preprofessional requirements and other occupational skills. What was left to the liberal arts curriculum as distinctively its own was the responsibility for introducing students to an understanding of their own world. The culture concept—the ability to objectify one's own culture—was a contribution of nineteenth-century anthropology, but in the modern liberal arts curriculum the task of interpreting Western culture was assumed by a number of subjects identified as basic or "core" subjects. Among these were literature, the fine arts, the social sciences, and the natural sciences. A central position was to be occupied by the history of Western civilization, a subject not conceived of or taught in the nineteenth century.

Insofar as the object of the core curriculum was understanding or appreciation the acquisition of knowledge as that word was understood in the technical fields was minimized. The student might acquire a feeling for the shape or tone of the culture without having much precise knowledge of it. Literary studies served this purpose very well and became a highly popular option. On the other hand, the new curriculum did not serve those who insisted that the acquisition of precise bodies of information was essential to more advanced work. Representatives of these fields dragged their feet and attempted to curtail or bend the core to their needs. This remained the basic issue at Iowa over the decades following the adoption of the core program, as resistance to it was voiced by those who knew specifically what their disciplinary objectives were and who resented the intrusion of what they felt to be vague and unfocused requirements into the curriculum: The clarity of the struggle was clouded, however, by the corrupting influence of bread-and-butter considerations, as various programs fought for inclusion among the core requirements in order to enhance enrollments and justify staff increases.

CHAPTER EIGHT

The Boyd Years

C oming as it did in the midst of mounting campus tensions, the need to find a successor to President Bowen posed a pressing problem for the Board of Regents. Various groups expected to be consulted, while time was short and the need for administrative continuity was great. The full board itself constituted a selection committee and agreed to consult with committees representing the Faculty Senate, Student Senate, Staff Council, and Alumni Association. State senator Minnette Doderer complained that there were no women on any of these committees—a portent of things to come. Bowen strongly urged the board to appoint the academic vice-president and dean of faculties, Willard L. Boyd, who was, of course, well and favorably known to board members. The campus committees endorsed the proposal, and no further search was conducted. Boyd was appointed president and assumed office on July 1, 1969.[1]

The new president's response to the campus disturbances has already been described. The university over which he was to preside for the following twelve years was altered by the turmoil in both tangible and intangible ways. The tangible changes were most apparent in the Liberal Arts College, where curriculum and administration were both altered by the force of student demands. A new degree, bachelor of general studies, was introduced. Designed for students who were not interested in a major concentration, the B.G.S. required only the skills course in rhetoric and a distribution of other course work among several subjects. Some of the regents wondered whether it represented a lowering of academic standards, but like the liberal arts faculty they approved the proposal without enthusiasm.[2] Changes also occurred in the program of courses. The student demand for a more "relevant" curriculum had resulted in the Action Studies Program previously described. Most of the Action Studies courses were outside of the departmental structure and carried no credit. Dean Stuit proposed a more formal response with the designation of Contemporary Issues courses. Each department was urged to select for a special listing those of its courses which had contemporary relevance. Changes in the

Willard Boyd. Courtesy of the University of Iowa Photographic Service.

content of certain of the core courses also reflected the new mood of the campus. Readings in such militant black writers as Baldwin, Cleaver, and Brown were introduced into the English literature core, much to the distress of certain traditionally minded members of the English department. As options to the traditional core course in Western Civilization the history department introduced a number of Problems in Human History courses, dealing with such specialized topics as The Twentieth-Century World Crisis, The Vietnam War, The European Left, and Conquest and Colonization.[3] In response to environmental concerns the science departments introduced a new interdepartmental course on The Chemistry and Physics of the Environment. For their part the students demanded and were granted representation on university and college committees. Parietal rules were relaxed, and certain dormitories were opened to both men and women students. The academic calendar was advanced in order to terminate the spring semester in May and thus deprive potential demonstrators of the warm spring evenings so conducive to riotous behavior. But perhaps the most significant consequence of the campus unrest was a new emphasis on civil rights. The student movement had originated in this issue, and it was only appropriate that it should culminate in affirmative action programs to recruit minority and women students and faculty members.

NEW DIRECTIONS

Howard Bowen had conceived of the university in conventional terms. His object had been to strengthen its programs and thus elevate its standing among American universities by providing the support necessary to attract and retain an outstanding faculty and superior students. He had found the university in a steady upward spiral of growth and had confidently expected that an expanding Iowa economy would be able to support his ambitious plans for the university. His successor had entertained different expectations, being dissatisfied with certain aspects of the educational program of the university. Willard Boyd again raised the question that had been posed by Hancher: should the university be conventional, or should it be unique? In his inaugural address to the faculty and frequently thereafter Boyd insisted that the university should assert its institutional autonomy in order to achieve individuality. He believed that the curse of American higher education was its lack of diversity. Every institution sought to emulate the same model. Powerful pressures to standardize were exerted by an array of scholarly, professional, accrediting, and governmental agencies. Boyd urged his colleagues to resist these pressures and have the courage to strike out on their own. The university would thus achieve its own distinctive character.[4]

While he encouraged diversification it nevertheless pleased the new president to think of the university as distinctive in its physical and intellectual unity. Surrounding its core of arts and sciences was a well-integrated cluster of professional colleges. He noted that the Faculty Senate and a single Graduate College with its intercollegiate faculty had promoted a growing feeling for the university as a single entity. At the same time he emphasized the importance of a decentralized and flexible administration as essential to achieving the uniqueness he sought. Decisions should be made by those most immediately involved, including the students. He informed the faculty that the time had come to reevaluate the university's programs and goals. The Senate Committee on the Future of the University was invited to initiate an ongoing study of university objectives. The program of departmental reviews initiated by the Medical College could also serve a useful purpose in helping to determine priorities, relevant courses, space needs, and enrollment projections. Boyd was a strong supporter of departmental reviews, which he proposed to extend throughout the university and repeat on a five-year cycle. He conceived of the reviews as an integral part of the planning process in which the faculty would be actively involved in shaping the future of the university. Unfortunately, the faculty was not yet up to the challenge. The Committee on the Future of the University complained that it lacked a focused mandate and recommended to the Senate that it be dissolved. With a few exceptions the departmental reviews dealt narrowly with current operations rather than with plans for the future.[5]

The happy blend of unity and diversity so pleasing to the president was not so apparent to the North Central Association accreditation team which visited the campus in 1978. The visitors were impressed with the fragmented nature of the university—its decentralized administration, high degree of collegiate and departmental autonomy, and weak horizontal relationships across collegiate and disciplinary boundaries. They noted the absence of agencies to implement university-wide standards of faculty quality, services, and facilities. They recommended that the Medical College practice of college-wide peer group reviews of faculty qualifications be adopted by the other colleges. They would also institute university-wide peer group review of candidates for tenure positions. A university, they observed, should be more than a mere federation of colleges. The unity which the president celebrated needed to be legitimated by standards accepted by all of its units. There was no immediate institutional response to this challenge.[6]

The president himself was not without innovative educational ideas. The time had come, he believed, to give up the expectation of continuing growth and to accept the idea that the university should be a medium-sized institution with a limited program, determined to excel in what it did. He saw no reason to feel threatened by the growth of the other regents' institutions or by the rapidly expanding junior and area community colleges.[7] He proposed a "relevant" curriculum of courses which would relate the traditional specialized fields of knowledge to the broader problems of society, permitting students to come to grips with current issues. Such courses would be interdisciplinary in nature, bringing the resources of two or more disciplines to bear upon common problems. Consistent with interdisciplinary courses and with the unfocused expectations implicit in the B.G.S. degree was the president's proposal of a University College. This would be a mechanism whereby superior students would be able to formulate their own academic programs without regard to departmental and even collegiate boundaries. The University College would have no separate faculty of its own, since the entire university faculty would potentially be involved. However, the professional colleges with their own preprofessional programs were not enthusiastic about the prospect of students who might wish to take some professional work for reasons of their own. For his part Dean Stuit regarded the proposal as aimed at undergraduates, and he pointed out that the new B.G.S. program served the purpose the president had in mind. The Educational Policy Committee of the Liberal Arts College declined to take up the matter, thus in effect killing it.[8]

Boyd qualified Bowen's unconditional commitment to a research-oriented faculty by distinguishing between functions which were properly fused together, thus revisiting the old battleground of teaching versus research. He acknowledged that university professors, all of whom were engaged in teaching graduate or professional college students, should properly be involved in the discovery as well as dissemination of knowledge. He knew that the university was increasingly dependent upon the external funding commanded by faculty members with established scholarly reputations. Nevertheless, for reasons difficult to identify he belittled the research effort by saying that there was much less research going on at Iowa than was generally assumed. He was prepared to compromise with the established expectation of excellence in both teaching and research by conceding that outstanding achievement in either area should offset short-comings in the other. Such a concession appeared to open the door to those who hoped to base claims for promotion on superior performance as teachers. Earlier, when dean of faculties, he had already extended a similar concession to medical faculty members heavily burdened with service functions.[9]

Another educational emphasis which was distinctively his own was his stress on the importance of interdisciplinary teaching. Again, this was a challenge to the established order of things. The university had grown up as a cluster of disciplinary specialties, each with its own agenda and self-selected faculty. Each of the professional colleges occupied a world of its own, and even within the Liberal Arts College many of its departments existed in a surprising degree of isolation from closely related subjects. Communication studies and journalism, drama and literature, sociology and social psychology, history and political science, to mention only a few, carried on their activities as though the neighboring organizations scarcely existed. Nevertheless, Boyd considered the disciplines not so much as ends in themselves but as foundations on which to build interdisciplinary work. In a given discipline the student learned a distinctive method of analysis; the method should be put to use in an interdisciplinary context where practical problems are addressed. There is more to education, he affirmed, than mere training. General studies of an interdisciplinary nature lead to an understanding of the self, of work, and of the community. He would even go so far as to require every faculty member periodically to teach an interdisciplinary course. Provost Heffner was ordered to form a commit-tee to consider ways to develop interdisciplinary studies. That committee threw cold water on the most comprehensive forms of intercollegiate study by declaring that education was an exclusive responsibility of each of the university's colleges.[10]

The Liberal Arts College had in fact a certain amount of experience with interdisciplinary studies, a review of which would have revealed some of the difficulties in offering such work. Over the years it was the English department which had shown a persistent interest in interdisciplinary studies. The program in American Studies sponsored by that department had for some years offered interdisciplinary opportunities without ever having arrived at the kind of synthesis which the president took for granted as the proper outcome of interdisciplinary study. A program in European Literature and Thought offered an impressive array of seminar type courses on such topics as Myth and Reason, The Good Society, Science and the Nature of Man, and Form and Milieu in the Arts, each taught by two or more specialists from relevant departments. But these courses attracted only a few students. It is conceivable that more might have been done to meet the president's expectations had Dean Stuit taken the initiative. The dean pointed out that when the general education program had been adopted in the 1940s the faculty had favored interdisciplinary courses to satisfy core requirements but had subsequently found that departmental courses were as effective as interdisciplinary courses in achieving the ends of general education. He candidly admitted that he was committed to a discipline-oriented education, believing that interdisciplinary programs should rest on a strong disciplinary foundation. "If a university is to be great," he warned, "it must be able to demonstrate quality in its basic academic disciplines." [11] In fact, the most successful kinds of interdisciplinary work involved research on a clearly focused topic, such as that being done in physics and astronomy, in biomedical engineering, or in biological and medical collaboration on problems in genetics.

Thwarted in his efforts to establish a University College, the president found another way to promote interdisciplinary study by creating University House, a center housing a miscellaneous group of interdisciplinary programs. The former tuberculosis sanitarium at Oakdale was converted to facilities housing the program in Regional and Urban Research, the Genetics Graduate Program, the World Order Studies Center, the Statistics Consulting Center, the Center for Environmental Studies, the Institute for Child Behavior and Development, and the Administrative Science Graduate Program. Boyd envisioned these programs as engaged in experimental studies. He referred to University House, perhaps unfortunately, as "an academic half-way house." [12]

The president's implicit criticism of the rigidity of collegiate and departmental programs related directly to his views on general education. No Iowa president took so grave a view of what he considered to be the current threat to the survival of liberal, or general, education. "Liberal education," he warned, "is under its greatest attack in American history." The federal government with its targeted funding programs was distorting the shape of educational institutions. State government with its threats of line-item budgets and reviews of duplicating programs inhibited institutional development. Perhaps the greatest threat came from the academic community itself, in the form of peer-group review by accrediting agencies which imposed a stifling uniformity and crushed unorthodox innovations. A particularly aggravating instance of the latter occurred in the School of Journalism, where Boyd had encouraged the development of a curriculum emphasizing investigation, analysis, and communication, leaving the more practical aspects of journalistic education to job training and continuing education. The school promptly lost its accreditation. Experiences like this reinforced Boyd's conviction that applied skills were everywhere more highly valued than basic skills and that disciplinary parochialism and vocational pragmatism dominated the educational scene.[13]

The president continued to insist upon the need for general education as the best means of achieving the individual flexibility required in a changing society. He liked to note that the average individual would change occupations several times during the course of a lifetime. Too specialized an education would clearly be a handicap. But Boyd was quite uncertain as to the most effective form general education should take. He was prepared to abandon the core course pattern as a lost cause and consider other approaches to the problem. His conception of general education was essentially functional: the student should learn to comprehend, to analyze, to explain, and to act ethically. It seemed of little consequence to him whether work in general education came first, last, or along the way. He favored interdisciplinary courses dealing with "big" topics, such as war, the environment, and human rights. He echoed Bowen's belief that there should be more emphasis on values and the emotions. If his proposed University College failed to win favor perhaps an all-university forum for general education comparable to the graduate faculty would serve the purpose as well, since every college in the university served the cause of general education in one way or another. His uncertainty was apparent in the fact that while finding general educational values suffused throughout the university he could at the same time propose the introduction of an associate in arts degree. This would be a two-year program designed specifically for those completing the general education requirements of the Liberal Arts College. But when Dean Stuit asked the president if he wished to have the Educational Policy Committee pursue the matter Boyd backed off, and nothing came of the proposal.[14]

MAY BRODBECK

The appointment in 1974 of May Brodbeck as academic vice-president and dean of faculties marked an important turning point in the history of the university. For the first time the central administration was to become systematically involved in the crucial process of recruitment, review, and promotion of faculty members, matters which had previously been left to the colleges and departments. Brodbeck had taken her Ph.D.

at the university. At the University of Minnesota she had built a distinguished career as philosopher and administrator, having served as president of the American Philosophical Association and dean of the Graduate School. Building on the efforts of Bowen and Boyd to invigorate the faculty she inaugurated procedures designed to provide a central administrative oversight of appointment and promotion decisions. Initial junior appointments would no longer be routinely approved by the dean of faculties. The academic credentials of proposed appointees accompanied by three letters of recommendation must now be forwarded for the dean's approval. She also announced that she would personally interview candidates for senior positions.[15]

In the past junior faculty members on term appointments had not always been informed as to the quality of their work or their prospects for advancement. Departments had occasionally neglected to evaluate the performance of junior colleagues until the time when mandatory decisions as to advancement or termination must be made, sometimes to the pain and distress of all those involved. Brodbeck now required that annual reviews of the performance of probationary faculty be submitted, with more intensive scrutiny during the third and sixth years of service or one year prior to termination of appointment. These requirements served both to assure fairness to the individual and to strengthen the faculty's sense of involvement in the academic careers of each of its members.[16] The official criteria for promotion which had been in place for many years were unexceptionable, but their application in certain instances had been less than rigorous. Brodbeck announced that recommendations for promotion to tenure positions must be accompanied by a full review of qualifications by the relevant departmental faculty and collegiate dean. The uncertainty surrounding the meaning of "service" was clarified by defining service as "other professional contributions." Attention had been focused on a presumed conflict between teaching and research, whereas in fact the real conflict was between research and service. In fields such as clinical medicine, dentistry, nursing, and social work where service was central to the discipline there tended to be a corresponding lack of interest in research. The difficulty inherent in resolving such conflicts was apparent in a crisis in the College of Nursing.[17]

Prior to the Second World War nurses had generally been trained in hospitals rather than in universities. When university colleges of nursing were organized their faculties had rarely received research training in that field. In order to obtain necessary credentials faculty members often took doctoral degrees in such non-nursing fields as psychology, education, or social work. Such training hardly prepared them for research careers in nursing. At Iowa a crisis was apparent in 1975, when some thirty-three assistant professors and instructors in nursing had reached the sixth probationary year without having satisfied the criteria for tenure appointments. They were then notified that they would be given six additional years, during which time neither the college nor the central administration took positive steps to encourage or assist them in developing and pursuing research programs. By 1979 it was apparent to Brodbeck that she must either grant tenure or terminate them. Since all were satisfactory teachers she chose the humane alternative and announced that twenty-two assistant professors and one instructor would be given tenure at their present rank (five of the original thirty-three had previously been promoted and five had resigned). Brodbeck knew that the decision would be controversial, and she was not mistaken. Many faculty members felt that so massive a deviation from established standards cast doubt on the university's determination to abide by its regulations. A Faculty Senate committee appointed to investigate recommended that instead of granting tenure the individuals in question be appointed clinical assistant professors, an annual appointment renewable indefinitely until such time as the tenure criteria might be satisfied. The council endorsed the recommendation and the president and Dean Brodbeck accepted it, reserving authority to make exceptions to the established criteria in rare and special cases.[18]

A 1974 statement by the president on academic vitality and tenure reaffirmed the established expectations of effective teaching and useful research. Security of tenure was confirmed for those who satisfied these requirements. Junior faculty members on term appointments were assured that there would be no quotas or limits on the number of faculty holding indefinite tenure. Assurance of promotion whenever merited was an important advantage to the university, since many universities placed limits on the number of senior positions, forcing promising junior faculty members to move elsewhere. Tenure decisions should preferably be made in the sixth year of probation, by which time the individual could reasonably be expected to have demonstrated accomplishments worthy of a permanent commitment. For those who received full-time faculty appointment as instructors without having completed doctoral degree requirements six years was in fact a short time in which to establish public scholarly credentials, and some questioned whether the years during which degree requirements were being met should be counted in the probationary period. If the university were to refrain from appointing instructors without appropriate credentials it risked the likelihood of losing promising candidates, especially in periods of rapid growth when young teachers were in great demand.[19] No satisfactory solution to this problem was found.

One of Dean Brodbeck's major objectives was to strengthen the scholarly and professional standing of the faculty. Doubtless aware of the rejection of Bowen's proposal to incorporate research time in the regular academic schedule she took a more traditional approach to the support of research. Carefully avoiding such terms as "leave of absence," "sabbaticals," and even "research," she favored "developmental assignments" to support work on special projects. Faculty vitality was best measured by involvement in the discovery of new knowledge, by contributions to improved teaching techniques, and by favorable recognition by one's peers. Developmental assignments at appropriate intervals would be made to support these objectives. Faculty members who submitted worthy projects would be given relief from teaching for one semester at full pay, or for a summer session at two-ninths of base salary. Individuals would be eligible at five-year intervals, and departments were urged to develop rotation plans. Applications would be reviewed by the collegiate deans and by a faculty committee reporting to the academic vice-president. Ninety-six of these assignments were made in 1977 for the support of research, improvements in instruction, and professional development.[20] In the expectation that developmental assignments would chiefly be made to senior faculty members Brodbeck initiated a Faculty Scholars Program for younger faculty, specifically those falling between the third year of an assistant professorship and the second year of associate professorship. The intent of this program was to single out especially promising scholars or creative people and provide them with an unusual opportunity to develop their talents. The faculty scholar would teach only one semester for each of the three years of the scholarship and would receive an added stipend for travel or research expense. Up to ten scholars would be appointed in the first year and five annually thereafter.[21]

An important stimulus to the intellectual vitality of the university resulted from the Ida Beam bequest of land worth $650,000. Ida Beam Distinguished Visiting Professorships brought to the campus for brief periods a succession of outstanding scholars in a wide variety of fields who contributed greatly to the enrichment of campus life. Of far greater magnitude was the succession of gifts from the industrialist Roy Carver, beginning in 1971. Carver funds supported professorships, Special Support Services, additions to the hospital and art museum, the Old Capitol restoration, a community health center in Muscatine, and artificial turf for Kinnick Stadium.

The president understood the practical importance of research in attracting non-state-appropriated funds to the university. He knew that the increasing proportion of the budget which they represented depended upon the capability and achievement of the faculty. In 1980 the university ranked 39th among the top 100 colleges and universities in the amount of federal research grants received. Within the Big Ten it ranked third in amounts received relative to the number of faculty members. During the previous decade it had received a total of $433,848,117 in external funds for the support of research, training, equipment, and student aid.[22]

The joint efforts of faculty and administration to advance the university, together with the determination of presidents Bowen and Boyd to cultivate a mutually supportive relationship with the faculty, resulted in a climate of opinion indifferent to the movement for collective bargaining which appeared on many campuses during the 1970s. Bargaining assumed an adversarial relationship between faculty and administration and tended to be favored by faculties which felt themselves to be isolated from administration and powerless to make their interests felt. At the university, on the other hand, where the active involvement of the faculty through its committees, Senate, and collegiate organizations in the decision-making process made it impossible to separate faculty and administrative functions, there was relatively little interest in collective bargaining. While certain categories of the nonacademic staff chose to adopt a bargaining relationship, a Senate poll of faculty opinion showed a substantial majority in favor of the existing relationships.[23]

AFFIRMATIVE ACTION

The coming of affirmative action might well prove in the long run to have been the most important event of the Boyd administration. As a public institution in a state predominantly white the university had never enrolled more than a token number of minority students. In response to the civil rights movement and the murder of Dr. King the university responded enthusiastically to Bowen's call for a program to provide educational opportunity for underprivileged minorities. It was perceived as a moral obligation, a humanitarian gesture, and a civic responsibility. The Office of Special Support Services was established in 1968 to recruit and assist educationally and economically disadvantaged students by providing financial aid, academic and personal counseling, tutoring, and other forms of assistance. Over the following decade, some 1,800 students were assisted, the vast majority of whom were black. Disadvantaged students were often educationally deprived, which meant that many of them had difficulty in satisfying academic requirements. The Office of Special Support Services, which was committed to increasing the number of such students, urged that remedial skills courses be offered and that students be guaranteed four semesters in which to establish themselves in good standing. But the question of adapting academic expectations to the needs of underprivileged students remained unresolved.[24]

President Boyd agreed with Bowen that equality of opportunity was "the foremost goal of our time," and he went on to celebrate the cultural enrichment presumed to flow from the presence on campus of numerous ethnic minorities. He was projecting an educational version of the newly emerging national attitude toward ethnic relations. The older public assumption of the assimilation of racial and ethnic groups to a common American type had been compatible with the ideal of general education as a unifying cultural experience. Now, however, the expectation of assimilation was in eclipse, replaced by integrated ethnic groups, each of which retained its distinctive identity. The appropriate educational response was to celebrate cultural diversity. Blacks were to be recruited not simply because they were entitled to advanced education—which, after all, they could receive at a black college—but because their presence on campus was believed to play an important role in exposing white students to Afro-American culture. President Boyd firmly believed that a diversified faculty and student body would improve the quality of both instruction and scholarship. In other contexts he stressed the value of interdisciplinary studies, but in this area, where cultural assimilation would seem to be the logical outcome of interdisciplinary work, he stopped short. Separate programs in Women's Studies and Afro-American Studies were established, and political constituencies appeared which gave every sign of permanently dividing the university community. Cosmopolitanism as the president understood it could appropriately be defined as the appreciation of cultural differences, although this was, strictly speaking, a social rather than an educational value.[25]

Affirmative action originated in a concern for the welfare of minorities, but it was quickly taken over by the majority—women—who were to become its principal beneficiaries. The university had long prided itself, no doubt with a certain condescension, on its coeducational tradition. But it was also a fact that women had been herded into the "cultural" fields appropriate to their peculiar social status, such as nursing, elementary and secondary education, home economics, and the arts. Save for nursing and education, established female occupations, these were fields appropriate for those who expected to have domestic careers. Seashore's reservations about the advanced education of women have already been noticed. As recently as 1958 Dean Stuit reflected a common ambivalence when he discussed the appropriate education for women in view of the fact that most of them would become homemakers. He noted the questions which were usually asked. Was a junior college education sufficient for women? Should scholarships and aid be awarded without regard to sex? In view of the high cost of professional education, should women be admitted to professional schools when there was an oversupply of male professionals? Merely to ask these questions suggested the willingness of educational officers to consider the imposition of social criteria upon the educational choices of students when they happened to be women. But Stuit backed away from the hard line these questions suggested. He believed that educational decisions should take note of the fact that women were first of all human beings, then homemakers, family members, civic leaders and participants, and also possibly gainfully employed. He acknowledged that many women were capable of doing professional and technical work. For such diverse expectations the best possible preparation was a sound liberal education.[26]

While the campus radicals of the 1960s sought to politicize the university in terms of public issues, President Boyd sponsored his own brand of politicization. Traditionally, the academic objectives of the university had been defined by the administrative officers and senior faculty members, most of whom were white males. While this had certainly been an academic political system it was one in which merit was usually recognized. The new politicization which Boyd promoted introduced a social, nonacademic factor. He envisioned the university as composed of various interest groups: men and women, blacks and other ethnic groups, students, and nonacademic staff. Academic decisions should be reached by agencies which represented each of these groups rather than by agencies constituted according to some conception of relevance to the academic purposes of the university. Accordingly, university charter committees were reconstituted to include women and minority faculty members, students, and staff. With the president's blessing women faculty members caucused in order to assure the election of women to committees, and wherever they failed to be elected Dean Brodbeck arbitrarily added women members. Eventually, although not during the Boyd years, the time would come when the administration would require that the next faculty appointment be offered to a woman regardless of the priority order of candidates adopted by the program in question.

Affirmative action at the university was inaugurated in the academic year 1971–72. Although it was mandated by the federal government through legislation and executive orders President Boyd welcomed it with every intention of complying with both the spirit and letter of the law. He announced that while the university had always stood for equal opportunity the time had come to take positive action to achieve this goal. The barriers to the employment of women and minorities must be overcome, beginning with the university itself. Opportunities for employment must be brought to the attention of all, and recruitment practices must be designed to identify and attract qualified women and minority candidates.[27] Dr. Cecelia Foxley was appointed director of the affirmative action office. A survey of the faculty showed that women for the most part occupied the lower ranks and received lower than average salaries. In order to rectify this situation a "matched-pair" methodology was devised in order to overcome the presumed discrimination. Women were matched with male departmental colleagues in terms of qualifications, seniority, rank, and experience. Salaries were then adjusted to equalize their incomes. Over one hundred women received salary increases totaling $101,257. In making these adjustments considerations of merit were disregarded; it was sufficient to correct a presumed injustice. In the academic year 1971–72, some 2,159 women students received financial aid in the form of loans, grants, or scholarships as compared to 2,339 males assisted.[28]

State restrictions on the employment of family members of public employees enacted during the Depression for the purpose of spreading employment income had fixed a precedent which lasted for decades and served as a significant barrier to married women who wished to pursue academic careers. These precedents were swept aside in October 1971, when it was announced that spouses of university employees were eligible for academic appointments so long as neither spouse was in a position to establish the status or pay of the other. Another significant victory for women was achieved in February 1972, with the decision that part-time faculty members, who were usually female, would be eligible for advancement as determined by the same criteria used to evaluate full-time faculty. The expectation that junior faculty members should qualify for indefinite tenure within seven years of initial appointment or be dismissed had presupposed full-time faculty status and worked to the disadvantage of the part-time appointee. Efforts to modify the regulation by lengthening the probationary period for part-time faculty were not immediately success-ful, perhaps due to the small number of individuals involved.

Federal supervision of affirmative action in academe was assigned to the Office of Civil Rights of the Department of Health, Education and Wel-fare, which became increasingly aggressive in implementing its com-pliance procedures. Each educational institution was required to adopt an affirmative action plan based on a precise enumeration of employees in each ethnic and gender group. Previous nondiscrimination policies had required that such distinctions be concealed; now they must be revealed. Underutilization was to be determined by comparing the number of targeted employees in each group with an appropriate pool of potential employees. Wherever underutilization was established a schedule of nu-merical goals and timetables was to be drawn up indicating future staff needs and the steps to be taken to increase the number of employees in each group in order to reach the indicated goal. Goals and timetables were the heart of the affirmative action effort, and as the program unfolded they became the principal point of contention.[29]

In the spring of 1972 each department and program was required to draw up goals for the following two years. The combined goal for addi-tional female faculty numbered 25 and for minorities, 6. For the adminis-trative, professional, and scientific category the goal was 235 females and 32 minorities. As it turned out, the goals were more than achieved in each category save for minority appointments in the latter category, which fell 9 short. The usefulness of projecting goals was limited by the fact that the number of appointments in any future year could not be predicted with accuracy. More openings proved to be available in 1973–74 than had been predicted, thus providing opportunities for appointments in the favored categories. In general, however, the 1970s were to be financially lean years, restricting the total number of openings. Nor did the summary figures in-dicate the fact that most of the female appointments were in programs tra-ditionally staffed by women, such as nursing.[30]

At a meeting of deans in November 1972 fear was expressed that if affir-mative action were vigorously pursued it could result in lowering the scholarly quality of the faculty. Pressure to reach employment goals within the specified timetables might lead to the appointment of less qualified women or minority candidates. President Boyd, Provost Heffner, and Dr. Foxley all insisted, however, that there would be no reverse discrimi-nation against white males. After an exhaustive search in which a good-faith effort had been made to identify qualified women and minority candidates for a vacancy the appointment would be offered to the best-qualified candidate. Employment goals must be realistic, in terms of the likely number of appointments to be made and the size of the pool of qualified candidates. The ultimate test would not be whether the goal was reached, but whether a good faith effort had been made to reach it. The president then added that in order to appoint in the favored categories and also maintain faculty quality it might be necessary on occasion to delay an appointment until such time as a female or minority candidate proved to be the most highly qualified.[31] If this was not reverse discrimination it might properly be called "delayed discrimination."

Federal investigators complimented the university on its program, but specified a number of areas in which improvements should be made, including goals and timetables; more minority and women appointees to senior positions, and to committees and boards; greater employment of faculty wives; improved grievance procedures; and the correction of wage and salary differentials.[32] Dean Stuit bitterly criticized these findings as outrageous and unrealistic. He was convinced that the government was using goals and timetables as an excuse for the imposition of employment quotas, and that the quality of the university would be jeopardized. He was wholly in sympathy with the principle of searching out qualified women and minority candidates and evaluating their credentials without discrimination. But the university should appoint the best-qualified person regardless of other factors. He insisted that salary scales should be based on merit rather than on age, seniority in rank, gender, or ethnic identification. He stubbornly declared that the university "is not a social welfare or political institution, hence it must not seek, as a university, to promote the welfare of *any* particular group." He objected to the setting of goals and timetables because it committed the university to objectives which if unachieved would expose the institution to hostile action.[33]

Although government officials agreed with university officers that nothing in affirmative action regulations required the university to employ an unqualified person, there was considerable difference over what was meant by "qualification." The university, and Stuit in particular, insisted upon the necessity of employing the most highly qualified person who could be found after an exhaustive search which included women and minorities. Government officials, on the other hand, maintained that there were large pools of qualified women and minority scholars and that the university could satisfy its scholarly expectations by appointing one of them if it searched widely enough. They thought of qualifications as applying to groups and were unable to appreciate the fact that professional and institutional competition had nurtured the concept of the uniquely qualified individual. For this reason they saw no conflict between goals and timetables and the university's need to appoint the most highly qualified person. Throughout the 1970s Boyd continued to insist that "the goal of the selection process had remained unchanged—to select the most qualified from among those available." [34]

By 1980, however, when Classie Hoyle, Cecelia Foxley's successor as director of affirmative action, sought clarification from the administration as to its position on the matter of qualification for faculty appointments she received a distinctly different answer. She asked whether an offer of appointment should be made to the best-qualified person or to a qualified member of an underrepresented group. Randall Bezanson, vice-president for finance and university services, replied that subjective elements were always present in such decisions. The benefits to be derived from cultural and racial diversity were always to be considered where merit was involved. In other words, affirmative action was now an integral part of merit, inextricably intertwining social with academic qualifications. [35]

After several years of affirmative action efforts women and minority representatives expressed dissatisfaction with the results, complaining of evasion and failure by the government to act more aggressively. New guidelines were issued in 1976, dividing the faculty into tenured and nontenured groups in order to monitor progress in each group. The numbers of women and minority faculty members in each group were to be compared with the percentage of such persons available in an appropriate labor pool in order to determine underutilization, if any. The Faculty Council reported that such comparisons were arbitrary because of the difficulty of identifying appropriate pools. [36]

Women proved to be the principal beneficiaries of affirmative action, while minorities complained that the program had been of little benefit to them. By the end of the Boyd administration, in 1981, sixteen percent of the tenured faculty were female, and twenty-one percent of the nontenured. Seven percent of the tenured faculty were minorities, a figure which included Asian-Americans, and eleven percent of the nontenured. Goals for tenure-track appointments had been met by one-third of the departments. The financial constraints of the 1970s had greatly restricted the number of new faculty appointments, while in several fields the lack of qualified candidates made it difficult to meet the goals. Under the circumstances, university officials professed to be generally pleased with the progress which had been made. [37]

FINANCIAL CONSTRAINTS

L ooking back on the years of the Bowen administration Dewey Stuit accurately characterized them as the "golden era," not only of the University of Iowa, but perhaps also of American higher education in general. The recruitment of better-trained and research-oriented younger faculty promised a higher standard of academic achievement, while the introduction of formal student evaluation of classroom instruction helped to keep teachers on their toes. Unfortunately, the bright prospects of those years were soon blighted by the restricted budgets of the 1970s, which threw the university on the defensive and forced it to confront the painful alternatives of eliminating certain programs or suffering across-the-board curtailment which would weaken all of its activities.[38]

The campus turmoil of 1968–69 was reflected immediately in an unsympathetic and often hostile attitude of the public toward the university, as reflected in the inadequate budget provided by the legislature for the 1969–71 biennium. The general education fund yielded merely a three percent increase for each of the two years, while growth in enrollment and inflation more than ate up the increase. It was necessary to raise tuition in order to provide modest salary increases. The added cost of from nine to twelve percent for the students was bitterly resented and added fuel to the campus conflagration of 1970. Certain board members objected to the third-place formula as a budget objective, proposing either to dilute it by adding other states to the comparison group or to substitute such factors as turnover rates, faculty resignations, fringe benefits, and recruitment experience in determining an appropriate salary base. Such proposals represented a weakening of the traditional determination of the board to make the strongest possible claims for support of its institutions. In preparing its budget requests the board had previously identified a "catch-up" sum needed to recover the university's third-place position and a "keep-up" sum to retain that position in the face of current increases by the comparison institutions. In 1970, greatly to Boyd's distress, the board abandoned the catch-up factor and recommended only a 6.5 percent keep-up increase in faculty salaries. A decade earlier Iowa had ranked eighth among the states in per capita support of higher education; now it ranked eighteenth.[39]

Continuing budget stringency in the 1971–73 biennium forced the president to consider more drastic alternatives, all of which bore directly on the educational program of the university. He could abolish programs outright. He could reduce the number of visiting professorships and research professorships. He could eliminate salary lines wherever departmental enrollments declined, thus in effect subjecting educational decisions to the curricular choices of students. Or he could institute the practice of budget rollback and reallocation. Choosing the latter alternative, he sequestered five percent of each salary and general expense budget for 1971–72, thus generating internal savings to be used for merit salary increases. He also closed the university elementary and high schools and the Institute of Gerontology. Ten buildings were "mothballed," and the custodial staff was reduced in order to achieve a saving of $332,000. These measures made possible modest salary increases in 1971–72, but there was nothing left for raises in 1972–73.[40]

In preparing his budget recommendations for 1973–75 the governor in turn adopted the reallocation procedure, ordering the university to prepare a base budget equal to ninety percent of that of the previous year, together with recommendations for salary increases, new programs, and general operating funds. He said that his object was to identify program priorities. The shoe was now on the other foot, and Boyd complained that the university would be badly hurt. He believed that it faced the greatest financial crisis since the 1930s. That this assessment was not exaggerated became evident when 108 faculty members resigned in 1974 to accept more attractive appointments elsewhere.[41]

Financing the increasingly expensive medical program presented special problems. Unlike other university programs, only thirty-four percent of the medical budget came from the state appropriation. Forty-two percent came from federal and foundation sources, and twenty-four percent from fees. The federal government was far more irresponsible than the state government in failing to recognize the necessity for stable and continuing financial commitment. Programs undertaken with federal funds and initiative were subject to sudden withdrawal of support, obliging the university to seek state support or to transfer funds from other university programs. In 1979 the university was obliged to request an additional state appropriation of $3,700,000 to replace lost federal funds, mostly in the health sciences. The extent of dependence on federal money in that year was apparent in the various forms in which it was received: capitation and formula grants; training grants; construction grants; cost of education allowances; work-study aid; basic and supplemental educational opportunity grants; direct loans; guaranteed loans; and fellowships and traineeships.[42]

The years 1975–80 saw a relative improvement in salary budgets, although they still lagged well behind the rate of inflation. Salary increases for those years ranged between 7.4 and 10 percent, although internal reallocations were necessary to support the medical budget. A Faculty Senate report of 1980 painted a grim picture of the financial losses suffered by the faculty in the previous twelve years. Consumer prices for the period had more than doubled, while faculty salaries had declined 19.6 percent in real dollars. As the report pointed out, "in effect, these dollars lost to inflation represent a subsidy from the faculty for the education of Iowa students and the operation of our institution."[43]

In 1980 the situation rapidly turned worse. While the regents were preparing a request for $6,000,000 in additional funds, Governor Ray proposed a cut in state spending which would cost the university $17,100,000. Building projects would be delayed, and the replacement of lost federal funds for the health colleges would necessitate the transfer of funds from other university budgets. The governor then ordered a $3,438,000 reversion to the state from the university general fund, approximately half to come from a freeze on hiring, and the remainder from supplies, services, and repairs. As of January 1, 1981, he ordered an additional one percent reversion. These orders came at a time when the regents were seeking a thirty-two percent increase in the salary budget for the 1981–83 biennium.[44]

That biennium proved to be decisive for Boyd. While the consumer price index was increasing at twelve percent annually, and the Iowa per capita income was increasing at ten percent, faculty salaries were increasing by only five percent. Federal employees, other state employees, and schoolteachers were all faring relatively better than university faculty members. Public universities in surrounding states were providing professorial salaries with fringe benefits which were eight percent higher than Iowa's. Nevertheless, the governor ordered a $4,400,000 reversion from the general education fund of the university at a time when student enrollment had reached the highest point in its history. Boyd announced that he would continue to press for the regents' $14,000,000 catch-up appropriation, which only earned him criticism from legislators for not supporting the governor's economy efforts. The president's resignation was now inevitable.[45]

The crisis in appropriated funds underscored the importance of finding alternative sources of support. The Medical College led the way by virtue of its long experience with various forms of income. By 1981 only twenty-four percent of its budget came from the state appropriation. An additional forty-six percent came from gifts, grants, contracts, and fees. The remaining thirty percent came from the Medical Service Plan. Increasing reliance on the plan was a cause of concern, however, since it represented a growing burden of patient care at the expense of other responsibilities.

Research grants, mostly in the health sciences, regularly increased, reaching $29,066,000 in the academic year 1977–78.[46]

Perhaps the greatest potential for future support lay in the private sector. As previously noted, the Alumni Association had been used initially as a lobbying organization, and a full-time secretary was not appointed until 1947. Under the leadership of the secretary, Loren Hickerson, the Old Gold Development Fund was established in 1956 to solicit alumni contributions for the support of university programs. In its first year of operation the fund received a modest $27,920.21 from 1,320 contributors. But the potential importance of this source of support became readily apparent as the volume of contributions increased rapidly year by year. The State University of Iowa Foundation was established in 1957 as a nonprofit tax-exempt corporation to solicit, receive, and manage gifts for the university's benefit. While the Old Gold Fund sought regular contributions from alumni and friends to be allocated to the support of specific projects, the foundation sought substantial gifts to an endowment fund or for projects specified by the donor. Darrell Wyrick succeeded Hickerson as director in 1966, and the two funds were merged in the following year. Contributions for current expenditures passed the million dollar mark in 1968, in which year the foundation also received over $2 million in deferred income. During the first twelve years the funds had received a total of $5,058,616 from 77,837 contributors.[47]

Important as the systematic cultivation of habits of regular giving was, equally important was the identification of wealthy individuals in a position to make substantial gifts, and to have the machinery in place to maximize the benefits of such beneficence. Thus it became possible to secure the Eliot art collection by successfully mounting a capital fund campaign to raise over a million dollars from nearly two thousand contributors to provide the museum in which to house the collection. Similarly, the construction of the Carver-Hawkeye Arena was made possible by a fundraising campaign to complement the munificent gift of Roy Carver. Altogether, in the first twenty-five years, the funds had received in gifts, pledges, and known bequests over $117,000,000 for the support of university programs. In addition to buildings these programs included distinguished professorships, scholarships and other forms of student aid, research support, library books, art works, and support of the University of Iowa Press.[48] The university was in the process of becoming a new type of mixed institution resting upon a public foundation of fairly dependable tax support supplemented by tuition and fees, federal grants and contracts, foundation grants, and a growing volume of private gifts from alumni and friends.

In the absence of what would eventually be called a "strategic plan" for its future the university throughout its history had always responded passively to the opportunities presented by growth. It either had allowed student enrollment choices to determine which programs should be enlarged and potentially strengthened or had permitted aggressive promoters to launch new ventures which tapped its resources and shaped its development. In the later decades of this century, faced with the prospect of increasingly stringent economies together with a stable or declining student population, it had to decide whether it could manage contraction more effectively than it had managed expansion. One tool for such management was budget sequestration and reallocation, although it begged the question as to which programs should be inaugurated or strengthened and which curtailed or eliminated. Such decisions were bound to be painful, and it remained to be seen whether the faculty and administration could formulate a program which would assure the university a useful place in the twenty-first century.

NOTES

References to collections of papers in the University of Iowa Archives are indicated as follows:

BDPC Boyd Presidential Correspondence
BNP Bowman Presidential Papers
BOPC Bowen Presidential Correspondence
GP Gilmore Presidential Papers
HPC Hancher Presidential Correspondence
HPS Hancher Presidential Speeches
JP Jessup Presidential Papers
MBP Macbride Presidential Papers
MLP MacLean Presidential Papers
OHI Oral History Project interviews

PROLOGUE: A PROVINCIAL UNIVERSITY

1. Vernon Carstensen, "The State University of Iowa: The Collegiate Department from the Beginning to 1878" (University of Iowa dissertation, 1936), 5–6. Common usage has restricted the term "land grant institution" to the agricultural and mechanical colleges that received assistance under the Morrill Act of 1862. This tends to obscure the fact that all of the western state universities were federal land grant institutions.
2. Leonard F. Parker, *Higher Education in Iowa* (Bureau of Education, Circular No. 6, Washington: GPO, 1893). Parker's succinct account of the early history of the university (76–121) is of particular value because of his close connection with it as professor of Greek between 1870 and 1887.
3. Ibid., 77.
4. Ibid., 66–68; Earle D. Ross, *A History of the Iowa State College of Agriculture and the Mechanic Arts* (Ames: Iowa State College Press, 1942), 21.
5. Ross, *History*, 39–44, 116–122, 137–138. William R. Boyd, untitled manuscript history of the State Board of Education, 1909 to the time of writing (n.d., State Historical Society library, Iowa City), 66–68 (hereafter cited as Boyd, "History").
6. Parker, *Higher Education*, 129–170; Carstensen, "SUI," 164–165.
7. John P. Irish, "The Origin of the Law College of the State University of Iowa,"

299

Iowa Journal of History and Politics, VIII (Oct. 1910), 553–557; Irish, "Some Episodes in the History of the Founding of the Medical College of the State University of Iowa," *Iowa Journal of History and Politics*, XVIII (Jan. 1920), 125–126.

8. Carstensen, "SUI," 304.
9. Silas Totten, *Plan of Organization and Course of Studies Adopted by the Board of Trustees* (Iowa City Reporter Office, 1860), 9–12, 17; Carstensen, "SUI," 201–205.
10. Totten, *Plan*, 4–9.
11. Ibid., 14.
12. Robert Keith McMaster, "A History of the Department of Philosophy at the State University of Iowa from Jared Stone to Herbert Martin" (University of Iowa dissertation, 1979), 20.
13. Carstensen, "SUI," 324–333.
14. George Thomas White Patrick, *An Autobiography: Together with Teacher and Philosopher, by Herbert Martin* (Iowa City: University of Iowa Press, 1947), 44.
15. *Report of the Joint Committee Appointed by the Twenty-second General Assembly to Investigate the State University of Iowa* (Des Moines: n.p., 1889), 10.
16. Carstensen, "SUI," 221–282.
17. James P. Wells, "Annals of a University of Iowa Department: From Natural Philosophy to Physics and Astronomy" (Department of Physics and Astronomy, University of Iowa, 1980); Nellie S. Aurner, "Charles Bundy Wilson," *Centennial Memoirs* (Iowa City: University of Iowa Press, 1947), I, 13.
18. Robin Beecher Prince, "History of the State University of Iowa: Charles Ashmead Schaeffer" (University of Iowa thesis, 1946), 57–63.
19. Jay B. MacGregor, "The Genesis and Growth of Control and Administration at the State University of Iowa" (University of Iowa dissertation, 1931), 50–53.
20. Parker, *Higher Education*, 113–114; Prince, "History," 47–49.
21. *Report of the Joint Committee*, 29–30.
22. MacGregor, "Genesis," 184–187.
23. Parker, *Higher Education*, 78; William J. Haddock, *A Retrospect: The State University of Iowa* (Iowa City: privately published, 1904), 57–58.
24. *University of Iowa Catalog, 1902–1903*, 5–6.
25. See below, chapter 1; Iowa, General Assembly, Joint Committee on State Educational Institutions, *Report to the 31st General Assembly* (Des Moines: State Printer, 1906).
26. H. J. Thornton, "Samuel Calvin," in H. J. Thornton, ed., *Centennial Memoirs*, 2 vols. (Iowa City: University of Iowa Press, 1947), II, 24–66.
27. Mary Winifred Conklin Schertz and Walter L. Myers, "Thomas Huston Macbride" (*Centennial Memoirs*), II, 26–27.
28. Walter F. Loehwing, "Bohumil Shimek" (*Centennial Memoirs*), II, 16–19.
29. Patrick, *Autobiography*, 89–97; McMaster, "History" 206–208.
30. Thornton, "Calvin," 50–51; Patrick, *Autobiography*, 86–87.

31. Parker, *Higher Education*, 117.
32. Karl D. Loos and Helen Loos Whitney, "Isaac Althaus Loos" (*Centennial Memoirs*), II, 37–66; Nellie S. Aurner, "Charles Bundy Wilson" (*Centennial Memoirs*), I, 32; Nellie S. Aurner, "Benjamin Franklin Shambaugh" (*Centennial Memoirs*), I, 9.
33. Prince, "History," 123–130, 150–154, 172–176.
34. Ibid., 73–74.
35. Carstensen, "SUI," 110–125.
36. Joseph W. Howe interview, University of Iowa Oral History Project (hereafter cited as OHI), Aug. 6, 1976, 55–57.
37. Thornton, "Calvin," 23–24.
38. The late Professor Gustav Bergmann referred to the period as "the age of the dinosaurs," correctly perceiving that by his time (the 1960s) leaders of this type had become an extinct academic species.

1. GEORGE MACLEAN AND THE NEW UNIVERSITY

1. [George E. MacLean], "Jottings: Fragmentary Notes on the MacLean Administration, 1899–1911, of the State University of Iowa" (typescript, University of Iowa Archives, May 28, 1934).
2. H. J. Thornton, ed., *Centennial Memoirs*, 2 vols. (Iowa City: University of Iowa Press, 1947), II, 66; MacLean to W. C. Spangler, Nov. 8, 1901, MacLean Presidential Papers (hereafter cited as MLP), Letterbook, Nov. 6, 1901–May 18, 1902, 41; "Regents' Records," University of Iowa Archives, June 13, 1904, 95–109.
3. Franklin G. Doty, "History of the State University of Iowa: The College of Liberal Arts, 1900–1916" (University of Iowa dissertation, typescript, 1946), 122–123.
4. *Twenty-first Biennial Report of SUI, for the Years 1897–98 and 1898–99* (Des Moines: Conaway, 1899), 15–16; "Regents' Records, 1894–1902," 251, 278–279.
5. MacLean, "Jottings," 1–8.
6. George E. MacLean, *A Decade of Development in American State Universities* (Lincoln: University of Nebraska Press, 1898).
7. Ibid., 12–28.
8. Delight Ansley, *First Chronicles* (Doylestown, Pa.: Gardy, 1971), 1–13.
9. Stephen Hayes Bush, "The Autobiography of an Ordinary Person" (typescript, University of Iowa Archives), 64–65.
10. Ibid., 64.
11. *University of Iowa Catalog, 1898–99*, 15–37.
12. Ibid., 141–177.
13. Ibid., 122–138.

14. Ibid., 196–207.
15. Robin Beecher Prince, "History of the State University of Iowa: Charles Ashmead Schaeffer" (University of Iowa thesis, 1946), 111.
16. Bush, "Autobiography," 69.
17. *University News Bulletin*, 1 (Oct. 1, 1899), MLP Box 1.
18. "Regents' Records," July 19, 1900, 336.
19. MacLean, "The Relation of Professional Schools to College Work," address at the University of Chicago, June 17, 1901, MLP "Speeches."
20. *Twenty-second Biennial Report of the Regents for the Years 1899–1900 and 1900–1901*, 25–29; "Regents' Records," June 6, 1900, 326–327. When MacLean asked what the president's duties were with respect to Haddock's functions the latter replied, "not a damned thing!": MacLean, "Jottings," 9; William J. Haddock, *A Retrospect: The State University of Iowa* (Iowa City: privately printed, 1904); *Up-To-Date: Postscript to a Retrospect* (Iowa City: privately printed, 1905).
21. "Senate Minutes," University of Iowa Archives, 1–21; MacLean, "Jottings," 11–12.
22. Bush, "Autobiography," 110–119.
23. William R. Boyd, untitled typescript history of the State Board of Education (hereafter "History"), State Historical Society Archive, Iowa City.
24. *Twenty-first Biennial Report of SUI*, 6–14.
25. Ibid., 6.
26. MacLean to A. B. Storms, Dec. 14, 1905, MLP Box 9–2.
27. Boyd, "History," 2.
28. "Regents' Records, 1894–1902," 220, 324; May 15, 1905, 430; Sept. 26, 1905, 13; MacLean to Law Committee, June 27, 1903, MLP Letterbook, April 21, 1903–Sept. 16, 1903, 376–377.
29. MacLean to T. M. Hodgman, Jan. 16, 1907, MLP Box 11-7.
30. Haddock, *Retrospect*, 50.
31. For admissions requirements, see the university catalogs for the years 1890–1910.
32. *Catalog, 1897–98*, 15; *Catalog, 1898–99*, 15, 32–34.
33. *Science*, N.S., vol. 29 (Jan. 29, 1909), 171–174.
34. MacLean to M. W. Jacobs, Feb. 8, 1905, MLP Box 8-7.
35. George E. MacLean, "What Constitutes a Liberal Education in the Twentieth Century," *Bulletin of the American Academy of Medicine*, X, no. 2 (April 1909), 1–11.
36. Laenas Weld to MacLean, April 9, 1907, MLP Box 11-3.
37. Carl E. Seashore, "Psychology and Life in Autobiography" (typescript, University of Iowa Archives).
38. President Hancher informed the writer in 1960 that he considered graduate dean Walter Loehwing, who had died earlier that year, to have been a "nobody."

39. Bush, "Autobiography," appendix, 1–2.
40. An informal photograph of the president in his Old Capitol office shows three telephones on his desk—bad news for historians!
41. MacLean to A. A. Knipe, June 25, 1902, MLP Letterbook, May 19–Oct. 4, 1902, 218; MacLean to T. D. Wood, Feb. 2, 1903, MLP Letterbook, Oct. 4, 1902–April 20, 1903, 471–472.
42. MacLean to G. W. Koontz, Feb. 12, 1900, MLP Letterbook, 1899–1900, 421.
43. MacLean to J. A. Beattie, Mar. 21, 1900, MLP Letterbook, Aug. 14, 1900–April 12, 1901, 834.
44. "Regents' Records," Jan. 8, 1904, 78–79.
45. MacLean to W. D. Tisdale, Nov. 21, 1900, MLP Letterbook, Aug. 14, 1900– April 12, 1901, 313; MacLean to Milton Remley, Jan. 9, 1901, 555.
46. MacLean to W. I. Babb, April 23, 1901, MLP Letterbook, April 12, 1901– Nov. 5, 1901, 58–59.
47. Bush, "Autobiography," 67–68.
48. MacLean to M. J. Wade, June 26, 1902, MLP Letterbook, May 19, 1902– Oct. 4, 1902, 227; MacLean to *Evening Gazette*, Burlington, July 19, 1901, MLP Letterbook, April 12, 1901–Nov. 5, 1901, 532.
49. "Regents' Records," June 13, 1904, 136–137.
50. "Regents' Investigation of Complaints against MacLean, June 14, 15, 16, 1904, Typescript of Stenographic Notes," 2–28, University of Iowa Archives.
51. Ibid., 28–36.
52. Ibid., 51–54.
53. Ibid., 90–93.
54. Ibid., 115–126.
55. "Regents' Records," June 16, 1904, 156–172; MacLean, "Jottings," 30–33.
56. MacLean to Frank Strong, Oct. 13, 1902, MLP Letterbook, Oct. 4, 1902– April 20, 1903, 47.
57. *Hawkeye for 1909*, 8–9; MacLean to faculty, Dec. 14, 1907, MLP Box 11-4; MacLean to C. F. Birdseye, March 6, 1908, MLP Box 13-3; MacLean to Mrs. J. G. Berryhill, Dec. 9, 1908, MLP Box 13-3.
58. *Centennial Memoirs*, II, 57.
59. MacLean to A. H. Whittemore, Jan. 14, 1903, MLP Letterbook, Oct. 4, 1902–April 20, 1903, 360–361; MacLean to C. F. Thwing, Jan. 4, 1902, MLP Letterbook, Nov. 6, 1901–May 18, 1902, 277.
60. W. R. Lane to MacLean, Nov. 8, 1905, MLP Box 8-2; H. B. Walters to Mac-Lean, May 13, 1904, MLP Box 7-3.
61. S. H. Bush to MacLean, July 9, 1904, MLP Box 7-3; C. R. Van Hise to Mac-Lean, Nov. 16, 1904, MLP Box 7-3.
62. A. R. Hill to MacLean, Nov. 30, 1910, MLP Box 25-1; MacLean to W. N. Romidy, Nov. 28, 1901, MLP Box 26-4; MacLean to A. R. Hill, Dec. 7, 1910, MLP Box 25-1.
63. *Des Moines Register*, Feb. 24, 1910.

64. Samuel Calvin, *Geology and Revelation: An Address* (Iowa City: privately printed, 1909).

65. MacLean, sermon at Macalester College, June 5, 1910, MLP "Speeches," 1910–11 folder; MacLean, address at Iowa College, Grinnell, June 13, 1900, MLP "Speeches," 1899–1906 folder; MacLean to E. K. Price, Oct. 7, 1899, MLP Letterbook, 1899–1900, 82.

66. MacLean to F. P. Graves, May 12, 1902, MLP Letterbook, Nov. 6, 1901–May 18, 1902, 962.

67. MacLean to P. C. Money, Aug. 29, 1902, MLP Letterbook, May 19, 1902–Oct. 4, 1902, 851–852; Thalia Cochrane to MacLean, Aug. 31, 1902, MLP Box 4-14.

68. *Des Moines Register*, April 8, 1908; Howland Hanson to MacLean, April 10, 22, 1908, MLP Box 14-1.

69. H. H. Fairall to MacLean, Mar. 31, 1909, MLP Box 19-5.

70. MacLean to Emory Miller, April 11, 1908, MLP Box 15-2.

71. MacLean to Isaac Petersberger, Sept. 24, 1908, MLP Box 15-4.

72. MacLean, address to Religious Association, *Religious Education*, IV, no. 2 (June 1909), 160.

73. MacLean to Joseph Cochran, Jan. 31, 1910, MLP Box 18-5.

74. MacLean, "Jottings," 29–30.

75. C. E. Pickett to MacLean, April 29, 1902, MLP Box 5-3; MacLean to W. I. Babb, April 24, 1900, MLP Letterbook, Feb. 1, 1900–Aug. 13, 1900, 317; MacLean to C. Wright, July 26, 1902, MLP Letterbook, May 19, 1902–Oct. 4, 1902, 409–410.

76. Iowa State Board of Education, *Records*, I (Jan. 7, 1911), 148.

77. MacLean to M. A. Braunon, Oct. 20, 1909, MLP Box 18-4; Board of Education, *Records*, I (Jan. 7, 1911), 148.

78. MacLean to W. L. Bryan, Dec. 15, 1902, MLP Letterbook, Oct. 4, 1902–April 20, 1903, 286.

79. MacLean to D. Utter, May 26, 1906, MLP Box 10-5; MacLean to N. M. Butler, Dec. 26, 1905, MLP Box 8-5.

80. Memorandum, MLP Box 12-4; J. R. Angell to MacLean, May 14, 1907, MLP Box 12-4; "Regents' Records," June 16, 1908.

81. MacLean to David Kinley, June 23, 1904, MLP Box 6-6; MacLean to Bowman, June 25, 1909, MLP Box 18-3.

82. Bush, "Autobiography," 72–74.

83. B. J. Lambert, "William Galt Raymond" (*Centennial Memoirs*), II, 15–16; N. C. Barrett, "History of the State University of Iowa: The College of Engineering" (Ph.D. dissertation, University of Iowa, 1944), 217–282; Boyd, "History," 13–16.

84. F. E. Bolton, "The New School of Education in the State University of Iowa," *Iowa Alumnus*, V (Oct. 1907), 1–7; *Catalog, 1907–1908*, 269.

85. Boyd, "History," 2–3; MacLean, "Jottings," 4.

86. MacLean to P. L. Campbell, April 26, 1909, MLP Box 18-5; W. G. Raymond to MacLean, May 28, 1909, MLP Box 21-5.
87. Boyd, "History," 16-28.
88. MacLean, "Coordination of Iowa State Educational Institutions," undated typescript, MLP "Speeches," 1899–1906 folder.
89. MacLean to C. A. Duniway, May 27, 1909, MLP Box 19-3.
90. Iowa General Assembly, Joint Committee on State Educational Institutions, *Report* (Des Moines: State Printer, 1906), 188–193; *Des Moines Register*, Feb. 18, 25, 1910.
91. MacLean to W. L. Brintnall, Feb. 6, 1909, MLP Box 18-4; MacLean to W. I. Babb, Mar. 18, 1909, MLP Box 18-2.
92. A. B. Cummins to MacLean, Mar. 27, 1909, MLP Box 18-5; MacLean to Cummins, April 1, 1909, MLP Box 19-1.
93. *Laws of Iowa: 33rd General Assembly (1909)*, chapter 170, 166–170.
94. Boyd, "History," 136.
95. W. I. Babb to MacLean, Mar. 21, 1909, MLP Box 18-2; Boyd, "History," 3–5.
96. Boyd, "History," 48–50.
97. Ibid., 89–90.
98. "Board of Education Records," I, 55, Iowa State Archives, Des Moines; Boyd, "History," 8–11; *First Biennial Report, Iowa State Board of Education*, 7–9.
99. Faculty Committee document, Nov. 23, 1909, MLP Box 19-6.
100. "Board Records," I, 42; MacLean to D. A. Emery, May 16, 1910, MLP Box 24-2; Trewin to MacLean, Oct. 27, 1909, MLP Box 22-4; Trewin to MacLean, Feb. 16, 1911, MLP Box 28-9.
101. Trewin to MacLean, Oct. 25, 1909, MLP Box 22-4; MacLean to Trewin, Oct. 26, 1909, MLP Box 22-4; "Board Records," I, 77.
102. "University of Iowa: Senate Proceedings," Dec. 1, 1909, University of Iowa Archives.
103. *Des Moines Register*, Feb. 10, Sept. 16, 1910.
104. C. R. Fischer to MacLean, Aug. 29, 1910, MLP Box 24-3.
105. MacLean to P. K. Holbrook, Jan. 16, 1911, MLP Box 28-6.
106. MacLean to Trewin, Jan. 30, 1911, MLP Box 29-2. The letter is quoted in Board of Education minutes, Feb. 1, 1911 (Board Records, I, 129). There is no record of previous board action on the matter; there was presumably an informal understanding that the resignation would be requested.

2. THE REIGN OF WALTER JESSUP

1. J. G. Bowman to G. E. MacLean, Feb. 16, 1907, MLP Box 11-3; Bowman to MacLean, April 8, 1908, MLP Box 12-4.
2. Board of Education minutes, Feb. 23, 1911; Bush, "Autobiography," 73–74.

3. Board of Education minutes, Mar. 15, 1911.
4. J. H. Trewin to Bowman, Mar. 11, 1911, Bowman Presidential Papers (hereafter cited as BNP), Box 5-1; Board of Education minutes, May 1, 1912.
5. Board of Education, *First Annual Report*, 1911, 9.
6. Boyd's description of the plan in his ms. "History" has a strong proprietary flavor (11–48).
7. Board of Education, *Second Annual Report*, 1912, 7–16.
8. Ibid., 10–22.
9. 35th General Assembly, *Iowa House Journal*, 1913, 2150, 1972; Board of Education minutes, April 3, 1913.
10. Boyd, "History," 42–48.
11. Bush, "Autobiography," 88–89.
12. Draft letter, Bowman to Board of Education, Jan. 2, 1913, BNP Box 2-133. The draft is marked "not presented," but there is little doubt that its substance was conveyed to the board.
13. D. A. Emery to Bowman, Sept. 18, Oct. 16, 1912, BNP Box 1-126; Bowman to A. Flexner, Jan. 23, 1913, BNP Box 2-151.
14. Boyd to Bowman, July 19, 1911, BNP Box 5-1; Bowman to H. M. Eicher, Mar. 7, 1914, BNP Box 5-1; E. P. Schoentgen to Bowman, July 22, 1913, BNP Box 5-2; G. T. Baker to Bowman, May 27, 1913, BNP Box 5-2.
15. Trewin to Bowman, Oct. 17, 25, 1913, BNP Box 5-1; Bowman to Trewin, Oct. 20, 1913, BNP Box 5-1.
16. Board of Education minutes, March 11, 27, 1914. Shortly before he left Iowa City someone removed most of Bowman's papers from the presidential office. He reported some years later that he suspected the identity of the thief, but lacking firm evidence he would not name the individual; Bowman to Nancy Mitchem, Sept. 19, 1932, BNP Box 5-4.
17. Board of Education minutes, March 27, 1914.
18. T. H. Macbride, "Darwin's Contribution to the Science of Botany" (n.p., n.d. [1909]), University of Iowa Archives.
19. T. H. Macbride, *On the Campus*, 2 vols. (Cedar Rapids: Torch Press, 1916).
20. Macbride to Sen. F. Larrabee, Feb. 23, 1915, Macbride Presidential Papers (hereafter MBP), 1915, #147.
21. T. H. Macbride, *Duplication in Separate Schools of Higher Learning, Supported by the State: Address to the National Association of State Universities, Nov. 10, 1914* (pamphlet, University of Iowa Archives).
22. Board of Education minutes, Aug. 9, 1916; Board of Education Records, #2, 455.
23. A. M. Schlesinger, Sr., *In Retrospect: The History of a Historian* (New York: Harcourt, Brace, and World, 1963); Bush, "Autobiography," 84–85; Dewey B. Stuit, OHI, 45–46; Allin Dakin, OHI, 10.
24. Walter Jessup, "Commencement Address, University of Missouri, June 6, 1928," Jessup Presidential Papers (hereafter cited as JP), 1927–28, #4.

25. Jessup, "Education in the Cabinet," n.d., JP, 1921–22, #94.
26. Jessup, "Problems in Higher Educational Administration," Baconian Lecture, Dec. 11, 1931, JP, 1931–32, #3.
27. Herbert Spitzer, OHI, 54.
28. Jessup, "Address to the National Association of State Universities," Nov. 12, 1923, JP, 1923–24, #4.
29. G. T. Baker, memorandum, n.d., JP, 1925–26, #13.
30. United States Bureau of Education, *State Higher Educational Institutions of Iowa, Bulletin #19* (Washington, D.C.: Government Printing Office, 1916).
31. *Bulletin #19*, 7–59.
32. *Sioux City Tribune*, Nov. 13, 1916, JP, 1916–17, #254.
33. *Bulletin #19*, 128–131.
34. Ibid., 62–65, 133–135.
35. Ibid., 59–62.
36. Ibid., 96–99, 83–87.
37. W. R. Boyd to D. D. Murphy, Nov. 21, 1916, JP, 1916–17, #14.
38. Boyd to Board of Education, Nov. 16, 1923, JP, 1923–24, #13; Finance Committee to Board of Education, Dec. 3, 1923, JP, 1923–24; Boyd to A. B. Lawther, May 1924, JP, 1923–24; Boyd to L. V. Carter, March 7, 1925, JP, 1924–25, #13 (Boyd).
39. "Report on the State Higher Educational Institutions of Iowa Prepared by a Committee Appointed by the Iowa State Board of Education," JP, 1926–27, #12 (3).
40. Board of Education, "Report to the Governor," n.d., JP, 1925–26, #13 (Board-General).
41. Board of Education, "Statement," Feb. 3, 1927, JP, 1927–28, #12 (3).
42. "Report on a Survey . . . by the Brookings Institution" (Washington, D.C.: n.p., 1933), excerpts in JP, 1933–34, #11.
43. Finance Committee to the Board of Education, Oct. 10, 1916, JP, 1916–17, #14.
44. *Bulletin #19*, 23–31, 125–128.
45. *University of Iowa Catalog, 1916–17*, 600.
46. Jessup, address to the National Association of State Universities, Nov. 1929, JP, 1929–30, #4.
47. *Bulletin #19*, 23–31, 34–37.
48. Ibid., 38–41; Frederick G. Davies, "History of the State University of Iowa: The College of Liberal Arts, 1916–1934" (University of Iowa dissertation, 1947), II, 879–883.
49. *Bulletin #19*, 107–108.
50. Carl E. Seashore, "Psychology and Life in Autobiography," (typescript, University of Iowa Archives), 100–101.
51. Board of Education minutes, Jan. 25, 1917, Feb. 8, 1923; W. R. Boyd to John Hammill, Dec. 27, 1928, JP, 1928–29, #11 (1).

52. Quoted in Mildred Throne, "The History of the State University of Iowa: The University Libraries" (University of Iowa thesis, 1943).
53. Jessup, "Iowa and Education," n.d., JP, 1922–23, #105; Board of Education minutes, April 15, 1925.
54. Davies, "History," II, 523. Dean Rienow's name would eventually grace a dormitory where minority students would share the facilities without discrimination.
55. U.S. Bureau of Education, 1916, Bulletin #6, "Statistics of State Universities and State Colleges for the Year Ending June 30, 1915," JP, 1916–17, #14.
56. *Bulletin #19*, 125; Board of Education to Governor and Legislature, Dec. 14, 1922, JP, 1922–23, #39 (d).
57. Davies, "History," I, 179.
58. *Bulletin #19*, 131–132.
59. Jessup, "Some Aspects of University Administration," Nov. 15–16, 1926, JP, 1926–27, #4.
60. Joseph Howe, OHI, 1–25; N. C. Barrett, "History of the College of Engineering."
61. Paul C. Packer, "The College of Education and the University," *Journal of Higher Education*, III (Dec. 1932), 493–495.
62. K. D. Loos and H. L. Whitney, "Isaac Althaus Loos," *Centennial Memoirs*, II (Iowa City: University of Iowa Press, 1947); Paul Olson, OHI, 8–17.
63. Board of Education minutes, March 11, 1914.
64. Herbert L. Searles, "The Study of Religion in State Universities," *University of Iowa Studies in Character*, I, #3 (Iowa City: University of Iowa, 1928), 46–53.
65. E. D. Starbuck, "Religion's Use of Me," in V. Ferm, ed., *Religion in Transition* (London: Allen and Unwin, 1937), 203–227.
66. Searles, "Study," 11–19; Bowman to Starbuck, Feb. 14, 1913, BNP, 3–186.
67. Searles, "Study," 40–45.
68. O. D. Foster to Jessup, May 4, 1921, JP, 1920–21, #53; Willard Lampe, *The Story of an Idea: The History of the School of Religion* (Iowa City: SUI Bulletin #704, 1955), 3–4.
69. Jessup statement, *SUI Newsletter*, VI, #10, March 10, 1921.
70. Committee memorandum, Feb. 1921, JP, 1921–22, #53 (a).
71. "Filling the Gap in Modern Education," National Council of Schools of Religion, *Bulletin*, II, n.d., JP, 1923–24, #53 (a).
72. G. F. Kay to Jessup, April 12, 1924, JP, 1924–25, #69; Board of Education minutes, May 22, 1924. While preparations for organizing the school were underway the press carried reports that Dr. John Morgan, assistant professor of psychology and director of the university's psychological clinic, had told the People's Church of Cedar Rapids that there was no afterlife in the conventional sense of the term. Jessup received a spate of letters demanding that

Morgan be repudiated or dismissed. In his embarrassment the president could only express his regrets and assure the complainers that the university had no desire to be "a meddler in religion." In establishing a School of Religion it was certainly "meddling" (Jessup to F. K. Nies and others, April 2, 1924, JP, 1923–24, #85).

73. T. B. Appleget to Jessup, June 10, 1929, JP, 1929–30, #11 (4).

74. Eugene Gilmore, "Religion in a State University," Gilmore Presidential Papers (hereafter cited as GP), 1938–39, #102.

75. William Koch to Gilmore, March 31, 1937, GP, 1936–37, #102; Gilmore to Koch, April 1, 1937, ibid.; Anonymous to Nelson G. Kraschel, Aug. 30, 1937, ibid.; Kay to Nelson G. Kraschel, Sept. 7, 1937, ibid.; Frank Horack to Gilmore, Dec. 9, 1936, GP, 1936–37, #102.

76. Gilmore to G. Thomas, Sept. 8, 1937, GP, 1937–38, #102.

77. Willard Lampe, "Religious Life at the State University," *Bulletin of the State University of Iowa*, n.s. 856 (July 25, 1936); Lampe, *Story of an Idea*, 3–4; Lampe, "Assumptions and Objectives of the School of Religion," May 1937, GP, 1937–38, #102.

78. M. Hotz to Gilmore, March 10, 1937, GP, 1936–37, #102.

79. G. F. Kay to R. Himstead, Aug. 26, 1939, GP, 1939–40, #102. Willard Lampe was less than candid when he told the physicist Arthur Compton of the University of Chicago that Jung was leaving on account of a reorganization (Lampe to Compton, June 23, 1939, ibid.; Kay to Himstead, Sept. 19, 1939, ibid.; Himstead to Gilmore, Oct. 2, 1939, ibid.; R. Lappen to Himstead, n.d., ibid.; Gilmore to Himstead, Oct. 7, 1939, ibid.; Himstead to Gilmore, Oct. 23, 1939, ibid.).

80. Draft program by Ansley, BNP Box 1–126; Board of Education minutes, Nov. 1, 1911; *University Catalog, 1912–13*, 149–169; Bush, "Autobiography," 74–75.

81. Davies, "History," II, 639–695; Susan Hancher, OHI, 7–10.

82. Board of Education minutes, April 15, 1930.

83. Jessup statement, n.d., JP, 1929–30, #68; Seashore to Jessup, Feb. 3, 1930, JP, 1929–30, #50.

84. Frances M. Flanagan, "The Educational Role of Norman Foerster" (University of Iowa dissertation, 1971), 100–151; Davies, "History," II, 812–820; Stephen Wilbers, *The Iowa Writers' Workshop: Origins, Emergence, and Growth* (Iowa City: University of Iowa Press, 1980), 73.

85. Howard J. Savage et al., *American College Athletics* (Bulletin #23; New York: Carnegie Foundation, 1929), 80.

86. Eric Wilson, OHI, 1–12; Board of Education minutes, March 13, 1924, Oct. 15–16, 1925.

87. J. L. Griffith to P. Belting, Jan. 26, 1928, JP, 1930–31, #67(A) (15); Baker to Jessup, March 11, 1929, JP, 1928–29, #11.

88. Belting to Jessup, April 26, 1929, JP, 1928–29, #11; Jessup to Belting, May 9, 1929, JP, 1928–29, #11 (1); Board of Education minutes, May 15, 1929.

89. John Gimbel, "A History of the State University of Iowa: Physical Education and Athletics for Men" (University of Iowa dissertation, 1951), 133–162.

90. Ibid., 162–186.

91. Bulletin #23, v–xxii.

92. Jessup to Baker, March 6, 1926, JP, 1925–26, #13 (Baker); Jessup to Baker, Aug. 23, 1928, JP, 1928–29, #11; preliminary draft, Biennial Report Relative to SUI (July 1, 1932), JP, 1932–33, #11 (1).

93. Jessup to Baker, June 27, 1930, JP, 1929–30, #11 (1).

94. Board of Education minutes, Feb. 16, 1932; Board of Education announcement, June 29, 1933, JP, 1933–34, #11 (1).

95. Board of Education minutes, March 2, 1929.

96. Board of Education minutes, April 9, 1929.

97. Jay B. McGregor, *Epsilon Bulletin*, XI (1939), 1–17.

98. Ibid., 18–68.

99. Leland Sage, *A History of Iowa* (Ames: Iowa State University Press, 1974), 267–292; *Des Moines Register*, June 28, 1931.

100. Neas to Jessup, Dec. 23, 1931, JP, 1931–32, #11 (1); Neas to H. W. Lundy, Nov. 20, 1931, ibid.; Neas to Jessup, March 24, 1933, JP, 1933–34, #11 (1); Board of Education minutes, Nov. 3–4, 1933.

101. W. H. Gemmill to Baker, Aug. 12, 1931, JP, 1931–32, #11 (4).

102. Board of Education minutes, Jan. 20, Feb. 12, Mar. 19, April 12, 1932; Boyd, "History," 79–83; *Cedar Rapids Gazette-Republican*, May 27, 1932.

103. Board of Education minutes, Sept. 26–27, 1932.

104. Boyd to Ed Brown, Sept. 27, 1932, JP, 1932–33, #11 (2).

3. SEASHORE'S UNIVERSITY

1. United States Bureau of Education, *State Higher Educational Institutions of Iowa*, *Bulletin #19* (Washington, D.C.: Government Printing Office, 1916), 131–132.

2. A. M. Schlesinger to Jessup, Nov. 18, 1930, JP, 1930–31, #50 (4); Norman Foerster, *The American State University* (Chapel Hill: University of North Carolina Press, 1937), 107: "Sometimes, as at Iowa, a great school was built up within the administration of a single dean."

3. Carl Seashore, *Pioneering in Psychology* (Iowa City: University of Iowa Press, University of Iowa Studies, #398, 1942), 4; Carl Seashore, "The District School," *Palimpsest*, vol. 23 (March 1942), 99–110.

4. Seashore, *Pioneering in Psychology*, 220–222.

5. Walter R. Miles, "Carl Emil Seashore, 1866–1949: A Biographical Memoir,"

National Academy of Sciences, *Biographical Memoirs*, vol. 29 (1956), 265–316.

6. Carl E. Seashore, preface to Norman C. Meier, *Aesthetic Judgment as a Measure of Art Talent* (Iowa City: University of Iowa Press, University of Iowa Studies, I, #19, 1926); Seashore, *Pioneering in Psychology*, 160–164.

7. Carl E. Seashore, "Psychology and Life in Autobiography" (typescript, University of Iowa Archives), 113–116; Carl E. Seashore, "A Pass-Key to the Domain of Educational Theory and Practice," *School and Society*, vol. 70 (Nov. 26, 1949), 337–338.

8. Seashore, *Pioneering in Psychology*, 160–164; George D. Stoddard, *The Pursuit of Education* (New York: Vantage Press, 1981), 39.

9. Walter Jessup, "Trends in Graduate Work," in John W. Ashton, ed., *Trends in Graduate Work* (Iowa City: University of Iowa, 1931), 174.

10. George W. Stewart, "Research in State Universities" (typescript), JP, 1921–22, #53.

11. "Report to the Graduate Faculty, Jan. 28, 1920," JP, 1919–20, #39 (2).

12. Stephen Bush, "Autobiography," appendix, 12; Seashore, "Autobiography," 107–109.

13. Quoted in Bernard Berelson, *Graduate Education in the United States* (New York: McGraw-Hill, 1960), 13.

14. Carl E. Seashore, "Trends in Graduate Work," in Ashton, *Trends*, 9–14.

15. Carl E. Seashore, "An Open Letter to the Graduate Dean," *Journal of Higher Education*, vol. 10 (Jan. 1939), 1–8.

16. Seashore, "Trends in Graduate Work," 14–25, 52–55.

17. Seashore, "Autobiography," 33; "Trends in Graduate Work," 27–28; *Catalog, 1915–16*; Donald F. Howard, "History of the State University of Iowa: The Graduate College" (University of Iowa dissertation, 1947), 141–144.

18. Howard, "The Graduate College," 69.

19. Carl E. Seashore, "An Open Letter Addressed to Women in Graduate Schools," *Journal of Higher Education*, vol. 13 (May 1942), 236–242.

20. Robert Keith McMaster, "A History of the Department of Philosophy at the State University of Iowa from Jared Stone to Herbert Martin" (University of Iowa dissertation, 1979), 277–282.

21. See the exchange of numerous letters among Seashore, Starbuck, Jessup, and students, JP, 1926–27, #50; JP, 1927–28, #50; Seashore papers, University of Iowa Archives, Seashore-Starbuck folder.

22. Seashore, *Pioneering in Psychology*, 6–18, 25–34.

23. Ibid., 15.

24. [Carl E. Seashore], "Researches Under Way at the University of Iowa," JP, 1929–30, #50.

25. Seashore, "Trends in Graduate Work," 9–60.

26. Stephen Wilbers, *The Iowa Writers' Workshop: Origins, Emergence, and Growth* (Iowa City: University of Iowa Press, 1980), 10–13, 17n.

27. G. W. Stewart to Jessup, Feb. 3, 1922, JP, 1921–22, #53 (a); "Announcement," ibid.; Graduate Council minutes, Oct. 24, 1922, Graduate Council folder, 1907–23, University of Iowa Archives.

28. Wilbers, *Workshop*, 39–40.

29. Ibid., 40, 57n, 22.

30. Seashore, "Autobiography," 75–76; *Pioneering in Psychology*, 123–126.

31. Seashore to Jessup, May 20, 1927, JP, 1926–27, #50; Seashore to Orton, June 8, 23, 1927, ibid.; Seashore, *Pioneering in Psychology*, 145–154.

32. Carl E. Seashore, *Psychology of Music* (New York: McGraw-Hill, 1938), 67–85; *Pioneering in Psychology*, 43–65.

33. Dorrance S. White, "A Biography of Philip Greeley Clapp" (typescript, University of Iowa Archives, 1960), II-7, III-2.

34. Carl E. Seashore, *Approaches to the Science of Music and Speech* (Iowa City: published by the University, University of Iowa Series on Aims and Progress of Research, #41, 1933), 3–15.

35. Lee Travis to H. C. Harshbarger, Oct. 3, 1975, quoted in H. Clay Harshbarger, *Some Highlights of the Department of Speech and Dramatic Art* (Iowa City: University of Iowa, 1976), 12.

36. Seashore, "Autobiography," 41–44.

37. Seashore to Glenn Merry, June 21, 1921; Jessup to Seashore, June 28, 1921, JP, 1920–21, #77; Merry to Harshbarger, Nov. 27, 1975, Merry folder, University of Iowa Archives.

38. Seashore, *Pioneering in Psychology*, 115. The dean's enthusiasm for applied science at times approached flatulence.

39. Seashore, *Pioneering in Psychology*, 117.

40. Harshbarger, *Highlights*, 17–19.

41. Seashore, *Pioneering in Psychology*, 39–43.

42. John M. O'Donnell, *The Origins of Behaviorism: American Psychology* (New York: New York University Press, 1985), 143.

43. [George D. Stoddard and Dorothy Bradbury], *Pioneering in Child Welfare: A History of the Iowa Child Welfare Research Station, 1917–1933* (Iowa City: SUI, 1933), 7.

44. Cora B. Hillis to George MacLean, Feb. 24, 1909, MLP Box 20-2.

45. MacLean to Hillis, Feb. 13, Mar. 1, 8, Oct. 27, 1909, MLP Box 20-2; MacLean to Seashore et al., June 2, 1909, MLP Box 18-3.

46. Hillis to MacLean, May 9, 1909, MLP Box 20-2. In later years, in his self-serving autobiographical writings, Seashore was happy to claim his share of the paternity of the Child Welfare Research Station, forgetting that his initial opposition had contributed to the delay of some seven years in its establishment. See his "Autobiography," 89–91, and *Pioneering in Psychology*, 170–189.

47. Seashore, *Pioneering in Child Welfare*, 7–25.

48. Carl E. Seashore, *A Child Welfare Research Station: Plans and Possibilities* (Iowa City: University of Iowa, Aims and Progress of Research, #1, 1916), 3–18.

49. Seashore, *Pioneering in Child Welfare*, 40–42.
50. George D. Stoddard, *The Second Decade: A Review of the Activities of the Iowa Child Welfare Research Station, 1928–1938* (Iowa City: University of Iowa, Aims and Progress of Research, #58, 1939).
51. Henry L. Minton, "The Iowa Child Welfare Research Station and the 1940 Debate on Intelligence," *Journal of the History of the Behavioral Sciences*, vol. 20 (April 1984), 160–176; Stoddard, *Pursuit of Education*, 51–56.
52. Robert Sears, oral interview by Hamilton Cravens, May 30, 1984, typescript, University of Iowa Archives, 19–30.
53. Seashore, preface to Meier, *Aesthetic Judgment*.
54. Earl E. Harper to Seashore, Sept. 21, 1944, Seashore papers, (Publications G), University of Iowa Archives.
55. Wilbur L. Schramm, *Approaches to a Science of English Verse* (Iowa City: University of Iowa, 1935).
56. Paul Engle to author, April 4, 1987.
57. Carl E. Seashore, "Professional and Preprofessional Schools or Divisions at the Graduate Level," *Proceedings, Association of American Universities*, 1927, 84–88.
58. Seashore to Eugene Gilmore, Mar. 1, 1933, JP, 1932–33, #50.
59. Seashore to Vernon Kellogg, Mar. 1, 1927, JP, 1926–27, #50; Carl E. Seashore, *Learning and Living in College* (Iowa City: University of Iowa Press, University of Iowa Studies, #21, n.d.), 5–14.
60. Seashore, *Learning and Living in College*, 5–102.
61. Liberal Arts College faculty minutes, Jan. 9, 1924, May 13, 1925, Jan. 13, 1926, University of Iowa Archives.
62. Seashore to Jessup, April 26, 1934, JP, 1933–34, #50.
63. Board of Education minutes, Dec. 10, 1935, Sept. 23, 1936.

4. VIRGIL HANCHER AND THE INERTIAL UNIVERSITY

1. Board of Education minutes, Jan. 3, 1940; Howard Bowen, OHI, 6; Herbert Spitzer, OHI, 16–17; J. B. Stroud, OHI, 4–5.
2. See the correspondence of Hancher, Hall, and Briggs, John E. Briggs papers, Box 7, University of Iowa Archives.
3. Hancher to Briggs, n.d., Feb. 8, 1940, Briggs papers; Hall to Briggs, n.d., ibid.; Susan Hancher, OHI, 1–16. Susan Hancher's bluntly expressed opinion that research conflicted with good teaching, which she considered to be a professor's "foremost qualification," may well have reflected her husband's distaste for dealing with independent faculty types (Robert Hardin, OHI, 43–45).
4. Hancher to Troyer Anderson, Jan. 25, 1945, Hancher Correspondence, University of Iowa Archives (hereafter cited as HPC), 1944–45, #87–90; Hancher to Sir Lionel Whitby, Dec. 5, 1946, HPC, 1946–47, #111; Hancher to D.

Stuit, Oct. 17, 1949, Liberal Arts file, Box 14, "Committee on Curricula and Instruction" folder, University of Iowa Archives.

5. Hancher, address to Iowa League of Municipalities, Aug. 19, 1942, Hancher Presidential Speeches (hereafter cited as HPS), 1940–43, University of Iowa Archives; Hancher, address to Teachers' Conference, Sept. 2, 1944, HPS, 1944–46; Hancher, "Moral and Ethical Problems in Education," Sept. 13–15, 1953, HPS, May 1953–Feb. 1954; Hancher, "This I Believe," July 14, 1952, HPS, July 1952–April 1953.

6. Hancher, speech at the inauguration of Dr. E. E. Voigt, May 25, 1942, HPS, 1950–Feb. 1951.

7. Hancher, "Education's Responsibilities for Freedom," Mar. 26, 1954, HPS, Mar.–Dec. 1954; Hancher, speech to Davenport Service Clubs, Dec. 16, 1957, HPS, Jan. 1957–June 1958; Hancher, "The Two Nations," June 10, 1956, HPS, 1956; Hancher to R. Ellsworth, May 29, 1948, HPC 1947–48, #110.

8. Hancher, "New Frontiers," Jan. 19, 1948, HPS, 1944–48; Hancher, "Higher-Higher Education," Mar. 5, 1964, HPS, April 1963–June 1964; Hancher, "Don't Blame the Teachers!" Sept. 1952, HPS, July 1952–April 1953.

9. Hancher, "Charge to the Candidates," Aug. 10, 1949, HPS, 1948–49; Hancher, address to Student Government Conference, Dec. 2, 1961, HPS, Feb. 1961–Mar. 1963; Hancher, "The New Anarchy" (not used), Sept. 21, 1948, HPS, 1948–49; Hancher, "Address to the Iowa State Bar Association," June 1–3, 1950, HPS, 1950–Feb. 1951.

10. Hancher, Phi Beta Kappa address (not used), 1947, HPS, 1944–48; Hancher, commencement address, Buena Vista College, June 3, 1949, HPS, 1948–49.

11. Hancher, address to the Charleston, West Virginia, Chamber of Commerce, Nov. 1, 1951, HPS, 1951–June 1952; Hancher, "Mid-Century and Beyond," May 11, 1950, HPS, 1950–Feb. 1951; Hancher, "The Third Choice," June 15, 1950, ibid.

12. Hancher, "The Constructive Mind," April 8, 1960, HPS, Aug. 1959–Jan. 1961; Hancher, "The Most Wonderful Work," May 4, 1955, HPS, 1955; Hancher, "All Things New," Mar. 12, 1961, HPS, Feb. 1961–Mar. 1963; Hancher, "The Case for Western Democracy against Russian Communism," *Junior College Journal* (May 1951), 482–493; speech draft (not used), Dec. 2, 1948, HPS, 1948–49.

13. Hancher to H. Newburn, Jan. 1942, HPC, 1941–42, #80.

14. Hancher, "Inaugural Response," May 24, 1941, HPS, 1940–43; Hancher, "Higher Education in a Changing Society," May 1948, HPS, 1944–48.

15. Hancher, "Some Problems of Higher Education," Aug. 22, 1960, HPS, Aug. 1959–Jan. 1961.

16. Hancher, "Commencement Address," Aug. 8, 1951, HPS, 1951–June 1952.

17. Hancher, "Remarks at the Dedication of the Library," Jan. 25, 1952, HPS, 1951–June 1952; Hancher, "Charge to the Candidates," Aug. 10, 1949, HPS, 1948–49.

18. Hancher, "The University When Peace Comes," Baconian Lecture, 1943, *Aims and Progress of Research*, #72, 111–120.

19. Hancher to Stuit, June 10, 1958, Liberal Arts file, rec'd 8/84, Box 10, folder 3.P.; Stuit to Hancher, June 16, 1958, ibid.

20. Stuit to H. Davis, Feb. 12, 1957, Liberal Arts file, rec'd 8/84, Box 10, folder (Z)D; Davis to Stuit, Mar. 28, 1957, ibid.

21. Agenda notes, deans' meeting, April 19, 1960, HPS, Aug. 1959–Jan. 1960; Hancher, address to the faculty, Nov. 13, 1956, HPS, 1956; Hancher, address to the Des Moines Alumni Club, Jan. 26, 1953, HPS, July 1952–April 1953.

22. State Board of Education Dinner for Press and Radio, June 29, 1950, HPS, 1950–Feb. 1951.

23. Hancher, "The Motivation of College Women," April 20, 1963, HPS, April 1963–June 1964; Hancher, outline of remarks to Association of American Universities, Oct. 26, 1954, HPS, Mar.–Dec. 1954; Hancher, "Education in a Free Society," Feb. 18, 1955, HPS, 1955.

24. Hancher, "Education's Responsibilities for Freedom," Mar. 26, 1954, HPS, Mar.–Dec. 1954; Hancher, "Some Problems of Higher Education," Aug. 22, 1960, HPS, Aug. 1959–Jan. 1961.

25. Hancher, remarks at Faculty Convocation, May 14, 1947, HPS, 1944–48; Hancher, "An Interpretation of the University Presidency," Aug. 31, 1962, HPS, Feb. 1961–Mar. 1963.

26. Dakin, OHI, 1–13, 17; McGrath to Hancher, Oct. 15, 1945, HPC, 1945–46, #82; Deans' Conference, Dec. 17, 1947, HPC, 1947–48, #82. The medical dean, Ewen MacEwen, objected strenuously to a directive from Hancher requiring that applications for research grants be reported to the graduate dean merely for informational purposes (MacEwen to Hancher, Mar. 26, 1946, HPC, 1945–46, #111; Hancher to MacEwen, Mar. 27, 1946, ibid.).

27. University organization chart, Dec. 30, 1946, HPC, 1946–47, #111; faculty convocation, May 14, 1947, HPS, 1944–48; Board of Education minutes, May 12, 1947.

28. Faculty convocation, Sept. 15, 1947, HPS, 1944–48; Board of Education minutes, Sept. 9, 1947.

29. Faculty convocation, Mar. 20, 1950, HPS, 1950–Feb. 1951.

30. Undated draft, HPS, 1948–49.

31. Hancher, "An Interpretation of the University Presidency," Aug. 31, 1962, HPS, Feb. 1961–Mar. 1963.

32. Eloise Ginter, "History of the State University of Iowa: Faculty Participation in Administrative Functions" (University of Iowa M.A. thesis, 1946), 13–64, appendices.

33. J. B. Stroud, OHI, 1–10.

34. Hancher to R. Ellsworth, Sept. 5, 22, 1947, HPC, 1947–48, #110.

35. Ellsworth to Hancher, Dec. 2, 1946, HPC 1946–47, #109; Dakin to Hancher,

Dec. 14, 1946, ibid.; Board of Education minutes, Mar. 10, 1947; Faculty Council minutes, May 26, 1948, University of Iowa Archives.

36. See Faculty Council minutes of 1947–48, 1947–49 folder.

37. R. Lloyd-Jones to Hancher, May 17, 1961, Faculty Council folder, 1/1/61–12/31/63, University Archives; Hancher to Council, June 27, 1961, ibid.

38. F. Kennedy to Hancher, Jan. 12, 1952; Hancher to Kennedy, draft, Mar. 1952; Hancher to Council, May 22, 1953, all in Faculty Council folder, 7/1/51–6/30/55.

39. "Summary of Council Activities," Sept. 27, 1954, ibid.; Faculty Council Report for 1956–57, University of Iowa Archives; "Policies Governing the Use of Limited Appropriations to Maintain a First-Rate University" [1958], Faculty Council folder, 7/1/58–6/30/59; J. W. Howe, OHI, 45–46.

40. Hancher to administrative officers, May 28, 1959, Faculty Council folder, 7/1/58–6/30/59; C. B. Righter, "University Faculty Council: A Study of Its Organization and Functions," June 19, 1959, ibid.

41. Council committee draft, Mar. 2, 1960; Faculty Council minutes, Mar. 15, 1960; Faculty Council folder, 7/1/59–12/31/60.

42. Hancher to G. Bedell and A. Vestal, Dec. 27, 1961, "Faculty Senate Documents," Faculty Council folder, 1/1/61–12/31/63; G. Bedell to Hancher, May 4, 1962, ibid.; "University Council: Basic Document," ibid.

43. Hancher to Bedell and Vestal, May 25, 1962, ibid.; open letter to the faculty, Nov. 11, 1962, ibid.; J. Baker document, Oct. 30, 1962, ibid.; Hancher to Lloyd-Jones, Nov. 1, 1962, ibid.; Faculty Council minutes, Nov. 6, 1962, ibid.; *Des Moines Register*, Dec. 20, 1962.

44. Hancher, "The Summing Up," Jan. 29, 1964, HPS, April 1963–June 1964.

45. Liberal Arts Faculty minutes, April 24, 1947, HPC 1946–47, #82; "Draft of Manual of Rules and Regulations for the Faculty of the College of Liberal Arts," HPC 1949–50, #82.

46. Committee minority to McGrath, April 12, 1948, HPC 1949–50, #83; McGrath to Hancher, April 8, 1948, ibid.

47. Hancher to McGrath, April 12, 1948, HPC 1949–50, #83; Hancher to D. Stuit, Oct. 17, 1949, ibid.

48. The first department to choose a chairmanship was history.

49. State University of Iowa, *Manual of Procedure of the College of Liberal Arts*, Iowa City, June 1950; Hancher to Stuit, Sept. 16, 1949, HPC 1949–50, #83; Stuit to faculty, Dec. 28, 1949, ibid.; Hancher to Stuit, Feb. 11, 1950, ibid.

50. Stuit, OHI, 36–41; Hancher, address to the faculty, Nov. 13, 1956, HPS, 1956; Hancher to board, July 31, 1958, HPC, 1958, Box "Letters to Regents."

51. TIAA draft, Jan. 23, 1939, GP, 1938–39, #117; SUI draft, April 4, 1939, ibid.; Gilmore memo, May 23, 1939, ibid.

52. Dakin, OHI, 34–35; Susan Hancher, OHI, 15–16.

53. University of Iowa Libraries, "Annual Report," 1940–41, University of Iowa

Archives; Stow Persons, "Ralph Ellsworth and the University of Iowa Libraries," *Books at Iowa*, no. 49 (Nov. 1988), 7–15.

54. Ralph Ellsworth, *University of Colorado Studies* (Nov. 1941), 38.

55. Ellsworth to Hancher, Feb. 25, June 16, 1944, HPC, 1943–44, #106; K. Keffer to Library Building Committee, June 16, 1944, ibid.; A. M. Githens to F. W. Ambrose, April 16, 1944, ibid.

56. Shambaugh's course offered a comprehensive survey of human culture from the Big Bang to the Big Depression. The political science department had found it impossible to provide a successor who could conduct the course with Shambaugh's showmanship and had abandoned it ("The Proposed University of Iowa Library and Instructional Center," July 15, 1942, HPC, 1942–43, #106).

57. Ellsworth to author, Nov. 18, 1987; Ellsworth to Hancher, April 16, 1945, HPC, 1944–45, #108; Hancher to Ellsworth, Sept. 21, 1943, HPC, 1943–44, #106; Ellsworth to H. Davis, Dec. 1, 1948, HPC, 1948–49, #114.

58. F. G. Higbee, "The Construction of the University Library," Nov. 6, 1952, HPC, 1952–53, #107.

59. [Ralph E. Ellsworth], *The Library as a Teaching Instrument* (Iowa City: SUI Publication, 1945).

60. R. E. Ellsworth, "Some Notes on the Proposed Library Building at the University of Iowa," HPC, 1944–45, #108; R. E. Ellsworth to Lewis Brown, Nov. 30, 1944, ibid.

61. Ellsworth to Lewis Brown, Feb. 1, 1945, ibid.

62. Ellsworth to Hancher, July 29, 1948, HPC, 1948–49, #114; Ellsworth to Hancher, Jan. 17, 1951, HPC, 1950–51, #105; Hancher to H. Davis, Mar. 9, 1951, ibid.

63. Ellsworth to Hancher, July 5, 1950, HPC, 1950–51, #105; Hancher to Ellsworth, July 12, 1950, ibid.; Faculty Council minutes, April 10, 17, May 8, 1951, folder "University Council, 1948–51"; Faculty Council minutes, April 14, 29, 1959; Faculty Council folder, 7/1/58–6/30/59; Hancher to W. L. Boyd, May 18, 1959, ibid.; Ellsworth to Hancher, May 16, 1953, HPC, 1952–53, #107.

64. Ellsworth to Hancher, April 16, 1945, HPC, 1944–45, #108; Hancher to Ellsworth, April 20, 1945, ibid.; Ellsworth to Dakin, April 1949, HPC, 1948–49, #114; Dakin to Ellsworth, April 18, 1949, ibid.; Hancher to Ellsworth, Nov. 15, 1949, HPC, 1949–50, #112; Ellsworth to Hancher, Nov. 16, 1949, ibid.; Hancher to Ellsworth, Dec. 20, 1949, ibid.

65. George D. Strayer, *Report of a Survey of the Institutions of Higher Learning in the State of Iowa* (Des Moines: State Board of Education, 1950), 7–13, 29–39, 57–72.

66. Hancher, "Moral and Ethical Problems in Education," Sept. 13–15, 1953, HPS, May 1953–Feb. 1954.

67. Hancher, "Liberal Education in Professional Curricula," Nov. 11, 1953, ibid.
68. Dakin, OHI, 28–30; Hancher, public statement, July 24, 1957, HPS, Jan. 1957–June 1958.
69. Hancher, "The State University and the American Dream," May 3, 1954, HPS, Mar.–Dec. 1954; Hancher to board, Nov. 7, 1955, HPC, Box "Letters to Regents."
70. Hancher, "The Summing Up," Jan. 29, 1964, HPS, April 1963–June 1964; Hancher, notes for Faculty Council meeting, Jan. 28, 1959, Faculty Council folder, 7/1/58–6/30/59; Dakin, OHI, 31–32; Hancher to board, Mar. 1, 1964, HPC, Box "Letters to Regents."
71. Hancher to Mason Ladd, Aug. 24, 1945, HPC, 1945–46, #78.
72. Hancher to board, July 8, 1960, HPC, Box "Letters to Regents."
73. Hancher, "Charge to the Candidates," Aug. 6, 1952, HPS, July 1953–April 1954.
74. Stuit to Hancher, Sept. 30, 1954, Mar. 14, 1955, HPC, 1954–55, #83; Aug. 1, 1955, HPC, 1955–56, #85.
75. Stuit, OHI, 1–12; when Loehwing was elected president of the National Council of Graduate Schools Hancher was surprised. He told the writer that he had considered Loehwing to be insignificant.
76. Stuit, OHI, 60–66; Stuit to Hancher, May 22, 28, Dec. 16, 1955, HPC, 1955–56, #85; Hancher to Stuit, Dec. 28, 1955, ibid.
77. Wallace J. Tomasini, "History of the School of Art and Art History" (n.d.), typescript, University of Iowa Archives.
78. Gilmore to Jessup, March 4, 1936, GP, 1935–36, #17; Seashore to Jessup, Sept. 30, 1935, ibid.; Stanley Longman, "History of the Art Department" (May 22, 1956), typescript, University of Iowa Archives.
79. Longman, "History," 17–24.
80. University of Iowa *News Bulletin* (Jan. 1934), 1–2; L. Longman to Fitzgerald, Mar. 16, 1937, folder "Grant Wood Controversy," University of Iowa Archives; Harper to Kay, Dec. 3, 1940, ibid.
81. Longman statement to *Time* magazine reporter, Nov. 18, 1940, folder, "Grant Wood Controversy."
82. Wood to Harper, Jan. 26, 1940, Grant Wood box, folder "Letters," University of Iowa Archives.
83. *Time*, Nov. 25, 1940; Wood to F. Martin, Nov. 26, 1940, Grant Wood box, folder "Photocopies of Correspondence," University of Iowa Archives; Longman to Kay, Dec. 9, 1940, folder "Grant Wood Controversy." Longman demeaned himself by pointing out to Dean Kay that Wood's New York dealer was Jewish.
84. Seashore to Wood, June 21, 1940, Grant Wood box, folder "Letters"; Harper, "Notes on the Art Department Crisis," Nov. 27 [1940], folder "Grant Wood Controversy"; [Harper], "Notes on a Conference between Wood, Kay, and Harper," Dec. 13, 1940, ibid.
85. Hancher memo, May 6, 1941, Grant Wood box, folder "Letters"; Hancher,

"Conference Notes with Park Rinard and Dan Dutcher," May 8, 1941, ibid.; Harper to Kay, Mar. 27, 31, 1941, ibid.; Wood to Hancher, June 18, 1941, Grant Wood box, folder "Photocopies of Correspondence"; Hancher to Wood, June 17, 1941, HPC, 1940–41, #79; Wood to Newburn, June 25, 1941, ibid.; Newburn memo, June 25, 1941, Grant Wood box, folder "Letters"; Wood to Hancher, Jan. 10, 1942, Grant Wood box, folder "Photocopies of Correspondence"; Harper to Newburn, Jan. 12, 1942, ibid.
86. Tomasini, "History."
87. Gerber, OHI, 22–27.
88. Donald K. Routh, "The Intellectual Progeny of Seashore and Spence," in Routh, ed., *Learning, Speech, and the Complex Effects of Punishment* (New York and London: Plenum, 1982), 213–229.
89. A. J. Marrow, *The Practical Theorist: The Life and Work of Kurt Lewin* (New York: Basic Books, 1969).
90. James A. Van Allen, *Origins of Magnetospheric Physics* (Washington, D.C.: Smithsonian Institution, 1983).

5. THE BOWEN REVIVAL

1. Hardin, OHI, 48–49. On Hancher's recommendation the regents consulted a committee designated by the Faculty Council, although Bowen, who was out of the country at the time, was unaware that a faculty group had been involved in the selection process (Faculty Council minutes, April 16, 1963, Faculty Council folder, 1/1/61–12/31/63; Howard R. Bowen, *Academic Recollections* [New York: Macmillan, 1988], 79–81).
2. Howard R. Bowen, OHI, 4–19; Bowen, *Recollections*, chapters 4–6.
3. Bowen, *Recollections*, 14–18; Bowen, "University Students and the Advancement of American Society," Jan. 15, 1968, Bowen Speeches, University of Iowa Archives, 1968–69; Max Hawkins, OHI, 20–26.
4. Hardin, OHI, 51–53; Bowen, OHI, 25–28.
5. Bowen, OHI, 30–31; Bowen, "Individuality," Dec. 5, 1964, Bowen Speeches, 1962–65.
6. Bowen, *Recollections*, 87–89; Bowen, "The President's Report, Sept. 1, 1966," 15–16, University of Iowa Archives.
7. Bowen, "Report to the Faculty, Oct. 29, 1964," Bowen Speeches, 1962–65; Bowen, 1966 report, 7, 14–15; Bowen, "Report to the Faculty, Sept. 1, 1965," 19–24, 30–31, University of Iowa Archives; Joseph Howe, OHI, 51–52.
8. Bowen, 1966 report, 20–24.
9. Bowen, 1965 report, 25–28, 59–63. The 61st General Assembly authorized leaves of absence for "study, research, or other professional activity" (regents' minutes, Dec. 9, 1965), University of Iowa Archives.
10. Bowen to Advisory Council, Sept. 4, 1964, academic vice-president file, Box 2,

Administrative Council folder, University of Iowa Archives; Advisory Council minutes, Sept. 9, 1964, ibid.; Academic Board minutes, Jan. 20, 1965, ibid.; Bowen, 1965 report, 28–29.

11. Bowen, letter to the faculty, April 12, 1966; Bowen Speeches, 1966–67.

12. Regents' minutes, Oct. 21–24, 1964; Bowen, *Recollections*, 89–90.

13. Bowen, *Recollections*, 82; Bowen, "The Next Twenty Years in Higher Education," *Journal of the Iowa Medical Society*, LV (July 1965), 349–351.

14. Bowen, 1965 report, 4–14; Bowen, 1966 report, 1–4.

15. Bowen, 1965 report, 17–18, 9–10; Bowen, *Recollections*, 97–98.

16. Bowen, housing policy statement, Dec. 14, 1967, Bowen Speeches, 1966–67; regents' minutes, Dec. 15, 1967; Bowen, speech to Panhellenic Interfraternity Council, April 26, 1968, Bowen Speeches, 1968–69.

17. Regents' minutes, Oct. 14, 1965, June 16–17, Nov. 10–12, 1966, Feb. 8–9, 1968.

18. Regents' minutes, Oct. 21–24, Dec. 9–10, 1964; Hickerson, OHI, 56–59.

19. Bowen, *Recollections*, 100–101, 81; regents' minutes, May 9, 1968; Bowen, "Statement on the Finance of Higher Education, Jan. 4, 1968," Bowen Speeches, 1968–69.

20. Bowen, OHI, 25–28; regents' minutes, Jan. 13, 1967; Academic Board minutes, Oct. 20, 1965; academic vice-president file, Box 2, 1964–69 folder; Bowen, "The Future of the University" (confidential), Oct. 17, 1966, Bowen Speeches, 1966–67.

21. Bowen, 1965 report.

22. Ibid., 40–47.

23. H. Bowen to R. Weintraub, July 23, 1964, Bowen Presidential Correspondence (hereafter cited as BOPC), 1964–65, #36. A comparable use of TAs had become a universal practice in American universities. Harvard employed them in roughly the same magnitude as did the University of Iowa (Bowen, 1965 report, 32–39).

24. [Faculty Council], "Memorandum of Discussion on the Graduate Teaching Assistant Program," Oct. 5, 1965, BOPC, 1965–66, #36.

25. Graduate College announcement, Mar. 15, 1967, BOPC, 1966–67, #36; Bowen to Deans et al., Oct. 15, 1965, BOPC, 1965–66; Bowen to D. Spriestersbach, Nov. 19, 1965, ibid.; Graduate College, "The Teaching-Research Fellowship Program," May 23, 1967, academic vice-president file, Box 1, Graduate College folder.

26. Board of Trustees, "Statement of Policy," July 31, 1964, Liberal Arts file, 1966–72, Box 2, School of Religion, "Directorship" folder, University of Iowa Archives; R. Michaelsen to F. Berthold, Jr., July 9, 1965, ibid.

27. Alfred Jospe to D. Stuit, May 17, 1965, ibid.; G. Forell to Stuit, Jan. 14, 1966, ibid.; Board of Trustees, minutes, May 12, 1966, ibid. Poor Bargebuhr, apparently unaware of his repudiation by his co-religionists, blamed the whole affair

on a Protestant plot to seize control of the school (Bargebuhr to Stuit, Feb. 9, 1966, ibid.; Stuit to Willard Lampe, May 29, 1967, ibid.).

28. F. Berthold, Jr., to Stuit, July 3, 1965, ibid.

29. Bowen to regents, Mar. 7, 1966, Bowen, Letters to Regents, 1964–67.

30. See the extensive correspondence among Bishop O'Keefe and Forell, Stuit, and Boyd, Liberal Arts file, 1966–72, Box 9, #37. Revised Articles of Incorporation embodying the new relationship were adopted in 1971.

31. Bowen, 1966 report, 17.

32. College of Liberal Arts, "The Next Decade," Feb. 1, 1966, Liberal Arts file, 1966–72, Box 1, Administrative Structure folder.

33. "Summary of Questionnaire Data on the Administrative Structure of the College of Liberal Arts," July 18, 1966, ibid.

34. "Report of the Committee on Administrative Structure of the College of Liberal Arts," Aug. 10, 1966, ibid.

35. Graduate Deanship folder, BOPC, 1964–65, #36; Spriestersbach, OHI, 28–30.

36. Stuit to Bowen, Feb. 4, 1965, BOPC, 1964–65, #60; Bowen to L. Merritt, Jr., Oct. 1, 1964, BOPC, 1964–65, #36; Spriestersbach to Bowen, June 30, July 3, 1967, BOPC, 1967–68, #36; Spriestersbach to W. Boyd and R. Heffner, Dec. 8, 1969, academic vice-president file, Box 1, Graduate College folder, University of Iowa Archives.

37. Spriestersbach to Bowen, Aug. 28, 1968, BOPC, 1968–69, #36; Bowen to Spriestersbach, Sept. 16, 1968, ibid.; Stuit to Boyd, Jan. 10, 1969, ibid.; Spriestersbach to Stuit, May 31, 1969, ibid.; University of Iowa News Release, Aug. 30, 1967, BOPC, 1967–68, #36.

38. Bowen, 1965 report, 49; Bowen to M. Huit, Oct. 29, 1965, BOPC, 1965–66, #93; C. Hougan to Bowen, Oct. 16, 1965, BOPC, 1965–66, "Demonstrations" folder; *Daily Iowan*, Oct. 26, 1965.

39. Bowen to regents, Dec. 5, 1967, Bowen, Letters to Regents, 1964–76; C. Grassley to regents, Feb. 9, 1967, BOPC, 1966–67, #60X; regents' minutes, Feb. 9, 1967; *Des Moines Register*, Feb. 17, Mar. 10, 1967.

40. *Daily Iowan*, Nov. 2–6, 1967; SDS brochures, BOPC, 1967–68, #93; Bowen statement, Nov. 1, 1967, Bowen Speeches, 1966–67; H. Ehrlich to Bowen, Nov. 6, 1967, BOPC, 1967–68, #93; M. Huit, news release, Dec. 1, 1967, ibid.

41. J. N. Kuhn to R. F. Dole, June 6, 1968, BOPC, 1967–68, #14.

42. K. P. Saylor, Monthly Detective Report, April 9, 1968, BOPC, 1967–68, #93; Stuit to Bowen, June 17, 1968, BOPC, 1967–68, #60.

43. *Daily Iowan*, Sept. 19, 20, 1968; H. Ehrlich, "Opening Remarks to the NUC," Sept. 19, 1968, Liberal Arts file, 1966–72, Box 6, NUC folder.

44. Bowen, "2000 A.D.," June 20, 1967, Bowen Speeches, 1966–67; Bowen, TV statement, n.d. [Dec. 1967], ibid.

45. SDS brochure, "Smash the Code of Student Life" (Oct. 1968), BOPC, 1968–69, #93.

46. Bowen, address to the faculty, Jan. 11, 1967, Bowen Speeches, 1966–67; Bowen, "University Constitution," draft, n.d. [1968], Bowen Speeches, 1968–69.

47. C. Varner to W. Sueppel, Jan. 14, 1968, BOPC, 1968–69, #93A; regents' minutes, Feb. 13, 1969; Bowen to Varner, Jan. 29, 1969, ibid.

48. J. Sutton to Bowen, May 2, 1969; Sutton to Bowen et al., May 16, 1969; Sutton to Bowen, Mar. 31, 1969; Bowen to Sutton, April 3, 1969: all BOPC, 1968–69, #93A; SDS brochure, n.d., BOPC, 1968–69, #93.

49. Bowen, OHI, 42–46; Bowen, *Recollections*, 90–97; Bowen to W. E. Sorenson, Nov. 27, 1968, BOPC, 1968–69, #93; Bowen to W. Binney, Dec. 26, 1968, BOPC, 1968–69, #14; Bowen statement, Mar. 17, 1969, BOPC, 1968–69, #93; regents' minutes, May 9, 1969.

50. W. L. Boyd statement, May 5, 1970, Boyd Speeches, 1969–75, University of Iowa Archives.

51. Bowen statement to students, May 4, 1969, Bowen Speeches, 1968–69; statement to the press, May 16, 1969, ibid.; regents' minutes, May 27, 1969.

52. Boyd statement to the faculty, Jan. 19, 1970, Boyd Speeches, 1969–75; Boyd statement, Mar. 26, 1970, ibid.

53. *Des Moines Register*, May 1, 1970; *Daily Iowan*, May 1, 2, 1970; NUC flier, n.d. (May 1970); *Daily Iowan*, May 8, 1970.

54. Office of the President, university memorandum, May 10, 1970; *Daily Iowan*, May 12, 1970; regents' minutes, May 14, 1970; *Des Moines Register*, May 13, 1970.

55. Faculty Senate minutes, May 12, 1970.

56. Liberal Arts College, Executive Committee minutes, May 15, 1970, Boyd Presidential Correspondence (hereafter cited as BDPC), 1969–70, #60. See the *Daily Iowan* for April and May 1970; also, the *Des Moines Register*, *Iowa City Press-Citizen*, and *Cedar Rapids Gazette* for the same period; *Des Moines Register*, Nov. 21, 1970; *Daily Iowan*, Nov. 21, 1970.

57. Board of Regents, "Campus Tensions—A Report on Iowa and Elsewhere," June 3, 1970; regents' minutes, June 10–12, July 9, 1970.

58. *Daily Iowan*, Feb. 9, 10, 1971; NUC, mimeographed sheet, Jan.–Feb. 1971, NUC papers, Box 1, University of Iowa Archives.

59. Loren Hickerson to his family, May 17, 1970, Hickerson papers, MsC 464, Box 2, "Campus Unrest at Iowa," University of Iowa Archives.

60. D. Ranney to Boyd, Mar. 31, 1972, BDPC, 1971–72, #60ZD; "Report of an Ad Hoc Committee of the University of Iowa Faculty Senate Appointed to Investigate the Circumstances Which Involved the Cancellation of a Research Seminar by Professor R. J. Herrnstein, Feb. 25, 1972," Faculty Senate file, 1970–71, "Herrnstein" folder, University of Iowa Archives.

61. Ad Hoc Committee report.

62. Ad Hoc Committee report.

63. Regents' rule 60.050; Boyd, "Statement by President Willard Boyd," Boyd Speeches, Mar. 7, 1972.

64. R. Herrnstein to R. Schulz, Mar. 10, 1972, BDPC, 1971–72, #60ZD.

65. Bowen, "The State of the University," Jan. 31, 1968, Bowen Speeches, 1968–69; Bowen to Carl Olson, May 16, 1968, BOPC, 1967–68, #93.
66. Bowen, "Student Unrest in the United States," Aug. 7, 1968, Bowen Speeches, 1968–69.
67. Bowen, "The Good Order of the University," Dec. 12, 1967, Bowen Speeches, 1966–67.
68. Bowen statement, Sept. 23, 1965, quoted in W. L. Boyd, confidential letter to A. Bonfield et al., Jan. 26, 1967, academic vice-president file, Box 2, "Academic Board" folder; Bowen, "The University: 2000 A.D."; Bowen, "The Good Order of the University."
69. Bowen, "University Governance," May 2, 1969, Bowen Speeches, 1968–69.
70. Bowen, "University Students and the Advancement of American Society" (draft) n.d. [1968], Bowen Speeches, 1967–68; collegiate deans' minutes, Jan. 10, 18, 1968, academic vice-president file, Box 1, "Collegiate Deans" folder (1); Bowen to regents, Feb. 1, 1968, Bowen, Letters to Regents, 1964–67; *Daily Iowan*, Feb. 8, 1968.

6. THE RISE OF THE MEDICAL COLLEGE

1. Abraham Flexner, *Medical Education in the United States and Canada: A Report to the Carnegie Foundation for the Advancement of Teaching* (Bulletin #4, New York: Carnegie Foundation for the Advancement of Teaching, 1910), 223–224; Mercy Hospital Brochure, MLP Box 19-6; Stow Persons, "The Flexner Investigation of the University of Iowa Medical School," *Annals of Iowa*, vol. 48 (1986), 274–291.
2. A. Flexner to MacLean, April 22, 1909, MLP Box 15-4.
3. A. Flexner, "State University of Iowa. Medical Department" (typescript, n.d., 6 pp.), MLP Box 19-6.
4. MacLean to J. R. Guthrie, July 7, 1909, MLP Box 19-7.
5. H. J. Prentiss to MacLean, July 12, 1909; E. W. Rockwood to MacLean, July 8, 1909; W. E. Bierring to MacLean, July 9, 1909; William Jepson to MacLean, July 19, 1909, all in MLP Box 19-6.
6. W. R. Boyd, "A Brief History of the Development of the College of Medicine of the Iowa State University, From 1909 to Date [1934]" (typescript, 16 pp.), appendix B, in Carl Cone, "History of the State University of Iowa: College of Medicine," typescript, 1941, University of Iowa Archives. Cone, whose research was done prior to 1941, had corresponded with Drs. Bierring, Dean, Whiteis, Van Epps, and Teeters, faculty members at the time of the investigation.
7. Abraham Flexner, *I Remember: The Autobiography of Abraham Flexner* (New York: Simon and Schuster, 1940), 127, 291–292; MacLean to W. R. Boyd, Oct. 28, 1909, MLP Box 18-3.
8. Flexner to J. H. Trewin, Nov. 8, 1909, MLP Box 19-6.

9. Dr. Jepson had in fact been appointed professor of surgery in 1902 with the understanding that he would move his residence to the Iowa City area, but he had subsequently repudiated the agreement on the ground that the university had failed to provide him with stipulated clinical assistance (Jepson to MacLean, Nov. 8, 1909, MLP Box 20-4).

10. Dr. R. H. Whitehead to Flexner, Nov. 7, 1909, MLP Box 19-6.

11. Flexner, *Medical Education*, 223–225.

12. Ibid., 159, 224.

13. "State University of Iowa: Medical Faculty Records," Dec. 7, 1909, 36–37, University of Iowa Archives; MacLean to Trewin, Dec. 9, 1909, MLP Box 22-4.

14. W. R. Boyd, "Letter to Alumni," July 11, 1910, MLP Box 23-3; *Des Moines Register*, July 17, 1910.

15. Boyd, "Brief History," 6–7.

16. *First Biennial Report of the Iowa State Board of Education to the Governor and 34th General Assembly for the Biennial Period Ending June 30, 1910* (Des Moines: Emory H. English, 1910), 10–11.

17. Boyd, "Brief History," 8; Board of Education, "Faculty and Finance Committee Minutes" (typescript, University of Iowa Archives, June 30, 1910), 264; Trewin to MacLean, June 4, 1910, MLP Box 27-2. Nearly half a century later, when Dr. Bierring wrote his *History of the Department of Internal Medicine, State University of Iowa, 1870–1958* (Iowa City: State University of Iowa, 1958), he referred in passing (45–48) to the Carnegie survey, but without mentioning Flexner's Iowa investigation. He did, however, describe his methods of clinical teaching at that time, and he referred to his hospital reports, copies of which have not been found. Apparently the Flexner criticisms still rankled.

18. R. Palmer Howard, *The Chief: Dr. William Osler* (Canton, Mass.: Science History Publications, 1983), 54–56; MacLean to Dr. Frank Billings, July 6, 1910, MLP Box 23-3; Cone, "College of Medicine," 172; MacLean to Boyd, July 20, 1910, MLP Box 23-3; MacLean to Faculty Committee, Board of Education, July 19, 1910, MLP Box 24-3; John G. Bowman to Jepson, May 22, 1913, William Jepson file, Medical College Papers, University of Iowa Archives.

19. MacLean to Dr. L. W. Dean, July 19, 1910, MLP Box 24-1; Bowman to J. L. King, Nov. 14, 1912, William Guthrie file, Medical College Papers; Bowman-Jepson correspondence, Jepson file, Medical College Papers.

20. Bowman to Trewin, Oct. 20, 1913, BNP, Box 5-1; Trewin to Bowman, Oct. 25, 1913, ibid.

21. "Board of Education Minutes" (typescript), University of Iowa Archives, April 10, 1910, 197; George Royal to Trewin, Jan. 21, 1910, MLP Box 26-4.

22. Iowa State Board of Education, *Second Annual Report*, 29–30, and "Finance Committee Minutes," Jan. 14, 1910, 133; letters in the Bowman file, Box 1-126, 4-206 and 208; "Medical Faculty Records," Mar. 12, 1912, 58.

23. *Journal of the Iowa State Medical Society*, I (1911), 127, 276–278; "Medical Faculty Records," n.d., 54; Bowman to Flexner, Sept. 18, 1911, BNP Box 2-151; *Des Moines Register*, Mar. 22, 1914.

24. H. W. Dunn to Bowman, n.d., rec'd Mar. 3, 1914, BNP Box 2-161; Bowman to H. M. Eicher, Mar. 7, 1914, BNP Box 5-1.

25. "Medical Faculty Records," June 7, 1915, 97.

26. Ibid., Dec. 13, 1915, 108.

27. Boyd, "Brief History," 9–10; *Laws of Iowa: 36th General Assembly*, chapter 24, 47–51; *Laws of Iowa: 38th General Assembly*, chapter 78, 86–88.

28. Boyd to Jessup, Jan. 26, 1920, JP, 1919–20, #39 (2); Flexner, *I Remember*, 291–297; Jessup to General Education Board, Oct. 28, 1922, JP, 1922–23, #39 (b); E. R. Embree to W. H. Gemmill, Dec. 8, 1922, JP, 1922–23, #39 (c); Flexner to Gemmill, Nov. 24, 1922, ibid.; Board of Education minutes, April 25, 1923. The *Iowa Homestead*, the Wallace family magazine, opposed the legislative appropriation on the ground that the Rockefeller stipulation of matching funds constituted outside dictation (JP, 1922–23, #39 [c]).

29. Robert Hardin, OHI; L. W. Dean to F. S. Paine, July 20, 1926, JP, 1926–27, #73; O. H. Plant to Jessup, May 21, 1927, ibid.

30. Jessup to Boyd, Oct. 10, 1922, JP, 1922–23, #39 (b); Jessup to Boyd, May 31, 1924, JP, 1923–24, #13; W. W. Brierly to Jessup, June 19, 1924, JP, 1926–27, #73; H. S. Houghton statement, n.d., JP, 1928–29, #11 (1); W. W. Brierly to Jessup, June 4, 9, 1926, JP, 1925–26, #73.

31. C. J. Rowan to dean, April 1, 1926, JP, 1925–26, #73; Steindler to Rowan, Mar. 24, 1926, ibid.

32. Boyd to Jessup, Aug. 21, 30, 1925, JP, 1924–25, #13 (Boyd); Jessup to Boyd, n.d., ibid.; G. T. Baker to Jessup, July 6, 1927, JP, 1927–28, #11 (2).

33. Elmer DeGowin, OHI, 16; W. B. Bean to author, Sept. 3, 1985; E. D. Plass to Jessup, July 1, 1927, JP, 1927–28, #73.

34. Medical faculty letter, May 30, 1927, *Des Moines Register*, July 24, 1927; Jessup to McClintock and Plant, June 7, 1927, JP, 1926–27, #73; G. T. Baker, press statement, May 26, 1927, ibid.; Baker to H. C. Shull, Jr., May 20, 1927, JP, 1930–31, #67A (16).

35. Baker to Jessup, June 1, 1927, JP, 1930–31, #67A (16).

36. Board of Education minutes, Oct. 11, 1927; Boyd to R. M. Pearce, Aug. 21, 1927, JP, 1927–28, #73.

37. Board of Education minutes, April 9, 1929.

38. W. A. Jessup to W. R. Boyd, Oct. 10, 1922, JP, 1922–23, #39 (b); H. S. Houghton memo, n.d., JP, 1928–29, #11 (1).

39. "A Good Investment," Medical file, (General), University of Iowa Archives.

40. A. C. Furstenberg, "Address to the Association of American Medical Colleges," Oct. 1945, ms., HPC, 1945–46, #111.

41. College of Medicine budget, 1941–42, HPC, 1941–42, #108–13.

42. V. Hancher to Boyd, Dec. 10, 1943, HPC, 1943–44, #109.

43. N. G. Alcock to E. M. MacEwen, Oct. 6, 1941, HPC, 1941–42, #108A–P; Hancher memo, Nov. 29, 1941, ibid.

44. Board of Education minutes, Dec. 11, 1928; MacEwen to Hancher, July 16, 1941, HPC, 1941–42, #58; Alcock to MacEwen, April 12, 1944, HPC, 1943–44, #109; Hancher memo, July 17, 1941, HPC, 1941–42, #58.

45. MacEwen to Hancher, Dec. 11, 1941, HPC, 1941–42, #108A–P; Hancher to MacEwen, Dec. 26, 1941, ibid.; Hancher memo, Dec. 31, 1941, HPC, 1941–42, #108A–P.

46. Hancher memo, Jan. 31, 1942, HPC, 1941–42, #108, pt. 1; Hancher memo, April 27, 1943, HPC, 1942–43, #109, pt. 1.

47. Hancher memos, June 13, 14, 16, 26, 1943, HPC, 1942–43, #109, pt. 1; Hancher memos, Sept. 1945, HPC, 1945–46, #111.

48. Hancher to MacEwen, Sept. 6, Nov. 26, 1945, HPC, 1945–46, #111; MacEwen to Hancher, Aug. 31, 1945, ibid.

49. Hancher policy statement, Jan. 2, 1946, HPC, 1945–46, #111.

50. Hancher notes, "Compensation and Status," Jan. 18, 1946, Medical College file, University of Iowa Archives.

51. A. W. Dakin, OHI, 23–26.

52. "Compensation and Status"; Medical Council minutes, June 3, 1946; H. S. Houghton to Hancher, May 14, 1946, Medical College file, #65A; Dr. Robert Hardin, who joined the faculty in 1945, believed that the "prime mover" in the formulation of the plan was Dr. Stuart Cullen, head of the section of anesthesia in the department of surgery. Dr. Hardin recalled that Dr. Cullen had proposed the supplemental fee plan to Hancher (Hardin, OHI, 54–60). As indicated above, however, that idea had been suggested by Dean MacEwen as early as January 1942 and had come to Hancher from several sources.

53. "Compensation and Status"; Hancher memos, Sept. 1945, HPC, 1945–46, #111. The plan, majority and minority reports, and the report of the Standing Committee on Medical Education and Hospitals are found in the *Journal of the Iowa State Medical Society*, 37 (July 1947), 303–313, (Sept. 1947), 420.

54. Board of Education minutes, Sept. 9–10, 1946; Hancher to Houghton, Sept. 6, 1946, Medical College file, #65A; Hancher memo, Aug. 7, 1947, HPC, 1947–48, #112R; *Daily Iowan*, Aug. 15, 1947.

55. Alcock to G. Hartman, July 23, 1946, HPC, 1946–47, #111S; Hancher memo, April 17, 1948, HPC, 1947–48, #112S; Alcock to MacEwen, Aug. 5, 1946, HPC, 1946–47, #111S; MacEwen to Hancher, Aug. 7, 1946, ibid.; A. W. Dakin to Alcock, Aug. 8, 1946, ibid.; Hancher to Houghton, Sept. 6, 1946, Medical College file, #65A; Houghton to Hancher, Sept. 12, 1946, ibid.; Dakin memo, April 8, 1947, HPC, 1946–47, #111; *Press-Citizen*, Aug. 15, 1947.

56. Hancher to C. Jacobsen (with copy to Alcock), July 5, 1947, HPC, 1947–48, #112S; Jacobsen to Hancher, July 9, 1947, ibid.; Jacobsen to Alcock, Aug. 6,

1947, ibid.; Hancher memo, April 17, 1948, HPC, 1947–48, #112S; Board of Education minutes, Dec. 9, 1947, Sept. 13, 1949.

57. College of Medicine, "Compensation Plan," #65A6, University of Iowa Archives; Robert Hardin, OHI, 54–63.

58. Majority Report, Medical Compensation Plan, Medical College file, #65A5; "Compensation and Status."

59. Jacobsen to medical faculty, Feb. 20, 1948, HPC, 1947–48, #112.

60. "A Prospectus for the Administrative Organization of the College of Medicine, Jan., 1963," George Kalnitsky papers, in his personal possession; [Robert Hardin], "Redraft of Prospectus," July 30, 1963, ibid.

61. Bowen to Hardin, n.d., BOPC, 1968–69, #65, "Reorganization" folder; Bowen to medical faculty, July 6, 1966, BOPC, 1968–69, #65, ibid.

62. Bowen to Hardin, July 5, 1966, BOPC, 1966–67, #65; Bowen to medical faculty, July 6, 1966, BOPC, 1968–69, #65.

63. Bowen, "Proposed Reorganization of the Health Sciences," June 17, 1967, BOPC, 1966–67, #65; Bowen to Hardin, Boyd, and Stone (not sent), Feb. 12, 1968, BOPC, 1968–69, #65; Hardin, OHI, 48–49; Bowen, OHI, 9–11.

64. Bowen, "Notes on Administrative Organization of the University of Iowa," May 23, 1967, BOPC, 1966–67, #65.

65. Committee on Faculty Participation (Ad Hoc Committee), "To Members of the Faculty," Oct. 27, 1967, Michael Brody papers.

66. Ad Hoc Committee, Working Document, Oct. 16, 1967; minutes of Oct. 6, 9, 12, 13, 16, 23, 31, Nov. 2, 3, 6, 7, 10, 1967, Brody papers. I am obligated to Drs. Michael Brody and George Kalnitsky, Ad Hoc Committee members, who graciously shared their personal records and recollections with me.

67. C. P. Gopelrud to R. Sheets, Nov. 6, 1967, Brody papers.

68. Committee on Faculty Participation minutes, Oct. 13, 1967, Brody papers; ibid., Oct. 6, 1967.

69. D. B. Stone to medical faculty, Dec. 15, 1967; Ad Hoc Committee minutes, Oct. 9, 1967; M. Van Allen to R. Sheets, Nov. 7, 1967, all in Brody papers.

70. Ad Hoc Committee to faculty, Nov. 30, 1967, Brody papers; *Manual of Procedure of the College of Medicine*, Jan. 1968, articles II and III.

71. Bowen to Hardin, Jan. 2, 1968; Ad Hoc Committee minutes, Jan. 10, 1968; Bowen to Ad Hoc Committee, Jan. 15, 1968, all in Brody papers.

72. "A Review of the Department of Pathology," May 1968; "A Review of the Department of Biochemistry," Sept. 1968; "A Review of the Surgery Department," Dec. 1968, all in Medicine file (Misc.), Box 1, University of Iowa Archives.

73. R. A. Dorner to R. Hardin, May 19, 1969, BOPC, 1968–69, #64.

74. Executive Committee minutes, Dec. 2, 1968, Medicine file, "Executive Committee" folder.

75. E. DeGowin, OHI, 1–11; R. Hardin, OHI, 1–10; P. Huston, OHI, 6–49; A.

Braley, OHI, 31–51.

76. Hardin, OHI, 10–18.

77. Bowen, OHI, 11–16; College of Medicine, statement for the regents, April 23, 1986, Medical College file.

7. GENERAL EDUCATION

1. Core Course, Box 6, Sub-Committee on Fine Arts folder, Report, June 25, 1943, University of Iowa Archives.

2. Hancher memo, Mar. 8, 1941, HPC, 1941–42, #79; memo, Dec. 20, 1940, ibid.; memo, Apr. 17, 1941, ibid.

3. Hancher memos, Dec. 20, 1940, Mar. 8, 11, Apr. 10, 19, June 17, 1941, HPC, 1940–41, #79; J. B. Stroud, OHI, 4–5.

4. Hancher inaugural address, HPS, Presidential Speeches, 1940–43, folder Jan.–June 1941; K. Porter to Hancher, Feb. 17, 1941, Core Course, Box 1, 1942; Hancher to Newburn, Jan. 1942, HPC, 1941–42, #80; Hancher to Newburn, Mar. 6, 1942, Core Course, Box 1, 1942.

5. Harry K. Newburn, "The Challenge to Liberal Education When Peace Comes," Baconian Lecture (1943), 99–109; Newburn, "The Post-War Responsibilities of Liberal Education," *Bulletin of the Association of American Colleges*, XXIX (1943), 275–299.

6. Core Course, Curriculum Revision, Box 1, 1941; HPC, 1941–42, #80, Box 2. For Newburn's papers dealing with the core course controversy, see the Liberal Arts file, received 8/84, Box 12, 4 accordian folders, University of Iowa Archives (hereafter Newburn file).

7. Frances M. Flanagan, "The Educational Role of Norman Foerster" (University of Iowa Ph.D. thesis, 1971).

8. Norman Foerster, *The Future of the Liberal College* (New York: Appleton, 1938), 87–88, 13–19; Foerster, *The Humanities and the Common Man: The Democratic Role of the State Universities* (Chapel Hill: University of North Carolina Press, 1946), 21–29, 10–18.

9. Norman Foerster, *The Future of the Liberal College*, 1–12; Foerster, *The American State University, Its Relation to Democracy* (Chapel Hill: University of North Carolina Press, 1937), 11–66, 95–96; Foerster, "Lowering Higher Education: The State Universities Face an Acid Test," *Scribner's*, vol. 99 (June 1936), 368–370.

10. Norman Foerster, *The American State University*, 200–208, 259–277; *The Humanities and the Common Man*, 37–45; *The Future of the Liberal College*, 64–77, 82.

11. Norman Foerster, *The American State University*, 106–112; *The American Scholar, A Study in Litterae Inhumaniores* (Chapel Hill: University of North

Carolina Press, 1929), 52–60; *The Humanities and the Common Man*, 45–51.

12. Flanagan, "Foerster," 112–118, 227; Stephen Wilbers, *The Iowa Writers' Workshop: Origins, Emergence, and Growth* (Iowa City: University of Iowa Press, 1980), 73.

13. Flanagan, "Foerster," 148–151; conversation with the late Baldwin Maxwell, Apr. 29, 1984; Flanagan, "Foerster," 100–148.

14. *University Catalog, 1941–42*, 198–200.

15. "Notes to Accompany Curriculum Proposal," Dec. 2, 1942, HPC, 1942–43, #80.

16. History Sub-Committee minutes, Apr. 30, May 14, 28, June 25, July 16, 1942, Core Course, Box 1, 1942 folder; Longman to Newburn, May 4, 1942, ibid.

17. Literature Sub-Committee minutes, May 25, June 1, 8, Oct. 12, Nov. 2, 1942, ibid.

18. Fine Arts Sub-Committee minutes, June 9, 16, 23, July 21, Oct. 13, 20, Nov. 3, 1942, ibid.

19. Social Science Sub-Committee, Report, Core Course, Box 6, 1942 folder; Social Science Sub-Committee minutes, July 16, Nov. 10, 1942, ibid.

20. Science Sub-Committee, Report, July 10, 1942, Core Course, Box 1, 1942 folder.

21. Sub-Committee on Skills, Report, n.d., Core Course, Box 6.

22. Steering Committee memo, Nov. 21, 1942, Core Course, Box 1, 1942 folder; "Notes to Accompany Curriculum Proposal," Dec. 2, 1942, HPC, 1942–43, #80; Liberal Arts Faculty minutes, Dec. 9, 1942.

23. Steering Committee memo, Jan. 30, 1943, Foerster papers, 1940–43 folder, University of Iowa Archives.

24. Steering Committee memo, Core Course, Box 1, 1942 folder; Liberal Arts Faculty minutes, Dec. 9, 1942, Mar. 10, 1943; Foerster to W. R. Boyd, Apr. 1, 1944, Foerster papers, 1944–45 folder.

25. Literature Sub-Committee file, Core Course, Box 2; "Proposed Core Curriculum," Foerster papers, 1942–43 folder.

26. Porter to Newburn, June 8, 1943, Newburn file.

27. Ibid.; Liberal Arts Faculty minutes, June 9, 1943; record of informal meeting, June 9, 1943, Core Course, Box 5, "Steering Committee materials" folder; *Des Moines Register*, Feb. 27, 1944.

28. Seymour Pitcher, "A Proposal for Curricular Reform," *Perspectives*, I, no. 1 (Mar. 1944), 11–12; Core Course, Box 5, Memorandum, Steering Committee folder; Steering Committee minutes, Nov. 20, 1943, Foerster papers, 1940–43 folder.

29. Hancher to Newburn, July 19, 1943, Newburn file.

30. Steering Committee agenda, Nov. 20, 1943, Foerster papers, 1940–43 folder.

31. Steering Committee minutes, Dec. 20, 27, 30, 1943, ibid.; Foerster to Steering Committee, Dec. 13, 1943, ibid.

32. Hancher memos, Feb. 3, 10, 1944, HPC, 1943–44, #80; Foerster to Hancher, Feb. 21, 1944, Foerster papers, 1944–45 folder.
33. Foerster to Newburn, Mar. 17, 1944, Core Course, Box 5, Steering Committee folder.
34. Foerster memo, Feb. 24, 1944, Foerster papers, 1944–45 folder; *Perspectives*, I, 12–17; *Des Moines Register*, Feb. 27, 1944.
35. Foerster to Boyd, Mar. 20, 27, Apr. 1, 1944, Foerster papers, 1944–45 folder; Boyd to Foerster, Mar. 21, 24, 29, 1944, ibid.
36. National Association of State Universities, *Transactions*, XLII (1944), 32–45; Foerster, *The Humanities and the Common Man*, 58–59.
37. Committee on Curricula and Instruction minutes, Mar. 18, 1944, HPC, 1943–44, #80; Liberal Arts faculty minutes, Apr. 5, 1944; informal minutes, Apr. 5, 1944, HPC, 1943–44, #80; Newburn memo, Core Course, Box 4, Steering Committee folder; Foerster to Boyd, Apr. 18, 1944, Foerster papers, 1944–45 folder. The secretary of the faculty, Bartalow Crawford, kept two sets of minutes, a longer informal set and a brief official record. Both are defective, and the official minutes were never subsequently corrected. The facts as stated here are probably an accurate account of what happened, in the light of information available.
38. Harry K. Newburn, *The New Program in Liberal Arts* (Iowa City: University of Iowa Publications, N.S. 1350, Jan. 1, 1945), 2–3; Hancher to Board of Education, Apr. 6, 1944, HPC, 1943–44, #80.
39. Boyd to Foerster, Apr. 6, 1944; Foerster to Boyd, Apr. 18, 1944; Foerster to Hancher, July 27, 1944; Foerster to Boyd, Aug. 2, 1944, all in Foerster papers, 1944–45 folder; *Iowa City Press-Citizen*, July 28, 1944.
40. Report of the Sub-Committee on Core Courses, July 12, 1944, Liberal Arts file, Box 3, 1944 folder; Proceedings, Sub-Committee on Core Courses, Dec. 7, 1944, ibid.; Report of the Sub-Committee on History, n.d., Liberal Arts file, Box 3, 1945 folder; K. Porter to H. Newburn, May 15, 1944, Liberal Arts file, Box 3, 1944 folder.
41. Hancher to McGrath, June 11, 1945, HPC, 1944–45, #82; McGrath to Seashore, May 28, 1945, ibid.; E. J. McGrath, "The General Education Movement," *Journal of General Education*, I (Oct. 1946), 3–8; McGrath to H. W. Bohlman, June 26, 1946, HPC, 1945–46, #82.
42. Hancher to J. Brandt, June 24, 1946, HPC, 1945–46, #82; E. J. McGrath, ed., *Toward General Education* (New York: Macmillan, 1948); Executive Committee minutes, Dec. 16, 1946; Liberal Arts faculty minutes, Dec. 18, 1946.
43. Hancher to I. L. Kandel, Feb. 7, 1947, HPC, 1946–47, #82; McGrath to Hancher, July 20, 1947, ibid.; Dakin to Mabie, July 18, 1947, ibid.; Mabie to McGrath, July 9, 1947, ibid.; Dakin to Hancher, Apr. 16, 1947, ibid.; Hancher announcement, Feb. 19, 1948, ibid.; Mabie to McGrath, Feb. 21, 1948, ibid.
44. Core Course Committee proposal, Apr. 14, 1948, HPC, 1947–48, #82; Report of the Committee on General Studies, n.d. [Apr. 1948], ibid.; Hancher to

McGrath, Sept. 30, 1948, HPC, 1948–49, #86; McGrath to Hancher, Oct. 4, 1948, ibid.

45. Hancher, "Liberal Education from the Point of View of the Professions," Mar. 20, 1953, HPS, July 1952–Apr. 1953; Hancher to H. Davis, Oct. 2, 1948, HPC, 1948–49, #86; [D. B. Stuit], "A Proposal to Study the Integration of General Education into Our Educational System," Mar. 27, 1951, HPC, 1950–51, #74; Liberal Arts faculty minutes, May 9, 1951, ibid.

46. Notice to the faculty, Dec. 10, 1952; Liberal Arts faculty minutes, Dec. 17, 1952, Feb. 18, Mar. 25, 1953; Educational Policy Committee minutes, Apr. 16, 1953, all in HPC, 1952–53, #76.

47. "Report of the Ad Hoc Committee on General Educational Requirements," June 1967, 1–10, Liberal Arts file, 1966–72, Box 3, Core Course folder.

48. Ibid.

49. Educational Policy Committee minutes, Jan. 4, Feb. 29, Mar. 14, 1968, Liberal Arts College file, 1966–72, Box 3, folder C; "Report to the Liberal Arts Faculty," May 22, 1968, BOPC, 1967–68, #60.

50. Bowen, "Students and their Learning," n.d. [1968], Bowen Speeches, 1967–68; Bowen, "Liberal Education in a Complex Society," Aug. 5, 1968, Bowen Speeches, 1968–69; Bowen, "Relevance," Nov. 12, 1968, ibid.; Bowen, "A New Era for Higher Education: Liberal Education and Governance," Mar. 4, 1969, ibid.

51. Bowen, OHI, 47–49.

52. *FYI*, Jan. 25, 1978.

53. W. Tomasini, "Why We Should Find Other Alternatives to the Literature Core Requirement," *FYI*, Apr. 12, 1978; "Interim Report of the Committee on General Education Requirements, July 20, 1978," *FYI*, Oct. 5, 1979; Sydney James, memo, Apr. 14, 1978, Sydney James file, University of Iowa Archives.

54. E. Obrecht, memo, Sydney James file; S. James, memo, ibid.

55. *FYI*, Apr. 11, 25, June 6, 1980.

8. THE BOYD YEARS

1. Regents' minutes, Feb. 13, 1969; Bowen, OHI, 41–42.

2. Educational Policy Committee minutes, Jan. 13, 1970, BDPC, 1969–70, #60; Liberal Arts College faculty minutes, Feb. 25, 1970, ibid.; regents' minutes, Apr. 8, May 15, 1970.

3. Liberal Arts College, "Contemporary Issues Courses," Liberal Arts file, 1966–72, Box 11, Contemporary Issues folder; Educational Policy Committee minutes, May 26, 1969, BOPC, 1968–69, #60.

4. Boyd, address to the faculty, Sept. 16, 1969, Boyd Speeches, 1969–75, University of Iowa Archives.

5. Boyd, speech to the faculty, Sept. 14, 1970, Boyd Speeches, 1969–75.

6. Report of a visit to the University of Iowa, Apr. 10–12, 1978, for the Commission on Institutions of Higher Education of the North Central Association of Colleges and Secondary Schools, 10–12, University of Iowa Archives.
7. Boyd, speech to Joint Service Clubs, Jan. 13, 1970, Boyd Speeches, 1969–75.
8. Boyd, address to the faculty, Sept. 16, 1969, ibid.; Educational Policy Committee minutes, Nov. 24, 1969, BDPC, 1969–70, #60; Stuit to Boyd, Feb. 20, 1970, Liberal Arts file 1966–72, Box 9, folder P; *FYI*, Feb. 21, 1972; Stuit to Boyd and Heffner, Dec. 27, 1972, Liberal Arts file, rec'd 8/85, Box 2, folder P.
9. Boyd, address to the faculty, Sept. 16, 1969, Boyd Speeches, 1969–75; Boyd, conference handbook statement, Sept. 1969, ibid.; Boyd, address to the faculty, Sept. 13, 1971, ibid.
10. Boyd, "Some Comments on Undergraduate Education," Mar. 2, 1970, Boyd Speeches, 1969–75; Boyd, "Our Mutual Problems," Sept. 13, 1969, ibid.
11. Stuit to Boyd, April 3, 1974, Liberal Arts file, rec'd 8/85, Box 2, folder P; Stuit to M. Brodbeck, Dec. 23, 1974, ibid., folder VP.
12. Boyd, "Implementation of University Statement on Vitality," Mar. 3, 1975, Boyd Speeches, 1969–75.
13. Boyd, "Who Decides What Is to Be Taught?" Oct. 12, 1978, Boyd Speeches, 1976–79; Boyd, "Proposition #1" [1973], Boyd Speeches, 1969–75.
14. Boyd, "Undergraduate Liberal Arts and the University," Apr. 27, 1972, Boyd Speeches, 1969–75; Boyd, "Educational Directions," Aug. 31, 1977, Boyd Speeches, 1976–79; Stuit to Boyd, Jan. 4, 1973, Liberal Arts file, rec'd 8/85, Box 2, folder P; Boyd to Stuit, Jan. 8, 1973, ibid.
15. M. Brodbeck to Stuit, Jan. 16, 1974, Liberal Arts file, rec'd 8/85, Box 2, folder VP.
16. Brodbeck to deans, directors, etc., Nov. 22, 1977, Liberal Arts file, rec'd 8/85, Box 2, folder VP.
17. Brodbeck memo to the faculty, Nov. 10, 1975, *FYI*, Nov. 10, 1975.
18. Faculty Council minutes, Dec. 18, 1979; *FYI*, Nov. 9, Dec. 18, 1979, Jan. 18, 22, Feb. 8, 12, 22, 1980.
19. Boyd, "Statement on Tenure and Academic Vitality," *FYI*, Feb. 18, 1974; Stuit to Brodbeck, Sept. 13, 1974, Liberal Arts file, rec'd 8/85, Box 2, folder VP.
20. Boyd, "Implementation of University Statement on Vitality," Mar. 3, 1975, BDPC, 1969–75; Brodbeck memo to the faculty, Oct. 17, 1975, *FYI*, Oct. 20, 1975.
21. *FYI*, Dec. 12, 1979.
22. Boyd, speech to Joint Service Clubs, Jan. 22, 1980, Boyd Speeches, 1980; Boyd, speech to the faculty, Aug. 28, 1980, ibid.
23. Report of the Faculty Welfare Committee, Apr. 1979, Faculty Senate file.
24. P. Jones to M. Ryan, Nov. 9, 1978, Committee on General Education file, University Archives; Special Support Services memo, n.d. [1978], ibid.
25. Boyd, "Martin Luther King, Jr., Celebration of Life," Apr. 3, 1977, Boyd Speeches, 1976–79.

26. Stuit, "Higher Education for Women: Some Questions," May 21, 1958, Liberal Arts file, rec'd 1/6/84, Box 5, Women's Education folder.

27. University memo, Dec. 6, 1971, BDPC, 1971–72, #106.

28. Annual Report of Affirmative Action Efforts, 1971–72, Affirmative Action file, University of Iowa Archives.

29. *FYI*, Jan. 3, 1972.

30. "Summary of . . . 1973–74 Affirmative Action Employment Program," BDPC, 1974–75, #2A; *Daily Iowan*, Apr. 1, 2, 1975. The summary also included figures for TAs and Merit System nonacademic employees.

31. Minutes of Collegiate Deans Meeting, Nov. 1, 1972, BDPC, 1972–73, #79; R. Heffner to deans and department executives, Dec. 8, 1972, ibid.

32. *Des Moines Register*, Feb. 13, 1973.

33. *Daily Iowan*, Mar. 27, 1973; Stuit to L. Kelly, Mar. 7, 1973, Liberal Arts file, rec'd 8/84, Box 1, Affirmative Action folder; Stuit to *Daily Iowan*, Mar. 7, 1973, Liberal Arts file, ibid.

34. T. Heath to Stuit, Mar. 28, 1973, Liberal Arts file, ibid.; Stuit to Heath, Apr. 3, 1973, ibid.; Boyd, "Statement on Tenure and Academic Vitality," *FYI*, Feb. 18, 1974.

35. R. Bezanson to C. Hoyle, Mar. 4, 1980, BDPC, 1979–80, Affirmative Action folder.

36. *Daily Iowan*, April 4, 1975; *FYI*, Oct. 6, 1976; Faculty Council minutes, Sept. 24, 1976; *FYI*, Oct. 13, 1976.

37. "University of Iowa 1981 Affirmative Action Program," Feb. 1982, Affirmative Action file, University of Iowa Archives.

38. Stuit, "Recent Changes in Higher Education," June 5, 1975, Liberal Arts file, rec'd 8/84, Box 3, folder S.

39. Faculty Senate minutes, April 25, 1969; regents' minutes, Feb. 12, Apr. 8, 1970; Boyd, report to the faculty, Sept. 15, 1970, Liberal Arts file, 1966–72, Box 13, folder P.

40. Regents' minutes, June 24–25, 1971; Boyd, address to the faculty, Sept. 14, 1970, Boyd Speeches, 1969–75; *FYI*, Mar. 1, June 28, 1971; Executive Committee minutes, Dec. 3, 1970; Boyd, university memo, Apr. 17, 1977, BDPC, 1971–72, #106.

41. Boyd, alumni luncheon speech, June 16, 1973, Boyd Speeches, 1969–75; Boyd, university memo, July 17, 1972, *FYI*, July 17, 1972; Boyd, fall 1972 speech to the faculty, Aug. 31, 1972, Boyd Speeches, 1969–75; Boyd, "The Pursuit of Quality at the University of Iowa," 1975, ibid.

42. *FYI*, Aug. 27, 1973; Boyd, testimony before House Committee on Education and Labor, June 10, 1974, Boyd Speeches, 1969–75.

43. *FYI*, Mar. 7, 1980; *FYI*, Special Report, June 16, 1975; Boyd, memo to the faculty, June 16, 1976, Boyd Speeches, 1976–79; Boyd statement, Feb. 26, 1977, ibid.; Boyd statement, May 1979, ibid.

44. *FYI*, Jan. 18, Apr. 18, May 2, Aug. 22, Oct. 17, Dec. 19, 1980.
45. Boyd statement at Budget Hearing, Dec. 9, 1980, Boyd Speeches, 1980; Boyd, "Educational and Budgetary Issues," Jan. 30, 1981, Boyd Speeches, 1981; *FYI*, Feb. 6, 27, 1981.
46. *FYI*, June 5, 1981; *FYI*, Oct. 4, 1978.
47. Annual Reports, Old Gold Development Fund and the State University of Iowa Foundation, 1956, 1957, 1968, University of Iowa Archives.
48. Annual Report, SUI Foundation, 1980, University of Iowa Archives; Boyd, remarks for the President's Club, May 10, 1980, Boyd Speeches, 1980.

INDEX